Religion, Theatre, and Perf

Routledge Advances in Theatre & Performing Studies

1 **Theatre and Postcolonial Desires**
Awam Amkpa

2 **Brecht and Critical Theory**
Dialectics and Contemporary Aesthetics
Sean Carney

3 **Science and the Stanislavsky Tradition of Acting**
Jonathan Pitches

4 **Performance and Cognition**
Theatre Studies and the Cognitive Turn
Edited by Bruce McConachie and F. Elizabeth Hart

5 **Theatre and Performance in Digital Culture**
From Simulation to Embeddedness
Matthew Causey

6 **The Politics of New Media Theatre**
Life®™
Gabriella Giannachi

7 **Ritual and Event**
Interdisciplinary Perspectives
Edited by Mark Franko

8 **Memory, Allegory, and Testimony in South American Theater**
Upstaging Dictatorship
Ana Elena Puga

9 **Crossing Cultural Borders Through the Actor's Work**
Foreign Bodies of Knowledge
Cláudia Tatinge Nascimento

10 **Movement Training for the Modern Actor**
Mark Evans

11 **The Politics of American Actor Training**
Edited by Ellen Margolis and Lissa Tyler Renaud

12 **Performing Embodiment in Samuel Beckett's Drama**
Anna McMullan

13 **The Provocation of the Senses in Contemporary Theatre**
Stephen Di Benedetto

14 **Ecology and Environment in European Drama**
Downing Cless

15 **Global Ibsen**
Performing Multiple Modernities
Edited by Erika Fischer-Lichte, Barbara Gronau, and Christel Weiler

16 **The Theatre of the Bauhaus**
The Modern and Postmodern Stage of Oskar Schlemmer
Melissa Trimingham

17 **Feminist Visions and Queer Futures in Postcolonial Drama**
Community, Kinship, and Citizenship
Kanika Batra

18 **Nineteenth-Century Theatre and the Imperial Encounter**
Marty Gould

19 **The Theatre of Richard Maxwell and the New York City Players**
Sarah Gorman

20 **Shakespeare, Theatre and Time**
Matthew D. Wagner

21 **Political and Protest Theatre after 9/11**
Patriotic Dissent
Edited by Jenny Spencer

22 **Religion, Theatre, and Performance**
Acts of Faith
Edited by Lance Gharavi

Religion, Theatre, and Performance

Acts of Faith

Edited by Lance Gharavi

Routledge
Taylor & Francis Group
NEW YORK LONDON

First published 2012
by Routledge
711 Third Avenue, New York, NY 10017

Simultaneously published in the UK
by Routledge
2 Park Square, Milton Park, Abingdon, Oxon OX14 4RN

Routledge is an imprint of the Taylor & Francis Group, an informa business

First issued in paperback 2013

Typeset in Sabon by IBT Global.
Printed and bound in the United States of America on acid-free paper by IBT Global.

Library of Congress Cataloging-in-Publication Data

Religion, theatre, and performance : acts of faith / edited by Lance Gharavi.
p. cm. — (Routledge advances in theatre and performance studies ; 22)
Includes bibliographical references and index.
1. Drama—Religious aspects. 2. Theater—Religious aspects. 3. Performance—Religious aspects. 4. Religion and drama. 5. Religion in literature. I. Gharavi, Lance. II. Title: Religion, theater, and performance.
PN1647.R46 2011
203'.7—dc23
2011032263

ISBN13: 978-0-415-89545-3 (hbk)
ISBN13: 978-0-203-13502-0 (ebk)
ISBN13: 978-0-415-71047-3 (pbk)

You can't understand the modern world unless you understand the importance of religious faith.

— Tony Blair

These people have no religion . . .

— Christopher Columbus

Contents

List of Figures and Tables xi
Acknowledgments xiii

1 Introduction 1
LANCE GHARAVI

PART I
Religious Actors

2 Religion, Ritual, and Performance 27
RONALD L. GRIMES

3 Spiritual Logic from Ritual Bodies 42
DONNALEE DOX

4 Embodying the Disembodied: Hesychasm, Meditation, and Michael Chekhov's Higher Ego 63
R. ANDREW WHITE

5 Becoming-Lucid: Theatre and Tantra 79
ANTHONY KUBIAK

6 Jew Media: Performance and Technology for the Fifty-Eighth Century 88
HENRY BIAL

7 Plain Speech Acts: Reading Quakerism with Theatre and Performance Studies 100
TAMARA UNDERINER

PART II
Dramas and Theatres

8 The Religious Drama of Egypt's Ali Ahmed Bakathir 117
MARVIN CARLSON

9 A Transdiasporic Paradigm: The *Afoxé* Filhos de Gandhy 127
ISIS COSTA MCELROY

10 The Decline of Israeli Society as a Black Mass in the Theatre of Shmuel Hasfari 155
GAD KAYNAR

11 Return to Tradition: The Symbolist Legacy to the Present-Day Arts 172
DANIEL GEROULD

12 Who Is Rama? 185
RICHARD SCHECHNER

PART III
Secularization and Its Discontents

13 Feeling Secular 195
ANN PELLEGRINI

14 About[/]Doing: Religion and Theatre in the Academy 210
LANCE GHARAVI

15 Performing Coexistence with Good Faith Intolerance 225
JOHN FLETCHER

Contributors 241
Index 245

Figures and Tables

FIGURES

9.1 Sons of Gandhy on Yemaya's day, Rio de Janeiro, 2 February 2011. 130

9.2 Sons of Gandhy on Yemaya's day, Rio de Janeiro, 2 February 2011. 131

9.3 *Reincarnation: bisavô do neto* (great-grandfather of the grandson). 133

9.4 Sons of Gandhy on Yemaya's day. 144

9.5 Sons of Gandhy on Yemaya's day. 145

TABLES

2.1 A Ritual Is Like . . . 36

2.2 A Ritual Is Not . . . 36

Acknowledgments

To all those whose efforts helped to make this collection a reality, I extend my warmest and most sincere thanks. I am particularly grateful to Robin Abrahams and Tamara Underiner, who provided insightful feedback throughout this process, and whose friendship and support were indispensable. Margaret Knapp's gracious and constructive responses also proved valuable in the early stages of this project. Marvin Carlson, Carolyn Roark, Heather Beasley, and Henry Bial all offered helpful guidance, advice, and encouragement. I also wish to thank Linda Essig, Jake Pinholster, Jennifer Setlow, and Courtenay Cholovich, who all encouraged and supported me in various ways. I am very grateful to Joya Scott, who assisted me in the final stages of production. My thanks also to the School of Theatre and Film, the Herberger Institute for Design and the Arts at Arizona State University, and Dean Kwang-Wu Kim for supporting the research leave that enabled me to undertake this project. To all the marvelous contributors to this volume who gave generously of their time, their prodigious intellects, and their vigorous imaginations, I extend my deepest respect and gratitude. I am also grateful to the editors and staff at Routledge who shepherded this anthology through the process and to production with such care. I am especially thankful to Anoush, Danna, and Sondra Gharavi for their endless support and patience as I worked on this project. Lastly, and most of all, I am grateful to Darius, to whom I dedicate this volume. He was, and remains, my daily blessing and inspiration.

1 Introduction

Lance Gharavi

> "Religion does not disappear even when it seems to be absent."
>
> —Mark C. Taylor

Recent decades have brought a remarkable explosion of robust scholarship in the fields of theatre and performance studies, enlivening these closely related disciplines in eclectic and exciting ways. Much of the most consequential work being done in these fields draws heavily from cultural studies and concerns issues of identity. The scholarship generated around theatre and performance through gender studies, critical race theory, queer studies, and post-colonial theory is among the most sophisticated, developed, and energetic in the disciplines. But comparatively speaking, theatre and performance scholars have had little to say about religion and spirituality. This may seem odd because religion is, among other things, a marker of identity that, like race, gender, and sexuality, overlaps, and often intertwines with, other markers. But this situation is changing.

In recent years, there has been a growing, though still nascent, energy in scholarship focusing on the intersections of religion and theatre/performance.[1] This collection is intended to advance this development by gathering together essays that address critical issues, provide illuminating case studies, identify crucial questions or points of concern, stimulate an expanding engagement with this rich area of research, and suggest fertile directions and apt models for further inquiry. It is my aim that this collection begin to sketch the outlines, contours, and flashpoints of a broad, but still focused, area of concern whose implications will have a meaningful and continuing impact on the ways in which we teach, practice, think about, and contest the fields of theatre and performance. The chapters in this volume are all written by experts in the relevant fields and are intended to be accessible to students and non-specialists, while also useful and challenging to professional scholars and artists.

WHY THIS BOOK NOW?

On 16 September 2001, the noted German composer Karlheinz Stockhausen earned an instant popular notoriety—and no small amount of scorn—when, during a press conference in Hamburg, he referred to the events that occurred in New York and Washington D.C. on 11 September of that year as "the greatest work of art that exists for the whole cosmos." Similarly, on the first anniversary of 9/11, famed British artist Damien Hirst cited the attack on the World Trade Center as "kind of an artwork in its own right." Both artists were excoriated in the press for their remarks, and both were at pains to publicly apologize and contextualize their statements afterward.[2]

Though I sympathize with the sense of what these artists, Stockhausen in particular, were struggling to articulate, I am skeptical of the usefulness or appropriateness—to say nothing of the wisdom—of situating 9/11 as art. That being said, it is far less controversial, even apt and obvious, to cite the events of that day as performances. If we circumscribe performance using my rather broad definition of "a conjunction of doing and witnessing," it is clear that those horrific events qualify as performances. Indisputably, there was both "doing" and "witnessing" involved; it is widely believed that the attacks that brought down the World Trade Center towers were witnessed—first-hand or via video—by more people than any other single event in all of history. Significantly, Stockhausen, in his controversial remarks, compared the attacks not to visual art (as did Hirst), but specifically to *performing* arts: "You have people who are so concentrated on one *performance*, and then 5,000 people are dispatched into eternity, in a single moment. I couldn't do that. In comparison with that, we're nothing as composers" (Tommasini, emphasis added).[3]

But what kind of performances were these? Certainly, they were political. That is to say, members of the media, politicians, journalists, pundits, writers, intellectuals, and public personalities, both individually and through their collective remarks, created narratives that framed the actions of the hijackers as incontrovertibly political acts. But they were also explicitly framed as religious acts. The stories told of that day were not simply of terrorists, but of specifically *Islamic* terrorists. Their motives and goals were narrated as intimately religious. And so, to some extent, were the reactions from the West. President George W. Bush, for instance, speaking less than a week after the attacks, specifically referred to his administration's imminent military response as a "crusade." And though the language of official Washington was quickly scrubbed of such historically loaded terms, the sense of the president's remarks endured. The myth (which is not the same as a fiction) that emerged from those early days, the urgently spoken and rupturing idea that "9/11 changed everything," became one of the principal guiding forces and persistent rationalizations for much of what followed—culturally, politically, militarily, and otherwise—in the U.S. and abroad. This myth carried overtones of revelation, of transformation, and of conversion. To this day, the events of 9/11 and its aftermath are, and may always be, inextricably bound up with religion, with holy war, with sacrifice, apocalypticism, and transcendence.[4] As such, 9/11 was, though not theatre, a historically monumental, pivotal, and harrowingly dramatic religious performance.

I begin this section by waving the spectacular and bloody banner of 9/11 because it illustrates, in an acutely vivid and visceral way, the crucial importance of attending to the intersections of religion and performance. I want to suggest a shift in perspective: religion should no longer be thought of as something that can be "safely" sequestered in the "private sphere." Nor—to reach beyond the level of how we "think" about religion—should it *actually* be. I argue this second point not for any social, moral, or political reasons, much less any religious ones, but simply because "should" implies "can." The attitude that suggests that religion *can* be so sequestered—an attitude characteristic of the West and of the ideology of post-Enlightenment liberalism[5]—is no longer tenable or particularly useful. It is plain that religion is a public force, one that stimulates and complicates public actions; that is to say, religion is a crucial component in a wide range of performances. Although we may cite certain activities (worship, prayer, rituals, etc.) as specifically religious, we may also identify a far broader array of actions and practices as influenced or inflected by religion.

As many social observers have noted, in the past several years, the U.S. and other countries have experienced a widespread revival of popular religious and spiritual consciousness. This phenomenon, as the example of 9/11 so grotesquely indicates, has not remained quarantined from the culture at large or from national and international politics. Examples are legion and familiar. Woven with other cultural and economic elements, lines of religion serve to form the grids upon which several large "abstract wars" are articulated and staged. These include the so-called "culture wars" of the U.S., the continuing "War on Terror," and the even larger "Clash of Civilizations" vividly imagined by scholars like Bernard Lewis and Samuel P. Huntington.[6] In recent years, the political resistance of Buddhist monks in Tibet and Myanmar opposing authoritarian regimes in their respective countries has been met with deadly violence and repression. Several European nations are vigorously debating—or have already enacted—bans on the wearing of the veil, headscarf, or *niqab* in public institutions, or even in public generally.[7] In 2004, Mel Gibson's Aramaic-language film, *The Passion of the Christ*, became a staggering international box-office success, even as it stirred immense controversy for its focus on violence and its depiction of Jews. The following year, a German production of Mozart's *Idomeneo* was cancelled for fear that its portrayal of the severed head of the prophet Mohammed would anger Muslims and lead to violence.[8] More recently, Trey Parker and Matt Stone's musical *The Book of Mormon* premiered, garnering rave reviews from audiences and critics alike. The production seized nine Tonys, including best musical, at the 2011 Tony Awards. The histrionics of Christian preachers, whether conservative or liberal, continues to ignite controversy and equally dramatic responses in the U.S. political arena, most recently as part of a wave of virulent anti-Muslim sentiment that swept through the U.S. in 2010 (a wave that still endures as of this writing). Finally, both inside and outside its various "theatres of war," the Middle East continues to prove a bustling multiplex of religious performances. In 2011, the previous decade's familiar repertoire took bold new form on the several (and too often blood-sodden) stages collectively and hopefully referred to as the "Arab Spring." The political gravity of these diverse performances in the Middle East serves not only to shape and align the cultural forces within these nations in material ways, but also to significantly tilt the axes of more powerful nations.

Regardless of whether religion has become somehow more important or wields a greater impact on the world today than in previous years, it is difficult to deny that the degree of discourse on, about, and around religion has increased in the U.S. since 2001. In the 2004 U.S. presidential election, an ambiguously worded exit poll question identified "moral values" as the most important issue among voters, edging out "the economy," "terrorism," and "the war in Iraq." Among the press, these so-called "values voters" were widely assumed to be representatives of the conservative, "traditional," church-going citizenry, and their values directly religious in origin.[9] These poll results led to a great deal of hand-wringing in the U.S. media over a suddenly perceived lack of reporting on religion, a marked increase in the coverage of religion by the press, and a spate of television specials focusing on religious—especially Christian—matters. The poll also provided a boost in political and cultural capital to the leaders of conservative Christian movements. The newly perceived cultural weight of religion brought a flood of bestselling non-fiction books on the subject and, inevitably and more recently, produced a backlash, a kind of counterattack in the religious-themed culture wars: a set of highly popular and passionately argued works pushing what has been collectively termed a "new atheism."[10]

But we need not appeal to the urgency of today's headlines, to the foam-flecked blogs, or the fickle barometer of recent bestseller lists to justify religion as a crucial area of scholarly and artistic concern. Many in the academy are coming to similar conclusions. When Jacques Derrida died in 2005, a reporter called the famous theorist and legal scholar Stanley Fish to ask him what he thought would succeed the concerns of race, gender, and class as the "center of intellectual energy in the academy." Fish answered without hesitating: "Religion" (Fish, "One University"). While Fish's response may prove an overstatement, scholars are increasingly coming to the opinion that neither the public nor the private sphere can be understood without adequately accounting for the role religious beliefs and practices play in shaping subjects and cultures (Taylor 1).

In short, intersections of religion, politics, and performance form the loci of many of the most serious issues facing the world today, sites where some of the world's most pressing and momentous events are contested and played out. That this circumstance warrants continued, thoughtful, and imaginative scholarly and artistic engagement from those within the fields of theatre and performance is one of the guiding principles of this volume.

Graduate and undergraduate students in theatre and performance studies typically receive a more or less thorough grounding in contemporary theories of gender, class, race, sexuality, post-colonialism, and the implications these discourses have for their fields and vice versa. But these same students rarely receive any scholarly perspectives on religion. One of the implicit arguments of the present volume is that this situation must change. In order to more fully appreciate and grapple with the complex ways in which theatre and performance are formed by, and formative of history, culture, politics, and subjectivities (not to mention literature, art, ethics, and even economics); in order to gain a greater understanding of how humans have related to one another and to the concentric and overlapping circles of their communities; and in order to achieve a firmer grasp of how these relations build and are built upon stories, representations, experiences, and performances, religion must be part of the picture. In short, this volume argues for a new perspective: an education in theatre or performance studies that does not take religion and spirituality into account is an incomplete one. Critical theories of gender, race, and post-colonialism are no longer the exclusive purview of specialists (although these still exist); they are now an expected part of the theoretical toolbox of nearly all scholars and students of theatre and performance. This volume argues that the same should be true of religion. The issues involved are too critical for the discourse to be left to the demagogues of TV or pulpit, too vital and ubiquitous to be cloistered in religious studies departments.[11]

In particular, we must overcome the notion that the study of religion and performance is not important because "it doesn't have anything to do with me." At my institution, we struggle to overcome a similar attitude among some of our white students who don't understand why they should study or support the production of plays by and/or about African Americans or Latino/as. The point of taking religion into account isn't merely to reinforce the multi-cultural, clichéd, and by now firmly institutionalized imperative to understand and celebrate "difference." There are other issues at stake.

"Difference" is a term that creates subject positions of self and other, constituting and dividing cultures and peoples in ways that are not always useful. The purpose served by avenues of understanding such as can be provided by scholarship, drama, theatre, and performance is not merely to achieve a greater appreciation of the experiences, victories, and challenges of "others." Nor is it to identify some idealized dream of universalism. It is also to explore how various subject positions and cultures are mutually formative and reinforcing, and how the boundaries that purport to delineate them are permeable and mutable in significant and material ways. Who you are helps create who I am. Your experiences affect (and effect) mine.

But difference, although an important conceptual schema, offers only a limited and limiting picture of the social/cultural scene. Religion, at least in the U.S., is not a context from which one absents oneself by not attending temple or church, mosque or yoga class, or even by unbelief in any "higher power" or binding "energy." This is because religion is not—or is not merely—something we may have or might be (like, some would say, "having" a gender, or "being" Latina). Nor can religion be reduced to some *sui generis* feature that is "out there" or even "in here." Rather, it is because religion is an ineluctable part of the cultural context, formed by and through that context, its performances and discourses. It is certainly not as though religion were something with clearly defined and neatly ordered borders, a remote curiosity confined to that odd-shaped building down the street. It is, if it is anything at all, more like part of the air we breathe. Religion is not a ghettoized part of culture, no matter how much the ideology of liberalism might wish to hedge it within the sphere of the private. There is no prophylactic around religion that prevents it from "infecting" the rest of society and all its members, nor is there any wall so impenetrable that it can fully and completely divide church from state. The history of religious belief, thought, practice, and writing informs and infuses laws, morality, art, literature, myths, the stories we tell ourselves about ourselves, our customs, the way we conceive of time, space, and nature, and, yes, our performances. Culture, in short.

We may abandon religious belief and practice, as individuals or as a society, but we cannot abandon our history. For many long centuries, religion was a foundational and momentously formative social and cultural reality for the West—no less, and perhaps more, than other regions of the world. Emerging from and as performance, narrative, and representation, religions guided the construction of ideals of human life, character, and relations. And these ideals endure into the present, even if aspects of their origins may have faded, even if the beliefs and practices from which they emerged have, in some instances, been rejected. As Jack Miles so saliently observed, we are all "immigrants from the past" (4). With this in mind, it becomes much more difficult to identify any space, any discourse, as wholly and exclusively secular. Not the courthouse, not the legislative chambers, not the classroom, the studio, or the theatre. As we seek to study, understand, and articulate the relations between theatre and performance on the one hand, and the complex matrices of histories, cultures, and subject positions on the other, engaging with the ways in which religion fits into this picture can serve to "render conscious and sophisticated what might otherwise be unconscious and naïve" (Miles 4). We would do well to remember our immigration status.

AN AWKWARD SUBJECT

When I was a child (and something of an awkward subject, myself), my mother taught me that it was bad manners to discuss religion or politics in something called "polite company." Today, one need only open the pages of a journal, attend a conference, or step into a classroom to discover that at least half of this quaint, common bit of wisdom has long been firmly rejected within the fields of theatre and performance studies. (Either that, or perhaps we're all just exceedingly rude company.) Discussions of politics are the daily bread of theatre and performance scholarship, and "*X* and the Politics of *Y*" is a common, even clichéd template for the titles of academic papers. Other supposedly uncomfortable subjects like race, sexuality, class, and the continuing legacy of Western colonialism have long been matters of acute concern for scholars of theatre and performance; their various aspects are explored with grace, comfort, and even relish in classrooms, conference halls, and in the pages of books and journals. But the same cannot be said—at least to the same extent—of the subject of religion. The other half of my mother's hoary old bit of social advice still seems to grip the field.[12]

This situation seems both odd and perfectly comprehensible given the historical relationship between theatre and religion. Artists and scholars as widely revered and respected as Tony Kushner, Harold Bloom, and Marvin Carlson have cited theatre and religion as "the world's oldest couple." As with nearly any long-term relationship—as Carlson takes pains to point out—this ancient couple has lived through times of great intimacy, synergy, and mutual support; periods of conflict, hostility, and estrangement; and stretches of uncertainty and ambivalence (5).[13]

The narration from which this "romance" is taken is a familiar one to students of theatre in the West. Theatre emerged in an intimate relationship with religion in the festivals of ancient Greece.[14] Other periods of closeness followed in the late medieval period (liturgical dramas, cycle plays, etc.), the symbolist movement of the late nineteenth and early twentieth centuries, in the work of various artists in the middle decades of the twentieth century (Artaud, the secular spirituality of Grotowski, Brook, etc.), and in both the experimental and commercial theatres of the 1960s and 1970s (The Open Theatre, The Living Theatre, the Performance Group, Bread and Puppet, *Jesus Christ Superstar*, *Fiddler on the Roof*, *Godspell*, etc.). These intimacies were separated by long stretches of hostility and mutual suspicion. Indeed, as Jonas Barish has so admirably shown in his seminal work on the subject, religion or religious authority was often behind, or at the forefront of, an anti-theatrical prejudice that has endured from Plato to the present.

But this narrative, common to Western theatre histories, bears a distinctly Christian and, of course, Western prejudice. These periods of "closeness" and the "breaks" that define them were not universal; they were not duplicated in all other cultures and religious traditions. The hostility between (secular) theatricality and religion typical of the "religions of the book," the latter's attempts to police the former and to situate theatricality as the exclusive domain of religion, followed different paths in each tradition, creating different sites of breach and closeness. Other traditions, of course, developed no hostilities toward "the theatrical" or, at the very least, developed different narratives and histories of the relations between performance and the practices of faith.

Further, this narrative of periodic intimacy and breach oversimplifies theatre, religion, and their relationship; it periodizes history in a way that causes us to see exceptions to the narrative as . . . well, exceptional. Such narratives set the margins of history and populate those margins to conform to established—indeed, themselves *establish*—lines of power.

According to a popular narrative, *ritual*—a key term in religious studies and a vital element in religious practice—was closely allied to the genesis of performance studies as a distinct discipline. The independent and occasionally collaborative efforts of Victor Turner and Richard Schechner twined together concerns and terminologies from theatre and drama with the anthropological and ethnographic study of religious ritual practices. Since that time, the boundaries that demarcate the disciplinary turf of performance studies have expanded, but the field still bears the traces, and often the propensities and prejudices, of its origins in what eventually came to be called ritual studies.

Yet despite these affinities and "periods of closeness" between theatre/performance, religion, and their respective academic disciplines, their relationship today is unclear and, from the perspective of theatre and performance studies, typically uncomfortable. Though there are a few journals, groups within academic organizations, and scattered specialists dedicated to studying the intersections of theatre/performance and religion, these have largely operated at the margins of the professional discourses. Given the aforementioned closeness and affinities, and even more, given the power of religion as a formative cultural and historical force, why this present and enduring discomfort?

The long history of anti-theatrical prejudice associated with religion, the familiar Western narrative fleshed out by Barish, may provide one explanation for theatre and performance studies' suspicious and sometimes hostile attitude toward religion as a subject of inquiry. Yet, ironically, in its developmental struggle for identity, as it sought to distinguish itself from—and even, at times, to supplant—theatre studies, the comparatively young field of performance studies has recurrently adopted a decidedly anti-theatrical prejudice, borrowing arguments and conceits that may be traced back to Plato and to polemics deployed against theatrical practice by religious authorities. Affinities, it seems, come in several different forms.

Another explanation for this discomfort is the place that "fundamentalism(s)" holds in the popular imagination and in the minds of many left-leaning—secular and otherwise—members of these disciplines. The positions of Christian fundamentalist evangelicals in the U.S. "culture wars"; the parts played by some Jewish fundamentalists in Israeli politics, policies, and the state's relations with the Palestinian peoples; and the equation of Islamic fundamentalisms with misogyny, the glib term *Islamo-fascism*, and terrorism all loom large in the minds of many otherwise sober academics and well-intentioned artists. The muscular and forbidding currency of "fundamentalism" in popular discourse can thus eclipse more complex and nuanced views of religion; it can color any mention of religion as a category with damning and overwhelming connotations of irrationalism and reactionary politics. In extreme cases, *religion*, *fundamentalism*, and *reactionary* become virtually synonymous and further fruitful inquiry becomes impossible.

But here, again, one may find strange and surprising affinities.

Fundamentalism was originally a term used to describe a movement in early twentieth-century North American evangelical Protestantism. In this context, *fundamentalism* denoted a culturally and denominationally specific movement that held the Bible to be the inerrant word of God, and that staunchly opposed both modernism in Christian theology and many of the findings of the natural sciences. Yet in recent decades, the term *fundamentalism* began to be applied to movements in Islam, Judaism, Catholicism, Hinduism, and other faiths, ultimately transforming into a general descriptor for a universal phenomenon, a blanket designation for a certain modern, ideological turn found in all "major" religions.[15] This use of the word served to create as much as name a new global religious species, one popularly caricatured as an atavistic reaction against modernity.

A dim view and sharp critique of modernity is, ironically, one of the defining characteristics of modernist theatre, performance, and art. The deleterious effects of industrialization, capitalism, and consumerism were the targets of, and inspiring force behind, much of the modernist avant-garde, which frequently saw these aspects of modernity as threats to cherished values and ideals of the human and human relations drawn from classical humanism, romanticism, and Marxism.

But the avant-garde has now arguably become merely another style in the variegated market of art and performance, its ideologies still cherished but no longer inspiring much faith and instead transformed into an almost aesthetic feature of the style's now Jamesonian pastiche. Many contemporary artists and scholars in theatre and performance studies have therefore turned the force of their criticisms toward the vicissitudes of late capitalism, onto the injustices, marginalizations, and cruel ironies wrought by the spread of neo-liberalism, the global market, and its accompanying monoculture. While these critiques typically assume an unspoken yet enduring ethic of universal human rights, they are simultaneously situated in language that calls into question universalized ideals of the human and honors values cited as culturally specific, whether such cultures are localized or rhizomatically linked by threads of shared interest, beliefs, or practices.

Similarly, the critique offered by many non-Christian fundamentalists is not against modernity *per se*, nor against science, technology, or modernist theology, but against the increasingly material reach of a neo-colonialist, neo-liberal force of global capital that overturns traditional and absolute values in favor of values that are equally absolute but exclusively capital-driven—an ideology that attends only to the [bottom] lines of the profit [*sic*]. After the failure of imported and remedial ideologies like Marxism, socialism, and secular nationalism, religion may be seen, in these instances, as a culturally specific corrective and avenue of protest for those who find themselves in the position of losers in a battle against the West, global capitalism, and its attendant political structures.

In this context fundamentalism is not an anti-rational dinosaur in the eco-system of a rational modernity. It is a reasoned and legitimate response, based on enduring and closely held principles, to continuing marginalization and injustice. It is a response to largely secular grievances, but a response fueled by and contextualized by religion. Peter Antes describes the critique succinctly:

> The Western system is seen as being strong in technology but weak in its ability to ensure and defend justice, moral norms and values. The reference to religious traditions is consequently not an irrational, premodern type of survival of religion but a clearly conceived model of religion as a socio-political factor able to intervene where the fundamental rights of people are in jeopardy. What is common to all these groups is their obligation to be a voice of the voiceless in society and to formulate their protest against all forms of social, economic and political exclusion. (444)

I vehemently disagree with Antes's suggestion that all forms of exclusion are anathema to fundamentalists. Yet I would note that the plea for culturally specific values, the protests in the name of social and economic justice, the critique of modernity, neo-liberalism, globalization, and marginalization offered by many non-Western fundamentalisms are—though there are obvious and significant differences—genuinely in sympathy with the concerns of many on the academic left, and in surprising consonance with much contemporary political performance art in the West.

Still another reason for the discomfort experienced by many theatre and performance studies scholars when it comes to discussing religion may lie in the continuing legacy of that loose collection of perspectives, theories, methodologies, artifacts, and polemics that is postmodernism. Still the dominant mode of scholarly discourse in many parts of the field, and a kind of philosophical Rubicon, postmodern critical theory, with its deep suspicion of authority, profound skepticism toward grand narratives, and its far-reaching critique of metaphysics, has seemed, and continues to seem for many scholars, irreconcilable with religion. Religion, of course, is widely associated with authority, whether that authority is situated in a bodied or disembodied god, an institution, an idol, avatar, oral tradition, a set of writings, or collection of practices. Religions, furthermore, may be cited for offering the grandest of grand narratives, whoppers dwarfing even those proposed by Marx's teleology or Enlightenment ideas of progress. Finally, many scholars view religions as based on a set of metaphysical propositions that purport to identify a "way the world really is." That these propositions are not empirically verifiable is not the point; postmodernists are not logical positivists. The problem is the specifically metaphysical character of these propositions, which identify a stable reality seemingly divorced from the constructions of culture, language, and performance.

Most sweepingly, postmodern critical thought constitutes an extreme epistemological crisis and pervading attitude of skepticism. Indeed, postmodernism amounts to an epistemological crisis so severe, profound, and far-reaching that it might be more appropriately termed a massacre. "Problematization" is a key mode, here. This characteristic postmodern skepticism runs up against the moral and epistemological certainties and absolutes offered by some religions, their affiliate institutions and authorities. For many in the academy, education—in theatre and performance studies or other disciplines—involves a process of breaking down these certitudes and purging the student of those "irrational" or unexamined "superstitions" often associated with religion. It is a process of urging the student toward a more sophisticated position of knowing unknowing. But despite criticisms from both the left and the right, this is no thoroughgoing relativism utterly bereft of values or foundation. It is a distinctive ideology that looks upon the discourse of ideas as a marketplace where free trade and exchange is the supreme and uncontested value—a kind of capitalist meta-epistemology—and the market itself—its mechanisms, history, and politics—the firmest object of study (e.g., Foucault). As Stanley Fish has observed, this ideology of discourse as a free market, a central concept in liberal democracies, drains the value from any of the actual speech itself or the ideas thus expressed.[16] This "liberal theology," as Fish describes it, is still a morality; but it is a "withdrawal from morality in any strong, insistent form" ("Our Faith"). Given the dominance of such theology in the West, and in the academy in particular, I would hesitant to term it, as Fish implies, "weak," for such a label belies and does injustice to the strength and durability of this mode. But I would argue that such a theology creates religion as its foe, and that it serves to produce both the academy and religion by positioning them in contradistinction to one another, even while it allows the academy to operate as religion's covert doppelganger. Yet though some scholars (e.g. Fish, Žižek, Neiman, Eagleton) express frustration at the perceived diminishing returns, dead-ends, and political and moral fecklessness of postmodern problematization, and seek a more positive way forward, few serious scholars believe the postmodern toothpaste can be put back in the tube.

One of the concerns some theatre and performance academics have with regard to addressing religion in the classroom or in their own research seems to be basically political. It is a concern that discussing religion constitutes a breach between the private and the public, between church and state, and, by extension, religion and the academy, and even religion and the arts. In the U.S. this concern may be particularly acute, *a fortiori* at state universities, because of the legacy of, and long discourse around, the First Amendment's religion clause. "The arts are public, the university is a public institution, but religion is a private matter," the argument seems to go.

Given the history of immigration in many Western nations, holding fast to these public/private distinctions—enshrining them in law, in policies, and in practices—may be understood as a tool for relieving potential pressures that arise from cultural pluralism. But the notion that religion is, by definition, a private and individual matter is ideological; it serves a modern political end and involves a false universalist consciousness. For some religious studies scholars, this popular definition—and even the concept of religion *as such*—is implicated as a product of the political history of the modern Western state.

As Talal Asad explains, the lines dividing the religious from the secular were redrawn several times prior to the Reformation. Yet despite these shifts, the Church always maintained its position of formal predominance. However, "in later centuries, with the triumphant rise of modern science, modern production, and the modern state," an idea of "religion as such" emerged; and this idea was increasingly identified with the moods, motivations, and beliefs of the individual. "Discipline (intellectual and social) would, in this period, gradually abandon religious space, letting 'belief,' 'conscience,' and 'sensibility' take its place" (39).

This ideology, moreover, is consonant with the anti-socialist, politically libertarian agenda of contemporary U.S. conservatism—a complex irony, to be sure. The concept of separate spheres termed public and private on the one hand and a normative understanding of religion as a matter of individual belief on the other are reciprocally maintenancing and mutually constitutive. One of the current political effects of this separation and its attendant understanding of religion is:

> the evisceration of substance, that is, collective aims, from the state. That is to say, the simple positing of religion is a covert justification for the modern tendency of the state to frame itself in increasingly negative terms: the secular state is an institutional apparatus by which the social body *prevents* the incursion by others into the personal and various other goals of individuals, rather than being the means of achievement for common projects and the collective good. This very definition of the modern democratic state in fact creates religion as its alter-ego: religion, as such, is the space in which and by which any substantive collective goals (salvation, righteousness, etc.) are individualized and made into a question of personal commitment or morality. (Arnal 32)

Under such a regime, alternative ideologies and potentially conflicting social worlds are privatized and made governable, subject to the discipline of the state and its attendant institutions that regulate the boundaries that ghettoize those social forces that might otherwise manifest as politically insurgent.[17] As such an ideology, such a regime, such a collection of institutions and practices are all also implicated in regulating and containing the efficacy of much contemporary politically resistant performance, theatre and performance scholars who seek to turn their deconstructive and critical prowess onto such systems, their histories and supporting narratives, have untapped but sympathetic allies in the field of religious studies.

Finally, another reason that many scholars of theatre and performance may eschew addressing religion is the widespread adherence to what is often termed the "secularization thesis." According to this thesis, secularization is a product, and one of the constitutive features, of modernity. As modernization and its constituent processes—global economic growth, industrialization, education, urbanization, advances in science and technology, etc.—ascend, religion declines. This decline is understood as functioning simultaneously on a macro and micro level; that is to say, secularization describes both a decline in the institutional power of religions over matters deemed civic and "secular" (e.g., an increasing separation of church and state and the reduction in the political power of religious authorities) and a decline in individual religiosity.

At the micro level, the secularization thesis often conceives of history as a parade of subtractions. As history, specifically modern history, progresses, the human understanding of the universe becomes less and less "enchanted." Misconceptions about the world and humanity's place in it gradually fall away, one after another. Over time, people slowly but inevitably relinquish illusions and superstitions, gods and spirits, myths, magical thinking, ideologies, and grand narratives. These are replaced by progressively more accurate naturalistic explanations emanating from the sciences and philosophy. "Maturation" is a common metaphor for this irreversible and inexorable historical process; secularization is understood as a kind of cognitive growing-up at the level of the species.

Perhaps some scholars look upon any serious engagement with, inquiry into, or discourse on religion as quaint, antiquated, and a wading against the tide of history. But the micro side of the secularization thesis is simply not supported by the available data (Stark). What's more, the macro side of this thesis can only be deemed plausible with significant (and perhaps fatal) qualifications. While the trend toward a liberal model of "separate spheres" continues, this does not imply that religion is losing its impact in the public and political arena. On the contrary, religious organizations and affiliations are increasingly serving as "interpretive communities" whose voices significantly impact not only the political discourse, but also the culture, material conditions, and public policy in otherwise ostensibly secular nations. As Jürgen Habermas explains, "Our pluralist societies constitute a responsive sounding board for such interventions because they are increasingly split on value conflicts requiring political interventions" (20). It may thus seem startling that scholars who otherwise enthusiastically excoriate and deconstruct grand narratives would so uncritically swallow the patently teleological tale constructed by the secularization thesis. Like so many other grand narratives, teleological histories, and utopian schemes, the secularization thesis has been a product of wishful thinking, one "constructed to flatter prejudged ideas" (Douglas 29).

But even if we assent to the evidence and accept the falsity of the secularization thesis, are there political reasons for its provisional adoption? After all, many post-colonial theorists and materialist feminists, while rejecting essentialist claims about colonial subjectivities and gender, argue for the adoption of a "strategic essentialism" as a political lever for progressive reform. Couldn't the secularization thesis be similarly utilized, in a winking sort of way, as a weapon in, for instance, the U.S. culture wars, or to coalesce an opposition to fundamentalisms?

Perhaps so. But I would argue that acceptance of such a thesis, however provisional or strategic, cannot be accomplished innocently or without the accompaniment of undesirable political implications antithetical to the concerns motivating such strategic adoption.

Modernity proposes its own set of "others" against which it defines itself. The binaries thus created form the polar conditions, the beginning and ending points, of the secularization narrative. They include oppositions like immature/mature, emotional/rational, primitive/sophisticated, superstitious/scientific, and obedience/freedom. These binaries are not cited as neutral or equivalent; one side is clearly privileged. The idea of secularization assumes that people and societies "outgrow" the former and embrace the latter. What's more, these binaries are not politically innocent. They are historically gendered—implicated in the historical subjugation of women and the creation and maintenance of masculinist social structures—and intimately tied to the justifications of historical colonialism. Finally, the political efficacy of these binaries is far from dormant. They continue to serve as polemical support for neo-colonialist enterprises, and provide the moral vigor to translate Huntington's "clash of civilizations" narrative into a "war on terror," penning a scenario in which a primitive, superstitious collection of totalitarian tribal groups called "Islam" is set against the rationalist science and sophisticated liberal democracies of the West. As was the case in the Cold War, binaries like these serve as a means by which the West produces its own other, and thereby itself. Today, such naïve and dangerous distortions exemplify and recapitulate the language that rationalized the colonialist adventures of Western nations in the nineteenth and early twentieth centuries—to catastrophic and murderous effect. Maturation, indeed.

A different strategy is in order. In recent years, the discourse on "postsecularism" has offered an intriguing, if elusive, promise in this regard. *Postsecularism*, like the related term *postmodernism*, is difficult to define. Its meaning is ambiguous and often contested. It is a term used to refer to a dispersed set of conditions in contemporary, secularized societies—particularly Europe, Canada, and sometimes the U.S. and other nations in the Western Hemisphere. The term typically designates a social or cultural consciousness—within a society deemed, or previously deemed, secular—predicated on a certain skepticism or "incredulity" toward the secularization thesis, and an awareness of the re-entry (usually conceived as *re*-) of religion into public discourse. Defined thusly, postsecularism holds the possibility of a new and heuristic dialogue on religion and secularism in the twenty-first century. This anthology constitutes part of a broader, more dispersed and diverse effort to bring theatre and performance studies into that conversation.

A WORD ABOUT THAT FIRST TERM . . .

The title of this volume indicates that the chapters contained herein will address religion, theatre, and performance. But what is religion? What is it, exactly, that we are talking about, here? Much like performance studies has a history of wrestling with the meaning of "performance"—in part, as a way to delineate both the methodologies and the perimeters of the field—so religious studies has struggled to define, redefine, and even un-define what it is that is its object of study.

But why this struggle? It is not as though arriving at a definition of religion is particularly difficult. It isn't—as the testimony of so many dozens of such definitions amply demonstrates. *Religion* is no more difficult to define than *theatre*, *performance*, *art* or *justice*. The difficulty lies in arriving at a definition that stands up to scrutiny and wins the consent of a wide range of experts and other interested parties. Scholars debate these definitions as a means of establishing the disciplinary horizons deemed necessary for serious study.

Whether we identify religion by reference to a set of necessary and internal attributes (e.g., belief in "non-obvious beings") or in relation to a function or set of functions (e.g., social cohesion or personal consolation), we are citing religion as something that is distinct from, and that cannot be reduced to, other phenomena or forms of cultural activity. Religion, thus understood, has an essence that can be identified by means of investigation and analysis. This essence is, moreover, antecedent to, and a precondition of, any identificatory investigation, analysis, or indeed, to any study of religion whatsoever. Religion, in other words, is *sui generis*.

Even a brief investigation into the current discourses around the meaning of the term *religion* reveals deep problematics that make any general discussion—even one as might be necessary for writing an introduction to an anthology like the one you are holding—seem hopeless without endless qualifications and hair-raising overuse of scare quotes. The problem isn't merely the typical and questionable objection that "without a precise definition, how can we know what we're talking about?" As Wittgenstein has pointed out, we can communicate perfectly intelligibly about concepts for which we have no precise and universally agreed-upon definition. The problem is that the history of the term suggests that assuming that there *is* any *thing* to talk about at all—i.e., that religion is *sui generis*, that it is an actual *thing* with an essence, rather than an epiphenomenon—is fraught with grim political implications and forbidding epistemological pitfalls.

Jonathan Z. Smith has been one of the most esteemed and widely cited critics of the notion of religion as *sui generis*. As he argues, though it is true that humankind has, throughout its history, venerated various gods and spirits, it has only relatively recently imagined something called *religion*.

> While there is a staggering amount of data, of phenomena, of human experiences and expressions that might be characterized in one culture or another, by one criterion or another, as religious—*there is no data for religion* [*sic*]. Religion is solely the creation of the scholar's study. It is created for the scholar's analytic purposes by his imaginative acts of comparison and generalization. (xi)

Smith is identifying religion as a historical artifact in the Foucaultian sense. As he points out, the idea of religion as a taxon covering a range of cultural and historical practices emerged only a few hundred years ago in the West. Derived from the Latin root *religio*, *religion* has equivalents in other Latin-influenced languages, but no equivalent in Latin or Greek (the language of the Christian New Testament), and often no equivalent in languages untouched by Latin. Can we simply conclude that, whereas the cultures of ancient Greece, say, or modern India possess(ed) no word for religion, they still had/have this thing that modern Europeans "discovered"? Given the history of European global conquest, of colonialism, and of enduring cultural hegemony, given also the term's previously cited ties to the development of the modern nation state in the West, it becomes easier to see the allure and arrogance of essentializing, universalizing, and transhistoricizing this relatively recent analytical category.[18]

So, just as scholars in recent decades have "discovered" is the case with so many other terms previously conceived as essential and universal, religion is a Western construct. For many, this means that there is "no such thing as religion," and some scholars have proposed discarding the term entirely.[19] But this seems an unsatisfactory conclusion. That a concept like religion was constructed, that it came into being at a certain time, under certain social and political conditions, and that its construction was in some way both generated by and generative of power is hardly surprising. And it is not, in and of itself, a convincing argument for discarding the concept. The term may still be useful and deserving of study, especially, as is certainly the case with religion, if it is in wide circulation and holds a powerfully creative position in cultural imaginaries.

Problematization is important, especially when scholars still ignore the histories, the constructedness, and the political birth and life-lines of a given concept. But this leaves us on the horns of a difficult dilemma. On the one hand, it would be a grave—if typically academic—mistake to discard the term *religion* as only and essentially an illusion. People do worship gods and goddesses, meditate, pray, and perform rituals. *Religion* is understood as a term that designates these activities. On the other hand, the notion that objects—like those activities and phenomena identified by the term *religion*—are not prior to the concepts manufactured to circumscribe them, but are themselves produced by those concepts in the context of specific historical power relations has an undeniable currency in contemporary academic thought. How then are we to move forward? We must recognize that religion as an idea, a category, and an object of discourse is constructed, and that its relation to any existing or historical practices is provisional and contingent at best. The term is simultaneously larger and smaller than any practices or phenomena it purports to designate. One cannot discuss these practices or these phenomena without said discussion being significantly conditioned by the limitations on thought imposed by the histories of, and discourses around, this term. The practices and phenomena themselves are not unmarked by the word, nor is what is said about them—including descriptions of religion as a historical construct—the product of thought that is free from the term, from its histories and prejudices.

As I have noted earlier, problematization can lead to diminishing returns. This is an observation whose consequences may seem dour for a collection such as this, calling the whole project into question. For given the difficulties surrounding the term religion, what is it that this collection of chapters that purport to address intersections of theatre, performance, and religion doing? *What is this book about?* I have suggested some of the problems involved in reaching agreement on the meaning of the term, so it should come as no surprise that the chapters in this volume do not collectively present a closed, lexical definition of religion. But neither is this an "anything goes" collection. The authors featured herein do share a set of common conceptions and concerns with regard to religion. These chapters address religion as a crucial object of discourse, an object that is formed by, and significantly formative of, subjects, cultural reality, and—more to the point—performances. Religion—whether we are "believers" or no, whether we accept it as *sui generis* or cite it as a construction—is a conceptual category through which we think the world. While I cannot vouchsafe that all the authors in this volume will agree with me, I would argue that any discussion of religion—and attendant concepts like spirituality or ritual—invokes the term in ways that are—explicitly or implicitly, self-aware or no—provisional, historically and culturally contingent, and strategic. But scholarship in art, in theatre, and in performance can move forward even as it acknowledges that its own approaches, however materialist they may be, involve a creativity and inventiveness that produce its object of study. Such is the case with the chapters in this volume.

IN THE BEGINNING WAS THE DEED . . .

In his manifesto on religious faith, *My Religion*, Lev Tolstoy declares, "A faith without acts is not faith" (202). In defending this declaration, he cites the passage from the biblical book of James: "faith without works is dead." The meaning of the latter, according to Tolstoy, is that faith motivates actions, and actions are manifestations of faith. I want to suggest an alternate reading, one that will frame the title of this collection: it is not that actions are expressions of religious faith, but that religious faith, religious identity, and religion itself are constituted by and as acts.

The idea that religion is made up of a set of beliefs is a familiar one. Corollary to this is the idea that such beliefs properly precede and motivate actions. "Practice what you preach" is a religious, as well as secular, commandment; to violate it is the very definition of hypocrisy. Some recent scholarship has called this first idea into question, however, suggesting that the equation of religion with belief is a fairly recent and Western development.[20] Other scholars question both ideas, suggesting performance, not belief, as a more appropriate candidate for the constitutive element of religion. Anthony Kubiak, for instance, describes religion as "ontologically charged theatricality" (271). Karen Armstrong, too, has recently suggested religion as a performative. "Religion," she claims, "was not primarily something that people thought but something they *did*" (xii, emphasis added).

Religion, whatever else it might or might not be, is a common marker of identity, and it should thus be no great leap to suggest that, consonant with other theories of identity performance, religious identity is constituted through performance. Situating religion as a performative may even be a less counter-intuitive move than doing so with other forms of identity, because religion is more obviously associated with performance—through the varieties of religious practice—than either gender or race, and rather less associated with a set of naturalized biological signs. Such a conception would reverse the direction of Tolstoy's understanding of "acts of faith." As Judith Butler has argued, gender performance is not expressive of some "inner" condition of an agent, both of which (condition and agent) precede and determine the performance. Quite the contrary. Performance is constitutive of gender and agency. The act is primary, though always historically and culturally specific. Similarly, if religion is a performative, it is not the religious faith that precedes the act, but the other way around. It is the act that precedes and produces religious faith *as its retroactive foundation*. Although such a formulation deserves greater attention than I can give it here, there is precedence for it. Žižek, for instance, argues that religious belief is not primarily an "inner conviction," nor are religious practices the products or expressions of a belief that precedes them. Rather, such practices are the very mechanisms that generate belief. Citing Althusser's discussion of Pascal,

Žižek explains the argument: "kneel down and *you shall believe that you knelt down because of your belief* . . . in short, the 'external' ritual performatively generates its own ideological foundation" (12–13). Belief, in this formulation, is an effect. It is an epiphenomenon produced by, rather than expressed by, the act.

So one does not merely or primarily *believe* one's religion. One *does* one's religion. And one does one's religion differently from one's ancestors, even if this difference appears only in relation to the differing historical and cultural contexts in which these doings occur. Such performances are always produced in relation to, or situated within, a pre-existing set of historically and culturally specific, materially and/or discursively operative institutions and regimes of representation that define performance's horizons and map its possibilities.

It may be objected that such a conception usurps agency with its accompanying and ostensibly private, individual, and interior conditions of belief. But the construction that is signaled by "performativity" is not opposed to the individual believing agent; on the contrary, performance is the necessary *scene* of such agency. Performance is the very mode (not to say "stage," for this metaphor would suggest an actor who is distinct from the space of performance) through which such agency and belief is "articulated" (not expressed) and comes into being as culturally intelligible (Butler 187).

It is not enough, therefore, to cite the connection between religion and performance as a matter of faith and acts, preaching and practicing, talking and walking, or, if I may, of *word* and *deed*. The connection is not one that either indicates or deflects hypocrisy. The connection is a matter of (to borrow a phrase from Marx that, in this instance, carries a theatrical pun) *the means of production*.

Religion, whether as a blanket concept or in specific instances like Lutheranism, is like Raymond Williams's concept of ideology and social orders: it must always be materially produced. It must always be actively made, and be *witnessed* (as performance is witnessed) being made. And it must do so actively and continuously or it will break down; it will wither and dissolve into oblivion (Williams 201). This I offer as a performance studies reading of "faith without works is dead." And it is in this manner that I situate the subtitle of this volume that binds together the concepts of performance and religion.

THIS BOOK

It is commonly said that great minds think alike. They don't—not always. And they don't in this collection. These chapters—written by some of the top scholars in the fields of theatre, performance studies, religious studies, and ritual studies—exhibit a wide variety of perspectives, approaches, and styles. In assembling this volume, I sought out contributions from notable thinkers—many, though not all of them, senior scholars—who've shown a distinctive concern for investigating the intersections of religion and performance. I purposely chose to place few limits on subject, perspective, or methodology beyond specifying that the chapters focus on modern intersections. More than anything, I was concerned with drawing out my contributors, inviting them to explore what they found most interesting, compelling, and important. The result is a collection that eschews a narrow methodological or perspectival uniformity, but that makes a happy virtue from the eclectic range of thought on religion and performance that characterizes the present moment.

The book is divided into three sections. The first, "Religious Actors," focuses on "acting" both in its theatrical, mimetic sense and in its more pedestrian sense of "doing." This section contains chapters that explore and situate the performer's relationships to ritual, religions, and religious practices. The chapters in the second section, "Dramas and Theatres," each analyze a particular body of dramatic literature, a specific work of theatre, or a performance company; the authors seek to map the complex relations between these works and the cultures and religious traditions from which they emerged. The third and final section, "Secularization and Its Discontents," features chapters that examine the diverse ways in which conflicts over religion and between religions are played out in discursive, representational, and performance sites within (ostensibly) secular societies.

This book is neither as diverse nor as comprehensive as one might wish. The mundane exigencies of our field and the material reality of publishing determine that an ideally diverse and comprehensive collection must always remain a fantasy. There are many people doing excellent research at the modern intersections of performance and religion whose work is not included in this volume. It is my hope that this anthology will stimulate, provoke, and inspire their continuing efforts. That being said, this is not primarily a volume dedicated to "preaching to the converted." Its purpose is also *evangelical*—but in a secular sense, denoting advocacy. This collection is both a (necessarily limited) means of, and urgent argument for, expanding the attention paid to religion as a crucial point of concern within theatre and performance studies.

NOTES

1. I use the term "intersections" to delineate a broad area of inquiry whose objects include, but are not necessarily limited to, performances (and dramas) about religion, performance in religion, religion in performance, and religion as performance.
2. In all fairness, both artists, Stockhausen in particular, were trying to make rather difficult and complex points about art. Given the media environment at the time, and the emotionally charged subject matter, it is unsurprising that their remarks were taken out of context and proved offensive to so many. For a more complete quote of Stockhausen's comments, see Tommasini. For Hirst's remarks, see Allison.

3. Compare this to the comments made by the famous Indian writer, Arudhati Roy, who described the November 2008 terrorist attacks in Mumbai as "theatre." See Roy.
4. In 2008, Republican presidential candidate John McCain regularly referred to "radical Islamic extremism" as "the transcendent challenge of the twenty-first century."
5. I use the term "liberalism" here, not in the U.S. electoral sense of implying leftist political values in contrast to right-leaning "conservative" values, but rather in the more general sense of the term as it emerged from Enlightenment thought.
6. Also see Barber.
7. Turkey, a predominantly Muslim nation with a secular state, is also debating this issue. In 2008, Turkey's parliament voted to lift a decades-old ban on wearing headscarves in public universities. This action was later annulled by a Turkish court. More recently, in 2011, the French government implemented a law banning the wearing of the *niqab* in public.
8. This occurred in the wake of the murder of filmmaker Theo Van Gogh. Mohammed Bouyeri, a Muslim man angered by the filmmaker's anti-Muslim statements and art, shot Van Gogh to death in the streets of Amsterdam on the morning of November 2, 2004.
9. Some challenged this conventional wisdom. See, for example, Langer.
10. See, for instance, Dawkins, Harris, and Hitchens.
11. I am not suggesting that other academic disciplines do not actively engage with these issues. Religious studies is, appropriately, an intensely multi- and interdisciplinary field. My point is that theatre and performance studies have not been sufficiently involved in the conversation, and that this situation is to the detriment of all three disciplines.
12. Admittedly, it's a very common piece of advice, passed on from generation to generation in the West. Not everything is my mother's fault.
13. As Carlson notes, Bloom and Kushner spoke similarly when they appeared as part of a program sponsored by the Classic Stage Company at New York University in 2004. Curiously, this metaphor of a sustained and rocky romance between theatre and religion, this perception of the two as "a couple," is more widespread than just these three examples. Prior to the instances I have enumerated, for example, Shimon Levy, in his introduction to *Theatre and Holy Script*, writes similarly of "Holiness" and "Theatricality." Levy cites what he terms their "symbiotic love" and makes extensive use of the language of romance to describe their "relationship." While an investigation into the reasons for the popularity of this metaphor and its implications are beyond the scope of this introduction, it does suggest a curious and possibly fruitful avenue for further inquiry.
14. While this idea has the status of a disciplinary truism, I must note that the ancient Greeks had no equivalent to the modern term *religion*.
15. I use the word "fundamentalism" here with caution, some reluctance, and principally to address the place the term occupies in the popular imagination. The most influential study of fundamentalisms in the general sense has been a series of volumes edited by Martin E. Marty and R. Scott Appleby. They describe fundamentalism as a militant and inherently political response to modernity. Citing what they term a "totalitarian impulse" in all fundamentalisms, Marty and Appleby identify fundamentalists as those who "*seek to replace existing structures with a comprehensive system* emanating from religious principles and embracing law, polity, society, economy, and culture" (824). Marty and Appleby's work, while undeniably valuable, has been controversial among some religious studies scholars. Many point out that not all groups referred to as "fundamentalist" are militant or seek to involve

themselves in political matters. Not all seek to replace existing structures with their own comprehensive system. Furthermore, the term "fundamentalism" is widely used by outsiders who deploy the word's negative connotations in the service of political polemics. For these reasons, many scholars prefer to use the word only in its original sense of referring to a movement in twentieth-century North American Protestantism.

16. For a similar critique of this ideology, see Žižek 15.
17. See McCutcheon 330.
18. See McCutcheon 327.
19. See, for example, Fitzgerald.
20. See, for example, Lopez.

WORKS CITED

Allison, Rebecca. "9/11 wicked but a work of art, says Damien Hirst." *Guardian*. Guardian News and Media, 11 Sept. 2002. Web. 7 May 2010.

Antes, Peter. "New Approaches to the Study of the New Fundamentalisms." *New Approaches to the Study of Religion*. 2 vol. Ed. Peter Antes, Armin W. Geertz, and Randi R. Warne. Berlin; New York: Walter de Gruyter, 2004. 1: 437–450. Print.

Armstrong, Karen. *The Case for God*. New York: Knopf, 2009. Print.

Arnal, William E. "Definition." *Guide to the Study of Religion*. Ed. Willi Braun and Russell T. McCutcheon. London: Cassell, 2000. 21–34. Print.

Asad, Talal. *Genealogies of Religion: Discipline and Reasons of Power in Christianity and Islam*. Baltimore: Johns Hopkins UP, 1993. Print.

Barber, Benjamin R. *Jihad vs. McWorld*. New York: Ballantine, 1996. Print.

Barish, Jonas. *The Antitheatrical Prejudice*. Berkeley: U of California, 1981. Print.

Butler, Judith. *Gender Trouble: Feminism and the Subversion of Identity*. New York: Routledge, 1990, 1999. Print.

Carlson, Marvin. "Theatre and Religion: The World's Oldest Couple." *Baylor Journal of Theatre and Performance* 1.1 (2004): 5–8. Print.

Dawkins, Richard. *The God Delusion*. New York: Houghton, 2006. Print.

Douglas, Mary. "The Effects of Modernization on Religious Change." *Religion and America: Spiritual Life in a Secular Age*. Ed. Douglas and Steven Tipton. Boston: Beacon, 1983. 25–43. Print.

Fish, Stanley. "One University Under God." *New York Times*. New York Times, 7 Jan. 2005. Web. 7 May 2010.

———. "Our Faith in Letting It All Hang Out." *New York Times*. New York Times, 12 Feb. 2006. Web. 7 May 2010.

Fitzgerald, Timothy. *The Ideology of Religious Studies*. New York: Oxford UP, 2000. Print.

Habermas, Jürgen. "Notes on Post-Secular Society." *New Perspectives Quarterly* 25.4 (2008): 17–29. Print.

Harris, Sam. *The End of Faith: Religion, Terror, and the Future of Reason*. New York: Norton, 2004. Print.

Hitchens, Christopher. *God Is Not Great: How Religion Poisons Everything*. New York: Twelve, 2007. Print.

Huntington, Samuel P. *The Clash of Civilizations and the Remaking of World Order*. New York: Simon, 1996. Print.

Kubiak, Anthony. "Virtual Faith." *Theatre Survey* 47.2 (2006): 271–276. Print.

Langer, Gary. "A Question of Values." *New York Times*. New York Times, 6 Nov. 2004. Web. 7 May 2010.

Levy, Shimon. *Theatre and Holy Script*. Brighton: Sussex Academic P, 1999. Print.
Lewis, Bernard. "The Roots of Muslim Rage." *Atlantic*. Atlantic Monthly, Sept. 1990. Web. 7 May 2010.
Lopez, Donald S. Jr. "Belief." *Critical Terms for Religious Studies*. Ed. Mark C. Taylor. Chicago: U of Chicago P, 1998. 21–35. Print.
Marty, Martin E., and R. Scott Appleby, eds. *Fundamentalisms Observed*. Chicago: U of Chicago P, 1991. Print.
McCutcheon, Russell T. "Critical Trends in the Study of Religion in the United States." *New Approaches to the Study of Religion*. Ed. Peter Antes, Armin W. Geertz, and Randi R. Warne. Vol. 1. Berlin: de Gruyter, 2004. 317–343. Print.
Miles, Jack. *God: A Biography*. New York: Knopf, 1995. Print.
Roy, Arundhati. "The monster in the mirror." *Guardian*. Guardian News and Media, 13 Dec. 2008. Web. 22 June 2011.
Smith, Jonathan Z. *Imagining Religion: From Babylon to Jonestown*. Chicago: U of Chicago P, 1982. Print.
Stark, Rodney. "Secularization, R.I.P." *Sociology of Religion* 60.3 (1999): 249–273. Print.
Taylor, Mark C. "Introduction." *Critical Terms for Religious Studies*. Ed. Taylor. Chicago: U of Chicago P, 1998. 1–19. Print.
Tolstoy, Lev. *My Confession; My Religion: The Gospel in Brief*. New York: Scribner's, 1929. Print.
Tommasini, Anthony. "The Devil Made Him Do It." *The New York Times*. New York Times, 30 Sept. 2001. Web. 7 May 2010.
Williams, Raymond. *The Sociology of Culture*. New York: Schocken, 1982. Print.
Žižek, Slavoj. "Introduction: The Spectre of Ideology." *Mapping Ideology*. Ed. Žižek. London: Verso, 1994. Print.

Part I

Religious Actors

2 Religion, Ritual, and Performance

Ronald L. Grimes

Religion, ritual, and performance are troublesome as categories. Because they are central to academic disciplines, their definitions are contested. Ritual presents double the trouble, because some scholars, assuming ritual to be both performative and religious, use it as a bridging concept between the other two.

Religion is a problem for two reasons. One is that many religious people neither know nor use the word. They keep to proper nouns such as *Judaism* and *Islam* or constructions such as *the Navaho way*. Others prefer generic terms such as *spirituality*, *faith*, and *belief*. Either way, people often object that *religion* connotes either a social sector or institution, and religion, they say, is rather a whole way of life, not merely some highly valued part of it. A second reason that *religion* causes conceptual trouble is that scholars investigating the history of the idea show that the word as we currently use it is of recent vintage and its purview, largely Western.[1] One prominent religious studies scholar even argues that religion is a category invented by scholars.

Like every other key academic concept, these have a history and come with baggage; it could hardly be otherwise. However, because most of us scholars continue using the terms, we have obligations. One is to say what we mean by the debated terms, but the other is to resist becoming so bogged down in terminological quibbling that we are disabled from conducting research among real people in actual situations.

It is increasingly common for North Americans to say they are spiritual but not religious. Because laying a conceptual wall between religion and spirituality is misleading, I define both terms in ways that assume their interconnectedness. *Spirituality*, I suggest, is life lived in search of, or in resonance with, fundamental principles and powers, usually symbolized as first, last, deepest, highest, or most central, and *religion* is spirituality organized into a tradition, system, or institution and typically consisting of a set of interacting processes:

- Ritualistic-performative processes (e.g., enacting, performing, imitating, singing, making, touching, wearing, giving, sharing)

- Experiential-personal processes (e.g., feeling, encountering, praying, being healed, being possessed, undergoing a revelation)
- Mythic-historical, or narrative-temporal, processes (e.g., telling stories, reciting, naming, remembering, recording, transmitting)
- Doctrinal-cosmological processes (e.g., believing, knowing, having a worldview, systematizing, ordering, arguing, thinking, explaining)
- Ethical-legal processes (e.g., prescribing, valuing, legislating, obeying, choosing, behaving, commanding)
- Social-cultural processes (e.g., instituting, organizing, exchanging, governing, being-kin-to, following, leading)
- Physical-spatial processes (e.g., building sanctuaries, making objects, leaving artifacts)

Conceived in this way, rituals are among the constitutive processes of religion, but, because rituals also appear outside religion, they are not exclusive to it. Although a ritual may be religious, ritual is not, by my definition, religious. Because I do not hold the view that ritual is necessarily religious, I prefer to say either "religious ritual" or "liturgy" when that is what I mean.

THE TERM *RITUAL*

In *Genealogies of Religion* Talal Asad offers a cursory history of the concept, ritual (55–79). Taking it as axiomatic that changes in institutional structures and in what he calls "the organization of the self" have precipitated changes in people's understanding of the term ritual, and generalizing from the example of St. Benedict's *Rule*, Asad claims that in the European Middle Ages *liturgy* did not denote enacted symbolism, nor did *ritual* denote a separate category of behavior. Rather, liturgy was a disciplinary program for acquiring Christian monastic virtues and ensuring that inner motives and outer behavior coincided.

Tracking entries in the *Oxford English Dictionary* and the *New Catholic Encyclopedia*, Asad says the word *ritual* designated the book that prescribed liturgical actions; it did not denote the actions themselves. Asad traces the rise, during the Renaissance, of a more individualistic and power-focused society and of a mind-body, private-public dualism that underwrote a distinction between figurative and real actions. In these circumstances, the concept of ritual, he claims, became less about the disciplining of a self or the creation of an attitude than about practices of representation and misrepresentation.

In the first *Encyclopaedia Britannica*, published in 1771, the term *ritual* designated the book that directs the ceremonies of the church. Books called "rituals" contained instructions for "rituals" and "ceremonies."[2] By 1910, in the 11th edition of the *Britannica*, "ritual" had quite a different meaning, and other religions, not only Christianity, now had rituals. In fact, ritual was no longer contained by religion at all. Ritual was a practice, specifically, a symbolic one, rather than a script prescribing a practice. This understanding of ritual as something in need of interpreting or decoding is entirely modern, says Asad (60).

In *Genealogies of Religion* Asad's argument in the chapter, "Toward a Genealogy of the Concept of Ritual," parallels the one in the chapter, "The Construction of Religion as an Anthropological Category." Although the first chapter is about ritual and the second about religion, in both cases, he wants to show the shift from a discipline requiring practice or obedience to that of a text, symbol, or code requiring a reading or interpretation. The conclusion in both instances is that neither concept, religion or ritual, is universal. Because each concept, religion and ritual, is culture- and history-bound, it is merely a beginning point and should be qualified or even displaced by the terms and meanings encountered in specific situations.

In *The Dangers of Ritual*, Philippe Buc advances an argument similar to Asad's. In rich detail, *Dangers* paints scenes of Medieval and Renaissance wrangling over ritual under varied names. A wealth of indigenous terminology is brought into play, not only *sacrament* and *ritual* but also *caerimonia*, *solemniter*, *honorifice*, and *cultus*. More remarkable than the wealth of participant terminology, which prods modern-day scholars to re-think their own usage, is the thick tangle of ritual descriptions. Buc is utterly skeptical that one can penetrate these accounts to ferret out the rituals behind them, because the descriptions themselves constitute a genre that was frequently mobilized as a political weapon. Consequently, one cannot afford just to look at *ritual* and other associated words. One also has to study the genres of the documents in which they are embedded, as well as the historical circumstances in which both the documents and the words are used. Doing so consistently is a tall order.

The basic claim of both Asad and Buc is that the word *ritual* has not always meant what it does now. Even so, each continues using the term much in the same way as it is used now, so their arguments, although historically convincing, provide no theoretical alternative.

CULTURAL PERFORMANCES AND SOCIAL DRAMAS

Performance, *drama*, and *theatre* are similarly debated and mobilized differently by various scholars. The academic use of dramatistic principles (*role* and *scene*, for instance) as interpretive analogs to social interactions dates back at least to the 1930s, but not until the mid-1950s did anything resembling cultural performance theory began to emerge. In 1954 Milton Singer visited India thinking he might study "the cultural pattern of India," but soon he began to wonder: Is this too large a unit of study? What, he asked, might be a more viable unit? Staggered by India's regional variations and its bewildering linguistic and religious diversity, he struggled to find the smallest manageable unit of research (25). When Singer asked his Indian friends and consultants how he should study the cultural pattern of India, they directed him to rites, festivals, recitations, prayers, and plays—in short, to what he called "cultural performances." These became "the elementary constituents of the culture and the ultimate units of observation" (27). He assumed rather than argued that such performances display what is central for a culture, that they more revealingly expose deeply held values than do other, non-performative aspects of the same culture. Besides being indigenous units, cultural performances had the added advantage of being bounded. They had clear beginnings and endings; they existed somewhere in particular; and, unlike ideas in the head or values in the heart, they were observable, even photographable. Cultural themes and values, Singer claimed, appear in performances, which utilize various cultural media such as singing, dancing, and acting. Given the limitations of human finitude and the constraints of cross-cultural field research, the only possible access to a whole culture, a "total civilization," is by way of its most revealing constituent parts: cultural performances.

More widely known than Singer's report was the use Clifford Geertz made of Singer's idea some twenty-five years later. What student of religion or anthropology has not been required to read "Religion as a Cultural System"? Some have been required to memorize its famous definition of religion, for which Geertz provided an article-length exposition: "A religion is: (1) a system of symbols which acts to (2) establish powerful, pervasive, and long-lasting moods and motivations in men by (3) formulating conceptions of a general order of existence and (4) clothing these conceptions with such an aura of factuality that (5) the moods and motivations seem uniquely realistic" (*Interpretation of Cultures* 90). Geertz attributed to ritual the power for generating religion's aura of factuality. Whatever metaphysical reality the gods may or may not have, he argued, they enter the human plane in "concrete acts," that is, in "performances" (112–113). Explicitly following Singer, Geertz claimed that scholars have access to things emotional and conceptual, to a people's ethos and worldview, by way of public cultural performances. Geertz was keenly aware that participants understand rituals differently from observers. For participants a religious rite is a constitutive action, whereas for an observer it is a mere entertaining spectacle, an aesthetic form. For observers, these performances may be "models of" what participants believe, but for participants these performances are "models for" what they believe; they have prescriptive force. "In these plastic dramas men attain their faith as they portray it" (114). A decade later, Geertz considered three genre-blurring analogies: social life as game, as drama, and as text. He found wanting the results of using the dramatic analogy on which he supposed performance theory depended. Although Geertz would later study the drama-oriented Balinese theatre state, which treated the royal palace as if it were a stage, and civil ceremony as if it were theatre, he never fully subscribed to the methods and preoccupations of Burke, Turner, or Goffman even though he employed dramaturgical language, often iconoclastically, in order to debunk "the pretensions upon which the society turned" (*Negara* 180).

THE RITUALIZATION OF SOCIAL INTERACTION

Sociologist Erving Goffman applied both ritualistic and dramatistic terminology to ordinary social interaction: greeting and departing are "ceremonial"; serving food in a restaurant is "dramatic." As he used them, the terms *ritual*, *ceremony*, and *drama* often sounded interchangeable, as if there were no significant differences among them. Social performance *is* ceremonial, "an expressive rejuvenation and reaffirmation of the moral values of the community" (*Presentation of Self* 35). Insofar as a performance is taken to condense reality itself (rather than being a mere simulation of it), the performance is said to be "ceremonial." Goffman's conception of ceremony or ritual was thoroughly Durkheimian.

Occasionally, Goffman discriminated between performance and ceremony. For instance, in *Frame Analysis*, he remarks, "A play keys life, a ceremony keys an event" (58). He seems to mean that a play simulates ordinary life in general, whereas a ceremony strips a deed of its ordinary context in order to create a highly focused event. In plays, he says, performers pretend to be characters other than themselves, whereas in ceremonies performers epitomize rather than pretend.

The idea of performance is important to Goffman insofar as it gives his theory its critical edge. Actions are deemed performances when they are not only done but also done to be seen. In being done to be seen, they inevitably misrepresent, thus the outcome of Goffman's theory is a hermeneutic of suspicion. The Goffman-inspired interpreter is a detective scouring backstage areas. There he or she hopes to spy the face behind the frontstage mask. From a Goffmanian perspective, all social interaction is performance, and performance becomes ritualized when someone insists on the sacred unquestionableness of what is being presented. To ritualize is to deny or hide the discrepancy between front- and backstage behavior.

Goffman is at his most ritually serious when he asserts, "The self is in part a ceremonial thing, a sacred object which must be treated with proper ritual care" (*Interaction Ritual* 91). In his view, a ceremony, or rite, is not merely a thing done or only an analogy for social interaction. Rather, ceremony is how the self is constituted. The ritually constituted self is essential to survival in society, a "sacred game." Goffman conflates ludic (play-driven), ritualistic, and dramatic language to present a view of contemporary, supposedly secular life in which the sacred, game-constituted self becomes a god: "The individual is so viable a god because he can actually understand the ceremonial significance of the way he is treated, and quite on his own can respond dramatically to what is proffered him. In contacts between such deities there is no need for middlemen; each of these gods is able to serve as his own priest" ("The Nature of Deference and Demeanor" 95).

Whereas the notion of performance allowed Goffman to question and expose, the notion of ceremony (or ritual) connoted the activity of tranquilizing questions, evading criticism. Thus, in his theory, the term *ritual* is suspect in a way that the word *performance* never is. This view is both the strength and weakness of his theory.

RITUAL TRANSFORMATION

For Victor Turner, as for Erving Goffman, society itself is inherently dramatic, creating the possibility for stage drama and the inescapability of performance in ritual. If Goffman was the ritual skeptic employing the idea of performance to debunk highly managed personae and expose ritual cover-ups, Turner was the ritual enthusiast using the idea of drama to transform the reigning conception of ritual. By construing everyday life as performative, Goffman saw it as riddled with pretense. By considering social processes as dramatic, Turner saw such processes as conflict-ridden but also culturally generative.

Like Milton Singer, Victor Turner believed he had discovered drama in the field, that he did not carry the concept of drama into the field with him. However, the phenomenon he tagged "social drama" did not consist of plays and celebrations, as it had for Singer, but rather of patterned social conflicts. They followed a predictable and universal form: breach, crisis, redress, and re-integration. This sort of drama, said Turner, is prior to, and the ground of, stage drama. The two kinds of drama feed one another.

Turner believed the redressive phase to be a primary source of ritual ("Are There Universals?" 12, 17). Because he held that the liminal phase of the ritual process gives rise to theatre, the implied sequence of emergence is: social drama, ritual, theatre. Turner put it another way that is perhaps truer to his intentions, because it makes the process sound less linear and more dialectical: "The processual form of social dramas is implicit in aesthetic dramas (even if only by reversal or negation), while the *rhetoric* of social dramas—and hence the shape of argument—is drawn from cultural performances ("Dramatic Ritual" 81).[3]

From the 1950s through the 1970s, *drama* was Turner's preferred term. In this period he wrote works such as "Frame, Flow, and Reflection: Ritual and Drama as Public Liminality," "Dramatic Ritual/Ritual Drama," "Social Dramas and Stories about Them," and *Dramas, Fields, and Metaphors*. But by the early 1980s, influenced by Richard Schechner and the emerging field of performance studies, Turner began to speak more frequently about performance in articles such as "Performing Ethnography" and "Liminality and the Performative Genres," and *The Anthropology of Performance*.

Turner never quite made theatre an object of study in the way he did ritual. Nevertheless, he celebrated theatre and attributed to it something of a privileged role as "the most forceful, *active* . . . genre of cultural performance" (*From Ritual* 104). In complex industrial societies, he held, theatre accomplishes many of the functions traditionally achieved in small-scale ones by rites of passage. But theatre, because it depends on the liminoid rather than the liminal, has the added advantage of being "suffused with freedom" (120). However generative of creativity the liminal phase of a rite of passage may be, it is replete—especially in initiation rites—with totalitarian dangers, whereas contemporary Western theatrical experience, because it is chosen, enhances rather than obliterates individuality.

Because Turner considered rituals to be essentially performative, he eventually felt the need to teach about them in a performative manner. What he called "performing ethnography" was an attempt to understand other cultures' rites by enacting them dramatically in classrooms and workshops ("Performing Ethnography"). In collaboration with his wife and collaborator, Edith Turner, Richard Schechner, and Erving Goffman, he turned his ethnography of the Ndembu into an "ethnodramatic" script, for which the agonistic social drama scheme provided the basic form ("Dramatic Ritual" 84). The workshops transpired in a series of nested frames. The ethnographically constructed ritual script was nested with a play-drama frame, and the play-drama frame within a pedagogical frame. Much of the learning occurred as students in the workshops experienced frame slippage, and as they failed to enter or sustain a frame.

Richard Schechner continues certain lines of thought developed by Turner and facilitates Turner's involvement in experimental theatre. Schechner refuses to isolate ritual from drama and play, treating all three as forms of performance, which he describes as "ritualized behavior . . . permeated by play" (Schechner and Wolford 52). The outcome of treating ritual as a species of performance is a theory of ritual that places it among, rather than above or outside, a large range of other cultural activities. In his discussion of "the magnitudes of performance," Schechner lays out a massive chart comparing sacred rites of passage with sandlot baseball, hostage crises, the Olympic Games, national network television, and a host of other human activities ("Magnitudes" 20–21). His aim is not to equate them but to demonstrate how they utilize the same basic temporal and spatial processes.

Schechner follows Turner in construing ritual as by definition transformative. Defining ritual in relation to other kinds of performance, Schechner distinguishes "transformation" from "transportation" (*Between Theater* 117 ff.; *Essays* 63 ff.). On the one hand, rites of passage effect a transformation of social state: a dead person becomes an ancestor; a man and a woman become one flesh, and so on. On the other, Euro-American actors are transported, carried away by, and into, their roles, but they are always returned to themselves. Their performances do not effect a change of status in the way a rite of passage does. Western stage actors re-enter ordinary life at the same point where they left it.

Even though Schechner emphasizes the similarities among drama, popular entertainment, and ritual, he does not ignore the essential differences, which he plots on a continuum running from efficacy to entertainment (*Essays* 75 ff.). For him, the basic opposition is not between ritual and theatre but between efficacy and entertainment. Both ritualistic and theatrical activity effect and entertain, but ritual *emphasizes* efficacy, and theatre, entertainment. Schechner's own theatrical values are such that he would reject a purely entertainment-oriented theatre. When a performance is efficacious, he teasingly calls it a "transformance." Although this sort of transformation is traditionally attributed to rites of passage, theatre has its own ways: Destructive behavior is displayed and thus rendered non-destructive; ordinary people are made into extraordinary characters, transforming actors into stars.[4]

For Schechner ritual and theatre have differences, but they are not absolute opposites. They become so only in specific cultures where aesthetic theatre emerges or where ritual is shorn of its entertaining functions. In certain cultures and historical periods, performance is a "braided structure" of efficacy and entertainment. Sometimes the braid is loose and sometimes tight. When it is tight, ritualization is rife.

Schechner's "restored behavior," like Turner's "liminoid" and "subjunctive," is an attempt to define an emergent ritual sensibility in the postmodern world. The tone, however, is different. Schechner's emphasis falls on the fictive, contrived nature of such events. In this respect his views are more akin to those of Goffman than those of Turner. Because ritualists "rebehave," they *never* act naively. There is no first, or original, act that charters subsequent performances. Because restored behavior is separable from performers, it can be composed into scenarios and directed by rubrics; it facilitates reflexivity: seeing ourselves act. Restored behavior allows performers to become someone other, or, as Schechner, in his impish manner, puts it "to rebecome what they never were" ("Restoration" 443).

A CRITIQUE

Although deeply influenced by the ideas of Singer, Geertz, Goffman, Turner, and Schechner, I have reservations about them. For one thing, it is important to notice both the similarities and differences between ritual and theatre and to resist forcing the one to be subservient to the other. As I use the terms, *ritual* and *performance* are only two children of the parent term, *action*. They have other siblings such as *play*, *sport*, *dance*, and *music*. The gerund *acting*, which emphasizes the processual rather than the static qualities of ritual and performance, has two connotations: that of pretending or playing a role and that of doing or accomplishing: "She was acting the part of Portia" and "She was acting in good faith." The first sentence carries the theatrical sense of the term; the second uses "acting" as a synonym for "doing."[5]

The verb *perform* has a duality similar to that of *acting*: "He performed in Aida," and "He performed his jury duties with integrity." When either term, *acting* or *performing*, is applied to ritual, especially to religious rites, conceptual confusion easily arises. Practitioners hear such usage as impugning their integrity, as if speakers were saying: "He was *merely* performing the (Roman Catholic) mass" or "She was *only* acting the part of a *loa* (a Haitian spirit in Vodoun)."

Schechner tries to avoid this dilemma by defining performance as the "showing of a doing," but few ritualists would say their primary intention is to show their doings. More characteristically they say they are doing, and that their doings may, incidentally, be seen or overheard. According to Schechner's usage, certain rituals, sequestered ones, for instance, would not count as performances at all. To show such rites would be to violate them. Also, certain examples of theatre are mere showings; they do not really constitute doings, that is, social transformations. When both terms are handled too loosely, rendering *all* human activity as performative showing and doing, Schechner's conception loses its utility.

Schechner's conceptual move is similar to that of Erving Goffman, for whom performance is "all the activity of an individual which occurs during a period marked by his continuous presence before a particular set of observers and which has some effect on the observers" (*Presentation of Self* 22). Both Schechner and Goffman imply that the mark of a performance is action in front of others, a showing before an audience.[6] Such a conception of performance is helpful insofar as it leads one to notice the performative dimension of all human activity, but it is not useful in discriminating among cultural domains.

In my view, it is less confusing to use *action* rather than *performance* as the parent term and to use distinctive verbs for what ritualists and performers do. When speaking technically, I prefer to say that ritualists "enact" rituals, whereas actors "perform" plays. One could still say about ritualists that, although they intend to "enact," they also sometimes "perform" occasionally or incidentally. One can still hear in "enact" the kinship with "acting," but the term's main connotation, "putting into force," reminds us that there are distinctions between ritual and performance that ought not be occluded.

There are other problems with the theoretical legacies of Singer, Geertz, Goffman, Turner, and Schechner. For example, there is no convincing evidence that rituals universally arise from social dramas, even though there are specific examples in which it does. In addition, Goffman and Turner tend to build value judgments into their definitions of ritual, in effect, making "ritual" mean "good ritual" or "real ritual," thus using it as a criterion.[7] Turner defined ritual and ceremony in such a way that "ceremony" merely confirms or consolidates, whereas "ritual" transforms. Schechner buys into Turnerian "transformationism," the view that ritual necessarily transforms. My view is that ritual just as often confirms the status quo or fails, and neither of these facts makes the event "not ritual." For Turner, drawing heavily on van Gennep, the primary model for transformation was the rite of passage, specifically the liminal phase of initiation. And if one examines his and van Gennep's sources, it is clear that the predominant examples are of male initiation. In the final analysis, Turner defined the whole of ritual in terms of a part, a very small one at that. Male initiation furnished the original paradigm not only for ritual in general but also for cultural creativity and change, opening this theoretical tradition to critiques of gender bias.[8]

In some societies rites are not thought to *transform*, that is, to change things fundamentally. Instead, rites of birth, coming of age, marriage, and death *protect* participants, or they *celebrate* transformations that have already occurred by other means. The Bemba say their rites *purify* women at the moment of first menses. This is a view quite different from one that holds that the rite transforms girls into women. It suggests that we cannot *assume* that rites transform any more than we can assume they conserve. Which rites transform and which do not should be a matter of observation, not of definition. Not all ritual actors intend to transform, but even if they do, the intention does not guarantee the results. A group may intend to transform and fail to do so. As Vincent Crapanzano has shown regarding the initiation of Muslim boys in Morocco, ritualists may say that a rite transforms when, in fact, it does not.

RITUAL AS A DOMAIN

Other than religion, the cultural domain most frequently and fully explored by scholars for its connections with ritual is theatre. Nervousness about too closely associating ritual with theatre has a long history. European Christendom was edgy about it. Actors, like prostitutes, were sometimes excluded from membership in the early church. The medieval church, which for a time tolerated and even nurtured plays, eventually put players back out on the streets. Not only were actors deemed unruly, theatrical performances sometimes provided stiff but dangerous competition for liturgical ones. This historical divide resulted in a conceptual one. The secularized and pluralistic contemporary European-American West is heir to this expulsion, leading us habitually to segregate ritual and performance. Because ritual and performance are associated with different social institutions (the synagogue and the theatre, for instance), Western scholars tend to stash them in different mental drawers.

My own interest in defining *ritual* comes from shuttling back and forth across the boundaries between religion and the performing and cinematic arts, and from attempting to connect ritual studies with performance studies. However interdisciplinary each academic field claims to be, Euro-American societies tend to stash rituals and plays in differing, sometimes even opposing, cultural domains. People singing, dancing, and orating occupy both physical and cultural space, jostling for people's attention and resources.

At the beginning of courses on ritual, I ask students to consider ritual as a cultural domain by handing them the following table with the far right column empty. I ask them to fill it out and then invite discussion. The right-hand column contains some typical responses (see Table 1.1).

The aim of the exercise is to uncover assumptions about ritual's "place" on students' cultural maps.[9] Later, aiming to explore what ritual shares with other kinds of human activity, I give them another, similar chart (see Table 1.2).

Usually, students find this second exercise more difficult than the first, so they begin to introduce conditions or sub-genres into their comparisons. By the end of the course most students would revise their responses.

Table 1.1 A Ritual Is Like . . .

A ritual is like a	party	insofar as	both can be fun, if the ritual is a celebration.
A ritual is like a	play	insofar as	participants sometimes play roles, especially in festivals.
A ritual is like a	performance	insofar as	people see other people act.
A ritual is like a	game	insofar as	both have rules and spatial boundaries.
A ritual is like a	spectacle	insofar as	they can be awesome to watch.
A ritual is like a	habit	insofar as	they may be done regularly without much thought.

Table 1.2 A Ritual Is Not . . .

A ritual is not a	party	because	parties are mainly about having a good time.
A ritual is not a	play	because	plays are make-believe rather than believed.
A ritual is not a	performance	because	performances are audience oriented and not really believed.
A ritual is not a	game	because	games are competitive, and there are winners and losers.
A ritual is not a	spectacle	because	rituals are not mainly about showing or being seen.
A ritual is not a	habit	because	rituals are more thoughtful and meaningful.
A ritual is not a	religion	because	religions are "sacred," require belief, and depend on institutions.

A WORKING DEFINITION OF RITUAL

Although I prefer to avoid definitions that reduce ritual to two or three essential characteristics, I recognize their usefulness in some situations, for instance, when interviewing ritual participants in the field or teaching introductory courses on ritual. In these circumstances, I sometimes relent, tendering a short, formal definition: *Ritual is embodied, condensed, and prescribed enactment.*[10] The advantages of this one are its simplicity and portability. Because the long list of possible qualities is shrunk to four qualities, students facing inquisitorial professors or curious interviewees can chant it, but the magic of a definition works only if you can offer an exposition of it.

Ritual is embodied. It is a human activity. People do it, and they do so in overt, bodily ways. Ritual is not only in the mind or the imagination even though it is both mindful and imaginative. If an action is purely mental, it is not ritual even though mental processes clearly underlie ritual action. However important ritually inspired memories or fantasies may be, we should not call them ritual. Ritual, insofar as it can become the object of study, is evidenced by gross motor movements (or a studied, practiced lack of them) in the body, hence the qualifier "embodiment." Because ritual is in and of bodies, it is also cultural, because bodies are enculturated.

Ritual is condensed. Although ritualization is rooted in ordinary human interaction, ritual is not ordinary action. It is more condensed or elevated than quotidian behavior. In this respect, it is like theatre. Just as theatre originates in the dramatization of everyday life, so ritual originates in the ritualization characteristic of the daily round. Rituals are made to stand out against the background of ordinariness; they are, we might say, extraordinary ordinariness. Because rituals are "condensed," unpacking is often necessary for both practitioners and outsiders to make sense of them, although rituals may also suffer from such unpacking.

Ritual is prescribed. Most human interaction is in some way prescribed. Cultures shape or channel behavior. As a result, we "just know" how to do certain things. Ritual illustrates this basic human fact but goes one step further. In ritual circumstances, things are overtly prescribed; one might even say "over-prescribed." There are right and wrong ways to enact rituals. Ritual is rubric-driven action. Etymologically speaking, a rubric is something "printed in red," words specifying what is to be done. Sometimes it is the "what" that is prescribed: say this; show that; walk here; go there. But sometimes it is the "how," the stylization, that is prescribed: clean the space attentively; dance with humility; intend this as a sacrifice.

Ritual is enacted. Ritual is a kind of action, but not just any action. So it helps to remind ourselves of its difference from ordinary action by assigning it a special verb: *enactment*. Because ritual acting is different from stage acting as well as from quotidian activity, we need a verb different from but related to *act*. Ritual action is special and in this respect similar to acting (the sort that transpires on-stage or in film), but ritual is not identical with pretending. However made up rituals may be, they are not regarded by participants as mere fiction or a game—hence the term *enactment*. To "enact" is to put into force or into play.

Outside field research situations and introductory courses, I prefer a family resemblance theory to a formal definition, because events cannot be usefully understood using only two options: "ritual" or "not ritual." Rather, they display *degrees* of ritualization. For this reason, ritual is a continuum, and events are more or less ritualized by:

- traditionalizing them, for instance, by claiming that they originated a long time ago or with the ancestors
- elevating them by associating them with sacredly held values, those that make people who they are, and display either how things really are or how they ought to be
- repeating them—over and over, in the same way—thus inscribing them in community and/or self
- singularizing them, that is, offering them as rare or even one-time events
- prescribing their details so they are performed in the proper way
- stylizing them, so they are carried out with flare
- entering them with a non-ordinary attitude or in a special state of mind, for example, contemplatively or in trance
- invoking powers to whom respect or reverence is due: gods, royalty, and spirits, for example
- attributing to them special power or influence
- situating them in special places and/or times
- being performed by specially qualified persons[11]

Because all of these qualities mark activity in various cultural domains (religion, the arts, politics, etc.), there is little temptation to regard them as the special purview of one domain. The obvious disadvantage of a family resemblance theory is that it complicates things, thwarting our desire to make simple, clear distinctions. But this vice is also a virtue. Seeing ritual's resemblances to other human activities, we are less likely to oversimplify, artificially severing the ritualistic from the ordinary.

NOTES

1. See Smith, Wilfred Cantwell; Asad; and Smith, Jonathan Z.
2. *Ritual* also has a second meaning: a religion's or tradition's way of celebrating divine services.
3. See also Turner, "Social Dramas" 153.
4. Michelle Anderson (106) has extended the analytical scope of Schechner's efficacy-entertainment continuum by showing how efficacious Voodoo ritual is regularly associated with closed spaces or back regions not accessible to

tourists; whereas entertainment Voodoo is consistently correlated with front regions open to the public.

5. Unlike the gerund *acting*, the noun *action* does not work both ways. We can say, "Her action was done in good faith," but we do not normally use the word *action* to mean "pretending" or "playing the part of."
6. I have written more about Schechner in Grimes, "Performance" (387 ff.).
7. A more fully developed critique of his definition can be found in Grimes, *Ritual Criticism*.
8. See Bynum; and Lincoln.
9. Over the years, the number of words in the second column has multiplied, and arguments occasionally break out about the clumping of terms.
10. Another variant: "Rites are sequences of action rendered special by virtue of their condensation, elevation, or stylization" (Grimes, "Forum on American Spirituality", 151).
11. The initial exposition of this idea is in my *Ritual Criticism*.

WORKS CITED

Anderson, Michelle. "Authentic Voodoo Is Synthetic." *The Drama Review* 26.2 (1982): 89–110. Print.

Asad, Talal. *Genealogies of Religion: Discipline and Reasons of Power in Christianity and Islam*. Baltimore: John Hopkins UP, 1993. Print.

Bynum, Caroline Walker. "Women's Stories, Women's Symbols: A Critique of Victor Turner's Theory of Liminality." *Anthropology and the Study of Religion*. Ed. Robert L. Moore and Frank E. Reynolds. Chicago: Center for the Scientific Study of Religion, 1984. 105–125. Print.

Buc, Philippe. *The Dangers of Ritual: Between Early Medieval Texts and Social Scientific Theory*. Princeton, NJ: Princeton University Press, 2001. Print.

Crapanzano, Vincent. "Rite of Return: Circumcision in Morocco." *The Psychoanalytic Study of Society*. Ed. Werner Muensterberger. Vol. 9. New Haven: Yale UP, 1980. 15–36. Print.

Geertz, Clifford. *The Interpretation of Cultures*. New York: Basic, 1973. Print.

———. *Negara: The Theatre State in Nineteenth Century Bali*. Princeton: Princeton UP, 1980. Print.

Goffman, Erving. *Frame Analysis: An Essay on the Organization of Experience*. New York: Harper, 1974. Print.

———. *Interaction Ritual: Essays on Face-to-Face Behavior*. Garden City: Doubleday, 1967. Print.

———. "The Nature of Deference and Demeanor." *Interaction Ritual*. Garden City: Doubleday Anchor, 1967. 47–95. Print.

———. *The Presentation of Self in Everyday Life*. Garden City: Doubleday, 1959. Print.

Grimes, Ronald L. "Forum on American Spirituality." *Religion in American Culture* 9.2 (1999): 145–152. Print.

———. "Performance." *Theorizing Rituals: Classical Topics, Theoretical Approaches, Analytical Concepts, Annotated Bibliography*. Ed. Jens Kreinath, Jan Snoek, and Michael Strausberg. Leiden: Brill, 2006. 379–394. Print.

———. *Ritual Criticism: Case Studies in Its Practice, Essays on Its Theory*. Ed. Frederick M. Denny. Vol. 10. Columbia: U of South Carolina P, 1990. Print. Studies in Comparative Religion. Print.

Lincoln, Bruce. *Emerging from the Chrysalis: Studies in Rituals of Women's Initiation*. Cambridge: Harvard UP, 1981. Print.

Schechner, Richard. *Between Theater and Anthropology*. Philadelphia: U of Pennsylvania P, 1985. Print.

———. *Essays on Performance Theory, 1970–1976*. New York: Drama Book Specialists, 1977. Print.

———. "Magnitudes of Performance." *By Means of Performance: Intercultural Studies of Theatre and Ritual*. Ed. Schechner and Willa Appel. Cambridge: Cambridge UP, 1990. 19–49. Print.

———. "Restoration of Behavior." *Readings in Ritual Studies*. Ed. Ronald L. Grimes. Upper Saddle River: Prentice-Hall, 1991. 441–458. Print.

Schechner, Richard, and Lisa Wolford, eds. *The Grotowski Sourcebook*. London: Routledge, 1997. Print.

Singer, Milton. "The Cultural Pattern of Indian Civilization." *Far Eastern Quarterly* 15 (1955): 23–35. Print.

Smith, Jonathan Z. *Map Is Not Territory: Studies in the History of Religions*. Leiden: Brill, 1978. Print.

Smith, Wilfred Cantwell. *The Meaning and End of Religion*. New York: Macmillan, 1962. Print.

Turner, Victor W. *The Anthropology of Performance*. New York: Performing Arts Journal, 1987. Print.

———. "Are There Universals of Performance in Myth, Ritual, and Drama?" *By Means of Performance: Intercultural Studies of Theatre and Ritual*. Ed. Richard Schechner and Willa Appel. Cambridge: Cambridge UP, 1991. 8–18. Print.

———. *Dramas, Fields, and Metaphors. Symbolic Action in Human Society*. Ithaca: Cornell UP, 1974. Print. Symbol, Myth, and Ritual.

———. "Dramatic Ritual / Ritual Drama: Performative and Reflexive Anthropology." *Kenyon Review* 1.3 (1979): 80–93. Print.

———. "Frame, Flow, and Reflection: Ritual and Drama as Public Liminality." *Performance in Postmodern Culture*. Ed. Michel Benamou and Charles Caramello. Madison: U of Wisconsin P, 1977. 33–55. Print.

———. *From Ritual to Theatre: The Human Seriousness of Play*. New York: Performing Arts Journal, 1982. Print. Performance Studies Series.

———. "Liminality and the Performative Genres." *Rite, Drama, Festival, Spectacle: Rehearsals toward a Theory of Cultural Performance*. Ed. John MacAloon. Philadelphia: ISHI, 1985. 19–41. Print.

———. "Social Dramas and Stories about Them." *Critical Inquiry* 7 (1980): 141–168. Print.

Turner, Victor Witter, and Edith Turner. "Performing Ethnography." *The Drama Review* 26.2 (1982): 33–50. Print.

3 Spiritual Logic from Ritual Bodies

Donnalee Dox

Culture and discourse have long provided a critical framework for analyzing performance practices. Performance practices with a religious or spiritual valence, however, require an additional layer of analysis. The bodies, objects, and words available to an observer in a spiritually oriented performance practice may involve sensibilities that are not observable—participants' sense of the numinous, for example, or of spirit presences. The critical effort to show how normative cultural practices construct performances easily occludes the significance of how such sensibilities inform the way performance is done and the ways people invest performance with meaning. Suspicion of the representational power of language can foreclose on the potential of language to emerge from the experience of internal sensations. Similarly, an overemphasis on language as discourses that construct people's experience limits readings of language as an expressive and sense-making capacity.

William Demastes recognizes the effects of these limitations on the study of performance in *Staging Consciousness*. Demastes asks whether there is more going on in performance than "a postmodern, theoretical pastime" (8, 18). Starting with the internal workings of the body, Demastes undoes the persistent dichotomy between mind and body by allowing for reciprocity between the ephemerality of consciousness and the materiality of the human body. Studying spiritually oriented performance practices benefits from a similarly open analytical orientation, one that investigates the interplay between the human body as a biological organism, the human body situated in culture and discourses, people's internal sense of something beyond the physical world, and performance (including language) as an expression of internal sensibilities.[1] For spiritually oriented performance practices, such as the neoshamanic ritual discussed in the fourth section of this chapter, performance is the site at which sensations within the body (feelings, thoughts, emotions, input from the five senses) and the observable components of performance practices (texts, spoken language, physical action, use of space, cultural influences, objects, bodies) intersect.

The category of ritual, in which performance studies most readily finds the sacred and spirituality, is, as Catherine Bell pointed out, an academic category oriented around material culture and social cohesion. Bell resisted an entirely functional approach to ritual, in which ritual serves as "a basic mechanism for resolving or disguising conflicts fundamental to sociocultural life" ("Constructing Ritual" 31). She advocated instead investigating the ways people invent rituals, and the conditions from which rituals emerge (*Ritual* 225). In the scope of this chapter, an emerging ritual becomes a mechanism by which people cultivate sensibilities they identify as spiritual and articulate a kind of logic based on those sensibilities in those conditions. Ritual performance occurs at the intersection of material culture (including practices, objects, artifacts, values, economies, and social hierarchies), the interior of the body (including feelings, thoughts, emotions, and sensations), and the processes of consciousness (including meaning making, logical thinking, descriptive thinking, and verbal expression).

As Demastes shows, performance involves more than meets the eyes and ears of an observer, more than culture and discourse construct for observation. The question becomes how to talk about the reciprocity between people's internal experience of spirituality, which cannot be observed, and the materiality of performance practices, which can be. In the neoshamanic drumming ceremony by *Kalumba* discussed here as a case study, the internal experience of spirituality is a vital and complex component of the ceremonial practice.[2] Experiential spirituality gives the ceremony its logic. But how are the internal sensations from which people's spiritual experiences emerge, the understanding of spirituality at work in the ceremony, and the ceremony's situation in multiple cultural frames interconnected? The question requires a perspective that looks into (as well as at) the body, and connects the experience of spirituality with both the body and material culture.

The chapter is divided into five sections. First, "Reconfigurations" addresses some of the challenges the study of spirituality faces in a materialist-oriented critical framework. The second section, "Sense and Spirituality," looks at physiological processes associated with spiritual experience. The third section, "Spirits, Bodies, Culture, and Critique," sets out the basic premises for discussion of the Sacred Drumming Ceremony. "The Drum is a Living Entity . . . " describes a neoshamanic practice at the intersection of culture and internal sensation. The fifth section, "Spiritual Logic from Ritual Bodies," returns to William Demastes's question and argues for the significance of what people claim as internal experience in the analysis of performance.

RECONFIGURATIONS: EMBODYING THE SPIRIT, MINDING THE BODY

Spirituality, as a kind of internal experience, poses a significant challenge to the configuration of mind, body, and spirit in the traditions of modern Western thought. The defining quality of spirituality, as a kind of experience, is its ineffability—a person's sense of something mysterious, just beyond the grasp of mental comprehension, something that defies representation except by metaphor. Many performative practices express this sensibility—religious theatre, music and dance, parades and festivals, architecture, public preaching and praying, religious and spiritual texts, advertisements for religious events, displays of glossolalia, mediumship, channeling, and psychic readings, and so on. Regardless of whether religious traditions or professions of belief frame these performance practices, their embodiment references a non-physical domain to human experience. Whether the mode of performance purports to represent, express, invoke, communicate, testify to, or celebrate that domain, there is always the possibility that the practice performs a logic that depends upon people's internal sensation of a metaphysical reality. Finding that logic requires opening the borders of performance analysis beyond cultural codes for spirituality, belief systems that define a ritual's meaning or efficacy, or the symbolic value of ritual bodies and objects.

Performance analysis tends to temper the potential significance of spirituality in ways that dismiss a perennialist approach to spirituality, and posit spirituality as emergent from social processes. First, affective qualities associated with spirituality—emotions, revelatory insights, a sense of being transported, a sense of the ineffable, ecstasy, heightened awareness, and so on—are generally not treated as authentic, but as functions of discourses or cultural norms (such as institutionalized religious beliefs) that structure certain kinds of experiences as spiritual. Spiritual experience is rarely given epistemological status or taken on its own terms as the impetus for, or logic underpinning, performance. Secondly, the human body in performance is posited as an object that is constructed by cultural and discursive forces and always situated in relation to social, political, and economic systems. To take the body as a biological organism and to locate the production of meaning in the body risk scientific reductionism on one side and humanist universalizing on the other, as well as disregard for the ways cultures identify bodies and discourses construct bodies as identities.

The tendency to temper the significance of spirituality is not unwarranted. In theatre studies, suspicion of religion as a conservative ideological force lingers as a legacy of the notion that the medieval church was hostile to theatre. The developmental "ritual-to-theatre" narrative, which ran parallel to anthropology's evolutionary model of human development, helped position religious or ritualistic performance as the primitive ancestor of modern, secular theatre. Though multi- and inter-cultural studies of performance have accommodated the religious sensibilities of non-Western cultures as constitutive of performance, and not in fact "primitive," the Western intellectual tradition still critiques, brackets, or "others" religion and spirituality.[3] Further, to the extent that religious experience is construed as irrational and anti-intellectual, spirituality remains anathema to academic inquiry.

Perhaps the most pervasive limitations on discussions of spirituality as a kind of experience have come from the effects of postmodernism. Modernism had effectively split aesthetic affect from Christian-inflected notions of spiritual transcendence, distinguishing religious belief and spiritual experience from reasoned thinking and the workings of the rational mind (Hufford and Bucking 33).[4] Thus, modernism could acknowledge, even embrace, the supernatural or metaphysical in non-Western or archaic cultures, but could not reconcile spirituality with Western formulations of knowledge. Postmodern thought likewise rejected metaphysics, the supernatural and institutional religion, but on different grounds. Claims of spiritual experiences or esoteric knowledge could be shown to be manipulations by systems of institutional power and organized around conceptual binaries (inner experience/outward expression, emotion/cognition, faith/reason, ineffable/material, self/other). As a critical framework, postmodern approaches to performance dismissed concepts fundamental to religion and spirituality (such as a subjective inner life, emotional response as authoritative, faith in the ineffable, an essential self, a metaphysical other); assumed religion and spirituality to be constructed by discursive formations (reality, truth, human, God); and critiqued religion's alliance with political ideologies.

If the postmodern critique of the metaphysics of presence exposed spirituality as a fiction, the body fared no better. Edward Slingerland observes that permutations of postmodern theory, which sought and found all thought to be constituted in existing discursive formations, itself failed to operate outside an epistemological framework that separated the intellectual and creative activity of the mind, the performative potential of the physical body, and metaphysical knowledge or experience (Slingerland 100). The body in postmodernism, as Slingerland points out, remained "a passive receiver of culture" and a "featureless 'site' for discursive power struggles" when it could have been allowed "an active role in the structuring of human consciousness" (Slingerland 94–95).

The distinction between mind and body Slingerland points to as an inherent limitation in postmodern theorizing also plays out in the ways ritual studies constructs ritual as a category of religious activity. Catherine Bell showed that the construction of ritual in academic study defines ritual by bodily actions rather than the logical faculties associated with the mind or cognition. Because ritual's functional power is thought to be grounded in its physicality, ritual studies subordinates the body to the mental, language-oriented processes of myth-making (Bell, *Ritual* 173). Ritual studies, Bell observes, takes "beliefs, creeds, symbols, and myths" to be the genesis for the physical activity of rituals (Bell, *Ritual* 30). Rituals themselves do not have epistemological status, but the myths that structure them do. Conversely, the mental processes that construct explanatory myths are not construed as embodied or active, that is, as the domain of the physical body (Bell, *Ritual* 27). However, as Carl Seaquist notes, "The symbolic approach to myth and ritual may seem intuitively obvious, because it has such a strong tradition in both scholarly and popular literature, from antiquity to the present, but there are good reasons to be skeptical of it" (Seaquist 206).

The privileging of mind over body has been fundamental to the constitution of ritual as a category of behavior, as has been the idea that ritual resolves social conflict.[5] Thus, experiential spirituality, either as the genesis or result of ritual practice, is left to hover outside mind and body. Certainly, this hierarchy holds in some ritual traditions. Christian theologian Theodore W. Jennings, Jr., for example, asserts that the physical activity of ritual "alters the world or the place of the ritual participant in the world" even as "[r]itual knowledge is gained through a bodily action" (Jennings 326). The distinction between mental processes and bodily activity is evident in Jennings's description of ritual as "corporeal rather than cerebral, primarily active rather than contemplative, primarily transformative rather than speculative" (Jennings 326, 332).

Catherine Bell and Edward Slingerland point to how conventional configurations of mind and body structure analyses of religious performance practices, and avoid the ambiguous liminality of spiritual experience. Yet, in practice the formulations of spirituality people develop may not be governed by the hierarchical configuration of mind and body operating in ritual studies and postmodern theory, and they may not limit the function of ritual to the social world. The organizing principle of a ritual may be acceptance of a non-physical domain participants can access, and the language and bodily action that constitute an observable ritual performance may be understood to emerge from that experiential component. Relegating spirituality to a cultural or discursive construction would limit analysis of such a practice. At the same time, ritual practices also rely heavily on the materiality of culture and discourses on spirituality to articulate the ritual's internal logic. The case study presented here is deeply invested in cultural practices, linguistic formulations, and the materiality of objects and bodies. Thus, studying performed spirituality requires traversing spirituality, corporeality, cognition, and the materiality of culture.[6]

THE SENSE OF SPIRITUALITY

"Sense" here has two meanings: internal corporeal sensation (sensing, feeling) and creating logic (cognition, making sense). Both are embodied, and both apply to spirituality. The body performs ritual, but the body is also the site at which people experience sensations of spirituality and from which people develop spirituality as a kind of logic that can be formulated in language. If the external body is the site at which we identify performative behavior, the interior of the body is the site of the sensations in which people ground spiritual experiences and which the performance of rituals supports and enhances.

Neurological research on ritual and spirituality offers an invaluable complement to humanities' investment in what Slingerland calls the "blooming, buzzing" variety of cultural practices (Slingerland 151). The body becomes a mutable, cross-cultural constant. Interestingly, early work on the physiology of spiritual experiences fits the neurological data into the functional model of ritual, privileging language as that which structures experience. [7] Eugene D'Aquili and Charles Laughlin showed that the rhythmic, repetitive actions of ritual generate limbic discharges, which in collaboration with other brain functions produce the sense of group cohesion and of the individual self dissolving. This finding supported ritual as a mechanism for resolving social conflict (D'Aquili and Laughlin 135). The location of spiritual experience in the limbic area, usually identified as a premammalian site of emotions and of a lower order than cognitive brain functions, also corroborated an approach to ritual as an adaptive, social, problem-solving activity.

However, following D'Aquili and Laughlin, there is also a neurological imperative to organize sensory data and construct models of reality by arranging concepts around antinomies and binaries, creating causal chains, and ascribing meaning (D'Aquili and Laughlin 139). This "higher" order brain accounts for the ways spirituality is conceptualized in myths, religious histories, and beliefs.[8] Mythologies provide the "cognitive matrix" for sensations that, in this model, have no epistemological content (D'Aquili and Laughlin 137, 133).[9] An integrated "causal operator" (a network of the anterior convexity of the frontal lobe and the inferior parietal lobule) links higher and lower order brain functions, which produces concepts of "gods, powers, spirits, [and] personified forces" people might sense in the performance of a ritual.[10]

Following Bell's critique, this neurological model of spirituality adopts an intellectual value system that privileges logocentric thinking (discourse) and social organization (culture). In a ritual practice, however, the sensations people experience in physical action and lower order limbic activity might well have epistemological value. Internally experienced sensations might have their own logic, which becomes the source for myths or other kinds of spiritual language, rather than requiring myth to explain them. In practice, sensations might have implicit significance.

Richard Schechner offers an excellent illustration of how the sensations of spirituality are intricately bound to the body and are recognizable apart from existing beliefs or mythologies. Schechner observes that the physical action of spinning in one place increases the body's endorphin production, which results in an opiate-like sensation of feeling "good," Freud's "oceanic" feeling. Schechner allows that recognition and description of this somatic experience require no interpretive symbol system, such as the poetry of Sufism or the ritual structure of Dervish whirling. Ideological, religious, or political constructs may be available to define the sensations as spiritual, or to give them epistemological content, but feeling and identifying the sensations do not depend on those constructs (Schechner 18).

Schechner is willing to bypass the binaries, oppositions, contradictions, and antinomies that undergird the functional approach to ritual as a mechanism for resolving social discord. He is also willing to acknowledge that the central nervous system (CNS) produces sensations, such as the sense that one's individual identity dissolves, or that binary thinking ceases. At the level of somatic sensation and feeling, Schechner suggests, "rituals communicate in their own code, whether or not I understand the code" (Schechner 25).[11] The sensations of whirling have their own corporeal logic, which might organize thoughts expressed in language or in gestures, rituals, images, and symbols. At the same time, the sensations of whirling might also lend themselves to explanation or interpretation through the existing hermeneutics of Sufi or Dervish traditions.

Theologian and neuroscientist Nina P. Azari's interpretation of the neurological correlates to spiritual experience supports the idea that internal sensations have an inherent logic. Azari holds that spiritual experience is not pre-constructed by myth, and has its own cognitive content. Azari makes the case that spiritual experiences are not reducible to pre-cognitive emotional and somatic sensations generated by the limbic system, which by convention have less epistemological value. Nor, she argues, are spiritual experiences reducible to representational systems that circumscribe beliefs in spirit entities, deities, spiritual domains, or a transcendent human spirit (Azari 2). Azari posits spiritual experience as distinct from the emotional states activated by the limbic system and possessing epistemological content that finds articulation in higher order brain functions (Azari 17).

These contrasting interpretations of the neurological correlates to spiritual experience have an important commonality. They suggest that what people experience as spirituality can be understood as a synthesis of physiological processes. These include what we recognize as mental processes, such the symbol systems of myths (mind). They also include internal sensations that are not cognitive or linguistic but grounded in physical activity (body). Leaving open the question of the existence of a metaphysical or supernatural domain, this line of inquiry does hold that spirituality is corporeal. The body links the experience of spirituality to the physical action of ritual, and the physical action of ritual to the cognitive formulation of myths.

The spiritual component that informs the performance of rituals, then, involves the body not only in the prescribed behaviors of the ritual but in the cultivation of internal sensations (including cognition). The formulation of concepts in symbolic systems that express internal sensations as specifically spiritual in nature—discourses on spirituality, myths, prayers, coded behaviors, symbolic gestures, touching sacred objects—also involves the body. Linking spiritual experience, cognition, and corporeality in the interior of the body in this way raises questions about how spirituality informs the communicative, observable aspects of performance. The questions lead from the interior of the body and individual experiences of spirituality to ritual bodies situated in culture and to shared constructions of spirituality encoded in ritual performances.

Some of these questions reflect the kind of analytical tendencies Catherine Bell observed in the study of ritual. Are we locating "spirituality" in the symbolic or representational aspects of ritual, the "cognitive matrix" of belief systems or myths? Or, can we assume that myths and belief systems derive from or emerge from sensations people already understand to be spiritual and cultivate by doing rituals? Does the physical action of ritual activate neurological activity that produces what people understand to be spiritual experience? Or is ritual, as Michael Winkelman suggests, a means by which people alter their brains (Winkelman 155)?

Other questions more directly address the emergence of rituals in cultural situations. By what processes do people come to identify certain sensations as spiritual (rather than, for example, as emotions or psychological aberrations)? How does ritual cultivate these sensations? What makes these sensations valuable as a kind of knowledge? How does the cultivation of internal sensation synthesize the cognitive processes of symbolic logic, formation of concepts about spirituality, and belief with the experience of spiritual sensations? The performance of ritual twists embodiment into a double helix by bringing people's internal physiological processes in contact with material culture. How do we investigate the interplay between experiential spirituality and material culture?

SPIRITS, BODIES, CULTURE, AND CRITIQUE

The previous section showed neurological models of how spirituality and cognition are interconnected in the body, which blurs rigid borders between cognition, corporeality, and spirituality. What is often lacking in efforts to find neurological correlates to spiritual experience, however, is how people identify spirituality as a specific kind of experience. Just as the logic of spirituality is, as I have suggested, derived from embodied practices, it is also deeply invested in the matter of culture. Catherine Bell asserts:

> [t]he contexts in which ritual practices unfold are not like the props of painted scenery on a theatrical stage. Ritual action involves an inextricable interaction with its immediate world, often drawing it into the very activity of the rite in multiple ways. Exactly how this is done, how often, and with what stylistic features will depend on the specific cultural and social situations with its traditions, conventions, and innovations. (Bell, *Ritual* 266)

Developing rituals, such as the Sacred Drumming Ceremony introduced in the fourth section, offer an optimal site for observing what Bell calls a ritual's facts of invention—the social, discursive, historical, and cultural components that together with somatic sensation and cognitive formulations constitute a ritual practice. Moving outward from the body's capacity for sensation and sense-making to the culturally coded (or loaded) objects and texts people engage invites some scrutiny.

For reasons given in the first section, critiques of spiritually oriented performance practices as naïve, fraudulent, manipulative, or simplistic "feel-good" activities sit more comfortably in research inquiries than do arguments for the epistemological value of spiritual and somatic experience. This is especially accurate for critiques of Western practices that draw on non-Western or indigenous cultures for inspiration. Modern neoshamanism and sacred drumming, the genre of contemporary spirituality into which the Sacred Drumming Ceremony falls, is no exception. Michael Harner's *The Way of the Shaman*, which popularized modern shamanism in the 1980s, earned a severe critique from Gary Laderman for promising an easy, quick method for "spiritual fulfillment and psychic transformation," for its facile cultural borrowings, and for its self-referentiality (Laderman 271). The analytical agenda of Laderman's critique will be familiar to performance studies scholars:

> Harner and other neoshamans extract a constellation of ideas and practices from a variety of cultural settings, historical circumstances, and individual encounters. They seek to produce seamless systems of shamanic practice available through texts, in workshops, or over the Web to eager novices looking for dramatic spiritual adventures and escape from the numbing routines and pains of daily life. One result of brokering the shamanic experience to a larger audience is the simultaneous distortion of local cultural histories and the invention of religious rituals that are customized for contemporary individuals living in the modern world. Harner draws on his own experiences and a wealth of cross-cultural knowledge to create his own version of shamanic ritual practice. (Laderman 270)

The critique of neoshamanism as a variation on popular, new age spirituality has merit as a caution against cultural appropriation, but it also limits the study of performative spirituality to cultural and discursive forces, writing out the interior of the body. It forecloses on whatever formulations of spirituality might be generated from the ritual actions of a given shamanic practice, and reduces cultural interaction to a manipulative, abusive marketing scheme.[12] Insofar as practitioners do develop practical epistemologies in and from the performance of rituals, and insofar as these might have value or influence in the larger culture, the experiential component warrants attention. Catherine Bell's call to recognize traditions, conventions, and innovations at work in specific rituals, plus the effort to focus on the interplay between physiological processes and culture, requires a different critical stance toward cultural borrowing than that taken by a critique such as Laderman's.

Philip Heffner, extrapolating from Mihalyi Csikszentmihalyi's concept of flow as well as from studies in neuroscience, suggests a stance that does not marginalize spirituality from critical analysis (see the first section) but from which spirituality

> refers to the way in which our consciousness is organized [. . .] so as to enable us to put our knowledge and experience of the world together in coherent ways that support values, viable lifestyles, and moral behavior. Spirituality refers to the organization of our consciousness that makes richness of life possible, for individuals and communities. (Heffner 124)

We might ask, then, what values, lifestyles, behaviors, and epistemologies does a ritual practice such as *Kalumba*'s Sacred Drumming Ceremony offer, and how do the internal sensations, symbolic expressions of spirituality, and culture come together to construct the ritual's spiritual logic?

Three premises guide the discussion of spirituality, corporeality, and culture in the fourth section. The first premise is that "spirituality"—a sense of being in relation with ineffability—can be investigated as a domain of human experience from which people formulate knowledge. The second premise is that spiritual sensibilities have physiological correlates, but that physiology does not explain the ways people experience spirituality. The third is that "spirituality" is identifiable as such in the interplay between the physical action of rituals, the formulations of knowledge people derive from sensations generated in rituals, and what is available in material culture through which people identify spirituality as a particular kind of experience.

"THE DRUM IS A LIVING ENTITY . . . "

In 2008 and 2009, I conducted fieldwork with *Kalumba*, a shamanic drumming practice in Tucson, Arizona. *Kalumba*'s founder, Mr. Martin Klabunde, offers retreats, workshops, meditation and relaxation sessions, private shamanic healing sessions, and classes in West African drumming. *Kalumba* is part of the Dambe Project, a non-profit organization for youth mentorship through music. "The drum," Mr. Klabunde wrote in an electronic announcement of *Kalumba*'s events and classes, "is a living entity, a spirit, and music is a sacred vehicle for pure intention" (*Kalumba* Announcement, November 2008). These words describe both belief and experience. Twice a month, *Kalumba*'s Sacred Drumming Ceremony and occasional Full Moon Drumming and Dance ceremonies created an experiential context that is the source for these words, and which these words inform.

During the time of my fieldwork, *Kalumba*'s Sacred Drumming Ceremony took place on weekend evenings at a ranch within the city limits of Tucson, sometimes in conjunction with a shamanic workshop during the day. Mr. Klabunde's sense that modern, technological society is infused with spirits motivated the creation and development of the Sacred Drumming Ceremony. The intent of the ceremony, which he describes in workshops and ceremonies as adapted from rituals he encountered during extended study with shamans in Uganda and Mexico, is to increase people's awareness of spirits that inhabit the three mountain ranges surrounding the city of Tucson. Ceremonial drumming is a means of communicating with these spirits, with spiritual forces or energies, as well as connecting consciously with one's spiritual self or soul.

"Come join us in this inner dance with one's own secret being. Learn to use the drum as the heartbeat of mother earth and a doorway to the stars." With these sentences, *Kalumba*'s 2009 electronic newsletters articulated the ceremony's spiritual logic: the action of the ritual synchronizes one's body with the bodies of natural cosmos, the earth and stars; that synchronization reveals an inner self, otherwise inaccessible. Spirituality is simultaneously communal and solitary, mediated by the action of hand drumming and also immanent. The Sacred Drumming Ceremony invests collective drumming with the potential for altering consciousness, coming to new awareness of self, and communicating with spirits:

> Through these ceremonies, one is able to transcend physical limitations and release one's own potential as a being connected with the stars and universe; part of a cosmic whole from this enlarged and peaceful state of awareness, one naturally discovers his or her own potential for self healing and guidance. (*Kalumba* Newsletter, January 2009)

The experiential logic of the ceremony assumes an essential self or soul that is capable of profound transformation leading to social transformation. The ceremonies do not hold out expectations for other kinds of more radical experiences associated with indigenous shamanism: a soul journey, visions, out-of-body experiences, a sudden transformation of consciousness, an initiation, communication with animals, ecstatic trance, self-representation in animals, self-identification with individual spirits, spirit channeling, or magic (though some of these are part of *Kalumba*'s other offerings).[13] Shamanism is overtly adapted for acceptance in a modern, urban, Western cultural setting.

The ceremonial space was a one-story, freestanding meeting room on the ranch, accessible by dirt roads leading off a major thoroughfare, with parking in an open lot between paddocks, an arena, and fenced horse pastures. The room comfortably accommodated thirty people in chairs arranged in a circle facing inward. Air circulated through high windows, which offered portals to the sky as dusk turned into night during the course of the ceremony. At about 7:00 in the evening, participants, numbering anywhere from ten to thirty, would gather on an open porch outside the meeting room. Mr. Klabunde's CDs, printed copies of two prayers, and a donation jar would be set out on a table, and participants asked to contribute $10.00 to offset the cost of renting the space. Some participants preferred to pay in advance through *Kalumba*'s website.

About 7:30, give or take a few minutes, Mr. Klabunde would quietly and informally invite participants to remove their shoes and enter into the ceremonial space. Each participant paused just inside the door to receive Mr. Klabunde's ceremonial cleansing with burning sage. Once inside the space, each participant chose a drum to play during the ceremony. Mr. Klabunde provided his own hand-made djembe and dundun drums, and African rattles for participants to use, and some brought their own drums. Mr. Klabunde makes djembes for sale on site and through *Kalumba*'s website, for a very competitive price of about $350.00. Each person took a seat on the chairs prearranged in a circle. Around a chair on the west side of the circle an array of drums were arranged for Mr. Klabunde to play during the ceremony.

When the group is seated with drums positioned between their knees, Mr. Klabunde gives a brief, quiet introduction to the Sacred Drumming Ceremony. The introduction is not standard, formulaic, or ritualized but depends on Mr. Klabunde's sense of what words and rhythms are right for that particular evening. He might, for example, give a bit of background on drumming as an ancient healing practice, talk about the migration of spirits from Africa to North America, set a simple intention for the ceremony (such as "life purpose"), advise participants to relinquish linguistic thought (to "take the brain out of it") in order to allow contact with spirits and energies, or offer ideas that will give participants an entry into drumming as a spiritual practice. Participants are asked to remain in the circle for the duration of the drumming (about ninety minutes), and not to re-enter if they leave the room for any reason.

After the introduction, Mr. Klabunde begins the ceremony. He stands in the center of the circle holding a conch shell. As he faces each of the four compass directions, he blows a long tone through the shell. Getting a clear tone sometimes takes more than one try, but there is no sense that this is a mistake or break in what should be a smooth, seamless ritual. Facing each compass point, Mr. Klabunde invokes the spiritual energies of East, West, North, and South. He then asks "Mother Earth" and "Father Sky" to bless the drumming. This action opens the ceremony for the collective recitation of two prayers attributed to Native American origins, a Navajo prayer "Walk in Beauty" and "Of Course It Was Not I," adapted from Black Elk. Participants read these prayers from the printed copies available on the porch before the ceremony began. Like Mr. Klabunde's introductory words, they provide formulations of spirituality that link the drumming with spirituality, but they do not proscribe a belief system or set expectations for what people will experience in the ceremony.

A hierarchy that privileges cognitive thought over corporeal sensation (see first and second sections) would read the prayers as a mythology that structures or explains the ritual. Taken as a cognitive matrix that structures the drumming, the prayers seem at first inconsistent. The word "spirit" is used in different ways. "Walk in Beauty" invokes a "big, beautiful spirit" in relation to a person's individual spirit ("my spirit"). "Of Course It Was Not I" speaks of "powers from the outer [spiritual] world" that can heal a person's individual psychic or physical wounds if a person releases ego-consciousness during the ceremony. As noted in the second section, D'Aquili and Laughlin posit that any cognitive matrix that identifies somatic experience as "spiritual" combines cortical functions with the processing of sensory input (D'Aquili and Laughlin 139, 140). Ritual can activate simultaneously both the "higher" order brain activity associated with the formulation of concepts and the "lower" order limbic system associated with the emotion, feeling, and mystical experiences.

These prayers do not explain drumming as inherently spiritual, or structure expectations for participants' spiritual experiences. Rather, the prayers put the physical action of drumming in relation to a domain of spiritual entities, to a spirituality immanent in the natural world, and to the human self (mind and body) as a spirit. They suggest a relationship between individuals and the numinous in which the individual self (ego) is open to a metaphysical domain, but they do not define that domain within, or as, a belief system. Perhaps more significantly, and not accounted for if the prayers are taken only as a cognitive matrix, this collective recitation is the participants' first physical engagement with the ritual. Collective recitation of the words initiates somatic as well as cognitive processes with the sensations of breath and vocalization. We can just as easily assume that corporeal sensations generated in the recitation of the prayers—the intake and exhale of breath, the formation of the words in the throat and mouth, the vibrations of the sound throughout the body—inform the word "spirit" in the prayers as assume that the word informs the sensations.

For people who have not studied shamanism or drumming, or attended a ceremony before, Mr. Klabunde gives basic instructions on the three tones and hand positions used for playing the djembes. He then teaches participants three simple rhythms, which when played together by roughly equal groups will create a synchronized aural environment. Once participants have mastered the rhythms, the remaining time (about seventy-five minutes) is devoted to steady, unrelenting drumming. Over the group's drumming, Mr. Klabunde improvises more complex rhythms on the array of drums set on the west side of the circle. He varies syncopation, speed, and volume over the steady ostinato of the group drumming. Some of the rhythms he learned during his tutelage with drum masters in East Africa, West Africa, and Mexico. Other rhythms are his own compositions, to which he attributes spiritual inspiration and healing power, a process of attribution very much in keeping with the ego-less sentiment of the prayer, "Of Course It Was Not I."

Around 9:30, Mr. Klabunde gradually slows his rhythms and plays more softly. Consciously or not, participants do the same. As people one by one stop drumming, the sound stops entirely. The ceremony ends with a few moments of silence. Eventually, without a formal end to the ceremony, people begin to get up, replace their drums, gather their belongings, and leave through the door onto the porch. By 10:00, Mr. Klabunde is packing up his drums, and participants have driven away on the unlit dirt road toward the highway.

SPIRITUAL LOGIC FROM RITUAL BODIES

Performance and ritual studies rely on parsing relationships between representations and their referents, whether through symbolic correspondences that define meaning, sign-systems that displace and defer meaning, or discourses that produce meaning. Performance and ritual studies are also deeply invested in how rituals are situated in human culture, and in the ways performance embodies cultural norms. Whereas the observable actions of rituals lend themselves to this kind of analysis, the physical actions also have a non-representational component in their potential to generate sensations and do not rely on cultural codes to construct those sensations, as in Richard Schechner's reflections on whirling. At the level of internal sensation, the Sacred Drumming Ceremony's repetitive physical action, the intensity of the sound, and the palpable vibrations can affect internal sensations in a variety of ways.

The physical activity synchronizes the discharge of slow brain waves, which in effect integrates what would otherwise be distinguished as mental, physical, and psychological functions. Michael Winkleman calls this the "integrative mode of consciousness" brought on and reinforced by repetitive actions, such as communal drumming (Winkelman 151). The integrative neurological model for somatic and mental processes proposed by D'Aquili and Laughlin identifies the rhythmic, repetitive actions of rituals with limbic discharges that do not produce emotional states in isolation but coordinate other brain functions, resulting in a sense of group cohesion and a loss of consciousness of the self as an individual (D'Aquili and Laughlin 135). The activity of communal drumming engages theta and alpha brain wave production, which ameliorates the mind's critical faculty and the impulse to think in binaries—precisely what Mr. Klabunde advocates as a component of the ability to relinquish ego and access or experience a spiritual realm.

Aural and kinesthetic activity such as sustained drumming generates, as Winkelman describes it, a "nonlinguistic channel" through which the perception of difference dissolves, self-identity dissolves, group cohesion is fostered, and non-linguistic awareness is heightened (Winkleman 150). The sensations of drumming may be experienced in as many ways as there are individuals—trance states, meditative states, out of body experiences, profuse sweating, auditory or visual hallucinations, release of muscle tension, restlessness or agitation, or pain are only a few possible experiences. Azari's relational model and the networking *causal operator* proposed by D'Aquili and Laughlin both integrate "higher" and "lower" functions. The content of the "lower" order brain functions, however, formulates knowledge in metaphors, images, and generalized affective concepts rather than in binary thinking or logical causality. And, as D'Aquili and Laughllin have proposed, the language that expresses physiological sensations as spiritual experience can loop back to affect and reinforce limbic and autonomic activity (D'Aquili and Laughlin 137). Michael Winkleman calls this physiological integration of cognition, physical activity, and spirituality the "integrative mode of consciousness" (Winkelman 151).

Activities such as communal drumming encourage neurological conditions in which people's sense of self-identity dissolves, group cohesion is fostered, and a kind of awareness that does not rely on language is heightened. Out of this sensation comes a formulation of sensation as knowledge, in which relinquishing the self as ego allows one to release one's self into a spiritual realm, even to communicate with spirit entities. The ability to sense individual spirits is characteristic of shamanism. It is one of the more difficult aspects of this practice to accommodate in performance analysis, in part because the spirits themselves are not observable performers. David J. Hufford and Mary Ann Bucklin observe that whereas sociological and anthropological data show belief in spirits to be "persistent and widespread" in modernized cultures, prevailing intellectual attitudes stigmatize belief in spirits as naïve, irrational, or pathological (Huford and Bucklin 26). The neurological correlates to spirit belief, however, suggest that far from being inherently absurd, perception of and communication with spirits emerges from non-verbal thinking. Winkelman concludes, for example, that spirit concepts are in fact based in the ability to infer the mental states of others, which is a form of social intelligence (Winkelman 152).

If the brain's response to activities such as coordinated group drumming is the conceptualization of spirit entities, the spiritual logic of this ceremony draws on cultural referents to formulate this relationship as non-linguistic communication with individual spirits and spiritual energy (Winkelman 151). The cultural borrowing that brings African spirits into the urban Southwest in *Kalumba*'s descriptions of the Sacred Drumming Ceremony presents a critical problem for performance analysis. Laderman critiqued neoshamanism as a self-serving distortion of local, indigenous histories irresponsibly brokered by self-styled shamans who provide spiritual adventures to relieve the numbing routines and the pains of modern life (Laderman 270). The way *Kalumba* describes the ceremony, however, preempts Laderman's critique. Cultural borrowing is understood to extend ritual practices from Africa and Mexico to a contrasting culture that is materially rich but spiritually inept.

The ceremony invites people to a "genuine Shamanic drumming ceremony," that consciously reveres and respects "the ancestors who keep these secret rituals alive by passing them on" (*Kalumba* Newsletter, January 2010). *Kalumba*'s educational and community service work is infused with a keen sensitivity to the disparities of wealth, health care, and material advantages of a highly industrialized culture against the material poverty of the cultures in which he learned shamanic drumming. There is no effort to reproduce a specific African ceremony and claim its authenticity, but rather an appeal to shamanic practice in general as "genuine." I observed no romanticizing or idealization of indigenous cultures, and the salvific effort of this practice does not flatter contemporary Western culture. Rather than offer a palliative to the demographics of a white, middle-class, urban demographic, the ceremonial drumming offers a corrective to the participants' home culture. The ceremony promotes social action through the discipline of the practice and individual transformations of consciousness. Efforts to access spiritual domains require adaptations to accommodate both the spiritual limitations and material advantages of modern, industrial culture.

In practice, Mr. Klabunde sometimes recommends that when drumming participants "take the brain out of it," to consciously release the binary thinking, linguistic formulations of knowledge, and cognitive frameworks that mark habits of thought in the modern world. At first look, this seems tautological. The prayers and introductions do not escape the binary thinking, linguistic constructions, and cognitive processes to which people are accustomed. But beating a drumhead intensely for an hour can raise endorphin and serotonin levels to produce sensations that one's consciousness is freed from representational or binary thinking, and that one's identity transcends the social world as a soul or spiritual self. Theta and alpha brain wave production can also usurp the mind's critical faculty and the impulse to think in binaries.

The suggestion to "take the brain out of it" implies that binary, linguistic thinking can be released without the physical action of the ceremony. If the conscious release of linguistic, binary thinking can happen even before the kinesthetic effects of the drumming kick in to affect internal sensation in the same way, what distinguishes the sensations of the drumming from a mental state of non-linguistic meditation? What is important in the suggestion to "take the brain out of it" is the desire for non-representational modes of thinking that can change habitual thinking and that leave internal sensation unstructured and open to communication with spirits. "Take the brain out if it" posits spirituality as knowledge that is not dependent on symbol systems for meaning, not structured by a cognitive matrix, and accessible at the level of experience.

The language that emerges from the ritual practice is also the discourse that constructs the meaning of the ritual practice. The spiritual logic is a matrix of cultural references, rather than a syllogism, which connects ritual traditions from non-European indigenous cultures with the authority of modern health science and personal transformation. The following description, from *Kalumba*'s June 2009 electronic newsletter, articulates points on this matrix. The ceremony makes unmediated and credible wisdom from ancient, indigenous cultures available through the spiritual power inherent in the drum and its use as a technology for healing people in a spiritually bereft culture:

> Indigenous cultures around the world recognize the use of the drum as a powerful spiritual tool that can be used to heal our spiritual, mental, and physical bodies.

Modern science verifies this non-scientific wisdom. Sacred drumming is a technique for psychological and physical health, and spirituality resides in the interior of the human body, not in a transcendent or immanent domain of spirituality:

> The act of playing the drum produces chemical changes in our bodies that boosts [sic] the immune system, reduces stress, depression and chronic pain and restores inner peace.

Ancient, indigenous cultures and modern, technological culture fuse in the sensations drumming generates. The final authority is the individual experience of drumming, through which a person can access a spiritual domain and improve personal well-being:

> drumming provides you direct access to universal energy and is a meditation that increases compassion, relaxation, serenity, joy and happiness. (*Kalumba* Newsletter, July 2009)

Ultimately, ceremonial drumming generates the sensation of

> one's own potential as a being connected with the stars and universe; a being, part of a cosmic whole, from this enlarged and peaceful state of awareness one naturally discovers his or her own potential for self healing and guidance. (Dambe Project and *Kalmuba* Announcement, January 2009)

The logic that somatic experience of the ceremony will yield spiritual transformations toward peaceful relations with self, society, and the numinous is evident in the testimonial of one anonymous participant who wrote:

> I feel something is there beyond what I am experiencing. I want more than just the experience of communal drumming. I want to experience a deep and meaningful connection with the drum, myself, other's [sic] and spirit when I play the drum. (*Kalumba* Newsletter, March 2009)

Whatever internal sensations allow for this fluidity between the observable, tangible world of matter and something ineffable happen in the process of performing the ritual. The neurological correlates to these sensations tell us that the materiality of the body and the sense of spirituality are inextricably linked. The cultural and discursive components of the practice tell us how those sensations simultaneously construct and express experience as spiritual, and what significance spirituality has in relation to material culture.

CONCLUSION

I have argued that ritual bodies are the sites at which internal sensations become experiences people identify as spiritual, but that the language of myths or cultural symbol systems does not necessarily mediate that transformation. Cognition is as much an internal process as are changes in neurotransmitter levels, activation of the limbic system, or suppression of the parietal lobe. From the internal sensations generated in the corporeal actions of ritual, people develop ways of thinking about the world. The logic of spirituality may not be a construction of discourses on spirituality and the artifacts of material culture that mark spirituality. Meaning-making can happen from the body as well as being written on the body.

Spiritually oriented performances might well emerge from and articulate a particular kind of knowledge. Whether specific internal neurological processes and sensations are inherently and only spiritual I will not argue. I do want to suggest that, at the level of physiological processes and perceptible sensations, the body fuses the meaning-making potential of language and culture. Ritual performance can be read as a mode of thinking that is not so much pre-cognitive or non-linguistic as it is simultaneously physical and ephemeral. The effects of the physiological processes are in reality those the spiritual practices cultivate and from which people formulate knowledge claims.

In practice, spiritual experience is not a stable category. It is as elusive as the spirits themselves. The descriptions of the ceremony, the prayers, Mr. Klabunde's introductory comments, even the anonymous testimonial, are not enough to construct the action of ceremonial drumming as inherently and always spiritual. In any given ceremony, some participants' facial expressions and body movements do suggest they have shifted consciousness and are immersed in the physiological sensations that produce trance, deep meditation, or conversations with spirits. However, other participants seem to be consciously performing a desired spiritual state, periodically checking to see if others are watching them or to see what other participants are doing. Still others appear amused, embarrassed, or bored.

Analysis of the physiological investment required by a ritual practice, the discursive articulations of spirituality associated with the activity, and the fluid exchange with material culture can help revise, (or complicate), the conceptual borders between mind, body, and spirit embedded in conventional analytical strategies. Such an investigation opens the possibility for more holistic discussions of religious and spiritual performance practices in general. The argument and approach taken here also suggest that spiritual formulations constitute a kind of knowledge formation at the intersection of the body and culture. This process, which posits the body as a biological constant in play with material culture, yields critical information about the circulation of ideas and practices across cultures.

Further research into other kinds of performance practices that claim a spiritual component (not all of which will evince a vision of social progress, personal transformation, or contact with spirits, and some of which may deliberately manipulate the somatic sensations discussed here) can prompt reconsideration of the modernist and postmodernist attitudes toward the affective potential of performance. This way of thinking about performance assumes that performativity involves a strong internal component, and can itself constitute a hermeneutic quest. The study of performance, as William Demastes hopes, does indeed extend beyond a "postmodern, theoretical pastime."[14]

NOTES

1. For the technical use of the word "performance" in ethnographic ritual studies on which this chapter relies, see Schieffelin.
2. Participant-observation of Sacred Drumming ceremonies and shamanic workshops offered by *Kalumba: Path of Light* was done in Tucson in November 2008, January 2009, and February 2009. At that time, the practice offered most of its shamanic healing work in Tucson and held the Sacred Drumming ceremonies bi-monthly. In February 2010, *Kalumba* was re-named *Collective Awakening* and restructured its website and electronic communications. *Collective Awakening* now offers a wider range of healing and spiritually oriented events, including ensemble musical performances, across the U.S. References are taken from *Kalumba*'s original newsletters and announcements, which were sent electronically to listserv subscribers, from the timeframe of my fieldwork.
3. For an example of an approach to spiritually oriented performance that takes spirituality seriously as component of a material theatre practice, see Mason. For an analysis of the antipathy to religion in the Western academy, see Hay.
4. See also Friesen for transcendence as a historical issue in theatre and performance studies.
5. See the foundational work of Clifford Geertz on ritual as social function and an approach to ritual as a symbol system, and the influence of cultural anthropology on theatre and performance studies in Balme.
6. The body in meditation has been a more conducive site for neurological research than the body in active ritual. See Newberg, "Religious and Spiritual Practices" and "The Neurobiology of Spiritual Transformation," esp. p. 190.
7. In a functional model, ritual fails if it does not unify, ease tensions, build community, create harmony, and otherwise heal social conflict. A failed

ritual is "one in which cultural and sociological categories are experienced as discontinuous" (Bell, "Constructing Ritual" 29). The evidence from studies in human physiology cited in this chapter suggests that an experience of discontinuity would also be a neurological or chemical failure, marked behaviorally by a person's disconnection with the world, and experientially by discomfort with that disconnection.

8. For an alternative understanding of cognitive theories of the relationship between myth and ritual, see Seaquist.
9. Prior willingness to accept such matrices as explanations for phenomena may be a factor in an individual's willingness to construe somatic experiences as spiritual. See Borg 1966.
10. For a similar mode of brain activity in the work of Antonio Damasio, see Azari 55–58.
11. Cf. Jennings 326. Jennings, though not focused on somatic sensation, suggests, "ritual action transmits the 'knowing' gained by the ritual itself."
12. For a useful description of the conflict between commercial neo-shamanism and traditional shamanic spirituality in a cultural context in which shamanism is indigenous and in which the issue of authentic spirituality is vital, see Levin.

    For an example of neo-shamanism in the West, see the website for Eagle's Wing College of Shamanic Medicine at http://www.shaminism.co.uk/. Based on his work on animism in hunter-gatherer cultures, journalist and author Robert Wright criticizes popular spiritual movements (and also Mircea Eliade's 1951 *Shamanism: Archaic Techniques of Ecstasy*) for unwarranted idealization of indigenous and ancient peoples. See Wright.
13. For an overview of perspectives on shamanism, with attention to shamanism as an emic and etic phenomenon, see Winkelman.
14. I am indebted to Mr. Martin Klabunde for his generosity of spirit and willingness to allow me to attend, participate in, and write about the Sacred Drumming ceremony. This project is undertaken with approval from the Texas A&M University Institutional Review Board.

WORKS CITED

Azari, Nina P. *Religious Experience as Thinking that Feels Like Something: A Philosophical-Theological Reflection on Recent Neuroscientific Study of Religious Experience*. Diss. Iliff School of Theology and U of Denver, 2004. Ann Arbor: UMI, 2004. Print.

Balme, Christopher B. "Cultural Anthropology and Theatre Historiography: Notes on a Methodological Rapprochement." *Theatre Survey* 35 (1994): 33–52. Print.

Bell, Catherine. "Constructing Ritual." *Readings in Ritual Studies*. Ed. Ronald L. Grimes. Upper Saddle River, NJ: Prentice Hall, 1996. 21–32. Print.

———. *Ritual: Perspectives and Dimensions*. Oxford: Oxford UP, 1997. Print.

Borg, Jacqueline. "The Serotonin System and Spiritual Experiences." *American Journal of Psychiatry* 160.11 (2003): 1965–1969. Print.

D'Aquili, Eugene G., and Charles D. Laughlin. "The Neurobiology of Myth and Ritual." *Readings in Ritual Studies*. Ed. Ronald L. Grimes. New Jersey: Prentice Hall, 1996. 132–145. Print.

Demastes, William. *Staging Consciousness: Theatre and the Materiality of Mind*. Ann Arbor: U of Michigan P, 2002. Print.

Eliade, Mircea. *Shamanism: Archaic Techniques of Ecstasy*. 1951. Princeton: Princeton UP, 2004. Print.

Friesen, Lauren. "The Problem of Transcendence in Modern and Postmodern Plays." *Theater, Ritual, Religion*. Ed. Ingrid Hentschel and Klaus Hoffman. Munster: LIT Verlag, 2004. 35–60. Print.

Geertz, Clifford. *The Interpretation of Cultures: Selected Essays by Clifford Geertz*. New York: Basic, 1973. Print.

Hay, David. *Why Spirituality Is Difficult for Westerners*. Charlottesville: Societas, 2007. Print.

Heffner, Philip. "Spiritual Transformation and Healing: An Encounter with the Sacred." *Spiritual Transformation and Healing: Anthropological, Theological, Neuroscientific, and Clinical Perspectives*. Ed. Joan D. Koss-Chioino and Philip Hefner. Lanham: Altamira, 2006. 119–133. Print.

Hufford, David J., and Mary Ann Bucking. "The Spirit of Spiritual Healing in the United States." *Spiritual Transformation and Healing: Anthropological, Theological, Neuroscientific, and Clinical Perspectives*. Ed. Joan D. Koss-Chioino and Philip Hefner. Lanham: Altamira, 2006. 25–42. Print.

Jennings, Theodore W. "On Ritual Knowledge." *Readings in Ritual Studies*. Ed. Ronald L. Grimes. Upper Saddle River, NJ: Prentice Hall, 1996. 324–334. Print.

Klabunde, Martin. "The Dambe Project and *Kalumba* Newsletters." Message to the author. November 2008–January 2010. E-mail.

Laderman, Gary. "Shamanism in the New Age." *Religions of the United States in Practice*. Ed. Colleen McDannell. Vol. 2. Princeton: Princeton UP, 2001. 268–283.

Levin, Dan. "Shamans' Spirits Crowd Air of Mongolian Capital." *New York Times* 21 July 2009, natl. ed.: A6. Print.

Mason, David V. *Theatre and Religion on Krishna's Stage: Performing in Vrindavan*. New York: Palgrave, 2009. Print.

Newberg, Andrew. "The Neurobiology of Spiritual Transformation." *Spiritual Transformation and Healing: Anthropological, Theological, Neuroscientific, and Clinical Perspectives*. Ed. Joan D. Koss-Chioino and Philip Hefner. Lanham: Altamira, 2006. 189–205.

———. "Religious and Spiritual Practices: A Neurochemical Perspective." *Where God and Science Meet*. Ed. Patrick McNamara. Vol. 2. Westport: Praeger, 2006. 15–31. Print.

Schechner, Richard. "Living a Double Consciousness." *Teaching Ritual*. Ed. Catherine Bell. Oxford: Oxford UP, 2007. 15–28.

Schieffelin, Edward. "On Failure and Performance: Throwing the Medium Out of the Séance." *The Performance of Healing*. Ed. Carol Laderman and Marina Roseman. New York: Routledge, 1996. 59–90.

Seaquist, Carl. "Mind Design and the Capacity for Ritual Performance." *Where God and Science Meet*. Ed. Patrick McNamara. Vol. 2. Westport: Praeger, 2006. 205–228.

Slingerland, Edward. *What Science Offers the Humanities: Integrating Body and Culture*. Cambridge: Cambridge UP, 2008.

Winkelman, Michael. "Cross-Cultural Assessments of Shamanism." *Where God and Science Meet*. Ed. Patrick McNamara. Vol. 3. Westport: Praeger, 2006. 139–159.

Wright, Robert. "Do Shamans Have More Sex?." *Slate*. Slate, 29 July 2009. Web, accessed 8/1/09.

4 Embodying the Disembodied

Hesychasm, Meditation, and Michael Chekhov's Higher Ego

R. Andrew White

After the eruption of the 1917 Bolshevik Revolution and ensuing Civil War, numerous members of the Russian intelligentsia either fled the country or defiantly converted from Marxist materialism to Orthodox Christianity (Tataryn 3–4). Later, throughout the 1920s and 1930s, Stalin's regime transformed the Russian arts into nothing more than an instrument of the Soviet propaganda machine. In the theatre, actors were expected to serve as a mouthpiece for the atheistic Communist Party. Faced with a narrow range of roles in a forgettable repertoire of Socialist Realism, numerous actors cast their attention toward the church and patristic literature for inspiration, examining more deeply the relationship between religious practices and acting technique. Consequently, particular tenets of Orthodox spirituality and monastic culture influenced the personal attitudes of several Soviet-era actors toward their creative process, including the legendary actor-teacher Michael Chekhov.

That Chekhov drew from Eastern spirituality and the ideas of Rudolph Steiner would raise few eyebrows, for his interest in yoga and his devotion to Steiner's Christian spiritual science known as anthroposophy are well documented and are, in part, why he emigrated from the Soviet Union in July 1928. Virtually unexplored, however, are apparent ways in which Chekhov was influenced by his own encounters with Russian Orthodox Christianity. In this chapter, I explore those influences to emphasize the connection between Chekhov's acting system (especially his notion of the Higher Ego) and meditative prayer. In particular, I focus on the Eastern Orthodox tradition known as Hesychasm: a form of contemplative prayer that flourished in northern Greece during the Byzantine Empire and became established as a system of organized monasticism in the fourteenth century.

What did Michael Chekhov know about Hesychasm, and where does he reference it in his texts? How did Hesychasm shape his acting system, and from what sources did he learn about it?[1] How does meditation fit into Chekhov's method, and what did he think it meant for an actor to meditate? Perhaps most important, what can theatre artists today learn from Chekhov's example of meditation for actors? In answering those questions through the format of a case study, I aim to shed light on a lesser-known influence on Chekhov's technique; however, on a broader scale, I hope to demonstrate how practices from the Christian meditative tradition, especially Hesychast prayer, can contribute to actors' creativity, use of imagination, and embodiment of the characters they play.

HESYCHASM, THE JESUS PRAYER, AND THE OPTINA PUSTYN MONASTERY

Sometimes referred to (rather misleadingly) as "Christian Yoga" (Kungurtsev and Luchakova 9), Hesychasm does indeed bear some similarity to yogic disciplines of the Far East. It is, nevertheless, a unique form of mysticism, the origins of which can be traced to the first Christian monks known as the Desert Fathers. Led by Saint Anthony, they sought God-realization while living as hermits in the Egyptian Sahara beginning in the third century CE. The monastic tradition they established is detailed in the *Philokalia*, a vast collection of spiritual writings from the Eastern Orthodox Church Fathers spanning a period of eleven centuries. It was compiled in the eighteenth century by Saint Nikodimos of the Holy Mountain and Saint Makarios of Corinth, both residents of Mount Athos—northern Greece's famed peninsula, where Hesychasm was established officially in the fourteenth century and which, to this day, serves as the center of Orthodox monasticism (Rossi 70–71).

The Greek word *hesychia* is commonly translated as "stillness," "rest," or "quiet." The translators of the English edition of the *Philokalia*, however, point out that *hesychia* means more specifically "a state of inner tranquility or mental quietude and concentration which arises in conjunction with, and is deepened by, the practice of pure prayer and the guarding of heart and intellect. Not simply silence, but an attitude of listening to God and of openness towards Him" (Palmer, Sherrard, and Ware 1: 364; Rossi 70). In addition, the derivatives Hesychasm and Hesychast "denote the whole spiritual tradition represented in the *Philokalia* as well as the person who pursues the spiritual path it delineates" (Palmer, Sherrard, and Ware 1: 364; Rossi 70).

In the late fifteenth century Nil Sorsky (also St. Nilius of Sora, 1433–1508), a former resident of Mount Athos who founded a colony of monks known as the Trans-Volga Hermits, was largely responsible for the spread of Hesychasm in Russia. Living up to their other name—the "non-possessors"—Sorsky and his followers claimed that spiritual salvation was possible only through worldly detachment, rejecting the church's acquisition of property and wealth as well as any sort of protection offered by the state. "Stressing prayer, contemplation, and an inner spiritual light, together with a striving for moral perfection," explains Bernice Glatzer Rosenthal, "they opposed ecclesiastical formalism and ritualism and insisted that church and state be independent of each other. Moreover, the state belonged to a lower order of reality, so it had no right to interfere in religious matters" (335).

Unsurprisingly, in 1503 the church backed Sorsky's rivals—the Josephite "possessors" (named for their leader, St. Joseph of Volokolamsk), who welcomed state involvement with church affairs and contended that the church must acquire wealth so that it could fulfill its obligation to serve society (Rosenthal 335–336; Stanton 31). Consequently, Russian Hesychasm all but disappeared until Ukrainian-born monk Paisii Velichkovskii (1722–1794), who became a priest and elder on Mount Athos, translated selected texts from the *Philokalia* into Slavonic and published them as the *Dobrotolubiye* in 1793 (Stanton 31–34).

Around 1865, with the publication of a text entitled *The Way of a Pilgrim*—literally *Candid Narratives of a Pilgrim to His Spiritual Father* (French xv)—interest in Hesychasm grew substantially among the Russian laity. In *The Way of a Pilgrim*, the anonymous author shares the story of his growth in Hesychast spirituality as he journeys through Russia studying Velichkovskii's translation of the *Philokalia* (Palmer, Sherrard, and Ware 1: 13). He also details the most important practice associated with Hesychasm—the Jesus Prayer, which, as James Aerthayil explains, "enables us to have a real encounter with the Person of Jesus at the core of our heart, an encounter that is at the same time transformative and divinizing" (541). As outlined in *The Way of a Pilgrim*, the Jesus Prayer "is a constant uninterrupted calling upon the divine name of Jesus with the lips, in the spirit, in the heart, while forming a mental picture of His constant presence, and imploring His grace, during every occupation, at all times, in all places, even during sleep. The appeal is couched in these terms, 'Lord Jesus Christ, have mercy on me'" (9).[2] In addition, the method of the prayer, which consists of four stages, is steeped in the psychophysical notion that the mind and body are indivisible, relying on the synergy of both to establish communion between the brain and the heart while keeping the exterior world at bay (Palmer, Sherrard, and Ware 4: 205–206).[3]

First, while focusing inwardly on the heart, one cultivates a state of quietude. Second, as Aerthayil notes, the individual employs practices to deepen concentration "such as physical immobility, control or suspension of breathing, fixation of the eyes on the heart, stomach and the navel in the order to [*sic*] 'let the mind go back into the heart'" (533). Third, the individual continuously repeats the words of the Jesus Prayer in rhythm with the breath (e.g., "Lord Jesus Christ" on the inhalation; "have mercy on me" on the exhalation). Later, mental repetition replaces vocal repetition. Eventually, when the inner prayer continues unconsciously, "even during sleep," it transfers itself from the mind to the heart, as when the anonymous pilgrim recounts that "my heart in its ordinary beating began to say the words of the prayer with each beat. Thus for example, *one*, 'Lord,' *two*, 'Jesus,' *three*, 'Christ,' and so on . . . I simply listened to what my heart was saying" (19–20, italics his). Hence, the Jesus Prayer makes possible Saint Paul's injunction to "pray without ceasing" (*Harper Collins Study Bible*, First Thess. 5.17). In the final stage, that "prayer of the heart" transforms into the "prayer of illumination and union" (Kungurtsev and Luchakova 10), and the individual experiences unity with Christ in an ecstatic, super-conscious state.

Once a Hesychast becomes divinized through experiencing the incarnation of Christ in his heart, he perceives what Orthodox Church Father Gregory Palamas (1296–1359) refers to as divine "uncreated light," which is the same light that the apostles Peter, James, and John saw emanating from Jesus during his Transfiguration when he conversed with Moses and Elijah atop Mount Tabor (Rosenthal 335; Aerthayil 539; Stanton 28).[4] As historian George Ostrogorsky clarifies, Palamas believed in certain "divine energies" that are revealed to humans on earth, "which are not created, but rather [are] manifestations of an endless operation of God. Such Divine energies are manifested in the wisdom, love, the grace of God, and the light seen by the apostles on Mount Tabor, and eternally made visible to the mystically illumined, was another such divine energy" (qtd. in Stanton 29). Unlike those who criticized Hesychasm, Palamas saw the possibility of what Ostrogorsky calls "an intermediary and a mediating power between God and man, which proceeded from God and revealed itself to mankind" (qtd. in Stanton 29). Thus, the deified Hesychast acquires the gift of clairvoyance and is designated as an "elder" (*starets* in Russian), becoming a mediator of God for others (Kontzevitch 29). For that reason, each Hesychast novitiate is placed under the guidance of a designated *starets*; however, in pre-Revolutionary Russia, the laity, too, sought the spiritual wisdom of the elders, and Hesychast monasteries became the destination of numerous God-seeking pilgrims. By the early twentieth century, the Optina Pustyn monastery had become the dominant spiritual center of pilgrimage in Imperial Russia and remained so until the Communists devastated the church, forcing Russian Orthodoxy to develop over the twentieth century in Western Europe.[5]

Founded in the fifteenth century and located approximately 130 miles southwest of Moscow in the remote forests of the Kaluga province, Optina Pustyn was, as Leonard J. Stanton documents, "a place where men seemed to succeed in their quest to become saints," where the elders, like the ancient Desert Fathers, were "[d]eified humanity, restored to its pre-fall condition" (49). The monastery's name, in fact, links it to Saint Anthony and his followers, for *pustynia* translates as "desert" (Stanton 47). No wonder that, from the mid-1800s until its closure by the Bolsheviks in 1923, Optina received thousands of pilgrims—nearly 25,000 per year just prior to 1913 (Stanton 69).[6] Among the most famous were the philosopher Vasily Rozanov, the poet Vladimir Soloviev, Nikolai Gogol (who claimed to have conversed "with the whole of heaven" (qtd. in Stanton 51) through his interaction with the elders), Fyodor Dostoyevsky,[7] and Lev Tolstoy (Stanton 210–213).[8]

In 1927, not long before joining the throngs of intellectuals who feared for their lives following the Revolution, Michael Chekhov made the first of several visits to the last surviving Optina *starets* of the Soviet period—Elder

Nektary (1856–1928), who spent the final five years of his life hiding from the authorities some thirty-three miles from Optina in the village of Kholmishche. The poet Nadezhda Pavlovich, who had lived near Optina at the beginning of the Soviet era, remained in touch with Nektary and, at his request, she frequently arranged secret visits from members of the Russian intelligentsia (Stanton 253). According to Chekhov, Pavlovich owned a photograph of him in the role of Hamlet. Upon viewing the picture, Nektary simply said to her: "I see a spiritual manifestation. Bring him to me" ("Life and Encounters" 38).[9]

HESYCHASM, ELDER NEKTARY, AND THE HIGHER EGO

Elder Nektary made a strong impression not only on Chekhov but also on other actors who visited him, many of whom—including Chekhov himself—later found inspiration reading the *Confessions* of Saint Augustine (Kontzevitch 447). Whereas historians often presume that Russian Orthodox clergy of the twentieth century condemned Augustine as the prime heretic responsible for dividing the Christian West and East, many actually studied his writings in detail. As Myroslaw I. Tataryn reveals, the leading theologians who immigrated to Paris regarded Augustine "with deep respect" (153). While they found his arguments to be ultimately insufficient, Tataryn continues, Augustine "was still perceived as making a valuable contribution to Christian thought" (153). Also, further evidence suggests that Gregory Palamas himself drew from Greek translations of Augustine's work in his own writing.[10] Whether Chekhov learned about Augustine through Nektary is unclear; however, because Augustine's entire body of work was published in Russian between 1879 and 1895 (Tataryn 15), Nektary was probably familiar with the patriarch of the Roman Church and might have recommended his work to any number of visitors.

Regardless, Nektary remained influential to Chekhov, as is evidenced in 1944 when he devotes an entire chapter of his memoir *Life and Encounters* to his visits with the elder. In that chapter, Chekhov details a broad range of conversations he and Nektary held about Rudolf Steiner, anthroposophy, and the theatre—all topics about which Nektary was surprisingly knowledgeable.[11] In discussing the considerable impact Nektary had on his life, Chekhov also echoes the author of *The Way of a Pilgrim*, who records an appearance of his own deceased *starets* in a dream (*Pilgrim* 36).[12] Similar to the pilgrim, Chekhov discloses: "Two or three times following the Elder's death, I dreamt about him, and each time he gave me advice that delivered me from emotional difficulties from which I, alone, did not have the strength to remove myself" ("Life and Encounters" 44).

Chekhov even invokes Nektary in *On the Technique of Acting*, in which work he praises the elder as "the last of the true religious mystics" who "had attained great spiritual heights" (24).[13] Significantly, Chekhov goes on to document that Nektary "radiated contagious humor, which arose purely from his Higher Ego" (24). That notion of the Higher Ego is a key element of Chekhov's acting technique and is one of what he calls "three different beings" that engage with each other to lead the actor into a state of creative inspiration. Chekhov dubs the first being the "everyday I" or the "lower self," which is the level of consciousness concerned with the emotions, voice, body, and day-to-day living (*To the Actor* 96).

In the English versions of his texts, Chekhov uses three interchangeable terms to refer to the second being or level of consciousness: the "higher I," the "higher self," or the "Higher Ego" (*To the Actor* 95–98; *Technique* 15–25)—all *vysshii ia* in Russian. According to Chekhov, the Higher Ego is the actor's "true self" (*On Theatre* Disc 2, Track 9) and "the real artist in you" for it "moves your body, making it flexible, sensitive and receptive to all creative impulses; it speaks with your voice, stirs your imagination and increases your inner activity. Moreover, it grants you genuine feelings, makes you original and inventive, awakens and maintains your ability to improvise. In short, it puts you in a *creative* state" (*To the Actor* 97, emphasis Chekhov's). Once the Higher Ego possesses the actor, Chekhov explains, "you begin to feel that you are standing apart from, or rather above, the material, and consequently, above your everyday self. That is because you now identify yourself with that creative, higher I" (*To the Actor* 96). Only with the "higher I" molding the raw material of the "everyday I," is the actor able to create the third being (or level of consciousness)—the character, which has a life of its own (*To the Actor* 98). Thus, in this "division of consciousness," Chekhov declares, "the higher Ego [acts] as the *source of inspiration* and the lower Ego as the bearer, the agent" (*Path* 147, emphasis Chekhov's).

The notion of duality is so deeply a part of acting, and Chekhov's need to discuss it is certainly not unique. In fact, his convictions about divided consciousness are remarkably similar to Constant Coquelin's (1841–1909) idea of the actor's first and second selves. For Coquelin, the actor's first self "is the one which *sees*, which should be the master. This is the soul, the [second self] is the body" (Cole and Chinoy 193, emphasis Coquelin's). With religious overtones, Coquelin argues that "the first self works upon the second till it is transfigured, and thence an ideal personage is evolved—in short, until from himself [the actor] has made his work of art" (Cole and Chinoy 192). Chekhov, too, establishes a strong connection of the religious to the artistic when he associates Elder Nektary with the Higher Ego (as noted earlier), for in doing so Chekhov suggests a correlation between acting in general and Christian meditative prayer. Indeed, in describing what drew Chekhov and Nektary to each other, Stanton affirms:

> The intensely personal approach Chekhov took to the actor's craft, his deep concern to realize the moral and spiritual potential of theatre arts, and even the psychosomatic methods of training Chekhov passed on to his students are all of a piece with the personally-centered,

> wholistic prayer and spirituality Nektarii [*sic*] and the other Optina elders taught. (254)

Certainly, Chekhov encountered influential notions of higher consciousness apart from his visits with Nektary. For example, Konstantin Stanislavsky, Chekhov's mentor, distinguished the actor's "higher 'I' which creates and shines forth" from "the one which eats, drinks and thinks about mundane affairs" (Stanislavskii 93).[14] Nor can it be coincidental that Chekhov's understanding of higher consciousness reflects concepts from yoga to which he was exposed during his work with Evgeny Vakhtangov and Leopold Sulerzhitsky in the First Studio of the Moscow Art Theatre (Carnicke 176). He also studied Theosophy, an occult system created by Helena Petrovna Blavatsky (1831–1891), with which he was ultimately dissatisfied. In his own words, Chekhov felt "unsettled by its extreme orientalism" and claimed that "it underestimat[ed] the significance of Christ and the Mystery of Golgotha" (*Path* 133). However, upon discovering the anthroposophical writings of Rudolf Steiner (who drew significantly from Eastern spirituality but emphasized the place of Christianity in his system), Chekhov was able to accept "orientalism" in a context that made more sense to him.

Chekhov's concept of the "higher I" certainly parallels Steiner's "levels of self" and "planes of existence" (Marowitz 78). Chekhov's notion, however, is undoubtedly steeped more deeply in Hesychast prayer. As Lendley C. Black reveals, Chekhov also uses the term "higher I" to define the presence of Christ dwelling within a person's body (10). In a letter to a close friend, Chekhov elaborates upon that perspective, explaining how Christ enters the human body and becomes one with the person as a higher form of that individual's "self" (or "I" consciousness) while compromising neither his own divinity nor the individual's humanity:

> When (and since) Christ comes into man as "I," this "I," while remaining Christ, becomes at the same time man. How is this possible? God, Christ, Gives Up Himself *without residue*. His sacrifice is *absolute*. Separating out in the capacity of the "I" part of His Essence and having transferred it to man, He speaks, as it were, to this part of Himself: "Now live and develop independently. Become an *individual* man, into which I have placed Myself. I give you freedom." This mystery of the "transformation" of God in man, this purely spiritual event, is wonderfully expressed in Christianity with the words: The Birth of the Christ-Child in the soul of man. (qtd. in Black 10, emphases Chekhov's)

Implicit in Chekhov's invocation of Christ, as Black posits, is the idea that "the actor's true creative state is a higher level of consciousness in which dwells Christ, God in man" (10). Moreover, when Chekhov claims that the "I" of Christ remains divine while becoming simultaneously human, he brings to mind the Hesychast notion of divinization as well as the proclamation of Orthodox Church father Saint Maximos in the *Philokalia*: "The whole man is deified by the grace of God-made-man, remaining entirely man in soul and body by reason of his nature and becoming entirely God in soul and body by reason of the grace and divine brightness of the blessed glory that quite becomes him . . . " (qtd. in Rossi 99–100). For both Maximos and Chekhov, the divine can dwell in the human and the human can merge with the divine without compromising the individual's identity. Furthermore, in contending that Christ actually speaks words of guidance, telling the individual with whom he has merged to "develop independently," Chekhov connects the concept of Hesychast deification to Saint Augustine's understanding of Christ as the inner teacher of truth. According to Augustine, "we seek advice not from the speaker outside of ourselves but from the truth within that governs our minds . . . And he to whom we go for aid is the teacher, Christ, who is said to dwell in the innermost man . . . " (142). Elsewhere, when writing about directing, Chekhov even goes so far as to lament "that the venality of our materialistic age frequently diverts the artist from thinking of the Higher Being within us; and yet it is exactly from that source, acknowledged or not, that we draw our greatest inspiration" (*To the Director* 31).

In *Life and Encounters* Chekhov clearly blends that religious belief with his approach to acting when sharing his thoughts on the character of Ahasver, the mythological "Wandering Jew" whose legend seems to have grown from European Christian folklore of the Middle Ages. As punishment for mocking Jesus during the walk to Golgotha, Ahasver was said to have been doomed to roam the earth, unable to die, until Christ's return. In contrasting Ahasver with the characters of Don Quixote and King Lear, Chekhov distinguishes Ahasver's humanity and (what Chekhov considers) his spiritual failure. Using rhetoric comparable to that of his letter cited earlier, Chekhov explains:

> Quixote was a demi-angel, Lear a demi-god, but Ahasver was a man: like you, me, him, all of us . . . Turning away from Christ, (but still led by the unseen Christ) [Ahasver] arrives at the knowledge that the essence of Christianity is neither in Christ's teachings, nor in His words, but *in Christ Himself, in His being, in the "I" of Christ.* Ahasver understands that merging with Christ, with the cosmic "I," is the aim and the crown of Christianity, that all of the disagreements, distortions, weakness, all the arguments about [Christ], and all the blood spilled "in the name of Christ" have been and will be until the time when the "I" of Christ becomes the "I" of you, me, Ahasver, until each of us will merge with Christ . . . until "not I, but Christ in me" will become reality. (116, emphasis Chekhov's)[15]

Here, while making an apparent attempt to proselytize his audience, Chekhov unquestionably echoes Rudolf Steiner who also identifies "the Christ as Cosmic Ego" (*Cosmic Ego*). Furthermore, by concluding with a paraphrase of Saint Paul's proclamation, " . . . it is no longer I who live, but it is Christ who lives in me" (*Harper Collins Study Bible*, Gal. 2.20), Chekhov aligns with Steiner's concept of deification. In a 1912 lecture, Steiner cites that same passage and interprets it as follows: " . . . when the Christ-Force penetrates the soul and absorbs it, man rises to the heights of the divine" ("*Bhagavad Gita*"). Also significant is Chekhov's use of the word "crown" (*korona*), because it is suggestive not only of the crown of thorns that Christ wore during the crucifixion, but also of the bride's crown worn in a Russian wedding. Hence, on a metaphoric level, it evokes the consummation of union with Christ, who is the lover or bridegroom (Carnicke, "Re: Translation"). Once again Chekhov echoes Saint Paul and, in this instance, also the author of the Gospel of John, both of whom refer to Jesus as the bridegroom of the church (*Harper Collins Study Bible*, John 3:28–30; Eph. 5:23–27).

Chekhov, however, appears to be more Hesychast than anthroposophist in the way he envisions the actor's overall path to creative inspiration. As Black remarks, like the method used by Hesychast monks to enter a heightened spiritual state and become one with Christ (i.e., the Jesus Prayer), Chekhov's "entire acting system is a technique for reaching creative inspiration, in which the actor's 'lower I' is transformed into the 'higher I'" (82). Or, stated more precisely: through using Chekhov's system, an actor (being inspired creatively by her "higher I") eventually transforms her "everyday I" into the "I" of the character. Important to note, however, is the fact Chekhov never contends that the actor must identify her higher self with the self of Christ. Only in his memoirs and personal writing does he deliberately reveal the connections of his Christian religious faith with his personal creative process. In writing about the spiritual underpinnings of Stanislavsky's System, Benjamin Lloyd draws a conclusion that might shed light on why the religious elements of Chekhov's teaching remain hidden. According to Lloyd, very little "will make the theatre academic more squeamish than [Stanislavsky's] relentless examinations of the spiritual component in acting" (73). Perhaps a similar sentiment, combined with the memory of Stalin's atheistic and intolerant regime, suggests one reason why, even after moving to Hollywood, Chekhov taught the principles of his acting method without naming the source.

Regardless, Chekhov's model of the creative process, like the Jesus Prayer, consists of four stages (*Technique* 146–158) and is grounded in meditation. In fact, with religious conviction, Chekhov insists: "It is necessary to consider theatre art in all its details *exclusively* as meditation . . . All the exercises are the ways towards this meditation of art" (qtd. in translation in Kirillov 231, emphasis Chekhov's). Much as the Hesychast uses the Jesus Prayer to invoke and eventually embody the person of Christ, the actor uses Chekhov's system to invoke and embody the person of the character. If the meditative Jesus Prayer enables the Hesychast monk to become a mediator of God for others, then Chekhov's system—itself a prayer of sorts—enables the actor to become a mediator of the character for the audience.

THE ACTOR AS MEDITATOR AND MEDIATOR

Thousands of actors benefit from practicing meditative exercises in acting classes and in warm-ups before performance. Engaging more deeply in a regular practice of sustained meditation can help actors in other obvious ways such as facilitating relaxation, enhancing concentration, improving their ability for memorizing lines, and helping to cope with anxiety induced by the daily stress of their profession. But when Chekhov classifies theatre art as meditation, he offers a unique perspective on what it means, in particular, for an *actor* to meditate. Because the overall art of the actor is itself the meditation here, Chekhov suggests that contemplative practices can serve as powerful and imaginative tools to transform the actor's everyday self into the self of the character. Specifically, Chekhov's point of view strongly suggests that meditating on a role means that the actor—through the use of imagination and visualization—prepares to empty herself and become an open vessel that receives the spirit of the character and eventually merges with it. According to Chekhov, the character exists at first as a disembodied entity, an image that visits the actor's mind, quite literally, from the spiritual realm (Kirillov 230). Hence, the first stage of Chekhov's technique requires the actor to turn the attention inward and perceive mental images of the character that "descend" into his or her consciousness from the Higher Ego (Chekhov, *Technique* 149)—much like the Hesychast experiences mental images of Christ when fervently practicing the Jesus Prayer.

In Hesychast prayer, the perception of images unrelated to the exterior world can be a sign of deepening consciousness. For instance, Nun Thaisia, a sister of the Kashirsky Convent who learned the Jesus Prayer from Elder Nektary himself, records in her journal becoming "flushed from the prayer" and experiencing vivid images of Jesus, heaven, hell, and even of her own guardian angel (Thaisia 379–380). In many cases, when the recipient of the images reaches a higher state of spiritual awareness, those images might actually be transcendent "spiritual knowledge" in the form of "celestial archetypes" that may be used to create religious art (Palmer, Sherrard, and Ware 1: 359–360). Both the iconographer and the actor bring the spiritual into the realm of the physical through their creative work—the iconographer through painting, and the actor through the process of embodiment. In *On the Technique of Acting*, however, when Chekhov urges the actor to draw pictures of those evolving images and keep them in a journal, he (perhaps unwittingly) makes a connection between the actor and iconographer that is quite literal (148). As a skilled cartoonist, Chekhov created numerous drawings of the characters he portrayed, an activity he saw as one of several valuable practices to help the actor embody the role.

Chekhov's idea of the character becoming incarnate through the actor's meditative practice also aligns closely with the Hesychast concept of deification, which depicts God as "Transcendent Person." In Hesychasm, as Vincent Rossi emphasizes, "God is forever present not as transpersonal Essence . . . but as trans-essential Person" (79). That "Transcendent [and uncreated] Person," Rossi continues, "gives itself to the created person through an uncreated grace in which the created person participates according to the degree of his or her purification and illumination. This participation occurs through the synergy of the benevolence of the Transcendent Person and the efforts of the created person" (81).

As part of the effort to merge with the character, Chekhov advises the actor to acquire knowledge of the character through engaging the evolving images in interior dialogue and asking them "Leading Questions" (*Technique* 96–97). Because part of the actor's meditation involves mental conversations with the disembodied spirit of the character, Chekhov evokes the principle outlined by the thirteenth-century monk Theoliptos in the *Philokalia*: "Prayer is the mind's dialogue with God, in which words of petition are uttered with the intellect riveted wholly on God" (Palmer, Sherrard, and Ware 4: 181). In his essay, "Meditation on Don Quixote," Chekhov relays the following account of an ongoing, interior dialogue he held with the disembodied character of Cervantes's insane knight errant:

> In the early years of my work in theatre Don Quixote once appeared in my inner vision and modestly declared his appearance with the words: "There is a need to play me . . . "
>
> "There is nobody to play you!" I answered him in excitement.
>
> I did not even ask him, "Why have you appeared *to me*?"—I knew: it was his mistake.
>
> . . . Many years passed . . . He appeared to me again and again, but now he said: "*You* should act . . .
>
> I was frightened: "Whom?"
>
> He disappeared giving no direct answer, but visited me repeatedly. He repeated his hints.
>
> Finally, I decided to explain to him on his next appearance that I just cannot, *cannot* embody all the mysterious profundities of his spirit, so full of suffering. I wished to explain to him that I have neither the means nor the strength—external or internal—which are necessary to embody him . . .
>
> Finally, he appeared and I started to prove it all.
>
> We were fighting for a long time. I was inspired by this battle. With the dexterity which is usual for people enjoying a fight I penetrated into him deeper and deeper . . . I was drawing him for himself . . . I told him: "This is what you are! . . . These are the things one must possess and what one has to go through to embody you!"
>
> . . . He spoke: "Look at me."

> I looked. He pointed at himself and said imperiously: "This is *you* now. These are *we* now!" (qtd. in translation in Kirillov 230–231, emphases Chekhov's)[16]

Chekhov goes on to record how Quixote persistently reveals himself in various manifestations of rhythms, melodies, sounds, movements, and gestures until Chekhov concludes that Don Quixote "who was always defeated . . . won this time. As for me, I accepted his destiny. I was defeated. And in my unsuccessful fighting, in my failure, I became Don Quixote" (qtd. in translation in Kirillov 231). Although a full production in which he played Don Quixote never came to fruition, Chekhov's account of his inner battle with Cervantes' "demi-angel" provides a clear example of what might be called an actor's prayer.

Because the character petitions the actor here (and not *vice versa*) Chekhov also presents the idea of religious vocation. While receptive to engaging with the image of the character, Chekhov resists violently Quixote's request for Chekhov to embody him on stage. Hence, Chekhov is quite literally *called* to play Don Quixote, who, similar to Hesychasm's uncreated "Transcendent Person," gives himself to the created person of the actor. Going so far as to call Quixote "a spiritual character" that "has a cosmic consciousness" (qtd. in translation in Kirillov 231), Chekhov further demonstrates that the actor's process can be interpreted in a way consistent with Douglas V. Steere's observation that fervent prayer, at its very core, "is a perpetual surrender to God . . . " (Steere 13).

Only after intensifying that inner work with the help of the director and other members of the company in the second stage of the creative process does the actor enter the third (and longest) stage, which Chekhov calls "incorporation," to give "real visible and audible existence to the images" (*Technique* 151). Again like Coquelin, who avers that the actor visualizes the character and "forces . . . his own face and figure into this imaginary mold" (Cole and Chinoy 193), Chekhov argues that the actor "recreates his whole body, limb by limb" (*Technique* 100) through envisioning in detail the character's body and then stepping into that "Imaginary" or "Invisible" body and working to move as the character. With theological resonance, Chekhov writes, "The imaginary body stands, as it were, between your real body and your psychology, influencing both of them with equal force. Step by step, you begin to move, speak and feel in accord with it; that is to say, your character now dwells within you (or, if you prefer, you dwell within it)" (*To the Actor* 87).

Chekhov's idea of the character and actor dwelling together in spiritual unity mirrors his explanation (cited earlier in this chapter) of the spiritual unification between Christ (as the "higher I") and the human wherein Christ remains divine but "becomes at the same time man." For the actor does not lose touch with her own identity any more than the Hesychast *starets* loses his individuality when embodying Christ. To apply the precept of Saint Maximos (also cited earlier) to the art of the actor, the character can dwell in the actor and the actor can merge with the character without compromising the actor's personal identity. That does not mean that the actor merely plays herself. Rather, upon reaching the fourth stage of the creative process, Chekhov contends, the actor enters a state of "inspiration" and "Divided Consciousness"—a condition he deems "the aim of the whole creative process, the true desire of the Higher Ego of the actor" (*Technique* 155). In that state the actor rises to a point of being able to inwardly observe the character as a separate entity, while avoiding the delusion that she has become the character. In fact, keeping one's own consciousness separate prevents the actor from confusing her own emotions with those of the character or from mentally blocking out the presence of the audience—both serious mistakes, Chekhov cautions, that "may lead to hysterics in the actor's private life" (*Technique* 157). For Chekhov, there is no room for such self-indulgency, and, he declares, when the Higher Ego guides an actor's creativity, the thought of replicating one's personal life on stage, indeed, seems "tasteless" (*Technique* 157).

Along those same lines, Thomas Merton maintains that one cannot "become a contemplative merely by 'blacking out' sensible realities and remaining alone with himself in darkness." Such a person, Merton criticizes, "is not alone with God, but alone with himself. He is not in the presence of the Transcendent One, but of an idol: his own complacent identity" (90). Through proposing a "meditation of art" whereby the actor not only imagines and embodies but, perhaps more significantly, *mediates for the audience* the spirit of an entity separate from herself, Chekhov demonstrates that a dramatic character—especially one as familiar as Don Quixote—is neither a role that an actor must interpret according to an expected standard nor a part that requires the actor to draw from analogous experiences in her personal life. Instead, any character can be thought of as a spiritual being or essence with which any number of actors may unify via their imagination, and literally *re-create* anew.

CONCLUSION

Through appropriating for the actor practices drawn from contemplative prayer, Chekhov demonstrates how meditation and imagination are intertwined, and if imagining is not meditation *per se*, it certainly is a meditative act. Through his model of the creative process, Chekhov provides a practical means by which actors can find creative inspiration beyond the boundaries of their own personalities and life experiences. In order to transcend one's everyday self, however, Chekhov prefers an expanse of time that, perhaps, a typical rehearsal schedule does not permit. From his film work in Hollywood, Chekhov certainly understood the realities of union contracts, production deadlines, and the necessity for professional actors to produce results in a hurry under less than ideal conditions. In fact, he devised shortcuts in his system to help his students adapt their method of working to the unforgiving demands of a film or television production schedule (Powers 159–172).

To grasp fully what Chekhov has to offer, however, one cannot ignore the importance he affords meditation and contemplative practice in his method of actor training. As Andrei Kirillov warns, " . . . as long as we are in a rush, Chekhov cannot help us. As long as we are 'practical' only, the pure idealist Chekhov will not answer our questions. We will use not more then [*sic*] five per cent of the advantages of his theatre and his theatre system" (228). Indeed, from the perspective of the commercial theatre Chekhov might appear to require impracticality of actors, but he also teaches us to exercise patience and to trust that inner contemplative work is productive and valuable. And if we are attentive to his message, Chekhov might compel us to stop, reflect, meditate, and consider that our inner vision of the character, aided and expanded by the breadth of our creative imagination, can lead us to transcend our familiar, everyday self and mediate for the audience what they come to the theatre to experience—something very much like divinity.

NOTES

1. For a brief discussion on the topic, see Black 10–11, and 82. Although Black sees a possible link between Hesychasm and Chekhov's concept of higher consciousness, he does not explore that connection in depth.
2. Variants of the invocation include "Lord Jesus Christ, Son of God, have mercy on me," and "Lord Jesus Christ, have mercy on me, a sinner," among others.
3. For a description of the four stages of Hesychast prayer, see Aerthayil 533–534.
4. For biblical accounts, see Matthew 17.1–9; Mark 9.2–8; Luke 9.28–36.
5. For a historical overview, see Tataryn 7–32.
6. Stanton notes, however, that just prior to the beginning of World War I, interest in Optina as a spiritual center was waning, and the monastery "was mainly a monument to its former glory" (69).
7. Numerous scholars claim that Dostoyevsky largely modeled Elder Zosima in *The Brothers Karamazov* after Elder Amvrosy, Optina's abbot from 1860 to 1891. For a detailed discussion see Stanton 164–178. Conversely, Tataryn cites Father Tikhon of Zadonsk (1724–1782) as Dostoyevsky's inspiration for the character (166).
8. Tolstoy visited Optina no less than five times during his adult life and paid his final visit in 1910 while fleeing from his family estate. He had been at Optina only three days before he lay dying in an improvised sickbed at the now-famous Astapova train station from 31 October to 7 November. According to Stanton, evidence is inconclusive as to whether Tolstoy, who had been excommunicated from the church, went to Optina seeking reconciliation (209–210; 226–227n).
9. This memoir was first published in Russian as a serial in New York's *Novyi zhurnal* [*New Journal*] from 1944 to 1945. Translations from Russian sources are mine unless otherwise noted.
10. For a detailed discussion, see Flogaus.

11. For a translation of a few brief excerpts of Chekhov's chapter on Nektary in *New Journal*, see Kontzevitch 446–451.
12. The pilgrim also documents visions of his departed *starets* when awake, and soon after feels "as though the soul of my *starets* made its way into my own, or gave light to it. I felt a sort of light in my mind, and a number of ideas about prayer came to me" (74).
13. Chekhov does not reveal Nektary's name but refers to him simply as "a hermit . . . living his last days" (24).
14. Here, Stanislavsky, like Chekhov, uses the term *vysshii ia*.
15. Unlike the version of *Zhizn' i vstrechi* published in *New Journal*, Chekhov's chapter on Nektary is not included in this edition.
16. For another example of questioning the image of Don Quixote, see *Technique*, 101–104.

WORKS CITED

Aerthayil, James. "Jesus Prayer and Stillness of Heart." *Journal of Dharma* 28.4 (2003): 529–542. *Academic Search Premier*. Web. 19 Feb. 2008.

Augustine. "On the Teacher." *Everyone a Teacher*. Ed. Mark Schwehn. Notre Dame: U of Notre Dame P, 2000. 132–147. Print.

Black, Lendley C. *Mikhail Chekhov as Actor, Director and Teacher*. Ann Arbor: UMI Research P, 1987. Print.

Carnicke, Sharon M. "Re: Translation Question." Message to the author. E-mail. 20 June 2009.

———. *Stanislavsky in Focus: An Acting Master for the Twenty-First Century*. 2nd ed. London: Routledge, 2009. Print.

Chekhov, Michael. *On Theatre and the Art of Acting: The Five-Hour CD Master Class with the Acclaimed Actor-Director-Teacher, Lectures Recorded by Michael Chekhov in 1955*. New York: Working Arts, 2004. 4 CDs.

———. *On the Technique of Acting*. Ed. Mel Gordon. New York: Harper, 1991. Print.

———. *The Path of the Actor* with excerpts from *Life and Encounters*. Ed. Andrei Kirillov and Bella Merlin. Trans. David Ball. New York: Routledge, 2005. Print.

———. *To the Actor: On the Technique of Acting*. New York: Harper and Brothers, 1953. Print.

———. *To the Director and Playwright*. Ed. Charles Leonard. New York: Limelight, 1984. Print.

Chekhov, Mikhail. *Zhizn' i vstrechi* [*Life and Encounters*]. Moscow: Iskusstvo, 2000. Print.

———. "Zhizn' i vstrechi [Life and Encounters]." *Novyi zhurnal* [*New Journal*] 8 (1944): 38–45. Print.

Cole, Toby, and Helen Krich Chinoy, eds. *Actors on Acting: The Theories, Techniques, and Practices of the Great Actors of All Times as Told in Their Own Words*. New York: Crown, 1949. Print.

Flogaus, Reinhard. "Inspiration-Exploitation-Distortion: The Use of St. Augustine in the Hesychast Controversy." *Orthodox Readings of Augustine*. Ed. George E. Demacopoulos and Aristotle Papanikolaou. Crestwood: St. Vladimir's Seminary P, 2008. 63–80. Print.

French, R. M. "Translator's Note." *The Way of a Pilgrim and The Pilgrim Continues His Way*. New York: Harper, 1998. xv–xvii. Print.

The Harper Collins Study Bible with the Apocryphal/Deuterocanonical Books. Ed. Harold W. Attridge. Rev. ed. San Francisco: Harper, 2006. Print. New Rev. Standard Vers.

Kirillov, Andrei. "Michael Chekhov and the Search for the 'Ideal' Theatre," *New Theatre Quarterly* 22.3 (2006): 227–234. *Academic Search Premier.* Web. 29 Oct. 2006.

Kontzevitch, I. M. "The Prima Vita of Elder Nektary of Optina." *Elder Nektary of Optina*, Ed. Kontzevitch. Platina: St. Herman of Alaska Brotherhood, 1998. 26–124. Print.

Kungurtsev, Igor, and Olga Luchakova. "The Unknown Russian Mysticism: Pagan Sorcery, Christian Yoga, and Other Esoteric Practices in the Former Soviet Union." *Everything Is According to the Way: Voices of Russian Transpersonalism.* Ed. T. R. Soida and S. I. Shapiro. Brisbane: Bolda-Lok and Educational Enterprises, 1997. 7–15. Print.

Lloyd, Benjamin. "Stanislavsky, Spirituality, and the Problem of the Wounded Actor." *New Theatre Quarterly* 22.1 (2006): 70–75. *Academic Search Premier.* Web. 10 Aug. 2007.

Marowitz, Charles. *The Other Chekhov: A Biography of Michael Chekhov, the Legendary Actor, Director, and Theorist.* New York: Applause, 2004. Print.

Merton, Thomas. *Contemplative Prayer.* New York: Image Books/Doubleday, 1996.

Palmer, G. E. H., Philip Sherrard, and Kallistos Ware, eds. and trans. *The Philokalia: The Complete Text Compiled by St. Nikodimos of the Holy Mountain and St. Makarios of Corinth.* 4 vols. London: Faber, 1979. Print.

Powers, Mala. "With Michael Chekhov in Hollywood: For the Motion Picture and Television Actor." *On the Technique of Acting.* Ed. Mel Gordon. New York: Harper, 1991. Print.

Rosenthal, Bernice Glatzer. "A New Spirituality: The Confluence of Nietzsche and Orthodoxy in Russian Religious Thought." *Religion and Spirituality in Modern Russia.* Ed. Mark D. Steinberg and Heather J. Coleman. Bloomington: Indiana UP, 2007. 330–357. Print.

Rossi, Vincent. "Presence, Participation, Performance: The Remembrance of God in the Early Hesychast Fathers." *Paths to the Heart: Sufism and the Christian East.* Ed. James S. Cutsinger. Bloomington: World Wisdom, 2002. 64–111. Print.

Stanislavskii, K. S. *Besedy v studii Bol'shogo teatra v 1918–1922* [*Lectures in the Studio of the Bolshoi Theatre 1918–1922*]. Moscow: Vserossiisnoe teatral'noe obshchestvo, 1947. Print.

Stanton, Leonard J. *The Optina Pustyn Monastery in the Russian Literary Imagination: Iconic Vision in Works by Dostoevsky, Gogol, Tolstoy, and Others.* New York: Lang, 1995. Print.

Steere, Douglas V. Foreword. *Contemplative Prayer.* By Thomas Merton. New York: Image Books/Doubleday, 1996. 9–14. Print.

Steiner, Rudolf. "*The Bhagavad Gita* and the Epistles of St. Paul, 28 December 1912." *Rudolf Steiner Archive.* The e.Librarian, 28 June 2010. Web. 16 June 2011.

———. "Cosmic Ego and Human Ego: The Nature of Christ the Resurrected, a Lecture by Rudolf Steiner, Munich, January 9, 1912." Trans. Frances E. Dawson. *Rudolf Steiner Archive.* The e.Librarian, 8 Jan. 2010. Web. 16 June 2011.

Tataryn, Myroslaw I. *Augustine and Russian Orthodoxy: Russian Orthodox Theologians and Augustine of Hippo: A Twentieth Century Dialogue.* Lanham: International Scholars, 2000. Print.

Thaisia, Nun. "The Jesus Prayer." *Elder Nektary of Optina.* Ed. I. M. Kontzevitch. Platina: St. Herman of Alaska Brotherhood, 1998. 374–381. Print.

The Way of a Pilgrim and the Pilgrim Continues His Way. Trans. R. M. French. New York: Harper, 1998. Print.

5 Becoming-Lucid

Theatre and Tantra

Anthony Kubiak

The present work is initiatory in a dual sense, both initiating (imperfectly and incompletely) a line of inquiry, and also theorizing the conception of initiation in a specific and, as it turns out, not so specific sense. The initiatory[1] performance I would like to frame is the practice of tantra, and tantra in the distinctively *Vajrayana* (Tibetan) Buddhist sense.[2] The point of the present chapter is not to suggest some superior and exotic Eastern performance practice from which Western theatre might have something to gain, nor is it to suggest the inferiority of Western theatre practice set against "more authentic" or "spiritual" practices of indigenous and emergent cultures. Rather, I am aiming here to demonstrate that tantric practices are rooted in some of the very impulses and conundrums that have driven Western drama before the Early Modern period and since, specifically in the riddles surrounding the manifestations of identity and its attendant emotions, and the thought processes that both shape that identity and feed it. In doing so I suggest that opening to these approaches might allow us richer responses to persistent questions of consciousness and materiality, questions that seem more amenable to tantric worldview than current "hard" materialisms. An additional reason for this inquiry is to propose that the ground for these materialisms is largely illusory, as are the various versions of history and theory that this materiality presupposes. Materialism and the presumptions of materiality—under increasingly skeptical questioning by a range of thinkers, both critical and scientific[3]—have shifted our experience of consciousness and world away from the dynamism that characterized previous epochs and toward a circumscribed linguisticism and/or historical empiricism that has, ironically, allowed mind and its matters rather easy commodification by the intellectual-economic forces that drive late Capital. The world, in other words, has been shrink-wrapped by language/theory (all claims to contingency and fluidity notwithstanding) and delivered to the shipping bays of Theory-Mart. As a result, the vitalism that characterized certain modes of poetic consciousness before poststructuralism has been displaced by various kinds of textualities and formalisms, the communications of one set of extra-human objects (tree, stone, river—world) displaced by another set of signifying objects, Texts (critical-theoretical, philosophical, political, Bible,

Torah, Quran). Our approach to a host of pressing political issues—both environmental concerns and humanist exigencies—has, as a result, become largely instrumental, academic, and, I fear, increasingly irrelevant. We are often no longer engaged with the suffering and injustices our analyses point to in the world, but have become mere theorizers of them. It seems that more vital connections with amateriality must be made in order to drive political action past the impasses of mere theory. A significant offshoot, then, and peculiarity, of this project is to suggest a reevaluation of the *animism* that has long been a part of our poetic and artistic tradition until its death at the hands of late-Capital and post-Marxist materialisms. This new animism, a repositioning of imaginal[4] consciousness fully in harmony with tantric worldview,[5] suggests a realignment with our living environment—both human and other—through performance, and a rapprochement with inspiration (breath), genius (mind), and the dreamtime that sustains it. I am suggesting here a reprise of the aesthetic as a category of action, an aesthetic emerging in part from the "feltness" of our social and political concerns. Tantra, both as spiritual and, as we will see, theatre practice, is one way to think about these issues.[6]

Tantra is often equated in the popular imagination with unusual and arcane sexual practices that culminate in clear awareness being maintained throughout orgasmic release. But whereas these do form part of the tantric tradition—emblematized by the figure of the *Yab-Yum*, the male and female deity in sexual union—within the context of spiritual practice, tantra has a much larger field of significance, and actually denotes the use of visualization, sound, and movement in order to effect the transformation of psychic force through the union of seemingly opposed impulses, transmuting anger, for example, into "mirror-like wisdom," or lust into discerning intelligence. Tantra requires a complete reimagining and reimaging of self and desire so that psychic power may be more effectively targeted toward the elimination of suffering and confusion, both within the self and in the extended world. Tantra is, in some sense, akin to psychoanalysis in its insistence on the necessity to reconceive or *reweave* the whole cloth of consciousness and its manifest identity.

Indeed, the etymology of the word *tantra* suggests such a weaving or weaving together of perception and knowledge into a "weft, context or continuum" (Fischer-Schreiber 217). *Tantra* is sometimes used relationally with the term *sutra*, which may refer to a more specifically textual and ethically based tradition of practice. *Sutra* is also etymologically consonant with the English *suture*, a tying or sewing together of differing tissues (texts, organs, skins), and as such is resonant with the word *tantra* inasmuch as they both suggest a weaving or sewing together. Sutra and tantra in this context make up two of three traditional approaches to *Vajrayana* Buddhist practice.[7] The other (apart from sutra and tantra) is *Mahamudra* or *Dzogchen* practice, a very particular non-objective meditational approach, which I will not discuss at length here.[8]

At the risk of over-extending the linguistic genealogy, I would note that the etymological resonance between the words *sutra* and *tantra* might begin to suggest the ways in which the alien term *tantra* in fact aligns with more familiar cognates in critical/theoretical terminologies, more specifically, with ideas of text and performance. *Text* denotes an enormous range of possible genres of writing, and, like sutra and tantra, is linked to other words that connote not only writing or inscription, but also the larger act of laying out lines in warp and weft within the loom of language: *textile, texture, context, pretext*. The word *text*, in its oldest root meaning, is also tied to the act of weaving, and, in extension, to weaving on a loom or within a frame. Both *text* and *textile*, in this sense, carry within themselves suggestions of tapestry art, scene, or figuration arising from the act of weaving and suturing, linking (however imaginatively) *text* and *textuality* to processes of both ideation (mind and text) and healing (bodies and the sutures that re-integrate them) through meditative *performance* (speech and song). *Performance* denotes this sense of making manifest: making something appear in the world from impulse, idea or text. This is one traditional understanding of magic—the power to make something immaterial manifest. Ideas of conjuring, notions of casting the spell, and the spell's intimacies with both time and articulation ("having a spell," "sitting a spell," spelling the word) support and inspire both textedness and performance. I would go so far as to suggest that all performance is spell, is incantation spelled out, is magic *at its root*.[9]

In its more extruded sense, then, text, tantra and performance signify, in part, a psychic practice, an imaginal interlacing out of which arises a vision in mind of a "selfless self" (which may variously be a character, the reader, the performer, or an extra-human entity, the *yidam*—see ahead) conjured initially through the lines and colors of spoken word and chanson. As Jeremy Safran describes it, tantric practitioners begin by visualizing the presence of the teacher or guru in a type of "transitional space" in which "the boundaries between subjective and objective realities are intentionally blurred" (20). Within this space of becoming, the person of the lama melds with the imaginal reality—what is called deity or *yidam*—and while perceived as real, this actuality is also realized through the process of visualization as pure illusion. The seeming contradiction here between the real and the illusory ultimately erases, through this particular meditative practice, the duality *between* the real and the illusory as categories of thought, creating a liminal space of unknowing which leads to the understanding that the dualities of self and other, this and that, are themselves both illusion and the *source* of illusion,[10] are, in other words, both illusion and a peculiar sort of Real that produces illusion—an apt conception, it seems to me, of theatre. A further point of this practice is the "imaginary construction of a world in which the normal boundaries of personal identity become permeable." In this visualization practice "the lama becomes identical with the Buddha, and the lama's mind becomes inseparable from that of the meditator. This identification helps to loosen the constraints of ordinary dualistic logic, and challenges the conventional self-other distinction" (Safran 20). Again, a pithy description of what we might conceive of as theatrical ontology.

Indeed, in the "imaginary construction of a world" we are well within the onto-phenomenal practices of an acting theory in which all constructions of the world are imaginary (or rather imaginal, preserving the real substrate of the purely phenomenal mind), and the permeability of identities becomes the very stuff of theatre. And, moreover, if we substitute the word *character* for the word *Buddha*, and the word *actor* for the word *meditator*, we see that the processes of tantric cross-permeability take on the basic timbres of acting practice. Indeed, in the shift from lama to Buddha and then to meditator, we sense something of the infusion of abstract character (The Buddha) with humanity (the lama), and the subsuming of that humanized character by the performer/actor (the meditator).

In this paradigm, the attempt through acting/practice to merge with the guru (either "actual" or as avatar) is to experience becoming, for example, *Menla*, the enlightened body of healing, the *pharmakon*.[11] It is to experience the coming or becoming of healing energy itself.[12] Thus the experience is not one in which the initiate simply moves toward something that is "outside" of self—it is not an Imitation of Christ. Tantra inoculates thought against mere belief through becoming. It operates as spiritual antigen, rather like acting and its katharsis move beyond simple pretense, simply "believing in" the moment of performance, and become something other, something potentially and potently curative. It is, moreover, ineffable, a indescribable, conscious, imaginal becoming-other which, in its indeterminacies, moves "beyond beyond," absorbing the attributes of both subject (the meditator) and object of meditation (the deity) and so erases the distinction, and finally erases mental *content* entirely, leaving only clear awareness. Tantrism, in other words, moves beyond mere belief because at practice's end, the instruction is to let all dissolve into emptiness, the emptiness of pure potentiality devoid of any specific attribute. This awareness of pure, undifferentiated energy (already too much conceptualized here) dissolves all belief, all certainty, and begins to erase ego itself. This erasure of ego, the "leaving behind" of the familiar, is—from the standpoint of normative culture—the *Unheimlich*, but it is also the *pharmakos*, that which, within the context of the socio-cultural, is deficiency itself—egolessness, the *pharmakos*, is the beggar, the slave, profound impoverishment within a culture of excess. Here empty awareness functions as *pharmakon* (and a hairsbreadth from the *pharmakeus*—the Deleuzean Becoming-Sorcerer), bringing, in the wake of deficiency, the therapeutic energy of unbounded potentiality. This might be hopelessly and naively "mystical" could we not summon the experience of the actor alongside these tantric practices as a kind of "shadow practice," the actor for whom the taking up of character represents an inverse process in which she is neither the same as, nor different from, the character she is presenting, and in which she also abandons ego in order to (hopefully) supersede it. Nor is she the same as or different from the person she is (or was) before the performance began. Her thoughts are neither her own nor someone else's. She, too, is at least momentarily bereft at play's end. The realization comes, throughout both processes (acting and meditative visualization), that one is always becoming, has always been becoming, becoming-Menla, becoming medicine, becoming *pharmakon* becoming *pharmakos*, becoming Other, becoming character, becoming enigma. But the difference between acting and tantra, of course, is crucial: whereas in tantra, the final dissolution of *yidam*, of self, of thought-content is liberation, in acting process, the final dissolution is indeterminacy itself, and as such a potential source of anxiety, uncertainty, fear, possibly terror. In the world of actor and *tantrika* (one who practices tantra), the destabilization of ego may have two very different outcomes—either the hyper-awareness of terror or the hyper-awareness of awakened mind, a synaptic gap apart.

This entire process through which one realizes the unceasing arising of self/other, and the utterly ungraspable nature of self or other as isolatable entities is an example of what Buddhism calls dependent co-arising—a kind of radical contingency theory in which nothing that appears in the world—either in mind or "in fact"—can be understood as having a stable identity or "essence" apart from everything else. I am not sure if acting or theory names this oscillating process of becomings, but tantric practice brings this insight into vivid awareness. Tantra might be understood, in fact, as a much older experiential mode of Deleuzean becomings, refusing, as does Deleuze much later, the molar in favor of the molecular. But *Vajrayana* pushes the case much farther. Here even the molecular, the capillary, the nearly instantaneous, is rejected in favor of what is absolutely ungraspable in time or place—emptiness.

Emptiness, or *sunyata*, then, is sheer creative potential, something akin to Deleuze's notion of virtuality. Indeed, the Buddhist idea of emptiness here functions in some sense as opposition to Western nihilism—the rejection of Lear's black hole, his "nothing will come of nothing." Buddhists reject this *nihilo ex nihil fit* in favor of something like the embryonic, creative, Einstein-Rosen bridge that emerges from the wormhole of meaninglessness and existential horror. All that is or can be emerges from an emptiness that is, in fact, the reservoir of all possibility—something more resonant, perhaps, with Romanticism's understanding of Imagination, or rather more precisely, with the planar flux of quantum foam.

What is also notable here is the complexity (but ultimately the simplicity) of becomings that tantric practice entails. The processes of becoming-other also disarticulate (better term than *deconstruct*) the presumed Foucaultian opposition between difference and sameness in which the Heraclitean Unity becomes the many by way of difference. Rather, in tantra, in acting the difference, we recall the unity beneath difference while at the same time coming to understand unity itself as continuous change, continuous becoming-other, pushing becoming-other well beyond its Deleuzean boundaries into becoming-emptiness, in which becoming itself becomes unlocatable and unbounded.[13] Moreover, and most importantly, noting the lack of ethical necessity in Deleuzean/Guattarian theory, the point of tantric practice is always and foremost the realization of compassion—being witness to suffering, a witnessing demanded of us as human beings—and becoming alive to a world that is, in each of its particles and particulars, alive.

This brings us again to animism. Beyond similarities in method and approach, literary text and performance often set out, as I've already said, to accomplish something quite similar to tantric becomings and transformation—transforming thought (idea, emotion, sensation) from one ideation into another through the use of image and trope. In doing so, the text speaks *to* us, and *speaks* us as the performance unfolds, and in doing so, performs us. In speaking to us, text and performance, like tantra, manifest agency. In agency, they conjure liveness. And although the very term "liveness," following the work of Philip Auslander, has been seemingly problematized, whether or how this liveness actually exists is, in the present context, quite literally immaterial. Whether voice and thought inhere in the text or performance itself, or is merely an impetus through which we (re) create its content is not important to the present discussion. What is relevant is that the text, in this sense, is alive. It is animate. It becomes possessed of voice, intention, and identity. It is the very locus of animist practice and manifestation. In tantra, a similar animistic manifestation occurs. Images, emotion, and thought emerge within the electro-chemical impulse of the brain. Pictures arise within the textures of mind, and through these, the world is shifted, and identity is changed. Things previously moribund come alive. And whereas both text and tantric practice engender performance, one might argue further that performance is absolutely central to each, a performance of transformation, through which transformation may actually occur—the counterpoint and mirror image of Aristotelian katharsis.

Of course the analogy is inexact. Although both tantra and theatre share similar ontologies, use technologies of mind that are deeply resonant, and effect, in different ways, transformations that are potentially life- and culture-changing, the presumptions of each practice are vastly different. The most important difference, to my mind, is the radically diverse situating of the Real and its manifest world. For Western cultures, the presumption still reigns that the world is, more or less, the way it seems to be. That it is, more or less, empirically verifiable, more or less solid, and not, ultimately, recondite. For many Buddhist traditions, the reality of the world is similarly assumed, but the nature of that reality is ultimately beyond our abilities to fully apprehend or explain it. The sensual apparatus given to us through evolutionary process provides us a very delimited and unlocatable notion of what the world is or might be, and intellect, being also a product of that evolution, will never decipher the central complexities of identity, consciousness, and the experience of life. The irony is that, in the Western artistic tradition at least, it has been theatre that has most powerfully suggested this conundrum. As Herbert Blau reminds us, theatre is precisely the locus which traces "the insubtantiality of self through the insubstantiality of performance" (156). This description of theatre is also perhaps the most succinct and apt description of tantric performance, summing and summoning the impossibility of Hamlet's fading invocation to the Ghost, "Stay, illusion!"

NOTES

1. "Initiation into tantra" is a kind of redundancy—tantra is itself initiation in the sense that every tantric practice within *Vajrayana* is a recognition of continuous "becoming," a "creation and completion" in the words of one of its central texts (*Creation and Completion* by Jamgön Kontrul) in which creation arises out of emptiness and dissolves back into it—virtualities arising from and disappearing back into the quantum foam of awareness-consciousness. The present chapter is a very partial foray into the ontological intersections between performance and spiritual practice.
2. For a full discussion of tantric practice, and more especially *Vajrayana* Buddhism as it is practiced, see Ray and also Samuel. I have avoided extensive citation of tantric ritual out of respect for those oral/aural traditions. There is much available on-line, but readers should be wary of sensationalistic websites and publications.
3. The authors and titles of works that have moved in this direction are too numerous to list here. My current favorite is Stengers.
4. The gesture here toward the imaginal is designed to underscore an important assumption of the present chapter: the choice to re-imagine (self, world) is no different than the choice to imagine in the first place. Within the various modes of contructivism, the assumption is that the constructed self is not reversible because it is *imagined and continuously re-imagined by the Other, by ideology*—but this speaks only of an inability to believe in the truly contingent nature of identity—that identity is in some sense unchangeable because of its situatedness within ideology. I simply don't believe this. Saying something does not make it so.
5. See Harvey—written for a wider audience, but still quite substantive and compelling. See also the work of David Abram, especially *Becoming Animal: An Earthly Cosmology*. See also his more widely known *The Spell of the Sensuous*.
6. I am aware of the various turns in this direction from Badiou to Žižek, as well as the rise of affect theory (Teresa Brennan and Elizabeth Grozs, among others), what I have called "The New Aesthetics" (or the New New Aesthetics, to differentiate it from the Frankfurt School's materialist misconceptions). These approaches remain, in my estimation (and often counter to their own claims), disembodied and at times oddly disengaged from the pain of the world they inhabit. For works that more directly engage with the intersections between tantric practice and affect, see Weinstone and also Holler.
7. What follows is a complex and variable interpretation of the various approaches within Buddhist history and practice. I am following Traleg Kyabgon's description of practice in his book *Mind at Ease: Self-Liberation through Mahamudra Meditation*. See especially page 137. However, this is, in the final analysis, my interpretation.
8. What is interesting in the meditational (*Dzogchen* and *Mahamudra*) approaches is the use of *Vipashyna*, or "mind-awareness" as a preparatory

technique. In *Vipashyna*, and more radically in *Mahamudra* and *Dzogchen*, the movement is a kind of distancing or spatializing of thought within a broader awareness—a process that has clear resonance with a much more limited and limiting Brechtian *Verfremdungsaffekt*. This, however, is beyond the scope of the present discussion.

9. I also think here of Lacan's dictum that his work stands between writing and speech. See the opening paragraphs of Lacan's "Instance of the Letter."
10. See Safran 20. The word "becoming" is sometimes used in Buddhist writings in the specific sense of "samsara," or illusion. I am using the terms becoming, becomings, becoming-other in the more Deluzean sense, but would like the terms to retain some of the Buddhist inflection.
11. Following, as throughout, the Platonic/Derridean play of these terms; *Menla* is also called the "Medicine Buddha."
12. And as a side note to this discussion of tantric practice, lest one be inclined at this point to view this practice as too much bound to devotional worldview in the usual sense, or rather too tame to be thought of in terms of raw-edged performance, we might view another, more powerful theatrical mode of tantric practice—*Chod*, or "cutting," in which one's body is offered through its own fear in a terrorizing play of mind, body, dance, and implement. *Chod* uses similar tantric modalities and visualizations, but here, one deliberately places oneself in terrifying places and times. *Chod* image and practice grew out of the practice of sky burial in Tibet, and was originally practiced in those charnel grounds among the decaying and half-eaten bodies of the poor and dispossessed. *Chod* is aversion therapy pushed to an extreme limit, and a "therapy" whose goal is not simply curing the practitioner of her phobias, but neutralizing fear itself so that one might become more fully free to act in the world.
13. I am aware that many Deleuzeans will claim that the Deleuzean project entails precisely this move into "creative involution." That may be, but I am claiming here a more radical presupposition for tantric practice which refuses to be grounded in an unprovable materialism.

WORKS CITED

Abram, David. *Becoming Animal: An Earthly Cosmology*. New York: Pantheon, 2010. Print.

———. *The Spell of the Sensuous*. New York: Vintage, 1997. Print.

Blau, Herbert. *Take up the Bodies: Theater at the Vanishing Point*. Urbana: U of Illinois P, 1982. Print.

Fischer-Schreiber, Ingrid, Franz-Karl Ehrhard, and Michael S. Diener. *The Shambala Dictionary of Buddhism and Zen*. Trans. Michael H. Kohn. Boston: Shambala, 1991. Print.

Harvey, Graham. *Animism: Respecting the Living World*. New York: Columbia UP, 2006. Print.

Holler, Linda. *Erotic Morality: The Role of Touch in Moral Agency*. New Brunswick: Rutgers UP, 2002. Print.

Kontrul, Jamgön. *Creation and Completion: Essential Points of Tantric Meditation*. Trans. Sarah Harding. Boston: Wisdom, 2002. Print.

Kyabgon, Traleg. *Mind at Ease: Self-Liberation through Mahamudra Meditation*. Boston: Shambala, 2004. Print.

Lacan, Jacques. "The Instance of the Letter in the Unconscious, or Reason since Freud." *Ecrits: A Selection*. Trans. Bruce Fink. New York: Norton, 2002. 138–168. Print.

Ray, Reginald. *Secrets of the Vajra World: The Tantric Buddhism of Tibet*. Shambala: Boston, 2001. Print.

Safran, Jeremy D. Introduction. *Psychoanalysis and Buddhism*. Ed. Safran. Boston: Wisdom, 2003. Print.

Samuel, Geoffrey. *Civilized Shamans: Buddhism in Tibetan Societies*. Washington: Smithsonian Institution, 1993. Print.

Stengers, Isabelle. *Cosmopolitics: I. The Science Wars II. The Invention of Mechanics III. Thermodynamics*. Minneapolis: U of Minnesota P, 2010. Print.

Weinstone, Ann. *Avatar Bodies: A Tantra for Posthumanism*. Minneapolis: U of Minnesota P, 2004. Print.

6 Jew Media

Performance and Technology for the Fifty-Eighth Century

Henry Bial

> "If Jews control the media, why don't we give ourselves better press?"
>
> —Jon Stewart *(Neuman)*

When I first began researching and writing about Jewish American popular culture in the 1990s, the history of Jewish artists in the American entertainment industry was still very much a story of "changing one's name for business purposes."[1] Despite the preponderance of Jewish writers, directors, and actors in theatre, film, and television, there seemed to be few overtly Jewish leading characters in these media, and those characters represented a very limited part of the spectrum of Jewish experience. Other scholars such as Andrea Most, David Zurawik, and Vincent Brook observed the situation similarly, noting that the fear of appearing "too Jewish" seemed to be a defining factor in shaping Jewish American cultural production in the latter half of the twentieth century (CE).[2] This mirrored contemporaneous conversations about Jewish American identity in "real life," and the mutual authentication between onscreen Jewishness and offscreen Jewishness proved a rich terrain for scholarly investigation.[3] The performance of Jewishness, I argued in *Acting Jewish*, was double coded, carrying one set of meanings for Jews and another for non-Jews, a strategic response to a perceived need to minimize or erase "Jewish difference" when communicating with "mainstream" culture. When I lecture about this to undergraduates today, they don't know what I'm talking about.

What can it mean to minimize or erase Jewish difference when Jon Stewart appears on national television five times a week, frequently "referr[ing] to himself as 'Jewey Von Jewstein' and crack[ing] wise on Jewish noses, circumcision, anti-Semites, Jews who play baseball (a short list), Israel as 'Heebie Land' and his grandma at Passover" (Gillick and Gorilovskaya)? When self-proclaimed "Hasidic Reggae Superstar" Matisyahu has a CD on the *Billboard* top 100? When the coffee table book *Bar Mitzvah Disco* is sold at Urban Outfitters stores nationwide, and even Salt Lake City's *Deseret News* runs a lifestyle piece headlined, "Hipster Judaism Is Popping

Up All Over" (Passy). Consider that in 2005, a year that many of today's Jewish undergraduates were bar or bat mitzvahed, cable network VH1 aired a special edition of its "All Access" series titled "So Jewtastic!" described by *TV Guide* as "A Celebration of All Things Jewish." As David Schneer puts it, "The assimilationist anxiety of the twentieth century is out, and cultural and sexual pride in the twenty-first is in, and this heady mixture has been very good for Jewish culture" (58).

While I agree with Schneer's assessment of the current landscape of Jewish American identity, his periodization of this phenomenon reflects the temptation common to many cultural commentators writing at "the dawn of a new millennium": the urge to identify a catastrophic change between past and present. This move to categorize what has come before as radically different from what will come after is especially attractive in the age of so-called "new media." As Jeffrey Shandler writes, "So often, the first responses to new media tend toward extremes [. . .]" (275). New technological innovations are regularly accompanied by utopian (or dystopian) prophecies, few of which turn out to be fulfilled. When the prophecy is particularly attractive ("cultural and sexual pride in the twenty-first is in"), the temptation to embrace it is even stronger, and the need for circumspection that much greater.

Hence my title: "Jew Media"—a poor pun, but one that serves two related but distinct purposes: (1) The phrase reflects the willingness of contemporary Jewish culture-makers to boldly self-identify, and to do so in a way that is at once ironic and "in your face"; (2) "Jew Media" also reflects the desire to reclaim the phrase from the anti-Semitic bloggers and hate groups who use it most often, usually as shorthand for "the public relations arm of the worldwide Jewish conspiracy."[4]

So I write here of "Jew Media" in the spirit of queer theory, as a way of re-centering the conversation, of refusing to accept the othering that, well, others, would force upon us. Placed as it is in ironic quotation marks, the phrase "Jew Media" signals my desire for a fluid, affective understanding of identity, as well as a more nuanced relationship to mass cultural representation than that provided by a conventional cultural studies model. Jew Media requires us to assume neither a sinister Culture Industry in thrall to an equally sinister Dominant Culture, nor a community imagined on a foundation of shared victimhood. Most importantly, it offers the Jewish media consumer an opportunity to assert that "Jewish" is a meaningful category of cultural experience, while keeping a certain critical distance from the impulse to generalize (or moralize) across that category. Jew Media is characterized by irony, a time-honored strategy by which the minority negotiates its relationship to the mainstream. Some critics, myself included, have suggested that an ironic outlook toward life has itself sometimes been a coded signal of Jewishness. In a postmodern age, we might further argue that such irony in self-identification is near universal. When irony no longer reads as Jewish, it is perhaps inevitably applied to expressions of Jewish identity itself. Irony, and I use it here in the Brechtian sense, is not just about humor, it's about seeing one's struggles and the struggles of one's identity group with a certain reflexivity or critical distance. This allows Jew Media to repurpose anti-Jewish stereotypes as a critique of anti-Semitism, allowing us to assert Jewish pride ("If Jews control the media, why don't we give ourselves better press") but to do so in quotation marks, as it were, to perform Jewish identity in a subjunctive mode, avoiding the pitfalls of essentialism or parochialism. Yet an examination of the history of Jewish American popular culture shows that this ironic assertion of Jewish identity represents not a catastrophic break, but a natural progression through multiple media, each of which was once "new."

My subtitle, "Performance and Technology for the Fifty-Eighth Century," then, is intended to address the understandable temptation to declare, "everything has changed." It plays on the now-familiar motif of utopian proclamations about "new media" and about cultural/social interaction more generally—e.g., careers for the twenty-first century. In such formulations, "the twenty-first century" is primarily an epistemic designator not a chronological one. It connotes technology more than time; dig into almost any document, exhibition, or website with "twenty-first century" in its title and you'll find references to computers, data networks, DNA sequencing, virtual reality. The phrase "For the fifty-eighth century" similarly designates not merely a time, but a way of thinking, one that is self-consciously Jewish. So calling this chapter "Performance and Technology for the Fifty-Eighth Century" signals another attempt to reframe the conversation in a way that marks the Jew as the insider, and everyone else as the outsiders, or (you should excuse the expression) the *goyim*. Like "Jew Media," "For the Fifty-Eighth Century" is a way of claiming, not without irony, that the Jewish worldview is an appropriate center or origin for my analysis. Unlike Jew Media, however, "For the Fifty-Eighth Century" requires the outsider to possess insider knowledge, in this case the knowledge that in the "Common Era" it may be 11 December 2010, but according to the traditional Jewish calendar, it is the fourth of Tevet 5771. And this deployment of insider knowledge is one way in which I signal my own Jewish identity.

Turning the tables in this way allows me to think differently about the question of new media. Instead of thinking about Web 2.0, social networking, etc., in the context of a catastrophic millennial shift, viewing developments in popular culture from the year 5771 prompts me to consider the Jew Media landscape as a natural progression of a process that can be traced back to the days of media that are no longer new: specifically film and television. Mass culture, after all, has been a critical site for the negotiation of Jewish identity in the United States since the 5680s. The explosive growth of new media has accelerated but not fundamentally changed the dynamics of that negotiation.

Even as I seek to reframe the debate in Jewish-specific terms, I also believe that Jew Media has lessons to offer all of ethnic and performance studies vis-à-vis the new media landscape. American Jews still present a problem for cultural critics: most approaches to racial and/or ethnic identity assume that a minority group (or group member) seeks either to assimilate entirely or to maintain a separatist, hyphenated identity. The desire to assimilate is usually framed as, to put it bluntly, "Bad." Assimilation is Bad because it represents the overwhelming discipline of the Dominant Culture, or because it represents self-hatred, or some combination of both. The desire to retain a separate identity is usually recognized as "Good." But this is problematic, too, as it challenges the universalist view of a society in which broader cultural norms can be shared. In either case, the theory most often deployed in media and performance studies doesn't reflect the actual situation on the ground, which is that most subaltern groups *want* to see themselves as different from the dominant culture . . . except when they don't.

Where performance intersects with technology and (new) media, identity-based analyses often fail to adequately explain the Jewish American experience. The bulk of our theory (not to mention our politics) is concerned with the notion of access. Minoritarian identities, according to most cultural studies scholars, are misrepresented or under-represented in the media because minority artists do not have sufficient access to the means of cultural production. It follows, then, that to redress this problem, we need to democratize access to the media in order to democratize representation and, by extension, the culture. This is the positive promise of new media: increased opportunity to produce and distribute content seems to imply that more culturally diverse content can be produced and distributed. Hence the urgency to assure that we as a society make access to the Web, to wireless networks, etc., as broad and deep as possible.

Access *is* important. But Jew Media shows us that access is only part of the equation. American Jews have had access to the means of mass cultural production for the better part of a century—access, even, in disproportion to their share of the general population. Yet this has not, by itself, solved the problem of Jewish identity. Access, it turns out, presents its own set of problems. Jewish American artists in the media, while certainly enjoying access at a level far from subordinate, nonetheless have tended to minimize the overt representation of Jewishness in their creative work, partly as a preemptive strategy to avoid accusations of "Jew-controlled" media.

Jew Media, then, is always contested, always in motion, imperfectly balancing the specific ("Jewish enough") and the universal (not "too Jewish"). How then, do we get a handle on it? When I consider a performance, be it new media, old media, or what we might call the "really old media" of live theatre, I bring to bear four questions[5] that structure the remainder of this chapter:

1. Who's Jewish?
2. How do you know?
3. Why do you care?
4. Is it good for the Jews?

WHO'S JEWISH

"Who's Jewish?" is a very delicate question because, by and large, the only people who care about the answer are (1) Jews; and (2) anti-Semites.[6] In the new media universe, this is evidenced most prominently by the disclaimer that appears when one enters the word "Jew" into the ubiquitous search engine, Google (a link to the disclaimer comes up first on the results list, under the heading "Offensive Search Results"): "If you recently used Google to search for the word 'Jew,' you may have seen results that were very disturbing. We assure you that the views expressed by the sites in your results are not in any way endorsed by Google." There follow three full paragraphs explaining, in broad terms, how the Google algorithm sorts keywords, and how "Jew" (rather than "Jewish" or other variants) is commonly used on anti-Jewish webpages. The actual results of such a Google search turn up a curious mix of sites, ranging from sites offering religious information and advice (www.jewfaw.org or www.myjewishlearning.com) to open source sites celebrating what Laurence Roth calls "Jewishness as brand identity" (www.jewtube.com or www.heebz.com), as well as the "very disturbing" hate sites (www.jewwatch.com) that document the alleged sins of the worldwide Zionist conspiracy. The keyword-oriented landscape of the World Wide Web makes such juxtapositions all but inevitable, and yet this phenomenon is not so different from the way such questions played out earlier in the fifty-eighth century. A search in a library card catalogue three or four decades ago would likely have revealed the same variation in response. Even leaving anti-Semites out of the conversation, we still have to contend with a wide range of conflicting answers, ranging from the religious to the cultural, from the dogmatic to the pluralistic. Often, it seems, the answer to "Who's Jewish?" is, somewhat counter-intuitively, determined by the answer to our second question . . .

HOW DO YOU KNOW?

In the early days of the fifty-eighth century, the Jews who (in Neil Gabler's memorable phrase) "invented Hollywood" were very circumspect about the films they made and the actors they showcased. They were trying to establish the movies as "all-American" and to do so they had to de-emphasize the ethnicity of the performers (Gabler). So, for example, when Jacob Julius Garfinkle (1913–1952) became an actor he decided of his own volition to change his name to Jules Garfinkle, and later to Jules Garfield (his friends called him Julie). But when he moved from New York, where he'd been a stage star, to Hollywood, the Jewish producer Jack Warner (of Warner Brothers) felt that even "Jules" was too Jewish, and suggested that he change it to James Garfield. The actor pointed out that there had been a president named James Garfield, and protested, "You wouldn't name a goddamn actor Abraham

Lincoln, would you?" To which a Warner executive replied: "No, kid, we wouldn't [. . .] because Abe is a name most people would say is Jewish and we wouldn't want people to get the wrong idea" (Gabler 301).

The studio's concern over Garfield's public image meant that he rarely got to play explicitly Jewish roles, although as Samuel J. Rosenthal has shown, this did not stop Warner Bros. from using the actor's Jewishness to market the film in the Jewish press. For example, in promoting the 1939 (5700) noir thriller *They Made Me a Criminal*, they ran an ad in the Los Angeles *B'nai Brith Messenger* with the tagline "Another Jewish Actor Rises to Stardom" (Rosenthal 175). Even at the beginning of the fifty-eighth century, one answer to "How do you know?" is: through extratextual information available only to the in-group. This is a clear example of using technology (here, the then-new media of advertising) to provide supplemental information about "who's Jewish" to a self-selected Jewish audience. The Jewish press has long served this function of supporting (not to say creating) a "Jewish interpretative community" by circulating information about Jewish celebrities, and such quasi-public identifications of prominent Jews have circulated in virtually every medium.

The Internet has magnified and dispersed this kind of extratextual knowledge. The question, "Is such and such famous person Jewish?" can be answered in moments from your cellphone, via any number of commercial and hobbyist websites such as JewOrNotJew.com, Heebz.com, and the ever-present Wikipedia (see: http://en.wikipedia.org/wiki/List_of_Jewish_actors). The immediacy of access to this kind of information, however, is matched by the questionable reliability of the source. This is less of a problem than it might seem, because such "crowdsourcing" of the question "Who's Jewish?" has a history that predates even the fifty-eighth century, though the "peer-to-peer networking" was conducted over coffee instead of over fiber-optic cable. More problematic is the attempt to craft a definition of Jewish that pleases all the users (consumers, producers, and "prosumers"[7]) on whom the site relies for its existence. Most address this dilemma with irony. The Heebz.com statement on "Who is a Jew?" is representative:

> We've decided to sidestep this issue in order to make everyone happy. As you probably know, there are a number of ideas on who is a Jew [. . .] So it is our plan to indicate maternally-Jewish Jews by some kind of icon and/or tag and/or filter. For the purposes of this site we will also include individuals with only a Jewish father. We will also include individuals who have undergone an official "conversion" process through any of the major Jewish groups. Is everybody happy now?[8] ("Famous Jews")

The irony and irreverence of the above statement are palpable. The tagline "Is everybody happy now?" is at once obsequious and confrontational, pandering and parodic. Roth suggests this kind of parodic opposition to "tired narratives" (like the debate about who is a Jew), "has become an important component in the cultural empowering of contemporary American Jewishness and in its marketing to both Americans and American Jews" (101).

Scholars use a variety of terms to describe the target audience for such marketing: "New Jews" (Kirshenblatt-Gimblett), "alterna-Jews" (Roth), and "Heebsters" (Cohen). There seems to be general agreement, however, that this phenomenon draws on multiple influences, including queer culture, zine culture, and a concerted effort by older, more conventional Jewish organizations and philanthropies to support "alt-Jewishness" in an attempt to keep a new generation of American Jews connected to their Jewish identity. This ironic and irreverent "branding" of Jewishness is evident not just in the extratextual means by which we interpret cultural products, but it is increasingly central to the performance itself.

Comedian Jon Stewart is a salient example. At first glance, Stewart's brand of intellectual, self-deprecating humor might seem to be simply an update on the classic Jewish comics Sid Caesar or Woody Allen. But in fact, Stewart is doing something different—he's joking about being an insider, not an outsider. For example, on accepting the 2005 Emmy Award for *The Daily Show*, Stewart declared, "When I first said that I wanted us to put together a late-night comedy writing team that would only be 80 percent Ivy League-educated Jews, people thought I was crazy. They said you need 90, 95 percent. But we proved 'em wrong" ("Sound Bites"). How do you know Jon Stewart is Jewish? Because he tells you, repeatedly. It's part of his act.

WHY DO YOU CARE?

For the Jewish consumer of Jew Media, caring about who is Jewish and who isn't is a way to enact one's membership in the imagined community of American Jews. In other words, the answer to "Why do we care?" is "Because by caring, we demonstrate that we belong." Lenny Bruce's infamous comic routine in which he divided the world into "Jewish" and "Goyish" (e.g., "Fruit salad is Jewish; Jello is Goyish") offers the prototype for this phenomenon, which I call "reading Jewish," a performance of identity via reading strategies. Bruce's routine has spawned a variety of imitators, including "Jewish vs. Goyish, Web Edition," drawn from the website bangitout, which bills itself as a "Kosher Comedy Community." A few selections from their long list posted by a user named Seth:

Jewish vs. Goyish, WEB EDITION

- PC is Jewish, Mac is goyish (the commercial says it all)
- Netflix is Jewish. Blockbuster is goyish.
- eBay is a shuk, Craigslist is the bais medrash bulletin board.
- Google is searching for chometz, AskJeeves is searching for the Easter egg.

Compared to Bruce's original routine, here the in-group jokes are both more out and more in. More out—in the sense of out of the closet—because they use Yiddish and Hebrew words to emphasize Jewish difference. More in because they require more specialized knowledge to understand. A *shuk*, for example, is a Middle Eastern market, and a *bais medrash* is a Jewish study center. Note that in this case, as in others, the pretense of Jewish and Goyish drops away entirely. The real purpose of the routine is to claim the world for the Jews. So when you laugh at this, and more importantly when you forward it, share it, *like* it, or *Digg* it, you signal your membership in the Tribe—as clearly and unambiguously as you would by wearing your "SUPERJEW," "Moses is my homeboy," or "Yo Semite" T-shirt—which is to say, very clear, but hardly unambiguous.

It's not just about belonging to the group, it's about making the group the center, and the general culture the outsider looking in. Yet the claiming of the center is always already ironic. As Kirshenblatt-Gimblett writes, "[i]rreverence is one of the forms that engagement takes, and effective parody requires considerable knowledge of its target. Paradoxically, then, making Jewishness uncomfortable—creative estrangement—is what makes it "comfortable" for this group, offering it a way to say yes and no at the same time" (4). Jew Media takes access, adds irony, and produces a performance that helps Jews negotiate their relationship with the broader culture.

Irony is, I'd suggest, a particularly useful tool for negotiating the new media landscape, because (at the moment at any rate), the interface encourages it. Everything on the Web is at one remove from reality. Everything is in quotation marks, visible or not. To the degree that we understand belief to be an essential component of Jewish identity, we may find this problematic. We might then wonder, for all the pleasures that Jew Media offers, about the answer to our fourth question . . .

IS IT GOOD FOR THE JEWS?

I began this chapter by noting that when I speak to college students about the erasure of Jewish identity in American popular culture, they don't really understand the circumstances under which their parents and grandparents engaged with Jew Media. The converse is also true. When I speak to older audiences (scholars and the general public) about contemporary performers such as Stewart, Sarah Silverman, or Sacha Baron Cohen (*Borat*), it is clear that these comics' parodic repackaging of Jewish stereotypes makes American Jews old enough to remember the Reagan administration very nervous. Such audiences are likely to have been raised to be hypervigilant about stereotypes, to prefer claims of universalism rather than separatism, to identify subtle discrimination and anti-Semitic code words ("New York media"). In short, this demographic (in which I include myself) has been raised to see every instance of Jewish representation in the mainstream through the lens of "Is it good for the Jews?"

As should be clear by now, in the fifty-eighth century it's not really possible to ask this question un-ironically. But this doesn't mean it cannot or should not be asked. "New technologies," Kirshenblatt-Gimblett reminds us, "are not only tools, but also social practices. They are also models for reimagining ways to be Jewish and to form Jewish connections" (7). To the degree that contemporary Jew Media functions to revitalize Jewish American culture, and to provide a new generation with a sense of engagement, a desire to act Jewish, then it is not perhaps too great a stretch to suggest that it can indeed be "good for the Jews." The positive promise of Jew Media, then, is the utopian prediction of technology bringing people together, preserving the best of what has come before, and encouraging radical innovation vis-à-vis what will come next. The darker side of Jew Media is partly the dystopian forecast that accompanies all new technologies: that its superficial quality and ease of use will cheapen our experience and make us stupid, that Jewish identity will be stripped of meaningful content, that the wisdom of generations and the divine presence cannot be meaningfully encountered through a screen. For those of us living in the fifty-eighth century, we also recall too painfully that new technologies offer their benefits just as freely to those who would persecute us. *If you recently used Google to search for the word "Jew," you may have seen results that were very disturbing.* These potential threats to Jewish identity—from within and without—ensure that "Is it good for the Jews?" however ironic it must inevitably be, remains an urgent and necessary question.

WHY IS THIS NIGHT DIFFERENT FROM ALL OTHER NIGHTS?

The four questions at Passover are actually framed by a meta-question—an overarching idea. Before we ask why we eat matzoh, why dip the greens, etc., we ask, "Why is this night different from all other nights?" And the meta-answer is, "You shall tell your child on that day, this is because of what God did for me when I was a slave in Israel"—not some remote person, but for me, because we are one people. We are timeless, not in the sense of unchanging, but in the sense of continually embodying and reenacting our own narrative. It is the questions, not the answers, that define the community.

To put it another way, the commitment to inquiry and debate about how Jewishness is defined is, arguably, a defining factor of Jewish identity. French Rabbi and philosopher Marc-Alain Ouaknin writes:

> The *Zohar* says: "When a man by means of inquiry and reflection has reached the utmost limit of knowledge, he stops at *Mah* (the what?),

> as if to say, what have you understood?" [. . .] The "What have you understood?" is not a negative result of the cognitive procedure: the "what?" adorned with its question mark is the positive result that should be achieved. We can say that "the essence of reason consists not in securing for man (*Mah*) a foundation and powers, but in calling him into question (*Mah?*)" (236).

Hank Lazer draws on Ouaknin's study of Talmudic hermeneutics, *The Burnt Book*, to suggest that the contemporary online world shares some formal similarities with this central text of Jewish thought. In Lazer's reading, the Talmud, with its multicolumn layout juxtaposing scripture with commentary with commentary on commentary, and so on, anticipates new media creations such as social network sites; it is a collective document that grows through individually actualized readings and writings. He writes (quoting Ouaknin):

> One might quite rightly talk about such textuality as an ongoing accretion, the page as a kind of palimpsest, or a perpetual additive thinking or conversing or interpreting. So that we might say that "the creation of meaning is a creation-production of time" (p. 171). Or we might acknowledge the pre-digital yet proleptic nature of that 1523 page and say it is an early example of Facebook or MySpace or an early blog or a Wikipedia entry. (Lazer 75)

The phrase "people of the Book" may seem to imply a kind of fixed, timeless identity formation. "As Israel has kept the Torah," goes the saying, "so has the Torah kept Israel" (Fackenheim 328).[9] But as Lazer points out, "The Book" is not single but multiple; not frozen in time, but continually being written.

It is precisely because of this that the meta-question is also, in a sense, a trick question. This night is *not* different from all other nights. The Passover seder does enact a catastrophic break from the past (the Exodus from Egypt), but it is a re-enactment. It is as much about looking backward as it is about looking forward; as much about continuity as it is about change. So too, with Jew Media. As Shandler writes, "True to the multiple meanings of the term media, new technologies effect their most significant innovations in religious life by establishing new connections and thereby creating new in-between loci. These are situated not on the frontier, looking into a limitless void [. . .] but rather at some new interstice, and so they look back and forth among known options" (281). In the world of Jew Media, every night poses its four questions. Reminding ourselves that we are not only Standing on the Dawn of a New Millennium but also heading into the final third of the fifty-eighth century is a good way to keep our perspective.

NOTES

1. This chapter first appeared in *TDR: The Drama Review* 55:3 (T211) Fall 2011, pp. 134–143 and appears here by permission of *TDR* and MIT Press. Special thanks are due the editors of the issue, Jill Dolan and Stacy Wolf, as well as *TDR* associate editor Mariellen R. Sandford, for their valuable suggestions. A much earlier version of this chapter was delivered as the keynote address for Texas A&M University's Race and Ethnic Studies Institute's (RESI) Race, Ethnicity, and (New) Media Symposium, 1 May 2009.
2. See also Jon Stratton, *Coming Out Jewish*; J. Hoberman and Jeffrey Shandler, *Entertaining America*; and numerous others.
3. On the fear of seeming "too Jewish" in everyday life, see (inter alia) Riv-Ellen Prell, *Fighting to Become Americans: Jews, Gender, and the Anxiety of Assimilation*; Eric Goldstein, *The Price of Whiteness: Jews, Race, and American Identity*; and David Mamet, *The Wicked Son: Anti-Semitism, Self-Hatred, and the Jews.*
4. Examples of the anti-Semitic use of the phrase "Jew Media" include blog headlines such as "Columbine: 10 Years of Jew media lies" (http://incogman.net/04/2009/columbine-10-years-of-jew-media-lies/) or "Viacom (Jew Media Control)" (http://nationalrevolution.blogspot.com/2006/04/viacom-jew-media-control.html). It is the more virulent version of the phrase "mainstream media" or "MSM" that can be found elsewhere in the blogosphere, though the term MSM has become so widely used that most contemporary uses seem to be innocent of anti-Semitic overtones.
5. This is, of course, another in-joke: a reference to the four questions asked at the traditional Passover seder.
6. My Kansas colleague, Tamara Falicov, points out that there is a third, smaller population concerned with this question: what we might call philo-Semites, non-Jews who have a fascination with things Jewish.
7. The term "prosumer" is used by web analysts to describe the user who functions as both consumer and producer of online content.
8. Heebz.com is widely seen as the successor to the now defunct "Jewhoo" (formerly found at www.jewhoo.com), which I discuss at length in Chapter 6 of *Acting Jewish.*
9. Fackenheim, a reform rabbi, cites this quote as a pre-existing aphorism.

WORKS CITED

Bial, Henry. *Acting Jewish: Negotiating Ethnicity on the American Stage and Screen.* Ann Arbor: U of Michigan P, 2005. Print.

Brook, Vincent. *Something Ain't Kosher Here: The Rise of the "Jewish" Sitcom.* New Brunswick: Rutgers UP, 2003. Print.

Cohen, Judah. "Hip-hop Judaica: the politics of representin' Heebster heritage." *Popular Music* 28.1 (2009): 1–18. Print.

Fackenheim, Emil L. *To Mend the World: Foundations of Future Jewish Thought.* 1982. Bloomington: Indiana UP, 1994. Print.

"Famous Jews: About." *Famous Jews.* Heebz, n.d. Web. 15 Sept. 2010.

Gabler, Neal. *An Empire of Their Own: How the Jews Invented Hollywood.* New York: Anchor, 1989. Print.

Gillick, Jeremy, and Nonna Gorilovskaya. "Meet Jonathan Stuart Leibowitz (aka) Jon Stewart: The wildly zeitgeisty Daily Show host." *Moment Magazine.* Moment Magazine, November/December 2008. Web. 13 Sept. 2010.

Goldstein, Eric. *The Price of Whiteness: Jews, Race, and American Identity*. Princeton: Princeton UP, 2006. Print.
Hoberman, J., and Jeffrey Shandler. *Entertaining America: Jews, Movies and Broadcasting*. Princeton: Princeton UP, 2003. Print.
"Jewish vs. Goyish, Web Edition." Comment posted by Seth. *Bangitout*. bangitout.com, 8 May 2003. Web. 15 Sept. 2010.
Kirshenblatt-Gimblett, Barbara. "The 'New Jews': Reflections on Emerging Cultural Practices." Re-thinking Jewish Communities and Networks in an Age of Looser Connections. Wurzweiler School of Social Work, Yeshiva University and Institute for Advanced Studies, Hebrew University. New York City. 6–7 December 2005. Lecture. New York University, n.d. Web. 15 Jan. 2010. <http://www.nyu.edu/classes/bkg/web/yeshiva.pdf>.
Lazer, Hank. "Is There a Distinctive Jewish Poetics? Several? Many?: Is There Any Question?" *Shofar: An Interdisciplinary Journal of Jewish Studies* 27.3 (2009): 72–90. Print.
Mamet, David. *The Wicked Son: Anti-Semitism, Self-Hatred, and the Jews*. New York: Schocken, 2006. Print.
Most, Andrea. *Making Americans: Jews and the Broadway Musical*. Cambridge: Harvard UP, 2004. Print.
Neuman, Joshua. "History of the World, Part 2: Jewish Conspiracy Theory: The Satire." *Slate*. Slate, 21 Oct. 2005. Web. 10 Sept. 2010.
Ouaknin, Marc-Alain. *The Burnt Book: Reading the Talmud*. 1986. Trans. Llewellyn Brown. Princeton: Princeton UP, 1995. Print.
Passy, Charles. "Hipster Judaism Is Popping Up All Over." *Deseret News*. Deseret News, 25 Mar. 2006. Web. 14 Sept. 2010.
Prell, Riv-Ellen. *Fighting to Become Americans: Jews, Gender, and the Anxiety of Assimilation*. Boston: Beacon, 1999. Print.
Rosenthal, Samuel J. "John Garfield." *Entertaining America: Jews, Movies and Broadcasting*. Ed. J. Hoberman and Jeffrey Shandler. Princeton: Princeton UP, 2003. 173–175. Print.
Roth, Laurence. "Oppositional Culture and the 'New Jew' Brand: From Plotz to Heeb to Lost Tribe." *Shofar: An Interdisciplinary Journal of Jewish Studies* 25.4 (2007): 99–123. Print.
Schneer, David. "Queer Is the New Pink: How Queer Jews Moved to the Forefront of Jewish Culture." *Journal of Men, Masculinities and Spirituality* 1.1 (2007): 55–64. Print.
Shandler, Jeffrey. *Jews, God, and Videotape: Religion and Media in America*. New York: New York UP, 2009. Print.
"Sound Bites: Special Emmy Edition." *Entertainment Weekly*. Entertainment Weekly, 23 Sept. 2005. Web. 30 Dec. 2010.
Stratton, Jon. *Coming Out Jewish*. London: Routledge, 2003. Print.
Zurawik, David. *The Jews of Prime Time*. Hanover: Brandeis UP and UP of New England, 2003. Print.

7 Plain Speech Acts

Reading Quakerism with Theatre and Performance Studies

Tamara Underiner

It might seem odd that an anthology examining relationships among religion, theatre, and performance would even include a chapter on Quakerism. By design, there are no theatrical elements in most Quaker meetings for worship, especially among those who adhere most closely to original Quaker meeting practice.[1] There are no rites, no rituals, no liturgy, no vestments, no incense, no stained glass windows, no draperies, no statuary, no masks, no art, no spectacle (though occasionally some music is allowed). In fact, from the very beginnings of Quakerism in mid-seventeenth-century England, Quakers were known for their deep suspicion of all things theatrical. Historians of U.S. American theatre point to the Quakers' anti-theatrical prejudice (an attitude they shared with the Puritans, who nevertheless persecuted them for other reasons) to help explain the relatively late start of theatre in the English colonies. Even today, the still-important Quaker call to simple living, coupled with a weekly worship practice whose performance repertoire is limited to sitting still in silence until one is moved to speak, and then to do so as plainly as possible, don't seem to lend themselves to the rich analysis that has long attended studies of fancier traditions like the Catholic Mass, say, or Yoruban Egungun festivals.

But I think the relationship between Quakerism and theatre is worth a closer look. For one thing, Quaker antipathy toward theatre has changed over the centuries, in keeping with changing understandings of theatre itself. For another, despite their small numbers—fewer than ninety thousand members nationwide remain[2]—Quakers have long performed symbolic and cultural labor as the "religious conscience for an expanding nation"—work that has been registered in literature, plays, films, and other literary and visual genres (Ryan). In this chapter, I argue that Quaker moral force was from the start deeply performative, despite Quaker suspicion against both theatricality and the taking of public oaths (that most performative of speech acts[3]). After briefly describing my own relationship to Quakerism, I introduce some basic history and operative tenets of Quaker religious practice in England and the U.S., as a way to understand the origins of the Quaker anti-theatrical prejudice and subsequent attitudes toward theatre and the arts. Drawing from the work of Quaker historian Michael P. Graves, I describe how these attitudes have changed over time relative to theatre and to public activism, and discuss implications for thinking about a Quaker performance practice. Throughout, I argue that such a practice is (and has long been) rooted in a Quaker preference for a "plain speech" that is also action. These actions—ranging from defenses of religious freedoms in early courts of law, to acts of private and public opposition to slavery, activism on behalf of women's rights, anti-war activism, and, more recently, calls for immigration reform—have tended, over the course of the centuries, to compel U.S. Americans to look at our most closely held beliefs about peace, social justice, and the experience of God.

QUAKERISM AND ME

I attended my first Quaker meeting on a Sunday not long after the Tuesday that was 11 September 2001. I had moved to Arizona a few weeks before, and already had begun to suffer a profound sense of disorientation in this place that was so different, in every way that seemed to matter, from the grey urban centers I had known best: Pittsburgh, Seattle, Minneapolis. When Phoenix erupted in red, white, and blue in the days after 9/11, at first I did not realize that the rest of the country was little different; I saw this eruption as a pathology unique to my new hometown. And so, seeking the company of people I trusted would advocate for something that didn't smell like blood, I went to the Meetinghouse of the Phoenix Quakers, conveniently located a few blocks from my new home.

At the time I knew very little of the Religious Society of Friends, a.k.a. the Quakers,[4] apart from their conscientious objection to all war on principle, and a bit about their reputation for having pursued progressive paths in U.S. American history in such areas as Indian relations in the seventeenth and eighteenth centuries, abolition in the nineteenth, and women's rights throughout. And, of course, that Quaker presence in the early days of English colonization had put a big damper on the development of theatre here, which I confess I thought was just . . . quaint. I brought my two-year-old daughter with me and we visited the tiny, unassuming First Day School[5] classroom, where I saw a handwritten sign one of the teachers had scotch-taped to the slump-block wall:

> The Society of Friends does not have an official creed (a set of beliefs) which all members must accept. Here is why:
>
> - Words often mean different things to different people.
> - Words can change their meanings over time.
> - God is always showing truth in a different way.
> - It isn't what we say that matters, it's what we do and feel.

I was struck in particular by the first three points: their unadorned resonance to poststructural understandings about the nature of language, and its relation to the unfolding revelations of history, if not God, "spoke to my condition" as a student of such things.[6] If the ex-actor in me felt concern that I might not be completely welcome among these Friends, the ambivalent Catholic in me gravitated toward their freedom from creed, and the scholar in me saw something kindred in the way the first three points cared about the relationship between language and revelation. My daughter and I became regular attenders. In the ten years since then, I have learned much about Quaker practice through the witness of other Friends, availed myself of the wisdom of our Meeting's elders and their suggested readings,[7] and pursued a rather idiosyncratic path of personal research and activism, which has led me to reflect deeply on the foregoing four points. All of which is to say: my words here are not those of a lifelong Quaker, nor one who is an expert or a spokesperson in any way for Quakerism in general or the Phoenix Meeting in particular. I offer this caveat not only in the familiar gesture of academic modesty, but also as a performance of Quaker practice. Quakers speak as a body only rarely; in fact, there is no one Quaker central body through which they could—only a few affiliating organizations that encompass various Meetings according to type (and even so, many Meetings remain independent). When one of these organizations—or Quaker action committees such as the Friends Committee on National Legislation, or the American Friends Service Committee—does make a statement about matters of some complexity, it is only after a long period of discernment that includes "threshing" meetings designed to reveal the variety of understandings and positions on the matter under consideration, toward mutual understanding. The resulting decisions and statements about them are also "seasoned" for a period before their release. In contrast, when a Quaker (or in my case, attender) writes about things having to do with Quaker values and practices in contexts such as the one in which I now write, it is understood that we do so as individual Quakers engaged at whatever level we are with those values and practices.

Since I arrived at the Quaker meeting that day in September of 2001, my own engagement with Quakerism has led me to take some issue with the foregoing fourth point, about actions and feelings being more important than words. Although I have come to see that Quaker practice (a "doing") does take precedence over theological doctrine, nevertheless it is also so that for Quakers, words *are* a form of practice. As such, they have always mattered a very great deal. This mattering is part of the reason for the suspicion of theatre that Quakers brought with them to the colonies from England, part of the reason for their enduring symbolism as a figure for uprightness in the U.S. American imaginary, and part of the reason for the ultimate efficacy of their activism in the various causes with which Quakers have been associated over time—pacifism, Indian rights, abolition, women's rights, prison reform, and now, immigration. By briefly historicizing this "anti-theatrical prejudice," I hope to show some of the thought that underlay both the proscriptions against theatre and later resonances with certain strains of theatre and performance studies perspectives.

QUAKERS ON THEATRE AND THE ARTS

George Fox founded the Religious Society of Friends of the Truth in 1652—ten years after the famous ban in England on the performance of stage plays, and four years after the Puritan-influenced British Parliament issued an ordinance ordering all playhouses to be pulled down, all performers to be seized and whipped, and all caught attending a performance to be fined. Quakerism would grow in England and across the pond during the energetic heyday of the theatre that followed the lifting of those restrictions—the period of Restoration comedy, a form not known for its moral rectitude. But these are not the most important factors affecting early and persistent Quaker ambivalence toward the stage, and it would be a mistake to consider the earliest Quakers as merely acting in consonance with the more general Puritan spirit of their times, or their continuing attitudes to be the result of mere orthodoxy. Although both Quakers and Puritans opposed the temptations of the theatre, their motivations came from markedly differing underlying worldviews.

As Quaker historian Margaret Hope Bacon describes it, "there was a joyousness about the early Friends that attracted adherents. In a day of doubt and gloom, based on a [Puritan/Calvinist] belief in the depravity of human nature, the Quakers proclaimed a faith in the perfectibility of humans through the workings of Christ, the Inward Teacher. No one needed to feel lost in sin or condemned to hell fire" (23). Perhaps the most important difference between early Friends and Puritans was the Friends' belief that one could access these divine workings directly, requiring neither authoritative scripture nor pastoral intervention. This autonomy the Puritans considered heretical—and traitorous, because Puritanism was for a time in England and later in the colonies a de facto form of state religion. Bacon also describes the various "joyous" ways the very first Quakers expressed their differences with Puritan beliefs, practices that over time would modulate considerably: preaching loudly in the streets, interrupting Puritan church services, and, on more than one occasion, stripping naked in public in imitation of the prophet Elijah. "One Friend stood on a street corner in London with a platter of smoking brimstones on his head," she notes (19), in what I can't help but see as a particularly vivid critique of the Puritan belief in hell fire. In return, the Puritans also dealt out punishments against the Quakers that were themselves spectacular: boring holes in their tongues, stripping Quaker women to the waist and dragging them through town; and public hangings (at least in the colonies; although persecuted on both sides of the Atlantic, no Friends were ever executed in England).

So whereas it can be argued, as Lori Stokes does, that the early Quakers were "as righteous a group of zealots as most Puritans," who shared with their persecutors a distaste for formal theatre and an apparent taste for other more public means of performing and preserving their respective faiths, it is important to remember that such displays were the results of fundamental differences between the two groups. George Fox and his society followed a more radically democratic kind of religious practice than did the Puritan reformers within the Church of England, one based on the conviction that individuals could experience the Holy Spirit (or "Light of Christ") directly, without the need for human intermediaries, and they considered this experience to be more authoritative than even the Bible itself.[8] So important was this direct experience of "the Light" that many early followers of Fox called themselves "Children of the Light." In order to have this experience, one needs to wait in silence on the Spirit, best done in collectivity with other Friends, so that the fruits of this divine communion can be shared. Although individual leadings, messages, prayers, and even prophesies are welcomed, "Quakers are happiest when they have what they call a 'gathered' meeting, and the same spirit and a similar message seems to have been reaching many of the worshipers at the same time" (Bacon 4).[9]

During unprogrammed Quaker meetings for worship, Friends sit together in silence, "waiting on the Spirit" until one is moved to speak, which may or may not happen. It is understood that the Spirit speaks through the individual person; although the vocabulary and style may be recognizably the person's own, the message is understood to emanate not from them but from the Spirit. (Quakers, as a rule, do not speak in tongues.) At times, less so today than in early Quakerism, the insight is accompanied by a trembling sort of delivery, which put the "quake" in "Quaker." This physical manifestation is held by some to be the sign of spiritual authenticity and by others (for example, frightened Puritans in Salem in 1692–1693) to be a sign of something less welcome, like witchcraft. In my own practice, I find very difficult the work of discernment it takes to distinguish my own impulses to share an insight from that of something greater than myself (and take this struggle as a probable sign that it's the pedagogue and not the Spirit in me that's moving). To help worshippers focus in on this task without distraction, most Quaker meetinghouses are rather austere places. The meetinghouse I attend, for example, consists of a large room with a glass wall at one end, opening onto a view of Piestewa Peak in the Phoenix Mountain Preserve, and at the other, two bookcases atop two tables, where there is a guestbook, some Quaker literature, and refreshments for the Rise of Meeting when fellowship occurs. In between there is nothing but long stretches of unadorned wall, until the very the west end of the room, where a handful of pictures were hung—but only after a long threshing process in which Friends debated the merits of hanging them at all.

For Quakers individually and together, discerning "that of God" or the "Inner Light" is the primary spiritual undertaking, and the practices that emanate from this undertaking affect every aspect of Quaker life, inside and outside of the gathered meetings for worship. They constitute "more a method of reaching God than a set of beliefs" (Bacon 88). As methods go, its simplicity is deceptive: one need only sit still in silence, but stilling the mind is always a difficult matter. And because Quakers distinguish the spiritual from the intellectual and the emotional, investments in the two latter arenas of human life can become obstacles to gleaning the Spirit's wisdom (an orientation shared by many of the world's more contemplative religious practices). I do scant justice here to the depth of the wisdom in most Quaker practice, but for the purposes of this discussion I want to underline that the Quaker practice of silence rather than stimulation in the form of liturgy, rite, ritual, movement, music, and spectacle come as much or more from a Platonic respect for the power of these worldly elements to sway the mind and heart, than from a Puritan-derived suspicion of them as inherently evil, wrong, or sinful. In the first two centuries of Quaker development, this in-meeting aesthetic traveled outside the meetinghouse as well, and manifested itself in a shunning of artistic pursuits in the secular realm.

Thus, George Fox "was moved to cry out against all sorts of music, and against the mountebanks playing tricks on their stages; for they burthened the pure life, and stirred up the people's vanity" (qtd. in Graves 240). The early and influential Quaker intellectual Robert Barclay, writing in 1678, was even more worried: " . . . these games, sports, plays, dancing, comedies &c do naturally tend to draw men from God's fear, to make them forget heaven, death, and judgment, to foster lust, vanity, and wantonness . . ." (qtd. in Graves 241).

> Even the sophisticated and courtly, William Penn, queried, "How many plays did Jesus Christ and His Apostles recreate themselves at? What poets, romances, comedies, and the like did the Apostles and Saints make, or use to pass away their time withal? I know, they did all redeem their time, to avoid foolish talking, vain jesting, profane bablings, and fabulous stories.' Barclay and Penn, of course, were writing in the notorious era of Restoration drama, and their views do not necessitate a rejection of all theatrical endeavor, but that is precisely how they were interpreted by their contemporaries and later Quakers, and the influence of these writers was enormous. (Graves 241)[10]

During the early 1700s, the Quaker-dominated governing assembly in Philadelphia repeatedly passed laws banning or regulating theatre, which were just as often repealed by the British Parliament (Johnson and Burling). But over the centuries Quaker attitudes changed, arguably in line with changing forms of and ideas about theatre itself in the larger society. Michael P. Graves, tracing the Quaker anti-theatrical prejudice in the U.S. from its founding to after the 1960s, sees the history of this attitude as one of a gradual accommodation to theatre before 1960, followed by an actual encouragement of it afterward, with Quaker actors, playwrights, and directors working in service both to the theatre (and film) and to Quakerism itself. By 1925, many Quakers were arguing for discretion over abstention in theatre attendance; the London Yearly Meeting, for example, now considered dramatic art as "one by which performers and spectators alike may gain a truer insight into human life, a deeper appreciation of its meaning, and wider sympathy with mankind" (qtd. in Graves 243). (Still, it should be noted that the same document also cautioned actors, whose work put them in spiritual peril through the constant representation of other characters.) Graves traces a significant shift from the tolerance of theatre to an active embrace, beginning in 1960, with a Swarthmore lecture on *The Creative Imagination* by British Quaker Kenneth C. Barnes, which opened an intellectual dialogue that fifteen years later could produce the following statement:

> What should be said to Friends in particular? Certainly that they should release themselves finally and completely from the mistaken view that gaiety in living, in form and colour and conduct, is touched with sin. Also from any thought that the arts are on the circumference of the activity of the spirit. They are at the centre. (Qtd. in Graves 245)

Three years after that, in his 1978 Swarthmore lecture, *Signs of Life,* Ormerod Greenwood called the forebears' shunning of the arts "a grave misreading of Divine purpose," a statement that inspired the formation of a Friends Theater Group in Philadelphia in 1992, which in turn formed the core of a new Fellowship of Quakers in the Arts established the following year. This Fellowship is based on its founders' "experience as Quakers that spirituality and art reinforce each other in healing brokenness on many different levels of existence. Failure to recognize the synergy between the two undermines our Society's spiritual health and our ability to make our witness known. Therefore, we are no longer willing to keep our Quakerism and our art separate" ("About the FQA").[11] Since 1996, the Fellowship has published a quarterly journal, *Types and Shadows,* devoted to writings on and about art. And the monthly *Friends Journal,* which comes as close as any publication could to representing the wide variety of contemporary Quaker thought and practice in the U.S., regularly publishes poetry, art, and creative writing.

QUAKER THEATRICAL PRACTICE

If actively embraced, then, what might a Quaker theatrical practice look like? There has been considerable debate about that in the decades since Barnes's writings, and there remains a strain of thought that privileges direct social action (such as service work in under-privileged areas of the U.S. and other countries), over the more indirect influence theatre might promote. But even among theatre advocates, the terrain is tricky. Given that

Quakers attempt to conduct all their affairs according to basic principles of egalitarian conduct, peaceful behavior, and inward experience, how do they wrangle with a form whose substance is conflict, for which the luxury of decision-making by collective threshing is not likely available, and for which "the actor doesn't have the Quaker option of waiting in the quiet until he feels like performing" (Lloyd, "Paradox" 226)?

As one might expect, each artist or group grapples differently with this question. Some Quaker theatre operates on familiar models of theatrical collaboration among various artists, is meant to be staged in a theatre space, and may or may not experiment with form. The 1983 musical drama *Children of the Light,* developed by George Fox University professor Arthur O. Roberts and composer David Miller, is an example of theatre so created and staged (Graves 248).

Other groups, interested in teaching lessons on Quaker values and histories or Quaker approaches to pressing social issues, often use collective devising to develop the work, which is then presented in meetinghouses and school settings. An example is the Leaveners, formed in 1978 in the British Yearly Meeting, which offer a number of music making and theatre and performance arts projects, some especially by and for youth. In general, such works grow out of individual contributions to a collective effort, often based on improvisation, relying more on group facilitation than directorial authority (*Leaveners*).

Contemporary Toronto-based Quaker performance artist Evalyn Parry works in a variety of genres—including spoken word, storytelling, song, and theatrical performance, often simultaneously, often irreverently—to promote a vision of social justice and personal change "across genders, genres and generations" ("About Evalyn"). Her work is not overtly Quaker, but her take on the subjects she cares about—which range from women's history to environmentalism—might be considered "Friendly." Last year, a YouTube video by Quaker spoken word poet, musician, and producer Jon Watt made the rounds under the headline, "Dance Party Erupts During Quaker Meeting for Worship." Breaking out of the silence of the meeting, Watts raps his solo "Friend Speaks My Mind," a combination of spiritual autobiography and Quaker history.[12]

Quaker actor Benjamin Lloyd describes a fascinating group research project in which he conducted "meetings for theatre" (a play on the Quaker "meeting for worship"). Working with both Quakers and non-Quaker actors, his aim was to explore the link between spiritual exploration and actor creativity specifically through Quaker understandings of "experience," "authenticity," "simplicity," "integrity," and "community." His attention to language is particularly relevant to the aims of this chapter, because I am interested in the way words do, as well as mean, things—and thus are actions of, in, and through speech:

> The language we use to describe what we do has a direct effect on what we do, and the quality of our participation in it. It mattered that

> we tried to call our gatherings "meetings for theatre", and not "workshops" or "classes". It mattered that we spoke of "leadings" as opposed to "impulses". It mattered that we wrestled with "discernment" and not "choices". It mattered that we "offered ministry", rather than "improvised" or "performed". [. . .] Using this new language forced us to carefully consider our actions and words in a way we are not used to as theatre artists. (Lloyd, "On Quacting")

I recommend his accounts of the experience for a deeper exploration of some of the paradoxes inherent in the relationship between Quaker practice and actor/show preparation.

Finally, all Quaker colleges now offer theatre programs, and the majority of them offer theatre majors as well. I have not yet had the opportunity yet to review their curricula, but I imagine they would yield a variety of answers to the question of how "an actor prepares" in Quakerly fashion.

QUAKER PERFORMATIVITY

So far I have been discussing Quakerism in relation to theatre that knows itself as such, but there is another strain of Quaker thought and history that resonates well with recent understandings of the "performance of everyday life" and its multiple individual and collective practices. Quaker ways of speaking and dressing, when approached deeply in the spirit of Quaker thought, provide another way to think through the relationship between Quakers and the kind of theatricality that is not merely representational, but also performative. Again, this requires a bit of background in Quaker thought.

As I mentioned briefly earlier, Friends structure their social relations on a central belief that there is "that of God" in every human being, which renders all equal: "that of God" cannot be quantified comparatively from person to person. All other Quaker practices and testimonies flow from this central tenet. One cannot do violence to another human being without doing violence to "that of God" within him or her. One needn't bow or doff one's hat to another of higher social rank, because that would imply that God's measure could be taken in human relations. One needn't employ both informal and formal modes of address, because that would affirm in speech those social distinctions. The famous early Quaker use of "thee" and "thou" instead of the more formal "you" to address even royalty follows from this and is part of the practice known as "plain speech," from which I draw the title of this chapter.[13] This attention to speech extends from a striving for everyday usage unadorned by rhetorical flourishes, to the still-operative Quaker refusal to take oaths, because to do so would imply two different standards of truth in speech: one for everyday use, and one for legal or civic purposes. "The early Quakers objected to oath taking and won for themselves and others with similar scruples the right to affirm, rather than to swear, in the court room," writes Bacon.

> In addition, Friends have opposed all loyalty oaths, not only because such oaths imply a double standard of morality, but because they invade the religious right of a person to think whatever one wishes in the privacy of one's heart, as long as one does not act in a manner detrimental to society. Furthermore, Quakers have questioned the practicality of such oaths in achieving their intention. As William Penn said: "The man who fears to tell untruth has not need to swear because he will not lie, while he that does not fear untruth, what is his oath worth?" (191–192)

Although once persecuted for their differences from Puritan beliefs and practices, Quakers soon earned a reputation for straight dealing and trustworthiness that prompted George Washington, in a letter to a Yearly Meeting of Quakers in 1789, to write, "Your principles and conduct are well known to me; and it is doing the people called Quakers no more than justice to say, that (except their declining to share with others the burden of the common defense) there is no denomination among us, who are more exemplary and useful citizens."[14]

The practice of plain speech was at one time accompanied by a requirement of plain dress, based on the understanding that one shouldn't dress "for" any occasion that might call attention to differential social rank. At one time, such dress itself became a hallmark of Quaker practice and constituted a kind of performance in its own right. Quaker parents and teachers like to tell the story of Hannah Severn to their children, which will serve to illustrate my point. Hannah was a young Quaker living in Philadelphia in the 1850s. The fashion of the day featured hooped skirts made of colorful fabric and hats with streams and streams of ribbons, and Hannah chafed under the Quaker restriction that all her skirts and bonnets be plain grey. She was embarrassed to be seen in such un-finery, and sometimes, after leaving the house, dashed her bonnet down the stairs and dressed her skirts up in borrowed sashes.

> One afternoon while running an errand for her mother, Hannah heard someone whisper to her from the dark recesses of a small alley. When she ventured into the shadows, she discovered a runaway slave woman and her baby who had been without adequate food or shelter for days. That night Hannah and her parents rescued the woman and her infant, harboring them in their home where they eventually nursed them back to health and helped them make their next connection north on the Underground Railroad. But before departing, the slave woman told Hannah about waiting two days for someone in a plain bonnet to walk by because she had heard that Quakers wore plain clothes and could be trusted to help. From that time on, Hannah Severn did not resent her

> simple clothes and bonnet because she now understood and respected the trustworthiness and compassionate values they represented. (Whitmire 74–75)

The point is, of course, that even in plain dress there was a certain theatricality that rendered Quakers visible *as* Quakers. Although a thaw in Quaker attitudes toward theatre was still almost a century away, this theatricality was performative as well as illustrative: it not only represented something good in and to people, but also in a way *did* good for people. As recognizable figures in society, then, by the nineteenth century "Quakers" had already become a stock religious stereotype on stage, in what Ryan calls a "usefully overdetermined designation suggestive of an extraordinary blend of piety, modesty, thrift, pacifism, sobriety, rectitude, and passivity" (Ryan 197). (Think of the Quakers in *Uncle Tom's Cabin,* who both shelter the Harris family of escaping slaves and nurse the man chasing them after he is wounded in the attempt.) By the time film entered the picture, Quakers had adopted more mainstream manners of speech and dress, but the stereotype of the Quaker as "antimodern, pre-modern and un-urban" (Ryan, 204) prevailed, and was often used to comment on current events (e.g., the threat of global war in 1942's *The Courageous Mr. Penn*), or contemporary mores (as represented by the outlaw Quirt Evans, played by John Wayne, redeemed by the love of a Quaker woman in the 1947 *Angel and the Badman*, discussed in detail in Ryan [212–217]).

Today, plain dress has largely been replaced by a value for simplicity in all things, dress included, but there is no longer a dress code. If the practices that marked Quakers off from the rest of the world in their "quotidian theater of daily social interactions" (Ryan 188–189) at times veered into affectation, self-righteousness, and stereotype, they grew originally as outward expressions of the inward spiritual experience. As early as 1761, for example, Quaker abolitionist John Woolman decided never again to wear dyed clothing, for he had heard that the process of making indigo dye damaged the nerves of the slaves who brewed it on the plantations. What is more important perhaps than his decision itself was the struggle he had in coming to and implementing it. In his journal, he attributes a terrible fever he suffered to the spiritual distress he felt about the subject, lifted only when he made the decision to forego such clothing. Still, it took him nine more months to actually do so, in part because of his Quaker thrift, but also because he did not want to be accused of calling attention to himself through what he feared his brethren would see as an "affected singularity" of dress. When he finally bought his first "fur-colored hat" (that is, one left in its un-dyed state), such Friends who reproached him for it he "generally informed in a few words that I believed my wearing it was not in my own will" and trusted that "the Lord in his own time would open the hearts of Friends toward me" without his having to preach much about it (121–122).

Woolman's ability to see "that of God" in slaves exemplifies an experience familiar to Friends who have struggled toward and with similar spiritual challenges and insights. After such an experience, one can no longer see distinctions among persons, and no reason to act differently according to context: one wears the same thing, and speaks the same way, whether in the presence of a commoner, a king, or a court of law. One can no longer participate in violence without self-injury, whether in word, or war, or human bondage. To the extent that a Quaker can remain true to her or his practice when between meetings, Quaker social being is a kind of action, from the smallest level of social intercourse to the largest level of participation in public activism.

AN INTERTWINED HISTORY OF PERFORMANCE

Graves characterizes the history of changing Quaker attitudes toward theatre as a "gradual rapprochement," in which over time Friends have become more theatre-friendly, pun intended. This leaves out part of the story, as this development tracks with the fields of theatre and theatre studies' own self-preoccupations. The two histories—of Quaker thought and recent theatre history—read better together, and the tensions and paradoxes that remain are still productive and instructive. Quakers didn't adjust themselves alone over time to a more liberal notion of theatre; secular theatre took itself to task over the same period of time. Theatre continues to refresh its relationship to social change in the subjects it explores on stage, to experiment with collaborative and collective processes to develop new work, to involve the audiences as co-creators of meaning, to consider theatre as a performative force as well as a representational practice, and to ask how to leaven its own pieties.

One of the principal overlaps in this mutual history comes as theatre studies has broadened to incorporate various insights and methodologies of performance studies, to consider the cultural work theatre can do off as well as on the formal stage. Such scholarship turns on an understanding that the body in performance, in concert with other bodies, activates long-standing cultural scenarios that serve to tell us who we are, alone and together (Taylor). It can help us approach anew the historical spectacle of a man standing on a London street with a platter of brimstone on his head, or the quieter performances of a Hannah Severn or a John Woolman, before such performances became reified into stage and film "Quakers." It offers a way to look back at much Quaker practice as both performance and performative, its speech acts plain but powerful—a view that in turn might serve to animate our faith in our own small acts of art and scholarship.

NOTES

1. There are four main "branches" of Quaker practice in the U.S., with many varieties within and among them. Liberal and Conservative Friends meet for

silent worship in unprogrammed meetings in which no pastor presides; what distinguishes the two from each other is their level of the Christo-centrism and commitment to social justice service projects. Pastoral Friends and Evangelical Friends hold meetings for worship that are similar to those of many Protestant denominations; they tend to be more Christo-centric, and share an interest in service and missionary work. For more information, see the information site of the Quaker-founded Earlham School of Religion (quakerinfo.org).

2. In 2007, the Quaker Information Center listed U.S. Quaker membership at 86,837, but this doesn't count regular attenders like myself, who have yet to make a formal application seeking membership in a monthly Meeting (or congregation). In the Meeting I attend, attenders and members are roughly equal in number; if this is a general pattern, the total of Quaker practitioners, in a general population of over 310 million, is less than 1 percent (www.quakerinfo.org/resources/worldstats.html).
3. I am, of course, referring to J. L. Austin's famous definition of performatives: words that *do* as well as *mean* something and thereby constitute "speech acts."
4. The original Society, formed in England in 1652 by George Fox, was called "The Religious Society of Friends of Truth." "Friends" was, and still is, the preferred short form and self-designation, but when English usage demands an adjective, "Quaker" is most commonly used. On the origin of the word, Quaker historian Margaret Hope Bacon reports that a Judge Bennett in England, when confronted with George Fox's chastisement that he should "tremble before the word of God," is said to have replied, "You are the Quaker, not I" (16). Originally a term of mockery, the word gradually became acceptable to Friends.
5. Early Friends referred to the months and to the days of the week by number rather than name, because so many of the names were pagan-derived. First Day School is thus the Quaker equivalent of Sunday school.
6. "Speaks to my condition" is a traditional way Quakers describe something they encounter that seems to relate specifically to where they are spiritually, or to their particular present and pressing circumstances.
7. In addition to the Bacon history that informs much of this chapter, I was introduced through the Phoenix Friends to the North Pacific and Intermountain Yearly Meetings' *Faith & Practice*, the journals of George Fox and John Woolman, Quaker writings on spirituality collected by Rick Moody, as well as to serial publications such as *Western Friend* and *Friends Journal.*
8. One result of this is that some Liberal Quakers no longer consider themselves Christian.
9. I find this gatheredness similar to what anthropologist Victor Turner has called "*communitas*" and in my experience, though it is rare, it is peculiarly powerful.
10. The internal quote is from Penn's *No Cross, No Crown*, 1682.
11. I don't know if they are members of this Fellowship, but it might interest readers to know that Quakers claim as their own actors Ben Kingsley, Judi Dench, and James Dean, as well as musical/performing artist David Byrne.
12. "Friend speaks my mind" is a traditional Quaker way of expressing agreement, which at the same time marks the nearer possibility of a group's spiritual cohesion on the question at hand.
13. There is some evidence that even by the mid-seventeenth century the use of thee, thou, thy, and thine was already in decline, so that to use these forms may have been less a matter of social leveling and more one of marking Quakers apart, linguistically (Firth).

14. I have also heard a story, possibly apocryphal, that Washington lamented in a more private letter his difficulty in dealing with "men who would not drink, and women who would not flirt." In the former he was mistaken: the minutes of early Friends meetings record the use of brandy as a stimulant to keep people awake for three and more hours of silent worship.

WORKS CITED

"About Evalyn." *Evalyn Parry*. Outspoke Music, n.d. Web. 27 Mar. 2011.

"About the FQA." *The Religious Society of Friends*. Quaker.org, 9 Dec. 2008. Web. 8 Apr. 2011.

Austin, J. L. *How to Do Things with Words*. Oxford: Clarendon, 1962. Print.

Bacon, Margaret Hope. *The Quiet Rebels: The Story of the Quakers in America*. Wallingford: Pendle Hill, 1999. Print.

"Distribution of Quakers in the World." *Quaker Information Center: A Gateway to Quakerism*. Earlham School of Religion, n.d. Web. 14 Mar. 2011.

Faith and Practice. N.p.: Intermountain Yearly Meeting of the Religious Society of Friends, 2007. Print.

Faith and Practice. 2nd ed. Corvallis: North Pacific Yearly Meeting of the Religious Society of Friends, 1993. Print.

Firth, Alan. "Summary: Thou and You." *Linguist List 7.599*. Ed. T. Daniel Seely. Quaker.org, 23 Apr. 1996. Web. 14 Mar. 2011.

Fox, George. *The Journal of George Fox*. Ed. Rufus M. Jones. Richmond: Friends United, 2006.

Friends Journal. Philadelphia: Friends. Print.

Graves, Michael P. "The Anti-Theatrical Prejudice and the Quakers: A Late Twentieth Century Perspective." *Truth's Bright Embrace: Essays and Poems in Honor of Arthur O. Roberts*. Ed. Paul N. Anderson and Howard R. Macy. Newburg: George Fox UP, 1996. 239–256. Print.

Johnson, Odai, and William J. Burling. *The American Stage, 1665–1774: A Documentary Calendar*. Madison: Fairleigh Dickinson UP, 2001. Print.

Leaveners: Raising the Creative Spirit. The Leaveners, Quaker Community Arts, n.d. Web. 8 Apr. 2011.

Lloyd, Benjamin. "On Quacting–Reflections on Revival." *The Actor's Way*. actorsway.com, 27 Nov. 2005. Web. 8 Apr. 2011.

———. "The Paradox of Quaker Theatre." *New Theatre Quarterly* 23.3 (Aug. 2007): 219–228. Print.

Moody, Rick. *Quaker Spirituality*. San Francisco: Harper, 2007. Print.

Ryan, James Emmett. *Imaginary Friends: Representing Quakers in American Culture 1650–1950*. Madison: U of Wisconsin P, 2009. Print.

Stokes, Lori. "Why the Puritans Persecuted the Quakers." *The Historic Present*. wordpress.com, 2 July 2008. Web. 8 Apr. 2011.

Taylor, Diana. *The Archive and the Repertoire: Performing Cultural Memory in the Americas*. Durham: Duke UP, 2003. Print.

Turner, Victor Witter. *The Ritual Process: Structure and Anti-Structure*. Boston: de Gruyter, 1969. Print.

Types and Shadows. Journal of the Fellowship of Quakers in the Arts. Philadelphia. Print.

Washington, George. "Letter to the Annual Meeting of Quakers." *TeachingAmericanHistory.org*. Ashbrook Center for Public Affairs at Ashland U, n.d. Web. 27 Mar. 2011.

Watts, Jon. "Dance Party Erupts During Quaker Meeting for Worship." *YouTube*. YouTube, 3 Aug. 2009. Web. 27 Mar. 2011.

Western Friend. Portland: Friends Bulletin Corp. Print.
"What Do Quakers Believe?" *Quaker Information Center: A Gateway to Quakerism*. Earlham School of Religion, n.d. Web. 20 Mar. 2011.
Whitmire, Catherine. *Practicing Peace: A Devotional Walk through the Quaker Tradition*. Notre Dame: Sorin, 2007. Print.
Woolman, John. *The Journal and Major Essays of John Woolman*. Ed. Phillips P. Moulton. New York: Oxford UP, 1971. Print.

Part II

Dramas and Theaters

8 The Religious Drama of Egypt's Ali Ahmed Bakathir

Marvin Carlson

One of the most widespread Western misapprehensions about the Islamic world is that because of Islam's opposition to depictions of the human figure, there is essentially no tradition of theatre in this vast area. This orientalist assumption has long been generally accepted not only by Europeans and Americans with only a casual knowledge of theatre, but also even in the basic works of theatre scholarship and theatre history produced by and for Western readers. Fortunately a more informed picture of theatrical activity in the Islamic world is beginning to emerge, although the impression still remains that when theatre has developed in this world, it has been in spite of or even in opposition to the beliefs and practices of Islam.

Whereas it is certainly true that historically and still today there is a serious opposition to theatre among many fundamentalist branches of Islam, there is also a significant and ongoing tradition of Islamic religious drama in Iran, the Ta'ziyeh, which has recently begun to attract serious attention in the West, and also a considerable body of more conventional drama, of which the West as yet has almost no knowledge, built upon Islamic belief. This chapter will provide a brief introduction to one important figure in this latter tradition, Ali Ahmed Bakathir (1910–1969), claimed by Yemen as their leading modern dramatist, but almost all of whose drama was in fact created in Egypt in the 1940s and 1950s, where he was considered one of the leading writers in the important generation that appeared in the footsteps of Egypt's great pioneer of the modern theatre, Tewfik al-Hakim.

Actually, Bakathir was born neither in Yemen nor in Egypt, but in Indonesia. His parents brought him as a child to Yemen, where he received a traditional Islamic education, but one affected by a reformist and modernist trend entering the schools at that time.[1] In Yemen, as in most of the Middle East, poetry is an essential part of the cultural life, and Bakathir's introduction to the theatre (which at that time was primarily a literary, not a performed art in Yemen) was in reading the verse dramas of the Egyptian Ahmad Shawqi, whose work was already considered a model for others throughout much of the Arab world. Bakathir, never before exposed to the genre of drama, was "amazed to discover that poetry could be transformed into a dialogue or discussion between two or more persons so that each person expressed his own personality and views" (Bakathir 3). He was sufficiently inspired to create his first play, a verse drama called *Humam* (*Gallant*) in direct imitation of the Egyptian author, and basically a tragedy of an ill-starred Islamic Romeo and Juliet.[2]

Humam was published a few years later, in 1934, and that same year Bakathir moved to Cairo to continue his education. Up to this point, he had no knowledge of any European language, but having heard of the richness and excellence of English poetry, he enrolled in a program of English study at Cairo University. The English poetic tradition fascinated him, but his interest in poetic drama led him, not surprisingly, to a particular passion for Shakespeare, and while still at the university, he produced a translation of *Romeo and Juliet* in Arabic verse.

Graduated from the university in 1940, Bakathir became a teacher and launched a major literary career, in the course of which he produced a number of novels, and over thirty plays, as well as an epic nineteen-volume dramatized account of Islamic history under the second Caliph in the early seventh century. The majority of his plays were drawn from Islamic and Egyptian history, although he also addressed such contemporary matters as the British occupation of Egypt and the creation of the state of Israel. The historical interest he shared with both the Yemeni literary tradition and the subject matter preferred by Shawqi, but to these Bakathir added a religious orientation and a passion for Arab nationalism which were distinct to his work. To these might be added a stylistic preference, because almost all of Bakathir's works, unlike those of Shawqi, were written in prose.

Bakathir's first original drama, *Ikhnaton and Nefertiti*, in 1940, indicated his historical orientation, his interest in religion, and also the particular way that religion often operated as a dynamic in his drama. Given his interest in the Arabic and Islamic traditions, his choice of a subject from ancient Egypt, which was neither, is somewhat surprising, and indeed Bakathir felt it necessary to defend this choice, on the somewhat dubious grounds that the history of a region inhabited by modern Arabs must be regarded as a part of Arab history (Freitag 7). In any case, Bakathir could point to the example of his inspiration Ahmad Shawqi, who among his historical studies from Arab history had also turned to the classic age for *The Fall of Cleopatra* in 1929 and *Cambyses* in 1931.

It is significant, however, that, unlike the more distinctly secular narratives of Shawqi, whose *Cleopatra* closely followed the model of Shakespeare and whose *Cambyses* traces the fall of the power-mad, *Macbeth*-like King of Persia, oppressor of Egypt, Bakathir turns to the story of the visionary Ikhnaton, primarily remembered for his early attempts to turn Egypt toward a monotheistic religion. Although Bakathir is clearly sympathetic toward his protagonist, he also presents him as a doomed figure, preaching a religious doctrine of harmony, peace, and love within a cruel and manipulative society unwilling or unable to share this vision. The image of a religious visionary too good to survive in a world devoted to deception, bad faith, and the struggle for power is clearly one that appealed deeply to Bakathir, and he returned to this situation in a number of dramas set in very different historical periods.

Bakathir wrote one more verse drama, a rather slight romantic pastoral, *The Howdah Palace*, before turning, like most of his contemporaries, to prose. He retained, however, a rather formal style, often employing words or phrases drawn not from the language of everyday life, but from the poetic tradition and in particular from the Qur'an, which remained central to his concerns. Almost all of his dramas present a Qur'anic verse as an epilogue and many include additional Qur'anic quotations by their characters. Bakathir wrote several plays in prose before creating a major prose work. The first three treated historical subjects, as do the majority of Bakathir's works. The only one to achieve much attention was *The New Shylock* in 1945, and that was for political more than artistic reasons. The work showed Bakathir at his most nationalistic and anti-Zionist, anticipating the rise of Israel and the increasing domination of the Palestinians.

The following year Bakathir wrote the first of his relatively few plays dealing with contemporary social issues, *Doctor Hazim*, a domestic drama with comic and satiric elements. The Qur'anic verses that end the play command children to respect their parents, and the play concerns the struggles of the Doctor and his wife to fulfill this obligation, despite the less than perfect relationship between generations.

The Secret of Caliph Al-Hakim, in 1947, was Bakathir's first major success in the prose drama and also his first to deal with a figure from Arabic Egyptian history. Its protagonist was the third Fatimid ruler, the darkest figure in a dynasty that was remembered for its extravagance and cruelty. From the time they came to power in Egypt, in 969, the Fatimids were resented and resisted by most Egyptians, and at the core of the tensions was religion. The most profound division within Islam, still powerful today, is that between the Shi'i and Sunni believers. Cairo was founded by a Shi'ite, and remained primarily dedicated to that branch. The Fatimids placed themselves outside this division, but were in most respects closer to the Sunni. In addition to questions of revelation and religious succession, the Fatimids represented a very different religious outlook from the Egyptian Shi'ites, being strongly devoted to a mystic, revealed, inner religion that seemed abstract and even foolish to the more practical Egyptians.

The first two Fatimid rulers of Egypt dealt with this tension in a fairly pragmatic manner, but Al-Hakim displayed a fundamentalism of the most extreme and unyielding sort. In the name of sobriety he ordered all vineyards uprooted, in the name of somber contemplation he banned banquets, music, and games, in the name of chastity he confined women to their homes. Matters came to a head when a religious mystic, al-Dazari, convinced Al-Hakim that both major branches of Islam were pure superstitions and that he was himself the divinity of a new religion. Rejecting the common view of Al-Hakim as an insane despot, Bakathir shows him undergoing a deep mystical experience, leading to a desire to transcend all human weaknesses and become as close as possible to God. His extreme demands on himself and others are turned to increasingly evil and destructive ends by Bakathir's version of the mystic, here Hamza, an agent from Persia who encourages the Caliph's illusions in order to destroy him and bring down the Egyptian Islamic state. Finally, Al-Hakim is led to a realization of his delusions by a mysterious unnamed person, perhaps some sort of heavenly messenger. He rejects Hamza, embraces Islam, and departs his palace to seek death in the desert in expiation of his crimes.

Much less popular than *The Secret of Caliph Al-Hakim*, but equally revealing of Bakathir's ongoing interest in religious themes, was his *The Tragedy of Oedipus*, created in 1949. *Oedipus* has proven one of the most attractive Western classics to Arabic adaptors. Voltaire's version of the play was one of the earliest major Western dramas translated into Arabic, by Najib al-Hadad late in the nineteenth century. Another version, by Farah Antun, was specifically created in 1913 for Egypt's leading theatre company at the beginning of the twentieth century, that of Georges Abyad. Tewfik al-Hakim, the first Egyptian dramatist to gain a major international reputation, published an *Oedipus* in 1949 with a major preface on the concept of tragedy in the European and Islamic cultures. Bakathir's *Oedipus* appeared the same year. More recently, during the 1970s, important new versions of the myth have been produced by Fawzi Fahmi and Ali Salem in Egypt and by Walid Ikhlasi in Syria.[3]

Although they differ considerably in plot details and tonality, the various Egyptian *Oedipuses* all turn away from the emphasis upon fate and use the myth primarily for political commentary. Both the Al-Hakim and Bakathir versions have been considered by at least some critics as deeply influenced by the British interference in internal Egyptian affairs in the early 1940s and by the defeat of the Arab armies in Palestine in 1948. Al-Hakim, in his comments on his version, did not himself mention these particular events, stressing instead a repeating pattern of character relationships within his dramas that he felt revealed his own modern tragic vision. Interestingly, Bakathir, strongly nationalistic and deeply troubled by the rising power of Israel, did specifically cite the 1948 war as a stimulus for the play, rather than situating it, as Al-Hakim did, within the body of his work. Even so, Bakathir's version is much more driven by religious than by political concerns, and the dynamic is best revealed if we consider the play in the light of Bakathir's previous work, and especially *The Secret of Caliph Al-Hakim*.

Both plays depict a powerful leader who is led into evil-doing by manipulative councilors, the Persian agent Hamza in *The Secret* and the wily, calculating high priest of Thebes, Lucasius, in *Oedipus*. Although there is obviously a political dimension to the intrigues of both of these villains, it is also striking that both of them operate from a religious base, disguising and justifying their plots by claiming to speak for the divine. Within both plays, however, there is a counter-religious force, which truly articulates the will of Allah and ultimately inspires the protagonist to turn to the path of the devout, even when this means his destruction in this world. This figure of good is very little developed in *The Secret*, even though he brings about the triumphant religious conclusion. In his *Oedipus*, on the other hand, Bakathir assigns this role to Tieresias, here a renegade priest rejected by the corrupt and worldly official priesthood, led by the evil Lucasius. In Al-Hakim's more political adaptation, Tieresias is an amoral intriguer, very much in the same mold as Bakatheir's Lucasius, but Bakathir makes Tieresias a devout, inspired, and articulate Muslim, a central figure in the play who speaks in a language redolent of the Qur'an, even to specific quotations.

Both the moral and the political dimensions of Bakathir's *Oedipus* are conditioned by religious concerns, here extremely close to those of the Muslim Brotherhood, one of the world's oldest and largest Islamic political organizations, founded in Egypt in 1928 with the goal of establishing the Qur'an and the Sunnah (based on the actions and practice of Muhammed) as the reference point for ordering the life of the Muslim family, individual, and state. The first major theoretical work of the leading intellectual of this movement, Sayyid Qutb, *Social Justice in Islam*, appeared the same year as Bakathir's *Oedipus*, and is so similar in its outlook that it might almost be utilized as an interpretive gloss on the play. In the face of a rising tide of Marxism and materialism in Egypt, Qutb called for an integrated, coherent, Islamic theory of social justice. Bakathir's play shows an Oedipus who begins as a kind of proto-Marxist, an atheist who preaches social equality and who confiscates the goods of the temple to distribute to the people. At last, through his entrapment and betrayal by Lucasius and the support and religious insight of Tieresias, he comes to understand that his social aims can be attained only by faith in God and total submission to his will.

At almost exactly the same time as he was writing *Oedipus*, Bakathir also created one of his most strongly Islamic plays, *al-Silsila wa al-Ghufran* (*The Chain of Sin and Forgiveness*), set in medieval Egypt during the reign of Ahmad ibn Tulun (d. 884 CE). Although the historical Ahmad ibn Tulun was a model Islamic ruler, generous, just, and a devoted follower and accomplished reciter of the Qur'an, Bakathir's play concerns not this ruler, but a fictional subject of his: one Abd al-Tawwab. The Qur'anic epigraph that ends the play concerns the importance of repentance and seeking God's forgiveness from sin, the only way to break the "chain" of the title. An act of adultery by the protagonist begins this chain, which Abd al-Tawwab eventually breaks by repentance and the performance of righteous deeds (indeed, the name Tawwab itself means "one who agrees to repent").

Arabic literary scholars have called Bakathir's *The Chain of Sin and Forgiveness* the first allegorical play in Arabic literature (Hassim 12). Its intended audience is seen as consisting of dedicated Muslims who are nevertheless susceptible, as all human beings are, to sin, and therefore in need of repentance and forgiveness by God, which they should then merit by leading lives of righteousness, dedicated to good deeds and providing an inspiration for inaugurating a similar process in the rest of their society. Among his prose plays, Bakathir's *Chain of Sin* is closest in its goal and dramatic method to his teaching plays for children, to which I will presently return.

Although Qur'anic phrases, stylistic expressions, and direct quotations appear throughout Bakathir's work, one play is based directly on a Qur'anic story. It appears in expanded form in al-Tha'alibi's tenth-century collection of popular religious stories, *Tales of the Prophets*. The title characters of the 1962 *Harut and Marut* are two angels who, after complaining to God of the wicked actions of men on earth, are sent to earth with the same desires as men to show them that they would fare no better. Chosen as judges in the ancient city of Babel, they indeed succumb to temptation, become as corrupt as their human fellows, and return to heaven chastened and more forgiving of human failings. The play has a kind of raisonneur in the person of Hermes, the king's wise councilor as well as a visionary prophet, who is strongly reminiscent of the holy Tieresias in Bakathir's *Oedipus*. Often the action of the play stops while Hermes delivers extended observations on the nature of God, the human condition, the need for international understanding, the inevitable triumph of the righteous, and even the necessity of putting space exploration to the cause of peace. Clearly for the play's author, these observations were at the center of his creation, although from a dramatic point of view they seriously compromise the forward movement of the work.

At approximately the same time as *Harut and Marut*, Bakathir completed another drama dealing with Islamic and Egyptian history: *Dar ibn Luqman*, set during the sixth crusade led by King Louis IX. Although the play has a long and complicated plot, primarily concerning intrigues among the Mamluk princes for the position of Sultan in Egypt, Bakathir's primary concern is to champion his Islamic protagonists, who, for all their flaws, can be seen as looking forward to the vision of tolerance and social justice described by Qutb, and to condemn the Christian crusaders, who are shown as dissolute bigots who cloak their greed and desire for booty under a guise of piety and religion. The play contains lengthy discussions contrasting Islam and Christianity, but in the end the contrast is between an enlightened and tolerant faith and a professed faith utilized to cloak dissolution, rapaciousness, and bigotry. The religious positions represented in *Oedipus* by Tieresias and Lucasius are here extended to large historical groups.

It is hardly surprising that a committed Arab nationalist and Islamist like Bakathir would tend to view the Crusades in such Manichean terms. Nor is it surprising that the same tendency may be seen in his various plays dealing with the more modern political conflict also based on competing religion: the ongoing conflict between Israel and its Arab/Islamic neighbors. The first of these, *The New Shylock* (1945), has already been mentioned, and despite its clear anti-Zionism, is Bakathir's most nuanced treatment of Islamic/Jewish tensions in terms of association of religious orientation with morality.

A number of his Arab characters are highly unsympathetic, and among his ruthless Zionists are Jews who call for peace, moderation, and tolerance. Two later Islamic/Jewish studies, written during the 1950s, are closer to the black and white world of *Dar ibn Luqman. God's Chosen People*, probably written in 1955, is set in a hotel in contemporary Tel Aviv which is, in the distinctly heavy-handed symbolism typical of the play, both a brothel and a meeting place for prominent Israeli politicians. Most of the action shows the politicians involved in various immoral and often financial schemes, such as manipulating markets and selling narcotics. Few Arab characters appear, but those who do are, in comparison to the Jewish renegades, models of honesty and probity, especially if they are also Egyptian.

The God of Israel, in 1957, presents a similar moral world, but is even more sweeping in its condemnation of the Jewish people, here considering them from perspectives much more typical of Bakathir's work as a whole, that is, depicted from a much broader historical perspective and from a much more distinctly religious orientation. The work is divided into three parts. The first, *Exodus*, takes place in the time of Moses. The second, *The Kingdom of Heaven*, takes place in the time of Jesus. The third, *The Serpent*, is set in the present day. The play, in epic form, is far too long to be acted in its entirety in a normal stage production, each part being more than the length of a normal dramatic presentation. There are other reasons why, despite its dramatic form, *The God of Israel* is really more suited for reading than performance. As is often the case in Bakathri's more polemic work, lengthy political and religious discussion replaces dramatic action, a tendency made even more obvious by the dramatist's decision not to bring such key characters as Moses and Jesus on stage, but to present them (according to widespread Muslim dramatic practice) only as off-stage voices.

By far the most interesting and dramatic character in *The God of Israel* is Iblis (Satan), the only character to appear in all three sections. The premise of the play is that in the time of Moses the Jewish people turned from their God to follow Iblis, who corrupted them with the promise of gold. It is Iblis who engineers the persecution and killing of Jesus by his followers, and in modern times fuels their rapaciousness and desire for world domination. Once again, however, as in *The Secret of Caliph Al-Hakim*, the overall structure of the drama suggests a kind of modern religious morality play, with the entire Jewish people here led, like the unfortunate Caliph, into destructive madness until the long-ignored God of justice intervenes. At the conclusion of *The God of Israel*, the long-silent voice of God finally condemns, from off-stage, the plottings of the now terrified Iblis, who is driven at last from the stage of world history.

Bakathir's major works of the 1960s still contain occasional attacks on the Zionists, but focus more on what he saw as the other major contemporary enemy to the Islamic faith and its people: Soviet Communism and its avowed doctrine of atheism. This concern appears in prominent dramatic form as early as 1953 in *An Empire for Auction*, a political fantasy that may be seen as a kind of continuation of *The God of Israel*. God has spoken, the state of Israel has disappeared, and the Jews have been once again scattered abroad. The action takes place in England, one of the sites of repatriation. This future England is so badly managed that a revolution breaks out, the country goes bankrupt, and in a kind of utopian Communist move, all citizens' wealth is confiscated and the entire country, and its Empire, put on the auction block, to be purchased, eventually, by African speculators. The play is meant to be a satire, not only of communism, but also of British imperialism, and, of course, of Zionism, but in fact, Bakathir's Britain, a country of which he has no first-hand knowledge, is really more a thinly disguised portrait of contemporary Egypt, and so the satire is often less than successful.

The Sole Leader (1965) is a more specific warning of the corruption and oppression of communist leadership, here represented by the Iranian dictator Qbd al-Karim Qasim, who uses communism as a justification for his tyranny over his people. *The Washing Line* (1965) continued Bakathir's campaign against Communist influence, but this time moved the attack to Egypt itself, blaming the leftist sympathies of the Egyptian intelligentsia under Nasser for most of the moral laxity, corruption, and opportunism in contemporary society and for the loss of religious moorings that Communism brought with it. Not surprisingly, the community attacked in this work struck back and even critics who had applauded Bakathir for his condemnations of Israel now accused him of putting polemic concerns before artistic ones, of creating caricatures instead of fully rounded dramatic figures, and of stilted and unnatural dialogue.[4] All of these problems had long been noticeable in Bakathir's work, even the "stilted dialogue," which in fact Bakathir had chosen, as have many modern Arabic dramatists, to give weight and significance to their drama by drawing upon the Qur'anic literary tradition. Only when they were turned against his literary contemporaries in Egypt itself, however, were they denounced as artistic liabilities.

Unquestionably, Bakathir allowed his devotion to political and even more centrally religious concerns to take precedence over dramatic effect. Nevertheless his extensive dramatic output contains many characters, scenes, and works of proven dramatic power. It would also be unfair to charge him, as some critics have done on the basis of his more polemic later works, of allowing his devotion to Egypt and to Islam to make him a creator of bitter and divisive theatre. Even in his darker satires there is always a measure of good-natured humor, and more important, his religious views also resulted in plays that, even when they contained evil or misguided characters like *Oedipus*, generally presented a world of stable, admirable, and ultimately victorious humane religious values.

I have already mentioned this aspect of Bakathir's work as it is manifested in such plays as *Doctor Hazim* and *The Chain of Sin and Repentance*. It is perhaps most directly and charmingly represented in the warm and engaging short moral plays for children that he created, utilizing characters from Islamic history, and preaching the virtues of piety, honesty, integrity, compassion, and forgiveness. Three of these plays have been translated into English by Yasien Mohamed, and show Bakathir at his most winning and also at his most dedicated to using the theatre to teach important religious insights. Like *The Chain of Sin and Repentance*, although in a much simpler and more direct manner, these works clearly are designed to operate as religious allegories.

The first, *The Ring*, will, for scholars of the drama, conjure up echoes of the Sanskrit classic *Shakuntala*, based on a story in the *Mhabharata*, with its magic and mysticism replaced by a focus on Islamic piety. In both plays a young prince meets a beautiful girl, weds her, gives her a ring, and returns to his palace. In both, while the wife and husband are separated, a son is born, grows to youth, and is eventually recognized as an ideal offspring by the father. Within this folktale frame, however, the versions differ markedly. Bakathir makes the prince one of the most famous figures in Islamic history, Harun ar-Rashid, the fifth Abbasaid Caliph, whose capital, Baghdad, was the center of the apogee of Arab-Persian Islamic civilization. For Westerners, his celebrated court is often associated with the stories of the Thousand and One Nights.

In the Indian version, a magic spell causes the king to forget his first love, but in Bakathir's more realistic story, ar-Rashid is simply distracted by the death of his father and the resulting demands of the state, including an arranged royal wedding to his cousin. When he returns to his first wife, Amina, and begs her to come to live in the palace, she refuses, fearing the jealousy of his new spouse. When the Caliph returns to insist, she has moved to an unknown location with her son.

Whereas in the Indian version the lost son grows up to become a mighty hunter, imposing his will on wild beasts, the Caliph's son Ahmed becomes an honest but humble laborer, trying only once, without success, to see his famous father and exhort him to lead a more religious life. In the Indian version, the king is at last united with his long-lost wife and son, but ar-Rashid's fate is a sadder one. Amina dies still separated from him and passes on the ring to their son, who in turn arranges for it to be sent to the Caliph after his own death. His conscience awakened by the ring, the sorrowing Caliph visits their graves and learns, through a series of flashbacks, of his son's pious and exemplary life.

The second "moral play," *The Orchard Keeper*, concerns Ibrahim Ibn Adham, a famous saint of the Sufi faith, a branch of Islam that sought purity through self-mortification, social isolation, and asceticism. Like Buddha, Ibrahim renounced family and property to lead a solitary life of wandering and meditation. In Bakathir's play a fellow Sufi finds the saint a position, in disguise, as an orchard keeper. When a beggar woman asks him for some fruit, he arranges with his supervisor to provide her with some and pays for it himself, much to the supervisor's surprise. His scrupulous devotion to his charge causes trouble when he unwittingly provides sour fruit to the owner of the orchard, never having sampled it himself to see which fruit was best. Exposed and humiliated, the saint departs, leaving the beggar woman, supervisor, and orchard owner to lament the loss of this human treasure after he has gone.

The third and last play in this group, *The Noisy Neighbor*, returns specifically to the theme of repentance, earlier considered by Bakathir in his first allegorical drama. The protagonist is another Islamic hero, the Iraqi theologian Abu Hanifa. Disturbed nightly in his prayers by the loud drunken singing of his neighbor, Abu Hanifa is never angry, but instead prays to Allah to guide the noisy neighbor to repentance. When the neighbor is arrested for his drunkenness and taken to prison, Abu Hanifa visits the governor to request freedom for his neighbor, and the neighbor, touched by such generosity, vows that he will repent to Allah and change his ways. The governor, also touched, gives the neighbor a reward and pardons all those arrested with him.

Thus in both simple and direct ways, in these dramatic parables for children, as well as in the far more complex and sophisticated dramatic structures of his historical and mythical explorations of similar themes, Bakathir continued throughout his dramatic career to be inspired by the guiding principles of Islam, and to demonstrate that, far from being a religion fundamentally opposed to dramatic expression, Islam could serve as an support and inspiration for a dramatist who is one of the most important and innovative in the modern Arabic theatre.

NOTES

1. See Freitag 2–4.
2. The play is analyzed in the light of contemporary religious and political concerns in Freitag 2–27.
3. Four of these works, including that by Bakathir, appear in English translation in the collection *The Arab Oedipus*, edited by Marvin Carlson.
4. See, for example, the lengthy condemnation of *The Washing Line* by the distinguished Marxist critic Mahmud Amin al-Alim, *Al-Wajh wa'l-Quina fi Masrahina al-Arabu al Mu'asir*, Beirut, 1973, 180 ff., cited in Badawi 129.

WORKS CITED

Badawi, M. M. *Modern Arabic Drama in Egypt*. Cambridge: Cambridge University Press, 2005. Print.

Bakathir, Ali Ahmed. *Muhadarat fi l-fann al-masrahiyya min Khilal Tajaribi al-shakhsiyya*. Cairo: Dar al Ma'rifa, 1958. Print.

Carlson, Marvin, ed. *The Arab Oedipus*. New York: Segal, 2005. Print.

Freitag, Ulrike. "Dying of Enforced Spinsterhood: Hadramawt through the Eyes of Ali Ahmad Ba Kathir." *Die Welt des Islams* 37.1 (Mar. 1997): 2–27. Print.

Hassim, Eeqbal. "The Significance of Qur'anic Verses in the Literature of Ali Ahmad Bakathir." *NCEIS Research Papers* 1.3 (2002): n. pag. Web (accessed 15 July, 2010).

9 A Transdiasporic Paradigm

The *Afoxé* Filhos de Gandhy

Isis Costa McElroy

This chapter has been propelled by a silent dialogue with Pravina Shukla's avatāra. I dedicate it to Ana Maria Gonçalves, who, on 3 August 2006, in Rio de Janeiro, wrote and signed a message on the opening page of her Kehinde's saga informing me: " . . . the history of what may have been if time preserved certainties . . . "

Brave breeze of these iyás. May it guide us. Much love, respect, and gratitude.[1]

It is eleven o'clock on a hot morning in the city of Salvador, in the northeastern coastal state of Bahia, Brazil . . . A large group of men have donned long white tunics, they have decorated themselves with white terrycloth turbans, each with a large plastic sapphire-blue gem sewn on the front. They wear white leather sandals, sapphire-blue socks, and many strands of plastic beaded necklaces, worn crossing their torsos. Among this gathering of hundreds of men is an old Black man carrying a staff and wrapped in a white toga-like sheet, wearing dark brown leather sandals. Behind him there is a crowd of yet more men dressed similarly, dancing and playing instruments, one man dancing while carrying a stuffed goat. The sash adorning their bodies reads *Filhos de Gandhy*. Sons of Gandhi. Gandhi, the slain pacifist who helped free India from British Raj, but he was not Black, nor did he wear terrycloth turbans with plastic gems on them, nor did he parade on the streets playing percussion instruments during carnival time. How did a stuffed goat fit in Gandhi's program? The men start to spray the crowd with pungent *Alfazema eau de cologne* as a blessing often used in Candomblé, the syncretized religion of Afro-Brazil. The procession begins. What is going on here?

—Pravina Shukla

The figure of Mahatma Gandhi fascinated me as a pre-teen living in São Paulo. I remember the enthusiasm with which I watched Richard Attenborough's movie *Gandhi* in the early 1980s. By then I had not yet seen, either live or on TV, images of the Bahian *carnaval* group Filhos de Gandhy ("Sons of Gandhi"),[2] but I knew quite well Gilberto Gil's musical tribute to the group. Through Gil, I first learned about this group of male performers who evoked the orishas and Gandhi as a prodigal son and protégé of Oshala, the creator deity, "king of the white cloth." Like other Brazilians, I must have "brazilianized" Gandhi in my imagination, and because of it must have felt a sense of kinship with the historic figure portrayed in the film. I remember how, when I later came across images of this "semi-religious *carnaval* group," or *afoxé*, I was enchanted by what I perceived as beautiful, poetic, political, and "carnavalistically" sacred. Nothing in my state of enchantment was threatened by a critical positioning or by uncomfortable perceptions of corruption, contradictions, or exotifications. Years went by. I persisted in following the group's development, its portrayal by the media, and its analysis by scholars. Even if my enchantment remained unbroken, as I zoomed into the group's symbolism, certain incongruent metaphors increasingly intrigued me.

Gil's song "Filhos de Gandhi" was composed after he returned from his London exile. Gil commented that the group had been one of the "strongest emblems" of his childhood and that his post-1972 participation in the group was a stimulus to "thicken the stew" (Rennó 146).[3] Other factors contributed to the national popularity of the Filhos de Gandhy. Toward the end of the 1970s, two major government tourist agencies—BAHIATURSA (state of Bahia) and EMTURSA (city of Salvador)—began sponsoring the Filhos de Gandhy. By the 1980s, the *bloco*[4] was able to put ten thousand "sons" on the street and had become an international trademark for Bahia and Salvador. Nowadays, the Filhos de Gandhy is occasionally accused of having been co-opted by government bureaucracies (Oliveira 303). The trajectory of the Filhos de Gandhy from the 1970s onward was inevitably conditioned by the consolidation of the cultural and telecommunications industries that took place during that time period, leading into the present transformation of *carnaval* as a mega-event in which each *carnaval* group functions as an industry within itself (and as such deals with other private and state industries, including those that promote sexual and afro-centric tourism).[5]

Mahatma Gandhi (1869–1948), the pioneer of *satyagraha*, the principle of non-violence as a form of protest and revolution, inspired generations of activists. In Brazil, Gandhi was transformed into a sacredly profane *carnaval* icon. Hindu anthropologist Pravina Shukla asks: "How did Gandhi shift from South Africa to India and end up in the heart of the African Diaspora in the sweltering heat of Salvador?" (39). In light of the awe and bewilderment of Pravina Shukla, I propose to reflect on the development and aesthetics of the Filhos de Gandhy from the following aspects: (1) the contextualization of the group within the performatic tradition of Bahian *carnaval*; (2) the question of gender in the group; (3) the cosmology of the group according to the narratives of its founders; and (4) the process of a Hindu-Muslim-Bahian aesthetic enunciation.

If I have indeed developed a hypothesis for reading some of the cultural paradigms of this *afoxé*, the enigmatic and contradictory aspects of this interpretive community reveal themselves as an analytic challenge that I can tackle here only within an open and metaphorically plausible reading.

THE CONTEXTUALIZATION OF THE GROUP WITHIN THE PERFORMATIC TRADITION OF BAHIAN CARNAVAL

The term *afoxé* has already been defined as "divination," "a plague or curse," "the enunciation that makes (something) happen," "royal entourage, in the representation of a group of noble hunters originally from Africa who carry as a symbol a black doll (the *babalotim*)," and "semi-religious carnival groups composed of Candomblé devotees wearing white tunics of West African-style and singing songs in Yoruba."[6] In the sense of entourage, *carnaval* procession, or "street Candomblé," the *afoxés* have their origin in afro-Brazilian performative festivals such as the *cucumbis*, the *maracatus*, and the processions of the *Reis Congos* ("Congo Kings") (Vieira Filho 51).

The first significant "afro-carnavalesque tide"[7] of Bahia occurred toward the end of the nineteenth century and was recorded by Nina Rodrigues, who described groups such as the Embaixada Africana ("African Embassy"), Filhos da África ("Children of Africa"), A Chegada Africana ("African Arrival"), and Pândegos da África ("African Merrymakers"). Muniz Sodré analyzed a major aspect of these groups especially in the pre- and post-abolitionist periods as a "tactic of collective penetration (with regard to time and space) in urban territory," that is, a "reterritorialization (the breaking of topographical limits imposed by urban social division on the Blacks)" (36). Two groups with high local visibility toward the end of the nineteenth century were especially paradigmatic: the Embaixada Africana and Pândegos da África, who would make their respective debuts in 1895 and 1896. Nina Rodrigues described them as follows:

> The richest and most important clubs to have emerged are Embaixada Africana and Pândegos da África. But, beyond small clubs such as A Chegada Africana and Os Filhos da África, etc., there are innumerable anonymous African groups and isolated African revelers. Two currents are revealed in the constitutions of these groups. In some, such as Embaixada Africana, the dominant idea of the most intelligent or most adapted Blacks is the celebration of survival, of a tradition. The personalities and motives are taken from the educated people of Africa, the Egyptians, the Abyssinians, etc. In others, if on the one hand the directors had intended to revive traditions, their popularity comes from their being genuine popular African celebrations. Their theme is the uncultured Africa that came enslaved to Brazil. (208)

These different tendencies of early Bahian *carnaval* performances registered by Nina Rodrigues suggest varying levels of participation and acceptance of afro-Brazilians in the *carnavais* of the 1890s. In the view of Kim Butler, when Embaixada Africana organized processions within the formats established by the white clubs and presented an image of a "civilized" Africa, the white elite was more accepting than were the black masses of Bahia. Despite adhering to the format of the white *carnaval* clubs, Pândegos da África had a lower level of acceptance, introducing aesthetics and rhythms of Candomblé. Finally, "the anonymous African groups and isolated African revelers" cited by Nina Rodrigues, those independent revelers currently known as *pipocas* ("pop-corn"), were then perceived as the subversive elements of *carnaval*. Nina Rodrigues mentions that these revelers horrified the white population. The urban penetration tactic of these later groups did not propose to follow the aesthetic or conduct of a "civilized Africa," or of an "enslaved Africa," but of a "Maroon Africa."[8] These were "guerrilla" performers interested in giving free expression to their emotions, critiques, and desires. Antonio Risério's study concurs with Butler, stating that the "afro-carnavalesque" displays of the end of the nineteenth century were hierarchized by the spokespersons of the dominant culture: the *clubes uniformizados* ("organized clubs") who imposed the theme of the

Figure 9.1 Sons of Gandhy on Yemaya's day, Rio de Janeiro, 2 February 2011. Photo by Cristiano Cardoso.

"cultured people" of Africa maintained their dominant position in the hierarchy, while the *afoxés* or *candomblés de rua* ("street candomblés") were condemned to a subordinate position as "expressions of primitiveness and barbarism that were an embarrassment to Bahia" (*História* 563).

Some changes appear from 1905 to 1914, when "the black-mestizo *carnaval*" was prohibited, but as Peter Fryer points out: "it was not so easy to take the streets away from black people in Brazil. And one of their responses was the creation of *afoxés* which took shape in Salvador in the 1920s" (23). The influence and visibility of the afro-mestizo organized *carnaval* groups declined. They became reduced to smaller groups and *afoxés* (such as Filhos d'Oxum, Lordes Africanos, and Filhos de Obá) until 1949 with the birth of the Filhos de Gandhy and the Trio Elétrico of Dodô and Osmar,[9] and the revitalization of these same groups with the symbolic landmark of the first performance of *Ilê Aiyê* in the 1970s. This was a time period that Risério refers to as the "re-africanization" of the Bahia *carnaval*. One could point to the Embaixada Africana as one of the matrices for the formation of the *escolas de samba*[10] of Rio de Janeiro, and Pândegos da África as the matrix for the creation of the *blocos* of Bahian *carnaval*.

Figure 9.2 Sons of Gandhy on Yemaya's day, Rio de Janeiro, 2 February 2011. Photo by Zaíra Bosco.

Raul Lody describes *Pândegos* as an *afoxé* whose performance included the parade of a central group of revelers adorned in the clothing and symbols of the orishas, and musicians dressed in Moorish style turbans, tunics with puffed-out sleeves, and *bombacha*-style pants. They carried with them the *babalotim*, a wooden totem that possessed magic powers and that had to be carried during the procession by a male child (*Afoxé* 13–14). As Lody explains:

> Only a boy could carry it; this was part of the mystery that surrounded the totem. Inside the doll a set of utensils prepared in the *terreiros* [Candomblé temples and sacred grounds] was deposited. This constituted the so-called Ashe, that is, the magic force or object that possessed this force. In this way, the totem represented the power and religious security of the group . . . animal sacrifices were carried out; birds and small goats were ritualistically sacrificed for the *babalotim*. (*Afoxé* 10)

According to Lody's analysis, the strategic positioning of the *babalotim* in the front of the group's parade formation served "as a true magical *abre-alas* ['lead-off contingent'], since the participants believed that this wooden sculpture emanated good things as well as repelled bad ones" (*Afoxé* 10). The connection between the *babalotim* of the *afoxé* and the *calunga* doll which remains present in *maracatu* performances of Recife and Olinda is evident. The crucial difference is that the *calunga* has to be carried by a woman, the *Dama do Paço* ("Lady of the Palace"), who marches in the front of the formation.

One of the founding members of the Filhos de Gandhy relates that the first group of Gandhys set out with "a black clothed doll," a *calunga* (Félix 45). The initial *calunga* has disappeared. Curiously, the figure of the *babalotim*, literally "the owner of the cachaza,"[11] was substituted in the Filhos de Gandhy, first by a figure known as Cândido Elefante, "a gentleman weighing over 200 kilos who could dance to the *ijexá* rhythm beautifully" (Félix 55). A second substitution of the *babalotim* came with an inclusion of a quasi-processional element or aspect of almost profane pilgrimage, with the incorporation into the parade of a portrait of Mahatma Gandhi (Risério, *Carnaval* 52).[12] The third and definitive substitution was the "materialization" and embodiment of the image portrayed by Raimundo Queiróz Lima, "Raimundo Gandhy" (1925–2006), a reveler who reports how he was informed one day, "You are going to represent the portrait" (*Filhos de Gandhy*).

Édison Carneiro explains that in the standard formation of an *afoxé*, the line of march would be: "the *arauto* [announcer]; the *guarda branca* [white guard]; *rei* and *rainha* [king and queen], *Babá l'ôtin*, *Papai Cachaça* [Daddy Cachaza], the masculine equivalent of the *maracatu* doll; the *estandarte* [flag-bearer]; the *guarda de honra* [guard of honor]; and the *charanga de ilús (atabaques)*, *agogôs* and *cabaças ijexás* [the band of *ilú* drummers, cow bells and shakers]" (52). According to Lody, the *ilús* are small, two-headed *atabaque* drums which are used in the ceremonies to Oshun, "a riverine deity,"[13] in the temples of Ijesha (*Afoxé* 6). In the *afoxés*, the *atabaque* drums are not taken to the streets "dressed" or decorated as they would appear inside Candomblé temples. The *afoxé* drums are not decorated with the *ojá* straps in the colors of the orishas worshipped during Candomblé ceremonies (17). The call and response melodies of *afoxés* sung by a soloist and repeated by a chorus are practically the same as the ones sung in afro-Brazilian temples that follow the *Ijexá* cosmology, while the choreography presents simplifications of the traditional steps and gesticulations of sacred Candomblé evocation dances. According to Lody: "What really matters when the *Gexá* [*Ijexá*] is danced—and this is what is danced in the *afoxé*—is the characteristic *ginga* swing, the movement of the shoulders and arms and the quick, short cadenced steps" (16). But what constitutes the Candomblé *Ijexá* performative repertoire? Is there, in

Figure 9.3 Reincarnation: bisavô do neto ("great-grandfather of the grandson"). This citizen [Raimundo Queiróz Lima] is the mascot of the largest carnival club, Filhos de Gandhy. Despite the theatrical element of "impersonation," there is also an aspect of genuine reverence to this figure. Where is the line between fantasy and sacred ritual, especially when a group is involved? Photograph and caption by Pier Armstrong. Salvador, during carnaval days, March 2000 ("Carnaval").

fact, a clear distinction between the sacred drumming and dancing of Candomblés *Ketu* and *Ijexá* (Yoruba cosmologies respectively originating from present-day Benin and Nigeria)? Risério is right when he affirms that "the term *ijexá* acquired a generic meaning from the fact that the majority of new afro-carnavalesque groups do not use *aguidavis*, that is, drumsticks, when playing the *atabaque* drums" (*Carnaval* 11–12). While followers of Candomblé *Ijexá* play the *atabaque* drums with their hands, those of Candomblé *Ketu* play them with drumsticks. The generic meaning of *ijexá* as a secular musical and dance style transcended the particular type of percussion and extended itself to the choreography and song, which do not follow a line strictly connected to any specific Yoruba-Brazilian cosmology.

THE QUESTION OF GENDER IN THE GROUP

Aside from the symbolic conversion of sacred Candomblé into secular Candomblé, and the influence of other secular performances such as the *maracatus* and *congadas*, less explicit influences may aid in understanding not only the figure of the *babalotim* but also the question of the male exclusivity of the Filhos de Gandhy *afoxé*. Olabiyi Yai has already pointed out the influence of the Geledé societies in the formation of Brazilian *carnaval* (Risério, *História* 563). In the Yoruba tradition, female ancestors are referred to as *Ìyámi Agbá* (my ancient mother). These ancestral spirits are worshipped in Nigeria by the Geledé societies, which consist exclusively of women. Oro societies also exist in Nigeria. Oro is considered the general representative of male ancestors and can be worshipped only by men. The Egungun societies carry out another form of male-ancestor worship. Only the spirits of deceased men can make apparitions, as it is believed that only men possess or maintain individuality after death; women are denied this privilege as well as the right to participate directly in worship. In Brazil there are two Egungun societies, both in the island of Itaparica in Bahia (Ilê Agboulá and Ilê Oyá). The Geledé and Oro societies did not have a "literal" continuity in Brazil. The Geledé societies actually existed in Brazil for a while and had as its last highest priestess Omonikê, Maria Júlia Figueiredo, "major purveyor of the devotion to Nossa Senhora da Boa Morte [Our Lady of Good Death], which was established in the 1820s by women who were members of the Irmandade dos Martírios [Guilds, Fellowship or Brotherhood of Martyrs]" (Silveira 81). The Irmandade da Boa Morte ("Sisterhood, or Sorority of Good Death") continued the Geledé ceremonial worship of female ancestors by a women-only group while absorbing and adapting Catholic referents. The Oro societies likewise appear to have been developed and transformed into the Filhos de Gandhy *afoxé*, and perhaps, even before the creation of this exclusively male *afoxé*, into some *Folia de Reis* ("Revelry of the Kings"), originally a Portuguese celebration which was transformed in colonial Brazil and which also did not allow women in their processional performances.

According to Yoruba cosmological principles, every person has his or her own orisha. The archetypical personality characteristics shared by orishas and their human protégés are maintained after death by the spirits, or *eguns*. Mahatma Gandhi, both physically and ideologically, recalls aspects of the archetype of Oshala. As in the Egungun societies, Gandhi is praised by the Filhos de Gandhy in his essential individuality, enjoying a privilege exclusive to male spirits. As in the Oro societies, he transcends his individuality in order to represent the power of a male collective ancestry.

The current president of the Filhos de Gandhy, Agnaldo Silva, offered a much more pragmatic explanation for the non-participation of women in this *afoxé*. According to him, since the group was formed by stevedores, and there were no women working unloading the ships, they could offer only "logistical support" by taking care of the costumes and "beautifying the turbans." But such a clear division of roles in this *afoxé* of dockworkers has not been the pattern in the formation and development of other groups. Carole Davies observes: "[t]he group remains all male exclusively. Thus the question of gender in *afoxé* becomes important. While some of the *afoxés* tend to incorporate both men and women, *Filhos de Gandhy* is principally a brotherhood" (Davies). Davies's analysis of the question of male exclusivity of Filhos de Gandhy looks beyond the easily refutable essentialism of Agnaldo Silva by pointing to an apparent reversal of roles when she states "the masculinist orientation of *afoxé* as represented in *Filhos de Gandhy* tended to relocate women to the periphery which they are not in *Candomblé* ritual" (Davies).

Far from occupying a peripheral position, the authority and standard of women in Candomblé have been experienced and perceived as central. This status quo leads one to question and reflect on the process that relocated the position of men from more centralized (in original Yoruba cosmologies) to peripheral (in the New World and mainly in Brazil). Lorand Matory analyzes both the process which has culminated in current understandings of Candomblé as a matriarchy, and the role that intellectuals such as Ruth Landes, Arthur Ramos, and Gilberto Freyre have played in the repositioning of men in Candomblé. Ruth Landes, author of *The City of Women* (1947), filled a crucial yet overlooked role in this process, as is evident in an article from 1940 in which Landes makes a surprising and unprecedented statement that subsequently reflects on her intentions and purpose:

> [A] mother of a Nago cult tries to avoid making 'sons.' She prefers instead an inconclusive ritual or cure . . . In very rare instances in the past men have acted as the heads of Nago cults . . . they made few sons and many daughters and forbade male sacerdotes to dance with the women or to dance publicly when possessed, and debarred male novices from certain female mysteries. In comparison with the women,

> they were only partially initiated, and tolerated in view of certain anomalies. (389–390)

As Matory observes, the figure of the gay man in Candomblé, the *adé*, was transformed into the antihero of the matriarchal nation as defined by Landes. "From the 1930s onward," states Matory, "the priestess became an object of public talk to the same degree that her *adé* antitype became an object of silencing" (199).

The silence surrounding the *adés* promulgated both a series of negative stereotypes more or less experienced in the practice of Candomblé, and a marginalization of heterosexual men who feel compelled to "prove" their heterosexuality by defining patterns of behavior in opposition to the *adés*. One of the stereotypes of the *adés* is to simulate possession, or *dar ekê* ("to give ekê"). *Èké* in Yoruba means "lie" (Cacciatore 109). As Patricia Birman explains: "[T]o give *ekê* means a paroxysmal exhibition of competence in this obscurely sexualized and feminine realm . . . although this is not exclusively a practice of the *adés*, it is, at the very least, a recurrent charge made against them" (118–119).

The terms *egun* ("ancestral spirit") and *elegun* ("one who has the power to receive and materialize the ancestral energy") are concepts that offer us other interpretative channels into the social paradigms reflected in the Filhos de Gandhy. In Yoruba, the meanings of the radical *gùn* involve references to mounting, saddling, and riding, and to spiritual or sexual possession. *Gùn* means to mount, as a horseman mounts his horse, or as an orisha mounts and "rides" a human. It also refers to the sexual act of a man "mounting" a woman or another man from behind. As Matory observes: "[since] a physically mountable man seems highly qualified, in a symbolic sense, to be mounted spiritually [. . . there is a] reluctance of 'real men' to be possessed in the Brazilian Candomblé" (212). This notion of "real man" resonates in the definition of the Filhos de Gandhy by one of the founders—curiously nicknamed Quadrado ("Square or Straight")—as a "*bloco* of respectable men" (Félix 57).

The development of a group of men that gradually incorporated Candomblé referents into their *afoxé*, a male group that uses the music and dance of the orishas without being "mounted," reveals an affirmation of ultra-masculinity. This is observable even in the song of Gilberto Gil that became a national hit and that reveals an inversion of roles between humans and orishas. In the lyrics, Gil—as a participant of the Filhos de Gandhy—evokes the orishas, the ancient *afoxés*, and *Nosso Senhor do Bonfim* (Our Lord of Good End), to evoke one another, to command each other to "come down" to the world of the living so as to watch the parade of the Filhos de Gandhy.[14] Thus, *the role of the gods and the ancestors becomes* that of *a voyeuristic audience: the Filhos de Gandhy* are not *evoking the gods* in order to be mounted but rather *to be seen and admired*. (If unfamiliar with Gil's lyrics of the song, refer to Note 17.) During the parade of the Filhos de Gandhy the performance is used to seduce the onlookers, who are cordoned off from the group. Shukla notes in detail:

> [O]ver 5000 men in one place for the days of carnival. This fact, inevitably, is appealing to young women interested in boyfriends for the duration of the carnival festivities. Gay men of Salvador, likewise, scope out the parading route of *Filhos de Gandhy* for precisely the same reason, to have a quick pick at the turbaned, majestic men of the carnival . . . Just as the perfume should be shared with others, in an act of good faith and symbolic blessing from Oxalá, members of *Filhos de Gandhy* have customarily carried a small stash of beaded necklaces to give out on the streets. Although many members of the *bloco* still give out beads, and increasing number of young men use the beads and a dab of perfume as barter, for a can of cold beer or a kiss . . . During the quest by many members of *Filhos de Gandhy* to look attractive in order to appeal to the young men and women of Salvador, the connection with the Mahatma's humble appearance and years of celibacy becomes ironic. Another strong incongruity between the Mahatma and the carnival revelers who impersonate him has to do, again ironically, with what Gandhi is most associated with peace. The *bloco Filhos de Gandhy* attracts many young men who exhibit violent behavior, and in fact, see membership to the group as an opportunity to enable aggressive tendencies while hiding behind the guise of a peaceful group of marchers . . . Members of the group often engage in more direct acts of violence, such as fistfights in the streets. (40–41)

The original fame of the Filhos de Gandhy as seducers and tough guys persists. Today they are called by the press "the *bloco* of smoochers," and fights with other, smaller *blocos* frequently break out in the various circuits in Praça da Sé, the heart of the city of Salvador. Present members of the group nurture images of courage, virility, and irresistible seduction. As an example of the consciously created image of desirable, brave men, we can note the taken-for-granted narratives of police aggression suffered by the Filhos de Gandhy the first time they participated in *carnaval*, and their courage in confronting the police.[15] Interestingly such accounts are not confirmed in any of the interviews that Anísio Félix conducted with the founding members of Filhos de Gandhy.

THE COSMOLOGY OF THE GROUP ACCORDING TO SOME OF THE FOUNDERS OF FILHOS DE GANDHY

Gandhi was assassinated in New Delhi in 1948. In the following year, a group of stevedores, a unionized labor elite, brought out to the streets of Salvador a *carnaval bloco* paying tribute to the Mahatma. As Anamaria

Morales explains, identification with the struggle for the independence of India, which had suffered economic and cultural oppression at the hands of the English colonizers, gave "an (un)disguised political character" to the debut of the Filhos de Gandhy (269). The foundational narratives of the group are, as with all oral traditions, multiple and poetic.

Founding member Manoel dos Santos, "Guarda Sol" ("Parasol"), relates, for example, that "'Vavá Madeira' [Durival Marques da Silva] would have been inspired by the newspaper headlines about the death of Gandhi" (Félix 41). Eduarlino de Souza, "Dudu," states: "We were sitting there under a mango tree drinking and chatting away when the wind blew a magazine our way; Antonio and Vavá looked at it, and there he was: Gandhi. Right then they got the idea to start a *carnaval* group named after him" (51). Djalma Conceição, ex-president of the Filhos de Gandhy, adds a new element to the story: "[O]ne of them had seen a movie called *Gunga Din*, they thought it was a nice name (the stevedores mixed up Gunga Din with Gandhi) and then a few of the guys suggested the name Sons of Gandhi because Gandhi was a man who had fought for peace" (13). Other participants and founders conferred a politico-religious meaning to the group. Humberto Café, a member of the board of directors of the Filhos de Gandhy, confirmed: "Gandhy was founded with the objective of bringing Candomblé to the streets. The offerings performed today by the members were the same as those originally performed by the founders when it started" (17). Nelson dos Santos, "Lobisomem" ("Wolfman"), has a different understanding: "[T]he fellows who inspired the creation of the group were more into booze than into religion" (62). Arivaldo Pereira, "Carequinha" ("Little Baldy"), composer of the hit song "Patuscada de Gandhi" ("Gandhi's Revelry"), is the founder who provides the most detailed version of the evolution of the performance of the group:

> Gandhy was formed as a *bloco*. Its music was percussion, just *batucada* drumming. In the second year, we were singing afro chants and by the third year it was transformed into an *afoxé*. As time passed there were a number of modifications in the costumes . . . In the second year, we had the goat and a small camel as *alegoria* floats. In the fourth and fifth years, we had the lancer, the gunner and for the big *alegoria* floats we had an elephant and a big camel. In the third year, the number of participants increased to about 200 men . . . Only after the third year, when the Candomblé people started showing up, did Gandhy begin leaning towards this syncretic side. From then on, we always did the *padê* [propitiatory Candomblé offering] before we started . . . The idea for starting the Filhos de Gandhy didn't come from *Gunga Din* like some people claim, but there was a connection, because the film had to do with India and their struggle against England. (22)

The association of the Filhos de Gandhy with the film *Gunga Din* (directed by George Stevens and released in 1939)—even if perceived as peripheral by the majority of founders, current members of the group, and researchers—still presents itself as yet another contradictory and revealing influence. The protagonists of the film are three British sergeants (one played by Cary Grant) and the Hindu water bearer Gunga Din[16] (played by the New York Jewish actor Sam Jaffe). The plot centers on the struggle between the British Army and a Hindu group, the Thugees, that worships the goddess Kali and proposes the extermination of the British colonizer. The group's war cry is "Kill for the love of Kali!" The destroyer/builder archetype, which Kali represents in Hindu cosmology, resembles that of orisha Ogun, "the violent warrior who, having water in the house, bathes in blood" (Verger 14). Ogun also represents, among many other aspects, and through his connection to other orishas: metamorphosis and "the primordial abyss"; this orisha is "associated with *brotherhood guilds*, *fraternal organizations* and *friendships*" (emphasis added, Mason 17–19). The Hollywood Thugees, as one would expect, are represented in the film as fanatic terrorists. Their revolutionary struggle fails due to the action of the water bearer Gunga Din, who, by sounding the alarm with a bugle, warns the British Army that they are walking into an ambush set by the Thugees. Gunga Din, previously treated with irony and condescension, is transformed into a hero worthy of an official burial; a stanza from the Rudyard Kipling homonymous poem is read in eulogy:

> You Lazarushian-leather Gunga Din!
> Though I've belted you and flayed you,
> By the livin' Gawd that made you,
> You're a better man than I am, Gunga Din! (30)[17]

One of the founding members of the Filhos de Gandhy states: "Gandhy was not inspired by the movie *Gunga Din*, like many people think, just the outfits" (Félix 57). Another adds, with respect to the figures: "There was a lancer and a water bearer . . . the water bearer isn't used anymore" (32). The lancer's role was to prevent people—"mainly women," added another founder—breaking past the security cordon that protected the group during the parade (41). Today, it is primarily women who patrol the security cordon, and the lancer has become a kind of supervisor. It is known that in the beginning there was a certain degree of concern with respectability and preventing confrontations with the police. As a result, alcoholic beverages were prohibited during the parade; in theory, this prohibition is still enforced. Originally there were revelers who performed the role of water bearers in Filhos de Gandhy, and one can no longer ascertain the ethylic properties of the liquid they were then bearing; nowadays it is primarily the women who accompany the parade who offer the "logistic support" in this arena, exchanging drinks for kisses and bead necklaces. The original figure of the water bearers appears to be a direct reference to the figure of Gunga Din. If costumes worn by the first Filhos de Gandhys were in fact inspired by the film, the source of inspiration was not the film's heroes, but the "bloodthirsty" Hindu Thugees.[18] Gunga Din could never be read as a pacifist or as a revolutionary. His association with Gandhi is nonexistent. But as a "water bearer" he shares, along with Gandhi, the archetype of Oshala. (As previously mentioned, Gandhi, physically as well as ideologically, represents aspects of the archetype of Oshala.) This aesthetic and cosmological similarity and approximation direct us to another reference point that helps to decipher the representation of the water bearer Gunga Din within the Bahian context.

A processional ceremony of a sacred character opens the liturgical calendar of Candomblé: the cycle of ceremonial feasts known as "Águas de Oxalá" ("Oshala's Waters"). In this auspicious ceremony, the devotees set out at dawn in search of the closest source of water in order to "cool" the sacred *quartinhas*, that is, to change the water of the vessels that contain the sacred rocks and symbols of the orishas. This procession and its chants recall the mythological voyage of Oshala and the battles between the Ile-Ife and the Oyo Empires. What we are dealing with here is a historic reference liturgically evoked in the narrative of the imprisonment of Oshala during the reign of Shango, an imprisonment that resulted in seven symbolic years of drought, unhappiness, and sterility, which ended only when Shango and his vassals dressed in white and went to beg forgiveness from Oshala (Beier 72). This narrative is used as a parable for the interpretation of the history of African slavery in Brazil as well as in Cuba.[19]

The cycle of "Águas de Oxalá" ceremonial feasts introduces two relevant aspects to our analysis: the metaphor of water and water bearers in the sacred universe of Candomblé and the reference to Oshala as symbolically "colonized" by a despotic power. The relation of the water bearer Gunga Din with the Filhos de Gandhy provides various supports for these metaphoric creations. Perhaps the major contradiction is that Gunga Din betrayed the Thugees. However, considering that the Thugees, rather than the British Army, inspired the costumes of the lancers, and that the iconic Gunga Din inspired the Filhos de Gandhy directs us to representations of the Bahian imaginary from a somewhat different historic moment when men dressed in white occupied the streets of Salvador: the Afro-Muslim-Brazilian Revolt of the Malês, which counted on the crucial support of the water bearers and was also defeated because of informers. In this sense *Gunga Din*, interpreted in Bahia in 1949, would at once represent the desire for liberation from colonial domination (which in Brazil prevented the separation of Bahia and the establishment of an independent Muslim state) and concomitant efforts toward the maintenance of the ruling powers.

The Revolt of the Malês (as the African Muslims in Bahia were called)[20] was the organized culmination of various insurrections occurring between 1807 and 1835. These African Muslims—notably included Hausas, Fulanis, and Nupes—were brought to Brazil in the final decade of the seventeenth century in the aftermath of the civil wars in the Oyo Empire. Islam in Brazil served as an afro-centric social and political organizing venue. The ethnic distinctions and historic enmities of the enslaved Africans in an area like Bahia lost their immediate relevance in light of organizing a liberation struggle and preparing for an Islamic seizure of power, as Décio Freitas describes:

> The rebels planned to carry out their struggle dressed in uniforms. As such, they manufactured the uniforms in advance. More than six months beforehand, Belchior and Aprígio had started working on them. The uniforms consisted of berets or hoods made of white and blue cloth, large camisoles or *roupetas* [tunics] worn over pants and fastened at the waist with white cotton belts. (Freitas 78)

According to Risério, the revolt of 1835 resulted in a:

> [F]rantic race against time—uncontrolled and bloody—through the rugged landscape of the city of Bahia, breaking out at *Água de Meninos*, at the cavalry barracks, the site of the crucial battle. Seventy Malês were killed, and Black Islam was defeated. The dream of the establishment of a Caliphate in Bahia died that night, the dream of an All-Black Bahia where the whites would be exterminated . . . and the mulattos turned into slaves. (*História* 335–336)

The saga of the Malês—despite being somewhat "nebulous"[21]—has endured in Brazil as a powerful source of mythic pan-African inspiration.[22] Raphael Vieira Filho recalls that as early as 1897, the *carnaval* group Embaixada presented a manifesto demanding reparations for the Africans killed during the Revolt of the Malês. References to the Malês are common in the theme songs and plots of *escolas de samba* and in a Filhos de Gandhy offshoot, the *afoxé* Malê Debalê (founded in 1979).

The testimonies of the Gandhy founders mention three tunes originally sung by the group: (a) "*Entra em Beco, Sai em Beco*" ("Get in an Alley, Get out on an Alley"), a reference to the meandering route of the group through the city, through the "rugged landscape of the City of Bahia"; (b) a melody from Candomblé "Êfila-la-e-ô de Balalaêôaa," a reference to the *filá*, a hat used by orisha Oshala (Castro 235), and to the somewhat conical cap worn by Black Muslims (Cacciatore 126); and (c) "Alá-lá-ô," a tune composed by Haroldo Lobo and Nássara for the Rio de Janeiro *carnaval* group Bloco da Bicharada ("*Bloco* of a Whole Bunch of Animals") in 1940, that refers to the Sahara Desert and to the beneficent Allah[23] (remembering that *alá* in the afro-Bahian context is also a reference to the white shawl that envelopes and protects Oshala). The fact that the Filhos de Gandhy presents references to Candomblé and to Islam merely reflects the religious syncretism that was well underway in Africa long before Europeans arrived.

THE HINDU-MUSLIM-BAHIAN AESTHETIC FANTASY

Abadá, a Yoruba word referring to the white tunic of Arabic origin worn by the Malês, is currently used to refer to the uniforms that participants wear in afro-Bahian *carnaval* associations (Castro 135). The members of Filhos de Gandhy wear a costume that consists of *abadás* and turbans. As we know, Gandhi did not wear a turban. A careful analysis of the turbans that the Filhos de Gandhy wear reveals that their turbans do not derive from a Hindu aesthetic, but are in fact closer to the headdresses of the Sikhs, the inhabitants of Punjab, the border region between India and Pakistan that was divided into an Indian Punjab and a Pakistani Punjab in 1947. This observation amazed me. Far from concluding that the founders or current participants in the Filhos de Gandhy would construct a metaphor based on this referent, what we perceive is a conscious and unconscious collage of signifier and signified elements leading to an inclusive performative discourse open to continuous interpretation. My amazement owes to the following: (a) Gandhi opposed any plan to divide India into two states, although this happened and resulted in a predominantly Hindu India and a predominantly Muslim Pakistan; (b) the *afoxé* Filhos de Gandhy developed into a quasi-processional spectacle in which men wearing Sikh turbans and Muslim *abadás* follow the mythical figure of a Hindu leader; and (c) the division of Punjab occurred a few years before the death of Gandhi. Gandhi's support of Pakistan was what in fact provoked his assassination. Punjab presents itself as a borderland between Hindus and Muslims, populated in the Indian section by Sikhs. This border area, a site of conflict and negotiation, is reflected in the aesthetic of the Filhos de Gandhy.

Today, almost sixty years after the death of Gandhi, the Hindu anthropologist Pravina Shukla visiting Salvador during *carnaval* observes:

> The parade float, white with sapphire-blue painting, features what are considered to be symbols of India—a camel, an elephants, and a goat—yet these are relegated to secondary place in the iconography when compared with the implements of the *orixás*, mainly the sword of Ogun, the crown of Oxalá, and the bow and arrow of Oxóssi, the *orixá* of the hunt. The carnival processions and any other important presence of *Filhos de Gandhy* also feature the Gandhi "look alike," a slender older Black man with an uncanny resemblance to Gandhi himself. This Brazilian Gandhi sits atop a white elephant effigy . . . The costume, said to emulate that of the Mahatma, consists of a long tunic dress, in the Brazilian carnival tradition of the requisite African *abadá*. The turban, as used in caricatures, conjures up images of majestic, "oriental," kings, surrounded by incense, rich foods and *harem* beauties, straight from a fantasy inspired by *A Thousand and One Arabian Nights*. In fact, the *Filhos de Gandhy* turban, with its huge plastic gem, does resemble some cartoonish illustration

> of a fairytale . . . It is not the dress of the simply clad, threadbare Mahatama, but rather the display of an African kingly man, in cool and flowing garments, adorned in the requisite turban that is worn because, as one informant told me, "everybody looks better in a turban." The turban not only frames the face, it adds a few inches to the height of the wearer, an important reason why many men opt to join the group: the choice reflecting, not political and musical affiliation, but pure vanity. (39–40)

Yet the turbans were already part of the afro-Brazilian reality well before India-via-Hollywood, as Raul Lody writes in observing the attire of a "traditional" Bahiana:

> On the head of the Bahiana, a shawl or a turban, usually white, forms an arrangement that resembles a crown . . . The turbans also demonstrate the influences of Muslim peoples in the constitution of this figure, which further involves bringing to the head a twig of *arruda*, of *guiné*, of *são-gonçalinho* or other leaf meant to protect the body. The association between Islam and the turban is not simple. If the head is the container of the design of our rational option between what is true, illusory, right, wrong etc., the turban symbolizes and reinforces spiritual consciousness. In the Muslim conception, the turban opposed all that is profane; it protects thought, which is always pre-disposed to dispersion and to forgetfulness. (*Cabelos* 79)

According to early descriptions, the turbans that the Filhos de Gandhy initially used were garlands tied with ribbons and garlic, much like the *selis* of the Sikh gurus, which are tied with strings.[24] The contemporary turbans follow the configuration of the Sikh turbans, the *dastaars*, which are decorated with a *khanda* (a broche) and which the Filhos de Gandhy replaced with a circle containing a plastic blue stone. The Sikhs decorate the *dastaars* with *khandas* in weddings, the *Anand Karaj*, or "blessing ceremony," representing the union of the individual soul with the universal soul. The *khanda* is therefore a metonymy of a ceremony that seeks the individual's fusion with the universe.

The mixture of geographical, rhythmic, and thematic references of the Bahia *carnaval* can be read, according to Milton Araújo Moura, as the expression of a conscience that perceives the multiplicity of the world and attempts to position itself in it in order to elaborate its identity (Dunn and Perrone 173). A cosmologically fertile and protean foundation allied to the political and poetic consciousness of the organizers and participants of the Bahian *carnaval* allows for the inclusion of foreign icons and elements. And these, especially when they are metonymies of other cosmologies, end up producing performatic creations of a metaphoric value unexpected even by the creators themselves.

Pravina Shukla argues that any observation of the Filhos de Gandhy would immediately reveal fundamental contradictions between the group and Gandhi:

> The Mahatma was simple; his "sons" are extremely vain, bejeweled, perfumed and beautiful. The Mahatma was celibate; his "sons" swap beads for kisses and hope for more. The Mahatma was a vegetarian; his sons eat the flesh of animals cooked and sold on the streets. The Mahatma was a pacifist; his "sons" are aggressive and unduly violent. A closer look at the bloco *Filhos de Gandhy* reveals not only that the reality of Gandhi is imagined, but also that the references to the orixás Oxalá and Ogun are idealized. (42)

But who is this Gandhi whom the revelers of yesterday and today celebrate? Agnaldo Silva, the current president of the Filhos de Gandhy, defines the group as a "Hindu-African entity," and adds that "*ijexá* fits right into the

Figure 9.4 Sons of Gandhy on Yemaya's day. Rio de Janeiro, 2 February 2011. Photo by Cristiano Cardoso.

Figure 9.5 Sons of Gandhy on Yemaya's day. Rio de Janeiro, 2 February 2011. Photo by Zaíra Bosco.

philosophy of Gandhi" (*Filhos de Gandhy*). A member of Gandhy stressed the importance of learning Yoruba, "the language of the secret," since according to him, "Gandhi also works his magic in Yoruba" (Morales 274). The group known as "the sorcerers of Candomblé" interpreted Gandhi as the greatest sorcerer (268). However, the lure of *carnaval* is sexual and carefree, the exact opposite of the self-control and self-discipline preached by Gandhi as the paths to divine truths. This apparent contradiction can also be explained according to Bahian logic, for a reading of Gandhi from within the cosmology of the orishas immediately invests him with sexuality—so much so that the *avatār* of Oshala portrayed in the Filhos de Gandhy is Oshaguian (a younger warrior Oshala) and not Oshalufan (an older Oshala). The sexuality of the orishas and their "children"—of the gods and human beings—is dealt with in quite different manners from what is found in Hinduism. The sexual potency of certain orishas is celebrated precisely as aspects of their divinity.

Pravina Shukla offers pertinent observations regarding the constructed caricature of an exoticized India as seen through the filter of second-hand Hollywood orientalisms.[25] The mass media of popular culture plays an undeniable role in the construction of *carnaval* performances. The old *afoxé* Mercadores de Bagdá ("Merchants of Baghdad") emerged in the same era that the Filhos de Gandhy, and "promoted recreations from movies with storylines of the East of the 'Thousand and One Nights' in their elaborate parades" (Oliveira 278). The *índio* or *caboclo afoxés* presented "costumes and plots inspired by the North American Indians of John Ford and other directors of Western films" (Risério, *Carnaval* 67). What perhaps escaped the perception of Pravina Shula is that these recreations or idealizations occur not only in the "profane" realm of *carnaval*, but also in the sacred realm of Candomblé and Umbanda, of religions and philosophies that have an inclusive, interpretive character.[26] So does the indigenous *caboclo* in Umbanda and Candomblé refer to afrocentric Bantu ancestry and not to the cosmology of the indigenous peoples in Brazil.[27] Although Gandhi has not yet—as far as I know—been included in the sacred repertoire of Umbanda, the secular reverence with which *carnaval* revelers receive him follows a similar process of interpretation and inclusion.

In 1999 the *afoxé* Filhos de Gandhy marked its fiftieth year. Lula Buarque de Hollanda filmed a documentary with scenes in which some members of the group parade through the streets of the city of Udaipur in India. If, for the anthropologist Pravina Shukla, the group was a source of awe, how might the figure of Raimundo Gandhy and his "sons" be perceived by the people of Udaipur? The documentary presents images of Sikhs and Hindus greeting Raimundo Gandhy and reverently touching the ground, but we do not know what they are thinking, or how they interpret this unexpected figure. According to one of the Filhos de Gandhy founders, the group is "almost a sect" nowadays (Félix 31). The people of Udaipur seem to have recognized this essential element—between devout and festive, between sacred and profane. Moa do Catendê, the creator of the *afoxé* Badauê (1979), recognizes the spiritual and political function of the *afoxés* when he says:

> They always demand a lot from us [the leaders of the *afoxés* and afro-*carnaval* associations], since for them we are spiritual nourishment. After all, in a certain way we made them wake up from a terrible sleep of recurring nightmares. And every step we take, during a rehearsal, or during a simple *carnaval* performance, through the strength of our culture, other perceptive Blacks can understand that our struggle is one and only; it is a struggle for black social integrity. (252)

In his analysis of the carnaval group Olodum, Piers Armstrong comments that the pragmatic procedure of the group is essentially a form of bricolage or type of intellectual cannibalism which simultaneously combines discourses of resistance and liberation alongside essentialisms, utopias, modernities, para-religiosities, and vanities ("Moralizing Dionysius," 38–45). And that summarizes some of the essential nature of Filhos de Gandhy: a transdiasporic paradigm that intersects Hindus, Sikhs, and Indian Muslims with Yorubas, Hausas, Fulanis, and Nupes, consistently recreating itself through North American cinema and in the complex afro-Brazilian cosmology.

POSTFACE

> The son asked his father:
> "Where is my grandpa? My grandpa? Where is he?"
> The father asked his grandfather:
> "Where is my great-grandpa? My great-grandpa? Where is he?
> The grandfather asked his great-grandfather:
> "Where is my great-great-grandpa? My great-great-grandpa? Where is he?"
> Great-great-grandfather! Great-grandfather! Grandfather!
> Aganju! Father Shango! Hail Egun! Baba Alapala!
>
> Gilberto Gil[28]

I recognize that some of this material may be difficult for a U.S. American readership. I quote myself (this is a new habit) from my imperfect dissertation, from the very first line of a Shahrazadian spiderweb:

> If my work was on Euro-Brazilian culture and literature, I would invariably start the report of my research with an introduction on the immigration of Europeans to Brazil. It would be expected of me to elucidate which nationalities, and within it which groups, made their way to Brazil. Much of the introduction of a Euro-Brazilian study could be left understated; I could assume my readers know where Italy is, that its citizens speak Italian and that although Sicilians and Calabrese have their specific sense of national identity, they all speak the same language and pray to the same god. The fact that we (living in countries determined and dominated by European/ North American philosophies and cosmologies) remain so ignorant on aspects of life in the African continent has often lead us to sweep our lack of knowledge under the carpet and to refer to Africa, or sub-Saharan Africa, as a uniform whole. ("AxéNgolo" 3)

This chapter is difficult not only "for a U.S. American readership," but for Brazilians as well, because too much has been taken for granted, and because my discipline is only now starting to receive some respect in Brazil. But the passage is long. We are not even in the middle of it. As Kamau Brathwaite explains, this is from inside an *Atlantic Trade Psycho-Physical Space Capsule*:

> To try to understand the nature and reality of the slave's religion in Jamaica (and the Caribbean/ New World), we have to begin with an understanding of the nature and reality of religion in Africa, where, as Herskovits and others have conceptualized it, *the culture focus is religious* i.e., that African culture, like most pre-literate/ oral, pre-industrial folk culture is what Europeans call theocentric: all aspects of

> life have religious reference and meaning; all artifacts and customs are based on or come out of religious belief, practice and symbolism; there is no real distinction between "secular" and "sacred," and the priest, who is essentially the center of the culture, is concerned with and/or is capable of more than "priestly'"(sacerdotal) function, but is/can be healer/physician (physical and psychological), artist (as, among other things, dancer/ choreographer), the maker/designer of symbolic cloth, the carver of stools, statutes and "fetishes," historian (the griot's function is a religious one), storyteller/ poet, diviner/prophet, politician (the chief and *okomfo* (priest) are always closely associated, often indistinguishable), warrior, philosopher, etc. . . . The significant feature of this African (religious) culture was that it was (is) *immanent*: carried within the individual/community, not existentially externalized in buildings, monuments, books, "the artifacts of civilization." (12–14)

But what happens when the scholar is the *okomfo*? I am often told I "do" performance studies. I don't mind it. Better to remain "in the closet"? And when we write? Should I refer to Richard Schechner? Perhaps. There is a lot I do not really know, and I am suspicious of foreign weapons. It's a guttural feeling. It's a legacy. But I occasionally get to them, observing from a distance. It takes time.

This goes to:
The Gunga Din in us, to the pseudo-quasi-cartoonish-would-be heroes "in a world of British adults." To we who can laugh, who are able to (despite the despites) at least try our damned best to be true to ourselves though our recognition of our stations, seasons, in life. To we who can drink from the same cup and cross bridges.

NOTES

1. A version of this chapter originally appeared in *Afro-Hispanic Review* 28.2 (2010).
2. Unless otherwise indicated, all translations are mine. The Filhos de Gandhy official website indicates that: "Vavá Madeira suggested the name for the *bloco*, which was inspired by the life of the pacifist leader Mohandas Karamchand Gandhi. The letter 'i' was changed into 'y' in order to avoid possible retaliations for using of the name of an important leader on the world stage. The *bloco* was therefore baptized with the name *Filhos de Gandhy*" ("Como Tudo Começou").
3. Gilberto Gil's song "Filhos de Gandhi" (1973) was recorded in Gil and Jorge Ben Jor's album *Gil Jorge Ogum Xangô* (1975). Many accept the perception of Gil as the "resuscitator" of a group in danger of extinction. Antonio Risério comments: "It must be stated once and for all: Gil is responsible for the resurgence of the Filhos de Gandhy" (*Carnaval* 53). But according to a recording by Anísio Félix, Camafeu de Oxóssi and the radio broadcaster

Gerson Macedo, and not Gilberto Gil, were the ones who actually revitalized the group. Nonetheless, Gil recorded the song "Filhos de Gandi" (1975) in an album symbolically entitled *Gil Jorge Ogum Xangô*, while the song "Patuscada de Gandhi" (1977) appeared in an album with an equally revealing title, *Refavela*. The tune "Patuscada de Gandhi" was originally composed by Carequinha (Arivaldo Fagundes Pereira) under the title "Papai Ojô." The two songs that Gil recorded effectively disseminated a cultural reference nationally, which had been restricted to Salvador and Rio de Janeiro (recalling that the Rio version of the Filhos de Gandhy began in 1952 with the participation of men and women). In Gil's support and popularization of the Bahian *afoxés*, Caetano Veloso played a parallel role in "thickening the stew" of the *trios elétricos*. Both the *afoxé* Filhos de Gandhy and Dodô and Osmar's *Trio Elétrico* were born in 1949. As Antonio Risério observes, these were "the two main trademarks of Bahian *carnaval*" that on the 1970s went through a period of revitalization (*História* 564).

4. "*Bloco[s] and bloco[s] afro*—Carni[a]val clubs in Salvador are called *blocos*. The *bloco afro* is specifically Afro-centric, created by and for the local Afro-Brazilian population and getting artistic inspiration from the Black diaspora (Africa, USA, the Caribbean and Brazil)" (Armstrong, "Carnaval"). An *afoxé* is a *bloco*, but of a special kind. *Afoxés* possess a specific cosmological archive of references.
5. For afro-centric or "root tourism" see Pinho. For the globalization and the commercialization of the Bahian *carnaval*, see Dunn and Perrone.
6. Definitions given by Raul Lody (*Afoxé* 31); Yeda Pessoa de Castro (144); Olabiyi Yai (qtd. in Risério, *Carnaval* 12); and Peter Fryer (23).
7. Term coined by Antonio Risério (*História* 562).
8. Maroon societies, or Quilombos, or Palenques. "The *quilombos* existed all through Brazil, from the Amazon to Rio Grande do Sul. In fact, as Kamau Brathwaite puts it, 'wherever there has been slavery, there has been maroonage.' According to the definition of the Portuguese colonial authorities, quilombos were all forms of habitations inhabited by five or more runaway slaves intending to secure their freedom by means of force. The quilombos represented geographical centers of resistance, i.e. insurrections would emerge from the quilombo and those planned outside often depended on the participation of the maroons" (McElroy, "AxéNgolo" 251).
9. "*trio elétrico*—A truck entirely covered with a huge array of very loud speakers" (Armstrong, "Carnaval").
10. "*Escola[s]-de-samba*—Literally, samba schools. The dozen or so large organizations in Rio [and other parts of Brazil] that compete with huge dancing parades. This is the model of carnival exported to the world, and is certainly its most extravagant manifestation" (Armstrong, "Carnaval").
11. "A large bottle was brought by the *Obá* as a symbol of his kingdom and worshipped by his vassals" (Ligiéro 93).
12. "African processional performances resemble Catholic ones when they formalize and dramatize some event of importance for the community. The event can be religious, political or social and can be functional as well as referential. . . . The event to which the procession makes reference can be recent, such as to honor a national hero, or a past one, as in the case of a procession in honor of a saint or martyr" (Ligiéro 86).
13. For a fuller explanation of the orishas, their archetypes and meanings, see Mason or Thompson (among many others).
14. The lyrics of "*Filhos de Gandhi*" by Gilberto Gil can be translated as: "Omolu, Ogun, Oshun, Oshumare/ Everyone/ *Come down to watch the*

Filhos de Gandhi/ Yansan, Yemaya, call Shango/ Oshosi as well/ Come down to watch the Filhos de Gandhi / Mercador, Cavaleiro de Bagdá/ Oh, Filhos de Obá/ Come down to watch the Filhos de Gandhi / Our Lord of Bonfim/ please do me a favor/ call everyone/ Come down to watch the Filhos de Gandhi/ Oh, my God in heaven/ It's carnaval down on earth/ call everyone/ Come down to watch the Filhos de Gandhi" (emphasis added).

15. "In the 1930s, the era of the resurgence of the *afoxés*, when the Filhos de Gandhy paraded for the first time in the streets, they were attacked by the police who charged that the group consisted entirely of Blacks, many of whom were trade unionists" (Pinho 125). "We witnessed in the 1930s and 40s a resurgence of the black *blocos* and *afoxés* with a much stronger political orientation, because its organizers were trade union activists and members of other organizations, such as the Stevedores and Dockworkers Union . . . The police attacked [The Filhos de Gandhy] the first year they came out on the streets on account of the group's consisting mostly of Blacks, workers and active trade unionists, and also because of their manner of dancing and singing, which upset all of Bahian society who found the style too African, too Black. It disturbed people and was a political affirmation of Candomblé, *ijexá* and of the Blacks" (Ilê Aiyê in Luz 34).
16. The character Gunga Din, inspired by the poem by Rudyard Kipling, is analyzed by David Birch, Tony Schirato, and Sanjay Srivastava as the elaboration of a hero within the framework of political and sexual power of the colonized. "*Gunga Din* (1939), for example, is a classic Hollywood film about three British soldiers who, with some timely help from a subservient Indian, overcome a rebellion that threatens British control of India. . . . The title character in the film is equally subservient and unimposing. *He is short, weakly built, and tends to break into exaggerated, childlike smiles whenever the British appear. Gunga Din is no way physical powerful or potentially threatening. . . . There is no way, given the codes of physicality operating in the film, that the character of Gunga Din can be taken seriously, be treated as an equal of the heroes, or be in control of his destiny. He is, in every way, an Indian child in a world of British adults . . . Gunga Din may not have had much formal education, but he was, nevertheless, noble and 'manly' because,* unlike groups such as the 'effeminate Bengali' (Sinha 1997), *he was true to himself through his recognition of his 'station in life*" (Birch, Schirato, and Srivastava 6–7, emphasis added).
17. In Rudyard Kipling's (1865–1936) "Gunga Din" (*The Barrack Room Ballads*), the poem that inspired the movie, Gunga Din is a water bearer serving the British Army at the end of the nineteenth century. He is beaten and looked down upon by the officers. ("*You limping lump o' brick-dust, Gunga Din!*"; "*You squidgy-nosed old idol, Gunga Din!*"; "*I'll marrow you this minute,/ If you don't fill up my helmet, Gunga Din!*") When he brings water to the soldier-narrator of the poem (Thomas Atkins), he is shot: "*But of all the drinks I've drunk,/ I'm gratefullest to one from Gunga Din.*"
18. Milton Araújo Moura points out a possible ambivalence in this aesthetic interpretation. According to Moura, the *carnaval* revelers "were, however, aware of the political difficulties related to the militancy of the Left; an icon such as Gandhi was the antithesis of the Communist stigma. Although their outfits recalled those used by Gandhi, they were also similar to those used by some soldiers loyal to the British crown. The appearance of the revelers associated them with the world of Gandhi without making the distinction as to whether they were specifically those of the pacifist leader or those of the loyalist troops" (Dunn and Perrone 165).

19. This is part of the answer to a crucial question I had when I started studying my "subject." I quote myself (why not?): "And I as I kept on trying to imagine the agony of being subjected to an enemy nation in one's home land, the excruciating trip to the shore, the 'horrors of the Atlantic crossing, euphemistically referred to as middle passage,' the days in the human market, the trip to some sugar cane plantation—what I kept on asking myself was, how were these men & women orienting themselves? What did they hold on to? How would they explain their lives to their children? How would the Babalawos, Tata Nkissi and other wise religious men and women explain and understand god in the midst of all this unimaginable terror? How did cosmological concepts of various African nations reach and transform themselves in the New World?" (McElroy, "AxéNgolo" 130).
20. "An expression possibly derived from the Hausa *malam* (master) or from the Yoruba *imalê* (muslim)" (Risério, *História* 335).
21. According to Nei Lopes: "for the Brazilian in general, the saga of the Malês remains known but *nebulous* . . . and so, now, when Blacks attempt to revive what unites them to their ancestry, searching to recuperate their lost identity . . . many can only gaze into the mirror of the Malês" (68). Nei Lopes refers to other black colonial struggles which may be not be chosen as "ideal," as "noble enough" mirrors in this quest for roots.
22. According to Risério: "the success of the afro *bloco* Malê Debalê, together with the popular revalorization of the Islamic revolts, has created a type of myth around the Malês. Today in Bahia, any informed Black, some with a certain degree of snobbery (understandable, but inexcusable) claims to be decedent of the Malês" (Risério qtd. in Lopes 69). According to Nei Lopes, "the Malê Islamism was one of the greatest and most efficient factors for unity which slaves in Brazil had in order to strengthen themselves and unite against oppression. By means of this, everybody, without distinction, was united under one banner and one nation: the Islamic nation" (58).
23. Translation of original lyrics: "It has arrived, our caravan has arrived/ We come from the desert/ Without bread, without banana/ The sun was unbearable/ It burnt our faces/ It made us sweat/ We come from Egypt/ And many times we had to pray/ Allah, Allah, Allah, my good Allah/ Send water for *Ioiô* ("masta") /Send water for *Iaiá* ("missy")/ Allah, my good Allah."
24. "Seli: A woolen cord worn by Guru Nanak around his turban. It was worn as a symbol of living in the world but not in worldly matters. It was passed on to each successive Guru up to Guru Hargobind who chose to wear the symbol of two swords of meri and peri instead" (Brar). See also Ji.
25. "Indian elements are representations of the representations of India made by outsiders . . . In Bahia, as in many parts of the world, images and caricatures of India created by the mass media become associated with symbols of deep spirituality and emotionality" (Shukla 42–43).
26. "Perhaps"? How could it *not* have escaped the perception of Pravina Shula? She must know how complex it is. She wrote a brilliant text. It was through her, through her *avatāra*, thorough her illuminated foreign amazement that I started thinking about the meaning(s) of one of my taken-for-granted passions.
27. Very few people have considered this. Very few Brazilians are aware of this, and/or treat it with (what I believe, should be) proper respect.
28. Translation of an excerpt of a 1976 song by Gilberto Gil entitled "Babá Alapalá." Baba or Father Alapala is the name of an ancestral egun. Further explanations and translations can be found at McElroy, "AxéNgolo" (453 and 587–588). For Gilberto Gil's original lyrics and translated adaption entitled "Alapala: The Myth of Shango," see Rennó 185.

ABOUT THE PHOTOGRAPHERS

The Brazilian photographers Zaíra Bosco and Cristiano Cardoso are social science scholars. Bosco is currently an MA student at ENSP-Fioxruz (Nacional School of Public Health). Cardoso is a member of the NUPEVI (The Nucleus for Research of Violence), where he is working on the production of a documentary film about religious intolerance and citizenship construction. Bosco and Cardoso live in Rio de Janeiro. The photographs that appear in this chapter are part of a larger photographic essay entitled "Sons of Gandhy on Yemaya's Day." The author of this chapter thanks Ana Paula Alves Ribeiro for putting her in contact with Cardoso and Bosco.

The Australian photographer Piers Armstrong studied and taught Brazilian literature at UCLA, before moving to Salvador, teaching at the Federal University of Bahia, and then the Universidade Estadual de Feira de Santana. His research focuses, among others, on aesthetic and social aspects of the popular cultural expression of Bahia. Armstrong is the author of, among others, *Third World Literary Fortunes: Brazilian Culture and Its International Reception* (Bucknell UP, 1999). The author of this chapter thanks Bill Hinchberger and Charles A. Perrone for putting her in contact with Armstrong.

WORKS CITED

Armstrong, Piers. "The Carnaval of Bahia: "From the Inside Looking Out." *BrazilMax*. BrazilMax, 13 July 2003. Web. 13 July 2011.

———. "Moralizing Dionysius and Lubricating Apollo: A Semantic Topography of Subject Construction in Afro-Bahian Carnival." *Luso-Brazilian Review* 38 (2001): 29–60. Print.

Beier, Ulli. *The Origin of Life and Death: African Creation Myths*. Oxford: Heinemann, 1966. Print.

Birch, David, Tony Schirato, and Sanjay Srivastava. *Asia: Cultural Politics in the Global Age*. New York: Palgrave, 2001. Print.

Birman, Patrícia. *Fazer estilo criando gêneros: Possessão e diferença de gênero em terreiros de Umbanda e Candomblé no Rio de Janeiro*. Rio de Janeiro: EdUERJ, 1995. Print.

Brar, Sandeep Singh. "Glossary of Religious Terms." *Sikhism, Religion of the Sikh People*. Sikhs.org, n.d. Web. 13 July 2011.

Brathwaite, Kamau. *Folk Culture of the Slaves in Jamaica*. 1971. London: New Beacon, 1981. Print.

Butler, Kim. *Freedoms Given, Freedoms Won: Afro-Brazilians in Post-Abolition São Paulo and Salvador*. New Brunswick: Rutgers UP, 1998. Print.

Cacciatore, Olga G. *Dicionário de cultos afro-brasileiros*. 1977. Rio de Janeiro: Forense Universitária, 1988. Print.

Carneiro, Édison. *Folguedos tradicionais*. 1974. Rio de Janeiro: FUNART/INF, 1982. Print.

Castro, Yeda Pessoa de. *Os falares africanos na Bahia*. 2001. Rio de Janeiro: Topbooks, 2005. Print.

Catendê, Moa do. "A política afoxesista." *Estudos Afro-Asiáticos* 8–9 (1983): 251–253. Print. "Como tudo começou." *Filhos de Gandhy*. N.p., n.d. Web. 13 July 2011.

Davies, Carole Boyce. "Re-presenting Black Female Identity in Brazil: Filhas d'Oxum in Bahia Carnival." *Ijele: Art eJournal of the African World* 2.1 (2001): n. pag. Africa Resource Center. Web. 1 Nov. 2007.

Dunn, Christopher, and Charles Perrone, eds. *Brazilian Popular Music and Globalization*. Gainesville: U of Florida P, 2001. Print.

Félix, Anísio. *Filhos de Gandhi: A história de um afoxé*. Salvador: Gráfica Central Ltda, 1987. Print.

Filhos de Gandhy. Dir. Lula Buarque de Hollanda. Latin American Video Archives, 2000. Film.

Freitas, Décio. *A revolução dos Malês: Insurreições escravas*. 1975. Porto Alegre: Editora Movimento, 1985. Print.

Fryer, Peter. *Rhythms of Resistance: African Musical Heritage in Brazil*. Hanover: Wesleyan UP, 2000. Print.

Fu-Kiau, Kimbwandènde Kia Bunseki. *Self-Healing Power and Therapy: Old Teachings from Africa*. New York: Vintage, 1991. Print.

Gonçalves, Ana Maria. *Um defeito de cor*. Rio de Janeiro: Editora Record, 2006. Print.

Gunga Din. Dir. George Stevens. RKO, 1939. Film.

Ji, Bhai Surinder Singh, and Bhai Tarlochan Singh Ji. "El turbante de los sikhs." *Red Sikh Hispana*. Red Sikh Hispana, n.d. Web. 13 July 2011.

Kipling, Rudyard. *Barrack-Room Ballads*. London: Heinemann, 1892. Print.

Landes, Ruth. "Cult Matriarchate and Male Homosexuality." Journal of Abnormal and Social Psychology 35 (1940): 386–397. Print.

Ligiéro, Zeca. "Performances processionais Afro-Brasileiras." *O Percevejo* 12 (2003): 84–98. Print.

Lody, Raul F. *Afoxé*. Rio de Janeiro: Funarte, 1976. Print. Cadernos de Folclore 7.

———. *Cabelos de axé: Identidade e resistência*. Rio de Janeiro: Ed. Senac Nacional, 2004. Print.

Lopes, Nei. *Bantos, Malês e identidade negra*. Rio de Janeiro: Forense Universitária, 1988. Print.

Luz, Marco Aurélio, comp. *Identidade negra e educação*. Salvador: Ianamá, 1989. Print.

Mason, John, and Gary Edwards. *Black Gods: Orisa Studies in the New World*. New York: Yoruba Theological ArchMinistry, 1985. Print.

Matory, J. Lorand. *Black Atlantic Religion: Tradition, Transnationalism, and Matriarchy in the Afro-Brazilian Candomblé*. Princeton: Princeton UP, 2005. Print.

McElroy, Isis Costa. "AxéNgolo Poetics: A Cultural and Cosmological Conceptualization of AfroBrazil in Space & Process." Diss. New York U, 2004. Print.

———. "A Transdiasporic Paradigm: The *Afoxé* Filhos de Gandhy." First version. *Afro-Hispanic Review* 29.1 (2010): 77–100. Print.

Morales, Anamaria. "O afoxé Filhos de Gandhy pede paz." *Escravidão e invenção da liberdade*. Org. João José Reis. São Paulo: Editora Brasiliense, 1988. 264–74. Print.

Oliveira, Paulo Cesar Miguez de. "A organização da cultura na cidade da Bahia." Diss. U Federal da Bahia, 2002. Print.

Pinho, Patrícia de Santana. *Reinvenções da África na Bahia*. São Paulo: Annablume, 2004. Print.

Rennó, Carlos, ed. *Gilberto Gil: Todas as letras*. São Paulo: Companhia das Letras, 1996. Print.

Risério, Antonio. *Carnaval ijexá*. Salvador: Corrupio, 1981. Print.

———. *Uma história da cidade da Bahia*. Rio de Janeiro: Versal, 2004. Print.

Rodrigues, Nina. *Os Africanos no Brasil*. 1932. Brasília: Editora Universidade de Brasília, 2004. Print.

Sansone, Lívio, and Jocélio Teles dos Santos, Orgs. *Ritmos em trânsito: Sócio-antropologia da música baiana.* São Paulo: Editora Dynamis, 1997. Print.
Shukla, Pravina. "Afro-Brazilian Avatāras: Gandhi's Sons Samba in South America." *Indian Folklore Journal* 1 (2001): 35–45. Print.
Silva, Agnaldo. "Filhos de Gandhi: entrevista por Emerson Nunes." *I Bahia.* Portal da Rede Bahia, 1 Nov. 2007. Web. 13 July 2011.
Silveira, Renato da. "Jeje-nagô, iorubá-tapá, aon-efan, ijexá: processo de constituição do candomblé da Barroquinha (1764–1851)." Revista Cultura 6 (2000): 80–101. Print.
Sodré, Muniz. *Samba, o dono do corpo.* Rio de Janeiro: Mauad, 1998. Print.
Thompson, Robert Farris. *Flash of the Spirit.* New York: Random House, 1983. Print.
Verger, Pierre Fatumbi. *Lendas africanas dos orixás.* São Paulo: Editora Corrupio, 1985. Print.
Vieira Filho, Raphael R. "Folguedos negros no carnaval de Salvador (1880–1930)." *Ritmos em trânsito:Sócio-antropologia da música baiana.* Ed. Lívio Sansone and Jocélio Teles dos Santos. Salvador: Dynamis, 1998. 39–58. Print. Programa a Cor da Bahia/Projet.

10 The Decline of Israeli Society as a Black Mass in the Theatre of Shmuel Hasfari

Gad Kaynar

FROM SOCIAL DRAMA TO DRAMA OF THE SICK COLLECTIVE SOUL[1]

This chapter deals with the complex correspondence in Israeli theatrical drama between religious ceremony and actual reality with its interpersonal, familial, social, and universal layers. It also deals with the interaction between this complex correspondence and the performance-oriented Israeli drama. This web of interrelations reaches one of its most extreme climaxes in the first trilogy—*Kiddush*, *Hametz*, and *Shiveah*—written by Shmuel Hasfari, one of Israel's leading and most controversial playwrights.

The correspondence between religion and performance in Israel is not new, and is firmly rooted in the pageants of the agricultural settlement movement from the 1920s onward. This is partly because this correspondence is based upon the paradoxical, ambivalent, and generative functions in the Jewish religion of the theologically permeated verb "to remember," a verb commanding evocation of a formative event or commandment either from the past, or that has taken place cyclically from time immemorial. This serves to turn remembrance into the activating factor that recreates the holiday or religious festival in whose framework the remembrance ceremony is conducted. Thus that primeval historical or mythical event is revived and, consequently, ensures the nation's continued existence. These remembrance ceremonies are based on scriptural commandments, such as: the biblical commandment "Remember the Sabbath day, to keep it holy" (*The Holy Scriptures of the Old Testament*, Exodus 20.8); Maimonides's injunction, "The Torah commands us to praise and sanctify the Sabbath day" (29:1); the commandment "In every single generation it is a man's duty to think of himself as one of those who came out of Mizrayim [Egypt]" (*Haggada* 31); the commandment "Remember what Amalek did unto you" (Deuteronomy 25.17); or the commandment to sit in mourning for seven days to decrease the "severity of justice" against the family mourning in accordance with the *Shulhan Aruh* (207: 5).[2] Yet despite the sacred and self-ritualizing origins of these ceremonies, the "rememberer" is rooted in the present, so that remembrance as a reality-creating mandamus is subjugated to the rememberer's worldview and interests. Moreover, remembrance in the religious ceremony manifests itself in a performative repertory of non-verbal gestures and theatrical speech acts, thus lending itself to a stage performance. The histrionic character of the stage performance emphasizes the performative nature of the remembrance ceremony, and this meta-theatrical emphasis enunciates the attitude of the playwright and director Shmuel Hasfari toward the dramatic characters who hold this ceremony or profane it, and toward the Israeli reality represented by them.

It is in this context that the first trilogy by Hasfari—*Kiddush*, *Hametz*, and *Shiveah* (religious rites and ceremonies whose meaning will be illuminated later on)—should be read. Shmuel Hasfari is an infuriatingly provocative playwright, in his works and personality alike, who comes from a liberal, national-religious home of Holocaust survivors, and acquired extensive knowledge of Judaism in his religious education. He studied at the Tel Aviv University Department of Theatre Art and left it, slamming the door behind him. He became a far more radical *Kahanist* than the racist Palestinians hater [Rabbi Meir] Kahane himself, and turned into a militant leftist with right-wing *modi operandi*. His first trilogy embodies both the ideological meaning of the playwright's personal abandonment of his religious roots, and the symbiotic, distorted, and manipulative connection created in Israel between traditional and secular cultures, and between the Jewish and Israeli crises of identity. This connection is reflected in the tense relationship between the religious ceremony in its original pattern, and its defamiliarization in the theatrical representation by Hasfari as playwright-director. This representation in and of itself simultaneously posits an ontological and formal, agnostic and homeopathic alternative to the same ceremony, a kind of Black Mass, as we shall see in the first play of the trilogy.

Kiddush—the first play of the trilogy and the major paradigm of this chapter—-depicts the growing animosity between Arieh and Pnina, a couple of Holocaust survivors, torn between their religious-spiritual origins and the secular-materialistic identity of Israeli society. The eruption of their subliminal hatred leads to the breakup of the family, reified by the gradual disintegration of the *Kiddush*, the ceremony that sanctifies the Sabbath and the family unity. The crisis culminates with the immigration of the couple's victim, their son Yossi, to the U.S.

Kiddush delineates a microcosmic representation of Israeli society on the background of the euphoric atmosphere following the glorious victory of the Six-Day War in June 1967. The sequel to this play, *Hametz* (meaning "leavened bread"), is an allegory in the form of a surreal family drama on the unrealistic and suicidal collective state of mind that drove Israel to the alleged defeat in the October 1973 Yom Kippur (The Atonement Day) War. The play takes place on the eve of Passover and the *Seder* ceremony (on the first night of the holiday). The protagonist Arik is an innate schizophrenic who is convinced, like Israeli society in general, that he is pursued by the entire world, and subjects his wife to psychological torture in order to repress the fact that his madness drove him to kill their son Yonathan. His sister Elisheva, on the other hand, tries—for the sake of obtaining compensation from the government—to convince medical authorities that Arik's mental condition ensues from his traumatic experiences as survivor of concentration camps and Israel's wars. At the *Seder* feast in Elisheva's house, in which the family members defile the sanctity of the event either by orthodox or secular excesses, and grapple with their painful memories of the past, Arik—about to be institutionalized in a mental hospital—is absent. Goaded by the Mephistophelean reincarnation of his dead son, Arik turns out as the "Jewish terrorist" who drives through Israel on his motorcycle and one by one destroys the Holocaust and war commemoration sites, thereby believing to release Israeli society from the syndrome of clinging to traumatic historical memories, ending up at Massada where he commits suicide.

The third play in the trilogy, *Shiveah*, revolves on the axis of another Jewish ceremony—the seven days' mourning over a deceased relative (Shiveah). The ceremony in this case is held in memory of Tuvia Hagorney, a religious, veteran teacher. Following a long, unhappy marriage, and having served as the object of contempt and derision for most of his family members, Tuvia secretly flies to London, on the very day in which his devoted son Shlomi joins the army, and his daughter-in-law bears his first grandchild. There he ends his life by falling from a hotel balcony, either by accident or as an act of suicide. Tuvia's funeral is held in the absence of his family members, who at the same time watch on television the historical peace mission of the Egyptian President Sadat to Israel. The sacrilege of violating the sanctity of the funeral rite is followed by profaning the Shiveah through ugly family strife that reveals the rifts among the dramatis personae, especially between the mother Devorah and her children. Ugly secrets about each of the family members are surfaced, ultimately leading to the suicide of the youngest son, the soldier Shlomi (a name ironically meaning "my peace")—who cannot get over the death of his beloved father—also by jumping off the balcony.

Hasfari's fundamental strategy in this trilogy is based upon creating an intertextual, synergic, and antithetical linkage between two apparently parallel representational systems that are, in fact, completely different. The first is the category of the religious ceremony that professes to represent traditional Jewish cultural values. Those who believe in and uphold the religious ceremony—any religious ceremony whatsoever—are *identified* with it and draw from it their collective identity, despite and because of its representational characteristics. It is a ceremony that in retrospect cyclically perpetuates and regenerates its signifier and subject—Israeli society. The second is the dual theatrical system: a) that of the theatre that stages the play, and through its fictional means presents the ceremony as a play-within-a-play. In this framework the actor is not *identical* with his role but *identifies* with it, just as the play's mise en scène and scenography are not instrumental in changing reality, but rather employ a purely aesthetic, mimetic, and non-pragmatic rhetoric. And b) that of the represented dramatis personae, who with their sham and specious behavior void the religious ceremony of its meaning. The performative element common to the ceremony and the play assists the theatrical text in tearing the mask off the play-within-the-play, i.e., the represented bogus religious ceremony.

It is the very provocation of profaning sanctity onstage by impairing the external characteristics of the ceremony, and not in the first place its critical-reformative purpose, that causes the implied spectators,[3] and sometimes even the real audience, to protest. This is how the critic Hillel Barzel describes the reception of the professional premiere of *Kiddush* by "religious circles and many members of the audience" at the Cameri Theatre of Tel Aviv in 1985 (343). Thus the playwright, who also directs his own works, succeeds in tearing the mask not only from the face of the characters—the agents of the implied audience—but also from that of that audience *in the course of the theatrical event itself.* The conflicts between the characters are therefore transposed to the conflict between the critical playwright and the implied spectators, who fall into the trap laid for them by the dramatist and protest against the means, not against the social and existential defects against which the playwright is warning.

Shmuel Hasfari's trilogy—*Kiddush*, *Hametz*, and *Shiveah*—dealing with familial-traditional ceremonies, entertains a ritual relationship among its three parts. This relationship is incorporated in a cyclical pattern built upon mutually detesting Holocaust survivor parents, victims who have become torturers, and their children, hapless victims of the victims. Its dramaturgy is also characterized by an additional strategy. This is the gradual and frantically escalating transition, which is not linear but simultaneous, from a stylized reality-like mode—employed as a lure to ensure the engagement of the implied spectators in the performance and their immunity, so to speak, against critical attack—to stylized, illusion-shattering modes characterized by a heightened theatrical consciousness and self-reference. The first stage in this transition process is a familiar, almost one-to-one representation of the traditional ceremonies with which the implied spectator is intimately acquainted, and for whom they constitute an identity and cultural icon. These include the ceremony symbolizing, first and foremost, remembrance of "the Creation," symbolized by family unity, which is manifested by the Sabbath prayer delivered by the father before the festive Friday evening meal (*Kiddush*); the collective commemoration of the exodus from slavery to freedom on the *Seder* evening in which the *Haggadah*, the exodus lore, is being read aloud (*Hametz*); or the ritual of death and personal remembrance incorporated in the week of mourning after the funeral (*Shiveah*). The next stage is the tragi-grotesque breakdown, autogenic repudiation, secularization, and profanation of the ceremony from within. This profanation is paradoxically reified through the zealous and self-defeating attempt of the participants to observe the prescribed form of the ceremony. This, however, is done in order to exploit the ceremony to advance materialistic objectives, to reinforce their social status and public image, to advance a belligerent ideology that runs counter to the spirit of Judaism, or to hurt despised family members bound together by a unity of contrasts. In the final stage, Hasfari resorts to the expressionist mode that with extreme theatrical images realizes the turning of the ceremony into a surreal nightmare, thus reifying the apocalyptic decline of Israeli society.

A fine example of this last stage is the metaphorical conclusion of *Kiddush*, when the mentally ill mother, Pnina, passes through walls on her way to the hospital for the mentally ill while the forlorn and totally forsaken father, Arieh, concludes the "foundation ceremony" of the family void by pouring the wine from the *Kiddush* goblet onto the bare table. Another example is the Malach family's Passover (*Seder*) table in *Hametz*, which suddenly soars upward in "Chagallic" flight, while the schizophrenic Arik holds an anti-ceremony and turns the *Seder* (meaning "order") into chaos. He speeds off on his motorcycle on a vendetta to burn down the country's various memorial sites, spurred on by the figure of a Mephistophelean angel of destruction with fly's wings, an agent of the "evil angels" from the Passover lore, who is none other than the persona of his own avenging son whom he murdered. The vendetta journey is directed on this occasion against Arik's Jewish family members and not against their archetypal enemies, the hostile Gentiles. A further example can be found in *Shiveah* with the appearance of Tuvia, the father, a humiliated husband and derided teacher, whose fate remains a mystery—he might have committed suicide or possibly escaped from his oppressive relatives. He reappears perhaps in the dream, perhaps in the reality of the family members, in order to demand reparation and expiation.

In these examples, particularly the last two, Hasfari employs—as mentioned earlier—a device of self-reference by heightening the theatrical consciousness of the performance in order to totally shatter the illusory veneer of familial-social unity. He converts the theatrical performance of the declining individual and society from an external, reality-like phenomenon, as in a large part of critical Israeli drama, into an internal experience of psycho-social and existential drama wherein the characters personify fractious typological voices in the substructure of the collective subconscious. Through this process, Shmuel Hasfari transforms what initially appears to be a social drama into the drama of the sick collective soul of Israeli society. The plays furthermore render the representation of self-destructive myths that established Israeli society, and that were absurdly nourished by the traditional religious arch-myths that the secular Zionist movement initially rejected, into a stunning sensory-poetic experience that constitutes a form of shock therapy.

THEATRICAL FICTION AS DENUNCIATION OF IDENTITY FICTION: THE TEXT AS A SELF-DEFEATING BOOMERANG

Kiddush, the grotesque social comedy written and first produced in 1980 at Tel Aviv University, had its professional premiere five years later at the Cameri Theatre. It depicts the decline and breakup of relations between the members of the national-religious, lower-middle class, urban Shiloni family. The parents, Arieh and Pnina, have met while being partisans during the Holocaust period, hiding in the woods and fighting the Germans. The father, Arieh, is an erstwhile Torah scholar who became a petty trades union activist. The mother, Pnina, is an ignorant, peasant-bred housewife. Their Israeli-born son, Yossi, is torn between his conflicting parents. Due to his inability to bear the hatred at home, which leads to total silence and non-communication between Arieh and Pnina, and his thankless role as mediator between them (the "telephone" as he defines himself), Yossi—the agent of the implied playwright—is driven to leave Israel. He thus damns his parents to madness and solitude. The arena of family events stretches between two significant rites of passage of an Israeli youth, from the preparations for his *bar mitzvah* to the conclusion of his military service and emigration from Israel. The depiction of the arena is inexorably intertwined with the narrative of the morally corrupt Israeli society, from the eve of the 1967 victorious Six-Day War to the "earthquake" that followed the "defeat" in the October 1973 Yom Kippur War. The status of the family metaphor as a microcosmic social allegory and a polyphonic representation of clashing positions in the normative climate of the Israeli macrocosm is supported by the documentary newscasts of the period, the architecture and interior decoration of the performance space, the prevalent linguistic codes, and the mimesis of quotidian life.

The first scene already reveals the manipulative correlation between religious tradition and an ideological-subjective worldview on the one hand, and a subliminal opportunist agenda relating to the social and economic image of the characters, driven by the irrelevant survival instinct originating in the Holocaust on the other. For Yossi's *bar mitzvah*, Arieh forces his son to learn by heart the entire portion of the Torah dealing with kosher and unclean animals. He does so not out of excess piety, but to enhance his own standing in his religious community. He exploits this ambition to justify to his son his dubious conduct as a combating partisan in World War II, when out of fear for the morality of armed Jews he got rid of a rifle he found. Yossi is torn between his father's opportunist ambitions and those of his mother, who forces him to practice the accordion because "anyone who could play [. . .] could be saved" (*Kiddush* 23).[4] His parents apparently try to inculcate both Jewish theology and non-Jewish artistic culture in their son, but from the outset it is clear that their motives are not the purest. The maltreatment of their child—also manifested in forcing him to wear orthodox identifying marks, which in turn leads to bullying by other children—are a role-reversal mini-reconstruction of the Nazis' maltreatment of them and their families. Tradition becomes an axe to grind, when it is totally distorted due to greed. This is blatantly revealed in the parents' willingness to travel by car on the Sabbath, a severely prohibited act, to obtain testimony that will ensure them reparations from the hated Germans, or as Pnina puts it, "Saving money takes precedence over the Sabbath" (23). Tradition is portrayed as a mechanism for moral suicide.

The *bar mitzvah* ceremony thereby becomes a purely performative act devoid of content. Its ludicrousness—amplified by the fact that the father has taught his son the wrong portion of the Torah—is emphasized on the meta-theatrical level by the son functioning as a Shakespearean fool who exposes the sham in his parents' hollow and histrionic behavior. Throughout the play, attention to the fact that ceremonies are devoid of religious content is reinforced by a series of deceptions. Thus, for instance, the father, Arieh, seeks to appear as orthodox-religious, while at the same time being prepared to desecrate the Sabbath to obtain reparations from Germany; he insists on holding the first Kiddush ceremony in the play in full, but does so only to show off his cantorial talents. He is then accused of hypocrisy by his wife since after the Sabbath eve meat dinner he has no compunction about visiting a secular family and enjoying cheesecake (which harshly profanes Biblical decrees), just as when he was a partisan in the forests he did not observe the Jewish dietary laws. The mother insists that Yossi, about to join the army, should put on phylacteries during his military service, while she herself openly desecrates the Sabbath, and so forth. The theatre, which is naturally founded on merely projecting non-pragmatic impressions as a terminal purpose, becomes a tool for exposing the speciousness of the Shiloni family's social pretense as a metaphor for the conduct of the entire Israeli society. In similar fashion, the costumes and sets display their status as mere theatrical paraphernalia: in their connection with the pseudo-piety of the characters. The yarmulkes worn by Arieh and Yossi do not denote faith. They are no more than a realistic item of the actor's costume intended to intensify the stage fiction's credibility, and the characters wearing the yarmulke, unlike the actors playing them, are nothing but failed and pathetic "actors of life" who have difficulty in maintaining the deceptive appearance they attempt to create.

In the original Cameri Theatre production the set by Yossi Ben-Ari made this use of theatrical means a lever for exposing the performative sham in the reality explicit, perhaps even too explicit. The designer did so by doing away with the walls and marking them on the stage floor, and also by marking merely the outline of the holy books Arieh purchases with the reparations money, without presenting the books themselves. The illusion of harmony, stability, and the scholarly and artistic enlightenment of Jewish family life is thereby clearly presented as self-eradicating. The same applies to the characters' names, which, as Hillel Barzel notes, expose their hypocrisy: "The father, whose name is Arieh [Hebrew = lion], is revealed as a coward while supposedly a partisan fighter"; the mother, "'Pnina' [Hebrew = ruby], whose tongue and deeds are inappropriate to the verse from 'A Woman of Valor,' the chapter from Proverbs that pertains to the Sabbath eve songs: 'For her price is far above rubies'" (343).

THE FIRST KIDDUSH

The four Kiddush ceremonies held in the course of the play endow it with its structural coherence, and by virtue of their connection to historical, familial, and social time they acquire the status of a chronotope as Bakhtin defines it: "Time, as it were, thickens, takes on flesh, becomes artistically visible; likewise, space becomes charged and responsive to the movements of time, plot and history" (14).

The beginning of the first Kiddush ceremony is planted in the middle of the play as a watershed that will lead to the decline and breakup of the family and society by their refutation from within, in an apparently completely realistic context. The scene takes place on a Sabbath eve in the winter of 1968, two years after Yossi's *bar mitzvah* ceremony, and one year after receipt of the reparations that improved the family's situation, but which, contrary to expectations, only deepened the schism between the parents. The mother, Pnina, is lying in bed cracking sunflower seeds, surrounded by newspapers, and listening to military commentator Haim Herzog, who is commenting on the air force's bombing raid in Jordan. In the dining corner, the table is festively set for the Kiddush meal when the father and son return from the synagogue. This is a reality-like scene with which many members of the implied spectators are acquainted from their own homes, and as such, it evokes a sense of familiarity and immunity. However, before the opening dialogue between Arieh, Pnina, and Yossi attests to the deep hostility between them, Hasfari exploits the synaesthetic and non-verbal stage rhetoric to anchor the family cell in the context of the broad socio-political fabric of Israeli reality. He modifies the components of the stage scene as personifications of the conflicting voices in the collective Israeli soul. Moreover, the mother lying in her bed and not joining her husband in the synagogue represents objectivized and brutalized Israeli secularism. The play as a prospective stage script creates a metonymic connection between her and the retrospective elation of the commentator boasting of the military might of the country, which is still in the grip of the post-Six-Day War militaristic euphoria. A similar relation is engendered between Pnina and the newspapers around her that represent the same arrogant phenomenological reality. These audiovisual relations pigeonhole Pnina into the nationalistic-belligerent-colonialist branch of Israeli society, to which, on the face of it, the yarmulke-wearing father should have belonged. But in order to radicalize the mother's socio-politically oriented critical characterization, the playwright contrasts her visual appearance with the icons of the Sabbath identified with peace and with the conception of Judaism as representing tolerance and humanism in the spirit of Levinas ("Monotheism as the driving force of Jewish culture [. . .] is Humanism. Only fools turn it into a matter of theological arithmetic" (355)) in a manner that turns the mother into a sort of realization of the same thuggish bestiality that the father, who brags about his supreme morality, attributes to her. And in order to further underscore this sub-cultural impression in contrast with the sublime spiritual-artistic culture symbolized by the Sabbath, the playwright allows Pnina to crack sunflower seeds, a clear and somewhat racist deictic marker of the habits of Israel's lower *Sephardi* (Oriental Jews) social classes.

Arieh stands with the goblet of wine, waiting for his wife, who intentionally delays her entrance. The *Kitzur Shulhan Aruh* (77: 3) expands on the commandment of blessing the wine, since the wine symbolizes sanctity, and sharing its sipping symbolizes familial unity and fraternity. Jewish law mandates performative behavior that represents respect toward the sanctity of the Sabbath, when it is incumbent upon the head of the family, who intones the Kiddush, not only to stand as he holds the goblet, but also to look at the candles that represent his wife, who kindled and intoned the blessing over them. The breakdown of family values in the Shiloni home is not underscored by negligence in fulfilling the Kiddush commandment, but the opposite: by extreme adherence to fulfilling it despite the destructive forces at work in the relations between the family members, thus emphasizing the grotesque and ludicrous sham of observing a commandment that has been voided of its meaning.

In this context, Pnina plays the role of the killjoy, even during the Kiddush itself. She demonstratively violates and secularizes its sanctity by appearing in a nightgown and bathrobe, is deliberately noisy as she brings in and lays out the plates, and responds "Amen" dismissively following her husband's entreaties. And all this, broadly speaking, to protest against the cultural framework to which she belongs by virtue of her bad marriage, as is proven in her regression to her farmer's daughter virginity when she loses her mind at the play's end, as well as in order, in this scene, to condemn her husband's self-righteous, pretended piety. She derisively enlists a lexicon of epithets from the world of the stage: she defines Arieh's cantorial ability when he recites the Kiddush as "spectacle," "opera," and him as "a *comediant*," a mealy-mouthed Alazon and Buffon pretending to be religious when his past contradicts it (37). The irony in this attack lies in the fact that Pnina, the dramatic persona captive in the reality of her fictional world, is unaware, unlike the implied spectators, that the humiliating performative metaphors—characteristic of Judaism's hostile attitude toward the theatre as "making a graven image or likeness" (Exodus 20.4), as clearly idolatrous art, and as deception and moral corruption—are spoken by an actress, and that this false art becomes a means of exposing the truth. In the face of Pnina's increasingly vicious barbs directed at his weaknesses—his questionable intelligence, his mediocrity as a professional, and his manhood, which Pnina does not hesitate to malign in the presence of their son—not only does Arieh incite Pnina's bestialization, but he, too, descends to her level and drags Yossi with him. The framework of the Kiddush, the festive repast, and the Sabbath songs become his weapons to attack Pnina. Yet turning the ceremony into a weapon of violence in a way that violates its very nature turns the very adherence to its continued existence, in a process of an uncontrolled tailspin, into an absurd caricature. It moreover becomes a nightmarish, expressionistic spectacle of sensory violence directed against the implied spectators to the point of "breaking," as the following excerpts will demonstrate:

ARIEH. (*Mutters [about Pnina's provocations]*) Bitch . . . (*Blesses the wine aloud in a traditional melody, trilling*) "Remember the Sabbath day, to keep it holy. Six days shalt thou labor, and do all thy work; but the seventh day is a Sabbath to the Lord thy God, in it thou shalt not do any manner of work, thou, nor thy son, nor thy daughter, nor thy manservant nor thy maidservant . . . (*During the Kiddush Pnina goes into the kitchen and returns with plates, glasses, silverware. Arieh is angered by the noise she is making, and emphasizes*:) nor thy cattle . . . nor the stranger that is within thy gates; for in six days the Lord made heaven and earth, the sea, and all that is in them, (*Pnina lays out the plates intentionally noisily, offers a plate to Yossi who is afraid to take it for fear of his father*) and rested on the seventh day. Wherefore the Lord blessed the Sabbath day and hallowed it. With your permission masters, rabbis and gentlemen, Blessed art thou, O Lord our God, who createst the fruit of the vine."

YOSSI. Amen.

ARIEH. (*To Pnina, who tries to take the wine goblet from him and take a sip from it*) Amen. 'Amen' I said. I said 'Amen'!

[. . .]

ARIEH. (*To himself*) God, where did I find this monstrosity?

PNINA. (*With bitter mockery*) Who found? You? Maybe I found you? Maybe I saved you? Maybe I fed you and dug potatoes out of the ice for you and picked lice and fleas from places on you that I'm ashamed to mention in front of the child? Those who wanted ate cabbage leaves because they were kosher. You had no problem eating the soup I made for you from non-kosher meat [. . .] What did you do there? Why did you cling to me? Who needed you, with your white hands, your stories, your stupid fairytales . . .

ARIEH. Cow . . .

PNINA. Cow? (*In a loud whisper*) At night you know very well what to ask for from the cow, right? I'd tell you a few more things, but I don't want the boy to hear . . .

ARIEH. Cow. When it was all over I should have sent you back to the village. "Every man with his own camp, every man with his own standard!" I made her into "a lady," "Frau Shiloni" . . . For who? For what? For a swineherd! It's a good thing my mother passed away before she could see the bargain I got. You saved me? Yourself! The war saved you, to this day you'd be sitting in a cowshed married to some peasant who'd be called up to the Reading of the Law and say the blessing over bread because he got mixed up . . . he thought it was potatoes. (*He laughs uproariously at his own joke, perspiring and flushed with anger*)

YOSSI. (*Laughing*) What?

ARIEH. (*Bangs on the table*) *Zemirot*! [Sabbath songs] (*Father and son sing, banging on the table*):

"This day is above all others,
For our Rock rested thereon,
Six days shalt thou labor
But the seventh day is a Sabbath to the Lord thy God,
In it thou shalt not do any manner of work,
For He did it all in six days,
This day is above all others
For our Rock rested thereon"

[. . .]

PNINA. [. . .] (*Spoiling for a fight*) [. . .] I know what you're going to say before you open your mouth, you're not at the union now, you zero. I won't buy any more Hasidic stories, you nobody! I'm not smart enough for you? You're top of my list, not number sixteen . . . (*A long oppressive silence. Pnina is enjoying herself*) So what? Do they know you as well, do they know what you're worth? Just wait, I'll show the whole world who you are, Deputy Head. Deputy-Head-of-the-Religious-Department. Deputy-Head-of-the-Synagogue-Collectors. Deputy-Head-of-the-Workers-Committee. Sham Deputy-Head-of-the-Charity-Fund-with-my-money, What a fake you are . . .

ARIEH. (*Lifts the laid table and slams it down*) Shut your mouth! (*Gets up and leaves the table slowly, before sitting down on the couch in the living room*)

PNINA. (*Hammers in a final nail*) You forgot Grace after Meals, you fake. (36–41)

The triumph of the "barbarous," "*Agraikos*," bestial, belligerent, right-wing Pnina, as a woman representing her counterparts in Israeli society, over the left-wing stalwart, the bleeding-heart, moralizing, Israeli "intellectual," is in her success in bringing the impostor Torah scholar, the Tartuffe who fraudulently stole her heart, down to her level of degradation. He descends to the level wherein he actively adopts, in his stage behavior, her vandalistic belligerence, and forgets the Grace After Meals, an omission that is not coincidental since this forgotten prayer contains an expression of gratitude to the wife, who prepared the meal.

The lethalness of the weapons that Arieh employs becomes increasingly grave. It begins with verbal abuse, leads up to a physical gesture of banging on the table during the Sabbath songs, in a manner reminiscent of drunkards' or neo-Nazis' behavior in a Bavarian beer-cellar, and culminates with the threat to overturn the table, of which it is written, "Whether at night or in the day, there is no Kiddush except at the place of the meal, as it is said, 'And you shall call the Sabbath a delight'" (Ganzfried 77: 3). From the perspective of the left-wing religious man who wrote this work three years after the upheaval that brought the militant Likud Party to power, Hasfari, through this titanic battle in the Shiloni home, realizes the process whereby Israeli society loses its soul, its humanist raison d'etre. At the end of the scene it is not by chance that the cyclical ceremony of welcoming the Sabbath by its sanctioning is replaced by the alternative ceremony in which the mother ritualistically reiterates to her son, "a million times" as he puts it (42), how his father chose morality and turning the other cheek over vengeance against the Gentiles. The new Israeli ethos invents for itself a new mythical narrative that is not rooted in the Book of Genesis or in the exodus from slavery to freedom. It originates in the weakness of the Holocaust that creates a mini-Holocaust in its image, as Yossi says to his mother at the second Kiddush ceremony in September 1972: "It's interesting [. . .] what it is that has managed to do to you what the Germans and the Poles and the Ukrainians couldn't" (60).

THE SECOND KIDDUSH

The second Kiddush is held in September 1972, five years after the previous ceremony that marked a point of no return in the Shiloni family's marital reconciliation. It takes place a year after Yossi's enlistment in the paratroopers in cahoots with his father, by forging his mother's signature on the consent form, against her refusal to allow her son to serve in a combat unit. This stratagem to circumvent Pnina's will leads to physical violence between Arieh and Pnina, which constitutes an escalation in their conflict, rendering the rift between them unbridgeable. And still, the warring couple continues to dwell, like Israel's torn society, in absolute mutual muteness under the same roof. The connection between the family rupture and the ideological crisis in Israeli society is once again represented by a radio broadcast of an interview with Pinchas Sapir, a leader of the ruling Labor Party. Sapir views Israel's presence in Judea and Samaria as an act of occupation, not liberation, and objects to the use of mystical concepts in the debate over the Occupied Territories. In an attempt to disengage from the legacy of the Holocaust and its implications for the present—a denial that paradoxically serves only to hone attention to the militant and inhumane implications of this past for Israeli reality—Sapir says, "If we believed in mysticism we would not have come to Eretz Israel; we would have remained there and we would have been annihilated together with all those who did believe in mysticism" (59). In other words, the moderate majority, which Sapir represents, repudiates the mystical messianic eschatology of the radical right, as exemplified by Pnina, but at the same time acknowledges the necessity of a military option as a response to the weakness manifested during the Holocaust. And nurturing this option, as opposed to acting toward achieving peace, by way of self-contradiction reinforces the mystics.

These signs of self-entrapment and socio-political eclipse are translated into metaphorical dramatic-theatrical terms in the characteristics of the scene. Yossi, in paratrooper's uniform, comes to the mother's home to conduct the Kiddush in her husband's place, and in so doing violates both the Zionist ethos—he absconds from his army base—and the Jewish ethos—he desecrates the Sabbath by driving on the sacred day. In other words, the very intention of conducting the Kiddush is performed by means that void it in and of itself.[5] Being a combat soldier, he brings his weapon with him, the reincarnation of that charged symbolic accessory imbued from the play's outset with the connotation of immorality and estrangement from Judaism's humanistic values of tolerance. In other words, the ideological violation of the Israeli ethos gradually invades the home itself, together with all the other symbols of militarism and secularity, and reverses the meaning of the Kiddush.

Furthermore, against the cumulative backdrop of rising violence in the home, Yossi's weapon obtains bi-polar functions: preserving the security of the state, and the need for a weapon to prevent further deterioration toward an act of deadly violence within the family, while the insinuated possibility of using the weapon as a means for moral suicide hovers, from the play's outset, in the background. This and more. The mother asks Yossi a question that acquires bitter dramatic irony in the eyes of the 1980s audience following the 1973 Yom Kippur War and Israel's embroilment in the Lebanese mire: "Will you be home for Yom Kippur?" Yossi answers: "If we're not put on alert. But I don't think we will. It's fairly quiet. A bit of tension is all" (60). The question and answer highlight the micro- and macrocosmic blindness of the dramatis personae and the society alike.

Moreover, the escalation in employing the Kiddush as a ritual that represents Jewish identity and culture in the service of the play's messages is also manifested in the manner in which the ceremony is performed. In the first Kiddush, the mimetic-realistic framework of the ceremony was preserved in meticulous detail, and even amplified. The effect was tragicomic, so that the intertwining of the *legomenon*, the discourse, and the *dromenon*, the dramatic action, together with the theatrical effects and the scenography in the second Kiddush, already entails a stylistic reversal. Tragicomic realism is replaced by a grotesque, nightmarish style, while still maintaining the realistic motivations. The latent shock effect that this device produces in the implied spectator is heightened by the wishes of the mother, who was earlier revealed as an avowed heretic, that the ceremony be conducted as prescribed by Jewish law. It is Yossi who makes a mockery of the ceremony when he chews gum as he holds the wine goblet and recites the Kiddush blessing. He rushes through it, repeatedly making mistakes in the canonical phrasing, and his mother corrects him. The cultural anomaly and deformation, from a traditional point of view, are patently obvious. The mother, an ignorant woman, non-Jewish in her peasant origins and lack of education, who is belligerent in her views, the mother who is gradually losing her mind, internalizes—as a kind of insane *dybbuk*—the role of the male, her absent husband, the apparently at least religious and well-educated head of the family. She thus undertakes a role that runs counter to her very gender and existential *raison d'etre*, just as her son does. *This is of course perfectly p.c., in line with updated feminist and current social policies, but collides head-on with conservative Jewish religion.* For the rather "traditional," let alone religious implied spectator, this situation seems like a totally grotesque and unbearably profane hodgepodge, which is affectively intolerable, of mixing genders, cultures, and ideologies. It moreover reflects, from the viewpoint of an audience that is conversant with Jewish tradition, a very distressing picture of the society in which it is the lunatic fringe that prophesies in the name of religion and leans on military strength that sets the tone. It is no coincidence then that the scene concludes with the mother's question: "Yossi, has this gun fired before?" (60) as a kind of insane subliminal mission with which the unbalanced Pnina charges her son, whereas only one scene earlier she objected to his going into the army.

THE THIRD KIDDUSH

The third Kiddush is conducted three years later, in 1975, at the height of the "earthquake" that shook Israeli society in the wake of the Yom Kippur War, shattering all the myths and truths on which it was founded. In the manner of its presentation, the play is transformed—in metaphorical correlation with society's state—from a grotesque to a theatre of the absurd piece that borders on a postmodern spectacle, for it constitutes the ritualization of a disintegrating anti-ceremony. The disengagement between Arieh and Pnina is final and absolute: in an appalling union of opposites, they continue living in the same small apartment, but in separate rooms and with no contact whatsoever between them, neither physical nor verbal. This is a deconstructive ceremony: instead of a family gathering and the organic flow of the ceremony, we are witness to anatomization, to the decomposition of the ritual, to the sanctification of divorce in unity. It is a ritual in which every stage is conducted separately by each of the partners, and each of them moves the chair in the dining corner in order that s/he has finished, in utter solitude, to perform a small part of the Kiddush ceremony that should have symbolized family unity. The movement of the chair has no meaning of its own; it is used only to notify the absent partner that a stage in the "operation" has been executed, and that the transition to the next link in the ceremony is possible. The fragmentation and anatomization of the ceremony of unity—breaking it down into its constituent parts, which transforms the collective rationale underlying it, voiding it of its meaning—underlines the absurdity of this Black Mass, and not only according to Eugéne Ionesco's definition of this term: "Absurd is that which is devoid of purpose. [. . .] Cut off from his religious, metaphysical, and transcendental roots, man is lost; all his actions become senseless, absurd, useless" (qtd. in Esslin 5). The absurd in this Kiddush is manifested in Pnina and Arieh's utterly desperate and insane attempt to observe the meticulous order of the ceremony in this anti-ceremony. Pnina, the Gentile in a bathrobe from the first Kiddush, now even wears an orthodox headcovering. However, even this parsimonious observance of the *Shulhan Aruh* merely serves to accentuate the baselessness and worthlessness of this ritual.

CONCLUSION: THE FINAL KIDDUSH

As an ironic counterpoint to the increasingly intense peace process in external reality, and as closing the circle that began with Arieh's attempt to hold the Kiddush ceremony despite the family rift, the final Kiddush is typified by the ultimate destruction of the ceremony and moral suicide. Arieh remains alone after his son emigrates, and it is he who refuses to have any contact with Yossi in recording audio letters that will never be sent. In the meantime, his wife has completely withdrawn and reverted to her original peasant-bred non-Jewish identity. She finally shatters the illusion of the home as a metaphor of family unity as she walks through the marked walls on her way to a hospital for the mentally ill. Following that, Arieh switches off the electric lights and the radio, but also extinguishes the Sabbath candles as if drawing a parallel of equal postmodern meaninglessness between the sacred and secular. He then addresses the absent members of his family, pours wine into his glass, recites the Kiddush blessing, and, when he gets to "With your permission masters, rabbis and gentlemen," (69) he stops short and pours the wine onto the empty table.

If the wine is the essence, the epitome of sanctity, then this purely self-referential theatrical act annihilates sanctity as well as its representation. Thus, Arieh's symbolic act on the stage evokes the intertextual and disintegrative references to other aspects of collective consciousness. One of them is the mother, whose appearance and speech characterize her as a kind of self-contradicting, insane pastiche. On the one hand, she is the incarnation of a religious Jewish mother as victim, and on the other, a Polish peasant, i.e., belonging to the population of torturers and sacrificers. As such, she is a visual human image that enunciates and epitomizes the apocalyptic chaos in which Israeli society exists. At the same time, this tragic unraveling also concludes the triple journey that Hasfari conducts throughout the play by means of the recurring and diminishing format of the Kiddush, through stages in the breakdown of the Shiloni family and the decline of Israeli society. These stages are at the same time gradual stylistic transitions from a satirical comedy into a tragedy, and stations on the continuum of artistic movements in modern art from realism to the grotesque, to surrealism and expressionism, and from the external reality to the inner distorted psyche of society.

However, it seems that the uniqueness of the final Kiddush is not primarily anchored in its immanent semiotic meaning, but rather in its modus operandi as a rhetorical stimulus that is intended to provoke the implied audience and turn the theatrical event into immediate evidence, here and now, of the hypocrisy and corruption of Israeli society. This is because it is not the painful motivations, thematic meanings, and social repercussions of spilling the wine—as well as the previous defamiliarizations and violations of the Kiddush ceremony—that are the topmost priority for the Israeli implied audience, but rather the purely formalistic, external aspect of violating the ceremony. In other words, the representational and distorted protagonists, Arieh and Pnina, are the unmistakable agents of this audience. And it is precisely the innate performative, "false," "pretended," "identifying," and non-instrumental nature of the performed play that thus transforms it—by driving the implied spectator to incriminate him/herself—into final proof of society's loss of identity and collective cohesion, a cohesion that should have been embodied by this implied audience and in the religious ceremony in its original, purist meaning.

Regarding the play from a more universal perspective, I might conclude that my analysis has demonstrated how macrocosmic and perverse social dynamics, sustained by opportunist religious belief, generate structurally and affectively correlative aesthetics, microcosmically devised to refute these dynamics from within.

NOTES

1. A version of this chapter originally appeared in *Motar: Journal of the Yolanda & David Katz Faculty of Arts, Tel Aviv University*. Ed. Gil Fishhof. Issue no. 16–17 (2010): 61–68.
2. The *Shulhan Aruh*—which in Hebrew means "*Set Table*"—is a practical codex of the "Oral Torah," the Jewish law, composed by Rabbi Joseph Caro in the sixteenth century.
3. The concept denotes "the processed image and acting role of the performance's addressees, as emerging from the rhetorical system of the theatrical text" (Kaynar 63).
4. All translations from Shmuel Hasfari's play, *Kiddush*, are my own.
5. Yossi himself makes a mockery of the religious act when he justifies his actions by distorting the precept whereby "saving a life takes precedence over

the Sabbath" turns into "saving a mother takes precedence over the Sabbath" (*Kiddush* 60).

WORKS CITED

Bakhtin, Mikhail Mikhailovich. *Forms of Time and of the Chronotope in the Novel.* Trans. Dina Markon. Tel Aviv: Kinneret-Zmora-Bitan, Dvir and Ben-Gurion U of the Negev, 2007. Print. [My English translation]

Barzel, Hillel. *Drama shel Matzavim Kitzoni'im: Milchama VeShalom.* Tel Aviv: Sifriat Hapoalim, 1995. Print.

Ben-Maimon, Moses (Maimonides). *Mishne Torah: Hilchot Shabbat.* New York: Am Chai, 1947. Print. [My translation]

Esslin, Martin. *The Theatre of the Absurd.* Rev. ed. New York: Anchor, 1969. Print.

Ganzfried, Solomon. *Kitzur Shulhan Aruh: A Compilation of Jewish Laws and Costumes.* Trans. Hyman E. Goldin. New York: Hebrew U, 1961. Print.

Haggada. Jerusalem: Israel Museum and Koren, 2006. Print.

Hasfari, Shmuel. *Hametz.* Tel Aviv: Or-Am, 2002. Print.

———. *Kiddush.* Tel Aviv: Or-Am, 1990. Print.

———. *Shiveah.* Tel Aviv: Or-Am, 2002. Print.

The Holy Scriptures of the Old Testament. London: British and Foreign Bible Society, 1965. Print.

Kaynar, Gad. "The Actor as Performer of the Implied Spectator's Role." *Theatre Research International* 22.1 (1997): 49–62. Print.

Levinas, Emmanuel. *Difficile Liberté—Essais sur le judaisme.* Paris: Editions Albin Michel, 1963 and 1976. Print. [My translation]

11 Return to Tradition

The Symbolist Legacy to the Present-Day Arts

Daniel Gerould

> For us everything has become cramped, stifling, unbearable. We are weary of conventional forms of society, conventional forms of morality, the very means of perception, everything that comes from outside. It is becoming clearer and clearer that if what we see is all that there is in the world, then there is nothing worth living for. We embrace all religions, all mystical doctrines rather than exist in this reality.
>
> —*Valerii Briusov* (172)

The present-day return to the spiritual in art, characteristic of both the visual and performing arts in the first decade of the twenty-first century, is part of a recurrent pattern, a periodic need to go back to eternal sources and re-establish contact with the deepest well-springs of human creativity in the sacred, however that may be defined. Prior to the present moment, the most significant manifestation of this phenomenon in modern times was the prominence of place given to the occult in the symbolist movement of *fin-de-siècle* Europe circa 1900. It is this legacy that I wish to examine in order to locate the origins of our new spirituality in the perennial rediscovery of older, hidden traditions. I intend to deal only with the broad ideas, omitting the tangled anecdotal history of the sectarian conflicts within and among the different groups of occultists.

Reacting hostilely to a smug, materialistic world, celebrated as *la belle époque*, which was obsessed by modernity and progress and prided itself on being technologically advanced, the French symbolists, at the threshold of modernism, shunned the surface here-and-now and sought reconnections with "lost" pasts rich in associations, analogies, and resonances.

Whereas co-existing positivistic naturalism embraced the contemporary world in all its specificity and unquestioningly accepted the premises of its reality, symbolism—as the first manifestation of modernism that challenged modernity—can be called an archaic avant-garde seeking legitimacy not in progress but in pre-history. Despite its apparently anti-modern stance, symbolism was a pivotal moment in the evolution of modernism because it undermined the whole edifice of a logical, explicable world of matter through which it discerned the lineaments of a higher order of the spirit. The seemingly solid façade of the nineteenth century was all illusion; reality lay beyond and below. Recognizing the illusory nature of the material world, the symbolists embarked on a journey back to the spirit.

Unlike subsequent bellicose and iconoclastic avant-gardes such as futurism or dada, which declared war on all that had gone before, symbolism—more contemplative and ecumenical—sought not a rejection of the past, but reclamation of large bodies of secret knowledge and reconciliation of older, forgotten wisdom with the latest perceptions and insights. As the archaeologist Heinrich Schliemann had recently made expeditions to Asia Minor in search of Troy, so the symbolists undertook mental journeys to unearth the deepest sources of divine wisdom in archaic Greek art and culture. However, rather than confining themselves to the narrow, rationalized neo-classical version of the Greek heritage upon which the official culture of the French state was founded, they found in the Dionysian mysteries analogues to Hindu, Egyptian, and Biblical mythologies. They looked back to a primordial fountainhead of transnational wisdom in the sacred books of the past at the same time that they looked within to create a new system of personal belief. The theurgic idea of art as benevolent magic was predicated on the ancient wisdom of old cultures with a common source in sacred rites of ancient and archaic Greece (see Berdyaev). The brilliant Russian director-playwright-theorist Nikolai Evreinov did ethnographic research on the origins of tragedy in goat-songs, traveling to sites in Asia Minor.

What is modern about the symbolist vision is not mimetic representation of the contemporary world, but its supersensible perceptions of a higher spiritual reality, apprehension of underlying patterns beneath the surface. In the case of Vassily Kandinsky (author of "The Spiritual in Art" and the abstract drama *The Yellow Sound* in 1911) and Piet Mondrian, this desire to portray spiritual realities eventually led to abstraction, and, in the case of Alexander Scriabin, to multimedia spectacle.

THE THEURGIC IDEA

The symbolists sought to re-establish continuities with both past and future through a synthesis of world religions that were imbued with non-denominational mysticism joining Eastern and Western traditions of belief. Pan was a reigning deity in *fin-de-siècle* art and literature. Earth-, sky-, and ocean-centered, symbolism viewed humankind as an element in a natural landscape, subject to the diurnal and seasonal cycles; sun, moon, and planets provided perspective. Thus, on the one hand, the symbolist vision was cosmic rather than social and collective. On the other hand, it was deeply subjective, located in the inner recesses of the psyche. And the two—macrocosm and microcosm—mirrored one another. The deep structure of the human mind corresponds to the deep structure of the universe.

Yet interiority was the point of departure and of return. Instead of dramatizing *faits divers*, usually stories of crimes of passion culled from newspapers, as was the practice of Zola and his followers, the artist looks within for what is essential, timeless, unchanging. Symbolists insisted on the primacy of spiritual realities, which, experienced subjectively, lead to the release of the creative powers of the imagination. The private could become public and effect social change only following inner transformation.

The symbolist legacy rests upon a powerful belief in the transformative power of art, and especially theatre, not as social action, but as spiritual enlightenment. The sacred is a human reality revealed by the prophets rather than an otherworldly revelation coming from a god outside humankind. The sole subject of art is "our veritable ego *[notre moi véritable]*, our first born: immemorial, illimitable, universal, and probably immortal" (Maeterlinck, *Buried Temple* 304).

For *fin-de-siècle* symbolists Theosophy—divine wisdom—was the synthesis of science, religion, and philosophy that served as the basis of their understanding of art. Not a matter of faith, but an acquired knowledge of the magical psychic powers latent in man, Theosophy explored the theurgic idea of occult art, involving rites and incantations for controlling divine and beneficent spirits. In 1888 Helena Blavatsky's *Secret Doctrine*, a work of comparative esotericism, set out the basic tenets of Theosophy, an alternative to materialism, rationalism, and positivism designed to resolve tensions between science and religion.

In 1901 Annie Besant and Charles Leadbeater's *Thought-Forms* discussed the power of thought to mold astral entities and expounded a theory of spiritual ideograms, mystical power of forms, colors, sounds, and odors. First published in 1889 and constantly republished, Edouard Schuré's *The Great Initiates* set out the central lines of an esoteric doctrine stretching from Rama and Krishna to Plato and Jesus. Beneath the diversity of rites, myths, and religions, there is a common doctrine of the mysteries.

A NEW MYTHOLOGY

Reaching back to the Greeks, to early Christianity, to gnosticism and the heretical sects and apochryphal texts, the symbolists re-interpreted myths eclectically and subjectively and created new mythologies that were intensely personal, subjective, and mysterious. Two myths not the subjects of drama in classical times, Orpheus and Narcissus, came to the fore as master myths of symbolism. Orpheus, the embodiment of music and poetry, undergoes Dionysian sacrifice to achieve an Apollonian triumph of his art (see Illouz 102).

Mythologies were less valued for their narratives than for their imagery and atmosphere as bearers of ideas and images. Alive and contemporary, myths became an embodiment of wisdom and prophecy for the present age. They are bearers of secret meaning.

Symbolist myths are the incarnation of human dreams and anxieties beyond time and space. Symbolists were the first to experience myth as multi-cultural and transnational. Cut loose from neo-classical moorings, the myths were set free to voyage, on the high seas; for the first time myths were set free as archetypal models. The mythic heroes were creators and receivers of poetry and the arts. They were voyagers, discoverers, and healers (see Cogeval 25).

RETURN TO ANCIENT TRAGEDY ON SACRED SITES

The mandate calling for a return to the sources of ancient tragedy led *fin-de-siècle* artists to envisage performances enacted on sacred sites. Following Nietzsche's speculations about the relations of audience to spectacle in *The Birth of Tragedy*, symbolist theorists and practitioners tried to recreate the spiritual dimensions of ancient tragedy. They designed, built, or imagined vast outdoor or intimate indoor theatres where their dramas could be enacted before audiences of initiates.

It was at this time that modern ideas of active audiences and collective creation first took shape. Symbolist theorists thought hard about how to achieve the participation of spectators. Turning to ancient sources of art and spiritual culture, the poet and playwright Vyacheslov Ivanov preached communality in the arts (*sobornost'*), hoping to bring about a universal brotherhood of spectators, actors, dancers, and choruses in a common ecstasy. "We have had enough of role-playing; we want a rite. The spectator must become an actor, a coparticipant in the rite. The crowd of viewers must merge into a choral body similar to the mystical community of ancient 'orgies' and 'mysteries,'" Ivanov maintained (Ivanov 104). Performances frequently took place in his fifth-floor St. Petersburg apartment, a corner rotunda called the Tower, where the symbolist artists and philosophers met regularly every Wednesday. Ivanov and his disciples sometimes arrayed themselves in ancient garb and re-enacted ancient ceremonies and rituals that were both Dionysian and Christian. Vsevolod Meyerhold, Alexander Blok, and Mikhail Kuzmin directed performances of plays involving choral singing and group dancing. After 1919 Ivanov favored choric actions, popular festivals, and outdoor performances of heroic legends.

Adopting Ivanov's notion of a Theatre-Temple, the Polish poet and playwright Tadeusz Miciński (a frequent visitor to the Tower), called for the creation of a universal temple of beauty in the Tatras Mountains, which he associated with the Himalayas and the origins of ancient Indian religions, "where in an amphitheatre of the dead and living, carved in the mountains, under the azure sky and among the deep forests, there will be revealed the mysteries of life on earth," and where Sanskrit dramas such as *Shakuntala* could be performed (Miciński, "Teatr-Świątynia" 435, 197). Panslavist, historiographer seeking the roots of Western civilization in India, and translator of the great thirteenth-century Persian mystic poet Jalal-Al-Din Maulavi Rumi, Miciński envisages theatre, at once primeval and social, that would unite East and West, reconcile Catholicism, Orthodox faith, and Hinduism, and bring Poland and Russia together on the basis of gnosticism and esoteric philosophy (Gerould, "The Magus" 58–59). In his 1905 essay "The Theatre-Temple," arguing for a theatre that purifies the soul, Miciński writes, "If we look at the Persian *ta'zie*, which mourns the death of the prophet Ali, or at the medieval mystery plays with Adam and Eve, Satan, the Apostles and Christ's Passion—everywhere at the sources of drama we find the sphinx of Religion" (Miciński, "The Theatre-Temple" 67).

Place is invested with special import. A pioneering site-specific performance took place in 1911 when Georgette Leblanc staged two performances of Maurice Maerlinck's translation of *Macbeth* in his castle in Normandy at the fourteenth-century Abbey of Saint-Wandrille bordered by a forest. For Maeterlinck *Macbeth* was Shakespeare's most profound occult work. The audience of fifty spectators moved about the grounds following the action from Macbeth's arrival on horseback at the gates to the terrifying events inside the castle (see Maeterlinck, *Maeterlinck Reader* 3).

The poet-playwright-painter Wyspiański envisaged a stage "on the sacred national soil" by the Royal Castle of Wawel in Cracow overlooking the Vistula, and at the same time dreamed of an enormous theatre under the open sky in the Tatras Mountains, with the lofty peaks serving as the wings and the deep blue waters of a small lake suggesting the auditorium. He conceived of his *Acropolis* as being played within the Royal Castle Wavel in Cracow; all the characters in the play are animated art works found in the castle (from the Bible or Homer) who have stepped out of their tapestries or off their pedestals (see Terlecki 60–61 and Kopszak and Szczerski 31–32).

SYMBOLIST COLLABORATIONS AND MULTIPLE VOCATIONS

Taking the unity of the arts as one of their cardinal beliefs, the symbolists totally rejected Dumas fils's "well-made" conception of playwriting as a special craft separate from other intellectual and artistic endeavors, and of the playwright as a technician skilled at manipulating stage effects who need have no broader or deeper concerns. Rather in their view theatre exists in relation to the other arts; at its highest points it represents a synthesis of the arts. The symbolists sought to bring about such a fusion of the arts by pursuing dual or multiple vocations and by collaborating with other artists.

The Lithuanian Mikalojus Ciurlionis, a musician who became a visionary painter, was able to devise a new pictorial language to express a religion of the cosmos by applying musical compositional forms and principles to painting. He developed his own cosmology. He translated his musical creative impulses into colors and shapes using the analogy of the seven colors of the solar spectrum and the seven tones of the chromatic scale. Inspired by neo-Platonic aspiration toward a higher existence, and endowed with cosmic memory, he transcends his own time and place, moving to a universality of the spirit. His perspective was that of the mind contemplating the whole universe. Moving toward the abstraction of spheres and circles, he composed visual sonatas portraying fantastic "infinite" landscapes imbued with mysticism in different movements about the sun, different planets, and signs of zodiac. The natural is supernatural. Admired by Ivanov and the World of Art (*Mir Iskusstva*) circle, Ciurlionis in a letter to his fiancée declared, "I should like to create a symphony out of the sound of the waves, the mysterious language of a hundred-year-old forest, the twinkling of the stars, out of our songs and my boundless yearning" (Gerould and Kosicka 15).

The symbolists saw theatre as a collaboration among artists, and in keeping with their belief in the unity of the arts, sought out like-minded artists in other media. No era was richer in collaborative alliances that established outstanding partnerships.

Poets worked with dancers, as in the case of William Butler Yeats and Michio Ito, a modern dancer who knew almost nothing about Noh, had had eclectic training, and was open to experiment (making him a perfect collaborator for Yeats). It was Yeats who brought the knowledge of Noh, which he had acquired from Ezra Pound. Ito came to study and appreciate Noh, and eventually brought the new form he had created with Yeats back to Japan in a Japanese translation of *The Hawk's Well* (see Fleischer 149–213).

For Yeats, the function of art was to invoke spiritual realities. Dedicated to séance going, Yeats considered spiritualism a modern religion and visited many mediums in the hope of contacting the dead, who he felt were always near. Believing in the power of mediumship (with its stars, special effects, farewell performances) to make superb theatre, Yeats collected information received from the dead. He invoked the doctrine of a world soul or Anima Mundi, from which creativity derived. This world soul, joined to the Great Memory, explains the symbolist exaltation of the playwright as a creator attuned to the collective unconscious.

The interdisciplinary collaboration between the Belgian painter Jean Delville and the Russian musician Alexander Scriabin was another milestone in the symbolist attempt to forge a new language drawing upon the various arts.

SCRIABIN'S MYSTERIUM

Beginning in 1902 Scriabin conceived of a ritual, with antiphonal dialogue of narrator and chorus that would enact a terrestrial and cosmic transformation, uniting feminine and masculine principles and transcending the "I" and "Non-I". Spectators would be votaries performing dances and assisting in the Dionysian rituals leading to the final cosmic apocalypse, which would be a world conflagration of matter, time, and space. A multimedia of sound, sight, smell, feel, dance, and décor, Scriabin's eschatological mysterium is a great cataclysmic work ushering in the end of the world, synthesizing all the arts and moving beyond the limits of the separate arts and of art in general.

For Scriabin, the theatre was essentially antireligious, and therefore sinful, because it substitutes for the truth a masque of multiple reincarnations and supports the illusion of life, whereas Scriabin rejects the concept of masquerade. The role of the mysterium was to overthrow theatre and restore the integrity of self-unity. Scriabin rejected the decadent theatrical life of Paris, the cult of theatre in Moscow, and Meyerhold's theatre of Masks, lamenting that "Our entire society is being converted into a theatrical production. It tries to achieve a semblance of life in its artificiality. Our own lives begin to acquire a theatrical character because of inner division and outer dispersion. We become stage actors performing for ourselves, possessed by a passion for self-analysis" (Schloezer 188).

In Moscow Scriabin frequented Tairov's Kamerny Theatre, where he particularly liked Kalidasa's Sanskrit drama, *Shakuntala* (1914), performed musically and rhythmically as an opera-ballet full of pantomime and processions. With Alice Koonen, Tairov's wife and lead actress, Scriabin created gestural pieces set to music, which she danced.

On an extended visit to Brussels in 1908 Scriabin became involved with a circle of friends drawn together by their shared interest in Theosophy. With Jean Delville, a symbolist painter and author of a treatise, "The Mission of Art," the Russian composer dreamed of creating an all-encompassing work of art combining colors, shapes, and sounds.

For his projected mysterium Scriabin worked on creating a new language that was derived from Sanskrit roots, but included cries, interjections, exclamations, and sounds of breath being inhaled and exhaled to suggest the breathing of the cosmos. "The Church, the sole true Church, is the Cosmos," Miciński declared (Gerould and Kosicka 8). For a public showing of Delville's monumental painting, *Prometheus*, there were light projections corresponding to notes played by Scriabin (see Bowers 72–73, 92–100, 124–126, and Morrison 184–241).

For his symphonic *Prometheus, Poem of Fire*, Op. 60 (1909–1910), Scriabin called for a keyboard of lights, or color organ, which could project colors on a screen or into the audience. The color music was to be determined by the notes. Delville did the cover design for the score, but Scriabin's project was not realized until 1967 at a performance by the Rochester Philharmonic at which Alex Ushakoff (a film producer and designer of space simulation systems for astronauts) scattered colors throughout the auditorium. Prometheus's fires, colors, and lights are meta-symbols of man's highest thoughts.

FUTURE UTOPIAS: SYMBOLIST SCIENCE FICTION

Looking beyond and through the here and now, the temporal and immediate, symbolists take a long view of the present from a dual perspective of past and future. Considering revolution as an act of the spirit and social change achievable through transformation of the individual, they are drawn to apocalypse, metamorphoses of humanity, and visions of utopia and dystopia. Symbolists were among the pioneers in the creation of modern science fiction: Villiers in *The Future Eve*, Jarry in *Dr. Fausterolle*, Briusov in his plays *The Earth* and novella *Republic of the Southern Cross*, Sologub in his epic trilogy *The Created Legend* (which Meyerhold planned to film), and Miciński in his *Nietota: Secret Book of the Tatra Mountains* (1910) and *Father Faust* (1913). These works, informed by demiurgic consciousness, draw heavily on the Faust myth in their portrayal of imaginary societies in conflict making use of weird inventions to forge mystical weapons. Their work reflects the resurgence of the supernatural in high art. Inspired by Platonic idealism, they experimented with horror literature, the grotesque, and the fantastic, including the mass culture motif of the puppet-soul in robots, androids, and cyborgs. Maurice Maeterlinck initially conceived his essay, "The Tragical in Daily Life," as "A Theatre of the Android," because he wished to eliminate the human actor and replace living human beings on-stage by simulacra.

Curious about all aspects of art and culture and ambivalent about the advance of civilization, a symbolist like Villiers de l'Isle-Adam did not reject modern science and technology, but incorporated them within a larger vision and higher wisdom capable of effecting a unifying reconciliation of spirituality and science. He tests the facile belief in progress characteristic of late nineteenth-century positivism. In his *Cruel Tales*, Villiers shows that the new technologies of advertising and mass marketing, when applied to the arts, will create a virtual world of fraud and sham, peopled by simulacra. But Villiers writes as a visionary thinker—in the company of mystics like Swedenborg, Blake, and Goethe—who are able to think in a spiritual arena where the religious and the scientific imagination can meet. In *The Future Eve*, Edison, who as the wizard of Menlo Park is a modern mythic hero of electricity, gradually assumes the lineaments of Prometheus, the bearer of light to humankind. Villiers is able to reveal old mythologies as antecedents of new (see Gerould, "Villiers" 391–398). The symbolists saw science not as superseding previous knowledge, but as part of an ongoing human quest for wisdom, a link in the chain of secret knowledge.

THE FADING OF SYMBOLISM

Although it enjoyed an enduring afterlife in poetry in a number of countries, the fortunes of symbolism on stage fell to a low point in the 1920s, 1930s,

1940s, and 1950s when a socially engaged, politicized theatre dominated by ideology gained ascendancy as a result of changed social circumstances. World War I, the Russian Revolution, the Great Depression, the rise of totalitarian dictatorships throughout Europe, Fascism and Communism, World War II, and the Holocaust made the idea of a "theatre of the soul" seem an elitist aberration, and its obsession with death and the other world decadent and unseemly. Social activists self-righteously condemned the symbolists as reactionary (although they had in fact been predominantly socialist and anarchist in political leaning). After the revolution, Andrei Bely left the Soviet Union to become Rudolph Steiner's disciple in Zurich, Valerii Briusov and Alexander Blok tried to embrace Bolshevism and come to terms with the new regime, whereas Sologub, who stuck to his anti-authoritarian symbolist beliefs in unfettered human creativity, was branded a formalist out of touch with Soviet reality and denied permission to emigrate.

For the next several post-1914 generations a "theatre of the soul" under the banner of transcendent spirituality could not help but appear a narcissistic and self-indulgent escape into vague private mythologies and somnambulistic introspection. The revival of ancient mystery cults with obscure rituals seemed a flagrant evasion of responsibility and a refusal to confront real issues in the real world.

REINSTATEMENT OF SYMBOLIST AESTHETIC

Symbolism was rediscovered and popularized in the 1970s, in large part because of major revisionism in the art-historical appraisal of the *fin-de-siècle* painters such as Gustave Moreau, Odilon Redon, Ferdinand Khnopff, and Jean Deville, who had always been regarded as of questionable taste and artistry when compared to impressionists like Renoir, Monet, Manet, and Lautrec, whose work set the standards for modernism in art.

Revisionism with respect to symbolist theatre was slower in coming, no doubt because the terrain was virtually unknown to the general public and the material was far less accessible. My Performing Arts Journal anthology of 1985, *Doubles, Demons, and Dreamers*—reprinted as *Symbolist Drama*, a simpler, but less evocative title—was an attempt to make available the amazing range of *fin-de-siècle* playwriting in the symbolist mode.

By the 1960s the impact of Artaud (an avowed admirer of Maeterlinck) and the vogue of the absurd helped prepare the ground for the rediscovery of symbolist theatre. Beckett and Ionesco were inheritors not only of the dramatic techniques and devices of *The Intruder* and *The Blind*, but also of the grotesque vision animating Maeterlinck's work. Starting with Villiers and continuing with Maeterlinck, symbolists always had a profound awareness of the fraudulence and absurdity of so-called "real life."

Transmission of symbolist concepts of a mythopoetic theatre took place in the second half of the twentieth century through the work of directors and creators like Grotowski and Kantor. Even earlier, the revival of poetic drama caused a re-awakening of interest in mythopoesis. A proponent of symbolist poetry, T. S. Eliot returned to myth in his plays *The Family Reunion* (Orestes) and *The Cocktail Party* (Alcestis) and showed how this could be done within the confines of literary drama and drawing room settings.

Two major forces for a return to the spiritual in modern theatre are Kantor and Grotowski, Polish artists whose idiosyncratic journeys back to their pasts have become paradigms for the future. Whereas Kantor pointed to his artistic predecessors and made contact with his family and local ancestors, Grotowski wished to find a common ground with distant progenitors, stretching back to Greeks, to early Christianity, to Gnosticism, and ultimately to archaic societies and their practices.

KANTOR

A prime lesson that Kantor learned from the symbolists was the importance of placing theatre within the realm of the totality of art. Although Kantor displayed verve and acumen in connecting his theatre to almost all the major avant-garde movements and artists of the early twentieth century, it is significant that his first work for the theatre was by Maeterlinck. Kantor started his theatrical career with a production of *The Death of Tintagiles*, a drama rendering palpable the invisible presence of death.

Kantor shared the symbolist obsession with first and last things, for entrances and exits, for genesis and eschatology. He regarded the stage as a vestibule between the worlds of the living and the dead where the departed could reappear not as ghosts, but as living beings. He created new myths out of old and old out of new. The returning soldier on his spiritual journey in *The Return of Odysseus* of Wyspiański haunted his work. A "painter of the soul," Kantor is a bridge from one age to another, from the *fin-de-siècle* circa 1900 to the turn-of-the-century circa 2000. His theatre is built on establishing contact with the other world and bringing the dead on stage as living presences.

Kantor, as master of ceremonies at a dramatic séance, creates a theatre of death where the stage is the antechamber between this world and the world beyond. Only the past exists, and it is irretrievable, but scraps and fragments of a lost past can momentarily be summoned forth by what Kantor calls "negatives of memory." The artist's discovery that life is best expressed by its absence, by vacancy, by sham, came about accidentally, as have all his most important "finds" (see Kłossowicz 67).

While vacationing on the Baltic in 1972, Kantor chanced upon an empty one-room village school house. Flattening his nose against the dirty pane of one of the windows, he peered into the past. Memory activated, time set spiraling backward, the theatre of death was born in that illusory return to the lost homeland of childhood. Looking through the window frame at the nonexistent world of the past, the artist saw himself as a six-year-old sitting on the bench. Only in memory can we detect the faded lines of our genealogy and save our most personal histories from forgetting and annihilation. Bits of old roles, scraps of past events are momentarily called up from nonexistence before falling back again into nothingness. On wooden benches, which he made himself, Kantor placed on stage thirteen old men and women, with their own childhood, in the form of manikins, attached to their sides and backs as emblems of mortality.

For Kantor the stage is a "poor room of the imagination," a place of community between the living and the dead—out of time and out of space—where a profane sacrum is celebrated each evening. "But isn't profanation the best way and perhaps the only way of making a ritual live?" Kantor asks (Gerould, "Iconographic" 324). "I maintain," Kantor asserts, "that the theatre is a fording place on a river, a plane across which dead characters from the other shore, from the other world, cross into our world, now, into our life. And what happens then? I can give you the answer: the Dybbuk, the spirit of the dead, who enters into the body of another person and speaks through him" (Pleśniarowicz 221).

GROTOWSKI

From his youth profoundly interested in esoteric spiritual literature and magic, Grotowski—adopting the religious formulation of his model, Juliusz Osterwa, the creator of the Polish ensemble Reduta—considered theatre to be a holy communion. Throughout his career Grotowski was engaged in a visionary quest for spiritual purification. Personal transformation was the goal of the theatrical event. The actor seeks spiritual liberation through exacting discipline in the holy act of psycho-physical performance before the spectator. Grotowski referred to the theatre in religious terms as a place where sacrifice leads to redemption and sanctity. Theatre, he argued, should return to the forms of ritual from which it arose. Then the actor becomes a celebrant in a secular mystery, acting for a community of spectators who take part in the ritual and join in the collective creation.

Grotowski approaches sacred theatre through myth and archetype in a profane ritual, a modern and ironic confrontation with mythopoesis that must be tested through blasphemy and sacrilege; in an age of disbelief only infernal mockery can rekindle sparks of feeling for the divine. In *Apocalypsis cum figuris* (1969), which combines passages from the Bible, liturgical chants, and texts by Dostoevsky, T. S. Eliot, and Simone Weil, the Christian myth of salvation achieved through Christ's sacrifice is put to the test of blasphemy and profanation, and the myth of the hero's spiritual transformation is radically restructured.

In his paratheatrical work between 1969 and 1975 Grotowski did away with the theatre building, the actor, and the spectator in favor of direct participation of one human being with other human beings in outdoor settings in forests and mountains, in events sometimes lasting days or even weeks, or in confined rooms for short periods, in order to reach the spiritual essence common to all men. Bringing together people of different nationalities, ages, professions, races, who met in different countries and settings, Grotowski strove to break down the barriers that prevent humankind from reaching what lies hidden in the soul.

Both the theatrical and the paratheatrical explorations conducted by Grotowski have been dedicated to the revelation of a secular mystery (the only kind possible in an age of disbelief), a ceremonial capable of making actor and spectator one, a communal and collective creation that will transform its participants and reorder their lives.

In the words of Ludwik Flaszen, Grotowski's longtime associate and literary advisor:

> Grotowski's performances wish to revive the utopia of those elementary experiences, supplied by the collective ritual, in whose ecstatic elation a community, as it were, dreamed a dream about its own essence, its place in total reality, not particularized into separate spheres, where Beauty was not different from Truth, emotions from intellect, spirit from body, joy from suffering; where man felt an affinity with the Totality of Being. (Burzyński and Osiński 59)

CONCLUSION

What the symbolists bequeathed to present-day theatre is a belief in the power of the creative imagination to transform first the individual, then society. They believed in the wholeness of experience, in the links between the exterior and interior, the microcosm and macrocosm, and in humankind's relation to the earth, thus anticipating present-day ecological concerns. Rejecting the official doctrines and dogmas of institutional religions and politics, the symbolists saw social change as effected through transformations of consciousness. The symbolist prepared the ground and cleared the field, making it possible for twenty-first century playwrights to range freely back and forth in time from ancient myths to science fiction projections into future times.

A version of this chapter originally appeared in *PAJ: A Journal of Performance and Art* 31.1 (2009): 80–90.

WORKS CITED

Berdyaev, N. A. *The Crisis of Art*. Trans. Fr. S. Jones. *Berdyaev Online Bibliotek Library*. N.p., n.d. Web. 30 June 2011.

Bowers, Faubion. *The New Scriabin*. New York: St. Martin's, 1973. Print.

Briusov, Valerii. "Ko Vsem, Kto ishchet, kak predislovie," *Sredi Stikhov, 1894–1924: Manifesty, Stat'i, Retsenzii*. Moskva: Sovetskii Pisatel', 1990. Print.

Burzyński, Tadeusz, and Zbigniew Osiński. *Grotowski's Laboratory*. Trans. Bolesław Taborski. Warsaw: Interpress, 1979. Print.

Cogeval, Guy. "Nostalgia for the Past: Myths." *Lost Paradise: Symbolist Europe*. Montreal: Montreal Museum of Fine Arts, 1995. Print.

Flaszen, Ludwik. "Po awangardzie." *Odra* 4: 59 (1967). Print.

Fleischer, Mary. *Embodied Texts: Symbolist Playwright-Dancer Collaborations*. Amsterdam: Rodopi, 2007. Print.

Gerould, Daniel. *Quick Change: Essays on Theatre*. New York: Martin E. Segal Theatre Center Publications, 324, 2011. Print.

———. "The Magus Tadeusz Miciński." *Theater* 7.1 (1975) 58–59. Print.

Gerould, Daniel, and Jadwiga Kosicka. "The Drama of the Unseen: Turn-of-the-Century Paradigms for Occult Drama." *Occult in Language and Literature*. Ed. Hermine B. Riffaterre New York: New York Literary Forum, 1980: 15. Print.

Illouz, Jean-Nicolas. *Le Symbolisme*. Paris: Livre de Poche, 2004. Print.

Ivanov, V. I. "Presentiments and Portents: The New Organic Era and the Theater of the Future." *Selected Essays*. Trans. Robert Bird. Ed. Michael Wachtel. Evanston: Northwestern UP, 2003: 104. Print.

Kopszak, Piotr, and Andrzej Szczerski. "The Young Poland Movement: Art, Nation, Modernity." *Symbolist Art in Poland*. Ed. Alison Smith. London: Tate, 2009. Print.

Kłossowicz, Jan. *Tadeusz Kantor: Teatr*. Warsaw: Państwowy Instytut Wydawniczy, 1991. Print.

Maeterlinck, Maurice. *Buried Temple*. Trans. Alfred Sutro. New York: Dodd, 1907. Print.

———. *A Maeterlinck Reader: Plays, Poems, Short Fiction, Aphorisms, and Essays*. Ed. and trans. David Willinger and Daniel Gerould. New York: Lang, 2011. Print.

Miciński, Tadeusz. "Teatr-Świątynia." *Myśl teatralna Młodej Polski*. Ed. Irena Sławińska and Stefan Kruk. Warsaw: Wydawnictwa Artystyczne i Filmowe, 1966, 435, 197. Print.

———. "The Theatre-Temple." Trans. Daniel Gerould and Jadwiga Kosicka. *Theater* 7.1 (1975), 67. Print.

Morrison, Simon. *Russian Opera and the Symbolist Movement*. Berkeley: U of California, 2002. Print.

Pleśniarowicz, Krzysztof. *Kantor: Artysta końca wieku*. Wrocław: Wydawnictwo Dolnośląskie, 1997. Print.

Schloezer, Boris de. *Scriabin: Artist and Mystic*. Trans. Nicolas Slonimsky. Berkeley: U of California, 1987. Print.

Terlecki, Tymon. "Stanisław Wyspiański and the Poetics of Symbolist Drama." *The Polish Review* 15.4 (1970), 60–1. Print.

12 Who Is Rama?

Richard Schechner

This writing is a prologue. The full account of Rama as a changing culture hero will be developed later. At the present moment, I can offer only an outline of a thesis. The Ramlila of Ramnagar—a thirty-one-day play enacted annually—is a unique performance, a complex interweave of theatre, religious devotion, and the embodiment of symbolic roles. Thousands of Ramlilas are performed across north India during the months of Bhadrapada and Ashvin (September/October). But the Ramlila of Ramnagar is the one regarded by Indians as the most realized, religiously and theatrically. Indeed, Ramlila is one of the world's great theatrical events.

The Ramlila enacts the life of Rama, Vishnu's seventh avatar, his wife, Sita, and his three brothers (all avatars). Called "*swarups*"—"the actual shape of"—pre-adolescent boys are inhabited by the gods while they perform. The Ramlila also features the Maharaja of Banaras, priests, chanters, hereditary and once-only actors, and a participating audience ranging from several hundred to more than fifty thousand on any given night. The Ramlila is theatre that exceeds theatre. It is embodied devotion, pilgrimage, and festival staged not in a theatre but "on location" over an area of many square kilometers dispersed in various specific environments constructed especially for Ramlila throughout Ramnagar. Many individual lilas (each daily performance is called a *lila*—and the word *lila* means "play") include the movement of performers, Maharaja, Ramayanis (chanters), technical staff, police, and large crowds from one location to another. This movement animates a real/symbolic terrain that maps India from Ayodhya in the north to the island of Lanka (Sri Lanka) off the southeast coast.

Ramlila operates within a cultural-religious-aesthetic system that supports simultaneous political action, religious devotion, and theatre-going. Ramlila is at present, and was during the years of its development in the nineteenth century, linked to notions of what constitutes "Ramraj" (the golden age when King Rama ruled; an epoch both before present human history, immanent in human history, and a promise for a future time in human history). Ramraj is an imagined perfect political system. This system haunts contemporary Indian politics. Understanding Ramlila can help us understand how India, ostensibly a secular nation, is also driven by believed-in religious performances. In Ramlila's case, it is a Hindu performance; but there are also, in India, strong Islamic performances such as the Ta'ziyeh of Shi'a Islam (an enactment of the martyrdom of Hussein, grandson of the Prophet). In fact, today's global situation demonstrates how deeply theatricality, religion, and politics are interlocked. Ramlila offers an excellent example of this process in action.

The many thousands who attend Ramlila comprise a representative cross-section of Hindi-speaking, mostly Hindu north Indians, from low-caste farmers to shopkeepers, professionals, high-caste brahmins, and *sadhus* (itinerant holy beggars devoted to "Sita-Ram," the conjoined deity of Rama and his wife Sita, incarnations of Vishnu and Lakshmi respectively).

Although Ramlila enacts a core Hindu myth, first told in Sanskrit in Valmiki's *Ramayana* (about fourth and fifth century BCE) and reconceptualized in pre-modern Hindi by Tulsidas in the sixteenth century), many Muslims work at Ramlila as image-makers, fireworks managers, and elephant drivers. And more than a few attend because of the sheer theatrical magnificence of the performance. People also come to the Ramlila because of its *mela*, a conglomeration of food stalls, goods for sale, games, and devotional *bhajan* singing in praise of Sita-Ram.

WHO IS THE MAHARAJA OF BENARAS?

There is an enormous gap between the popularly imagined ancient line of devout and heroic kings of Kashi-Banaras-Varanasi and the actual emergence of the ruling Narain Singh family, who are descended from a landlord-rent collector (*zamindar*) favored and employed by the British in their struggle for domination of the subcontinent in the eighteenth and nineteenth centuries. This colonial and then post-colonial social drama involves a complex triangular tension among Hindu Indians, Muslim Indians (later Pakistanis and Bangladeshis), and the British (first the colonizing power, later allied with the forces of globalization—which many of today's Indians have joined or wish to join).

As the nineteenth century proceeded, at one level the Narain Singh family needed to legitimize itself, to act royal in order to become royal. At another level, the family had to cede much of its recently acquired economic, political, and military power to the British. What was left to them (and other "royals" under British colonialism) were ceremonial duties and effects. Certainly, Ramlila became one of the grandest of these. During the reign of Ishwari Narain Singh (1835–1889)—a period of great upheaval and change in India, including the first major military challenge to British rule, what the British called the "Mutiny" of 1857 and the Indians call the "Rebellion"—the Ramnagar RL as we know it today took its shape.

During each of the thirty-one episodes, the "*samvads*," or 'dialogues' in modern Hindi assembled-written most probably in the 1860s to 1870s, were performed alongside the chanting of Tulsidas' Hindi *Ramcharitmanas*. The more modern Hindi *samvads* added a distinctly theatrical tone to the Ramnagar Ramlila, which had previously been mostly ritual spectacle reinforced by the chanting of the sacred *Manas* text. Also, during the nineteenth century, the presence of the Maharaja of Banaras became an expected and necessary component of the Ramlila.

In effect, the maharaja became the "sixth *swarup*," the moving Shiva, who people greet with the shout, "*Hara, Hara, Mahadev*!" ("Shiva, Shiva, great god!") as he passes to and from the Ramlila sites. But the Maharaja is not only the moving Shiva who validates Ramlila by attending it; he is also—or was, before the end of colonial rule in 1947—a king-of-this-world who selects, oversees the training, and pays the performers of Ramlila, including those who are gods. The formal abolition of the "princely states" with the advent of democratic secular India (on the official level) did not abrogate the royalty of the Maharaja of Banaras—the only Indian potentate to retain in the minds of his "subjects" (if one can call them that) a semblance of the old reality of "really being a king." As it turns out, the Maharaja is king because he ordinates the Ramlila; and the Ramlila of Ramnagar is unique because it is guided over by a king. The two systems—mythic and unreal from one perspective, actual and effective from another—support each other much as two playing cards leaning against one another form a perfect triangle with the ground they both rest on.

The complex layering of authorities and identities enacted in Ramlila is manifest most clearly in the final days of Ramlila and in the day after Ramlila is over. On the next-to-last day there occurs the Kot Vidai ("Farewell"), a scene unique to Ramnagar. At Kot Vidai, the Maharaja of Banaras receives Rama, Sita, and the other *swarups* at his Fort. The Maharaja greets them, touches their feet in worship and respect, feeds them, and presents each with a single silver rupee. They honor him with their visit; he worships them. But everyone knows that the Maharaja has selected the five boys who are the gods. So what is going on?

The Maharaja is playing multiple roles here, embodying as well as bridging secular-political, mythical-poetic, and devotional positions. He is a devout Hindu worshipper of Sita-Ram; he is king of Banaras welcoming the king of Ayodhya. But the next day, the Maharaja's "real" role is patent. He orders cannons fired to signal the end of Ramlila and the restoration of the status quo ante. Then the Maharaja summons the "boys," no longer *swarups* but subjects, and pays them each a token R500 for their "work" in Ramlila. This used to be a large amount of money—but no longer; yet the meaning of the payment is clear. The upside-down-world of Ramlila, when real kings bow down before boy-gods, is terminated in favor of the everyday reality of the other eleven months of the year, which usually begins in perfect weather. Perhaps the Maharaja after all is the agent of "Ramraj," the golden age of Rama's reign.

The emergence of the Ramlila—its development into a major pilgrimage site, ceremony, drama, and moving *durbar*—served both the Narain Singh family and the British colonial power. But what about after Independence?

GANDHI'S RAMA VERSUS BJP'S RAMA

Mahatma ("great soul") Gandhi constructed Rama as an "all-India perfect king/ruler." Like the sixteenth-century Banaras poet Kabir, Gandhi wanted to efface the differences that have caused so many bloody confrontations among Hindus, Muslims, Christians, Sikhs, Buddhists, etc. Gandhi wanted one India—but not Nehru's socialist-secular India. Gandhi's vision was infused with the notion of Ramraj, but figured in a different way than that offered to the people by the Narain Singh royal family. The King Rama that Gandhi summoned is the embodiment of a *dharmic* just, right-doing ruler. Obviously, in retrospect, one can see that Gandhi's project had to fail; perhaps we should not be surprised that in 1948 the Great Soul was gunned down by Nathuram Godse, a Hindu extremist. Gandhi's last words were, "Ram, Ram . . . "

During my most recent observation of and participation in Ramlila—2000, 2006—I have seen Rama worshipped not only in a devotional way, but also as the embodiment of Hindutva, a resurgent Hindu nationalism. Hindutva—India for the Hindus—is the guiding ideology of the Bharatiya Janata Party (BJP, holders of the majority in parliament until 2004). The BJP's published ideology as of 16 July 2011 states, in part:

> In the history of the world, the Hindu awakening of the late twentieth century will go down as one of the most monumental events in the history of the world. . . . The vibrancy of Hindu society was noticeable at all times in that despite such barbarism from the Islamic hordes of central Asia and Turkey, Hindus never played with the same rules that Muslims did. . . . The old foundation crumbled in the 1980s and 1990s when Hindus respectfully asked for the return of their most holy religious site, Ayodhya [the birthplace of Rama]. . . . a national hero, a legend whose fame and respect stretched out of the borders of India into southeast Asia, and even into Muslim Indonesia. A hero who existed before there was anyone in India who considered himself separate from Hindu society. . . . So long as freedom to Jews meant that symbols of the Holocaust in Europe were condemned, so long as freedom to African-Americans meant that the symbols of racial discrimination were wiped out, and so long as freedom from imperialism to all people meant that they would have control of their own destinities, that they

> would have their own heros, their own stories, and their own culture, then freedom to Hindus meant that they would have to condemn the Holocaust that Muslims reaped on them, the racial discrimination that the white man brought, and the economic imperialism that enriched Britain. Freedom for Hindus and Indians would have to mean that their heros such as Ram, Krishna, Sivaji, the Cholas, Sankaracharya, and Tulsidas would be respected, that their own stories such as the Ramayana and the Mahabharata would be offered to humanity as examples of the brilliance of Hindu and Indian thinking. . . . Hindus are at last free. They control their destiny now and there is no power that can control them except their own tolerant ethos. India in turn is finally free. Having ignored its history, it has now come face to face with a repressed conscience. The destruction of the structure at Ayodhya was the release of the history that Indians had not fully come to terms with. Thousands of years of anger and shame, so diligently bottled up by these same interests, was released when the first piece of the so-called Babri Masjid was torn down [in 1992]. It is a fundamental concept of Hindu Dharma that has won: righteousness. Truth won when Hindus, realizing that Truth could not be won through political or legal means, took the law into their own hands. (Bharatiya Janata Party)

It is this kind of energy that I felt in 1997, again in 2000, and continuing in 2006. Groups of boys and young men aggressively elbowed their way to get a better "*darshan*" ("view") of Rama. Fewer *sadhus* attended because, as one told me, "We now have our own real Ayodhya to defend."

This kind of Rama definitely was not Gandhi's Rama. In 1929 Gandhi said:

> By RAMARAJYA I do not mean Hindu Raj. I mean by Ramarajya Divine Raj, the Kingdom of God. For me Rama and Rahim are one and the same deity. I acknowledge no other God but the one God of truth and righteousness. Whether Rama of my imagination ever lived or not on this earth, the ancient ideal of Ramarajya is undoubtedly one of true democracy. . . . Even the dog is described by the poet to have received justice under Ramarajya. (305)

SOCIAL DRAMA AND AESTHETIC DRAMA

The relationship between social drama and aesthetic drama can be configured as an "infinity loop" (as first depicted in my "Selective Inattention"). This loop shows the dynamic positive feedback in which social dramas drive aesthetic dramas (Shakespeare's "mirror held up to nature") just as aesthetic dramas give meaningful shape to social dramas (Goffman's "the performances of everyday life," Turner's four-phase theory of "social drama"). Every social drama is imagined in terms of underlying aesthetic principles and specific theatrical-rhetorical techniques. Reciprocally, each culture's aesthetic theatre is performed in terms of the underlying processes of social interaction. To put this in terms of today's Ramnagar's Ramlila: Rama's story is acted out not only as a "lila" in the religious sense, but also as a drama comprehensible narratively in terms of crisis, response, climax, and resolution. Conversely, Rama's story is understood as the Hindu struggle for power and identity—not by all Indians, or even all Hindus for that matter, but by a significant number of Indian Hindus.

Instituted both as a devotional performance and as a means of authenticating and strengthening a relatively upstart royal line; used also to assert in the nineteenth century Hindu/Indian autonomy from the British: at that point Rama's army of monkeys and bears could not actually challenge the ruling colonial army, but those in attendance at Ramlila, following and identifying with Rama's brave, resourceful, and successful war against the ten-headed demon king Ravana, got the message. Ramlila was in those days one of the cultural weapons of what was to become a political revolutionary movement. Bharatendu Harishchandra, the composer of the *samvads*, the spoken dialogues of Ramlila, was a vehement Indian Hindu nationalist who insisted on a language separate from Mogul-inflected Urdu or colonially imposed English. Harishchandra's rallying cry was "Hindi, Hindu, Hindustan." Harishchandra's Rama is closer to the BJP's Rama than to Gandhi's. But for many people, Gandhiji's ideal lives: the month-long Ramlila is a time and place to set aside daily cares, including India's intense politics. This not to deny that what happens in the "real" Ayodhya several hundred miles from Ramnagar is felt in Ramnagar.

RAMLILA NOW AND INTO THE FUTURE

How this will play out under the rule of Anand Narain Singh, now just eleven years into his reign, remains to be seen. Vibhuti, his father, ruled for sixty-three years, from 1938 to 2001. Since the abolition of the Princely States with Indian Independence in 1947, there has not been a "real king" at all anywhere in India. But Vibhuti began his rule as a real king—if there can be such a thing under the aegis of colonialism—and ended his life as revered figure, beloved by thousands in and beyond Ramnagar and Varanasi-Banaras. Anand has no such cache to draw on; nor does he have anywhere the stage presence his father had an abundance of.

In 2006 and again in 2011 I asked people about Anand. The answers were guarded to negative. "He is always in Delhi." "There is trouble in the family." But during Ramlila, Anand sits in his *howdah* atop the royal elephant and plays the regal role required of him by the throngs of Varanasi who still regard the Raja of Kashi as the moving Shiva witnessing, honoring, and sustaining the story of their great hero god king Rama.

WORKS CITED

Bharatiya Janata Party. "Hindutva: The Great Nationalist Ideology." *Bharatiya Janata Party*. Bharatiya Janata Party, 9 Feb. 2009. Web. 15 July 2011.

Gandhi, Mohandas K. *Young India* 19 (19 Sept. 1929): 305. Print.

Schechner, Richard. "Selective Inattention." *Essays on Performance Theory*. New York: Drama Books Specialists, 1977. Print. Reprinted in all subsequent editions of *Performance Theory* published by Routledge.

Part III

Secularization and Its Discontents

13 Feeling Secular

Ann Pellegrini

This chapter continues a set of questions I have recently been pursuing regarding performances of belonging and exclusion, with a particular interest in how affect is transmitted and bound. Trauma is one such vehicle for transmission; so is religion via what I have come to call "queer structures of religious feeling." To ask into the religious is also to ask about the construction of the "secular." These categories are co-constitutive.[1] Thus, alongside my interest in religious feelings, and the subjects and worlds they make, I am also interested in "secular feelings" and the question, what does secularism feel like? As a first tentative answer let me pose the following: it feels a lot more like religion than we commonly suppose. In what follows, I offer a more detailed, albeit still provisional, analysis of the "queer" connections between horizons of experience that are generally posed as opposites, even as antagonists.

In the past decade, *affect* has emerged as a critical term across disciplinary and divisional divides. Within queer studies alone, affect has served as both object and method of analysis. Just a brief sampling of some key queer studies books published since 2000 includes: Chris Nealon's *Foundlings* (2000), Elizabeth Freeman's *The Wedding Complex* (2002), Eve Kosofsky Sedgwick's *Touching Feeling* (2003), Ann Cvetkovich's *Archive of Feelings* (2003), Sara Ahmed's *Cultural Politics of Emotions* (2005), Kathryn Bond Stockton's *Beautiful Bottom, Beautiful Shame* (2006), Heather Love's *Feeling Backwards* (2007), Dana Luciano's *Arranging Grief* (2007), Jasbir K. Puar's *Terrorist Assemblages* (2007), Lauren Berlant's *The Female Complaint* (2008), and José Muñoz's *Cruising Utopia* (2009). Looking beyond queer studies *per se*, we could add literary studies scholar Sianne Ngai's *Ugly Feelings* (2005), anthropologist Kathleen Stewart's *Ordinary Affects* (2007), media studies scholar Brian Massumi's influential *Parables for the Virtual* (2002), and some wonderful work by historians of American religion: notably, Marie Griffith's *God's Daughters: Evangelical Women and the Power of Submission* (first published in 1997, reprinted in 2000), John Corrigan's *Business of the Heart: Religion and Emotion in the Nineteenth Century* (2002), and Molly McGarry's *Ghosts of Futures Past: Spiritualism and the Cultural Politics of Nineteenth-Century America* (2008).

This list—as long as it is—scarcely exhausts the books, articles, and journal special issues in which "affect" serves as organizing keyword for investigation. What connections might we map between what sociologist Patricia Clough calls "the affective turn" and larger cultural currents? This is to ask not just why affect, but why affect *now*?

To be sure, this turn to affect is not so much new as renewed, or returned. Jasbir Puar and I jointly contributed a short keyword on "affect" to the hundredth issue of *Social Text*.[2] To contextualize the politics of affect and of affect studies for the readers of *Social Text* 100, we went back to issue 1 of the journal, to a 1979 article by Fredric Jameson on "Reification and Utopia in Mass Culture." In this essay we can already see Jameson outlining an argument that will culminate in his famous diagnosis, some five years later, concerning the waning of affect ("Postmodernism" 61), which he traced to "postmodernism, or the cultural logic of late capitalism" in an essay of that same name. The "waning of affect," he argued in that 1984 essay, does not deflate or eradicate expressive forms, but rather shifts their register from the realm of substantive feelings to fleeting "'intensities'" ("Postmodernism" 64). This shift is also, then, a loss of depth—in particular the depth that is the modernist subject. Later, and also in the pages of *Social Text*, Jameson spells out more clearly the transformation he has in mind: a move from "hermeneutic emotion"—anxiety was his paradigmatic example—to "what the French have started to call *intensities* of highs and lows." These intensities, he says, "really don't imply anything about the world, you can feel them on whatever occasion. They are no longer *cognitive*."[3]

As Puar and I outline, Jameson's own thinking about affect was itself part of a larger and longer conversation; for example, he draws on Raymond Williams's language of "'residual' and 'emergent' forms of cultural production" ("Postmodernism" 57). The "affective turn" as a whole (and think of this whole as a collective that is not one) draws across older formations of sentiment studies; theories of emotion; British cultural studies (via Williams); the work of Leibniz, Spinoza, Bergson, and Deleuze and Guattari, among others; and science and technology studies. Accordingly, what appears to be a "new" critical, conceptual lens that has gained significant intellectual and scholarly caché in the last decade is in fact indebted to multiple, and often contradictory, genealogical threads.

These contradictions have produced rich and fruitful debates over what affect "is" and/or "does" as well as exposed intellectual tensions about the relation and difference between affect and terms such as *emotion*, *feeling*, and *sensation* with which it is sometimes used interchangeably. Ultimately, Puar and I are less interested to delimit the boundaries of what affect is than we are compelled by the generative and productive multiplicity of its deployment as an analytic and political frame. (This may also represent our own polite compromise between psychoanalysis and affect.)

In light of this quick and dirty genealogy, let me reframe my initial question: why the return to affect now? One of the things I am tentatively wanting to venture is that some of the force behind the return to affect post-1979 is the anxiety that secularists, including and especially secular intellectuals in the U.S. academy (which has a distinctively liberal Protestant formation), had at the resurgence of religion post-1979. This anxiety formed in response not just to any religion, but to religion understood as "fundamentalist": 1979 is the date of the Iranian revolution, and also marks the emergence or re-emergence of a certain kind of U.S. Christian fundamentalism. Jerry Falwell names his "Moral Majority" as such in 1979.[4] As Janet R. Jakobsen has argued, within the traditional terms of the secularization narrative, which identifies secularism with modernity and asserts the privatization of religion as key to civil peace, the public presence of conservative Islam in Iran and conservative Christianity in the U.S. could only appear as dangerous anti-modern throwbacks (Jakobsen with Pellegrini, "Introduction" 11).

These twinned emergences have shaken the epistemological foundations of large segments of the U.S. academy for whom secularism has been and remains a kind of guiding sentiment. I do not want to overstate my case, and certainly not at so preliminary a stage of analysis; but, there is to me something intriguing in the way the religious politics of 1979 forward, and in so many quarters of the globe, betoken not just new forms (better, new alliances or assemblages) of/for social movement, but also new shifts in the culture of U.S. public feelings.

There are, of course, important caveats to offer. The secular anxieties I am tracking post-1979 do not everywhere take the same form; it might thus be desirable to speak of uneven developments around the religion question. Accordingly, this periodization would need to take into account important disciplinary differences and questions of field formation, such as who gets to ask about or study "religion"—and for what reasons, on what justifications? Certainly, I have been struck by the way queer studies, in its dominant Anglo-American mode, proceeds through a secular imaginary within which, religion, if it is to appear at all, must be made to appear as arch-conservative enemy of progress. In another place, Jakobsen has aptly summarized this position thus, with queer secular protagonists proclaiming: "'Of course they hate us. . . . They're religious'" (Jakobsen, "Can Homosexuals" 49). However, as Jakobsen goes on to note, this alignment of the queer with the secular and of sexual conservatism with the religious may actually reinforce the claims of the right to a monopoly on religion. Moreover, insofar as U.S. commonsense tends to conflate religion and morality, this alignment also cedes the language of values to the most conservative versions of religion (Jakobsen, "Can Homosexuals" 49–50).[5]

This "logic of reduction" (to use Jakobsen's terms) has had unfortunate political effects, obscuring possibilities for other kinds of alignments—between religious progressives and movements for sexual justice, for example. It has also, I would argue, had a distorting effect on the formation of queer studies as a field and has long impeded feminist studies as well.[6] Seeing religion as enemy (a seeing that is also a kind of structured un-seeing) produces a "white" genealogy of both queer and feminist studies by, among other things, leaving to the side the women of color and transnational feminisms whose relationships to religion have historically been far more complex and variegated. This is not the same thing as unambivalent.

In *Terrorist Assemblages: Homonationalism in Queer Times*, Puar offers a related mapping of the secular biases of Anglo-American queer studies and U.S. lgbtq organizing. Writing post-9/11 and during the state of affective emergency that is the war on terror, Puar persuasively documents the dependence of the "queer liberal imaginary" on the Muslim terrorist (11). The figure of the Muslim terrorist, whether conjured in or out of clerical garb, functions to assure the freedom and modernity of secular queers. If some secular queers can now allow for accommodations between homosexuality and some forms of Christianity and Judaism, she suggests, no such compromise is imagined for or with Islam, which has now "supplanted race as one side of the irreconcilable binary between queer and something else" (13). In the face of this, any assertion to agency by queer Muslims as both queer *and* Muslim is a kind of nonsense. As Puar writes, "The queer agential subject can only ever be fathomed outside the norming constrictions of religion, conflating agency and resistance" (13).

A fascinating example of this "dis-ease" with religious agency appears in Saba Mahmood's *Politics of Piety: The Islamic Revival and the Feminist Subject*, an ethnography of the women's piety movement in Cairo, Egypt. Writing from within the U.S. academy, Mahmood offers her study as a counter to the "overwhelming tendency within poststructuralist feminist scholarship to conceptualize agency in terms of subversion or resignification of social norms." In contrast Mahmood wants to "detach the notion of agency from the goals of progressive politics" so that she can responsibly attend to "dimensions of human action" that fall out or make no sense when "agency is conceptualized on the binary model of subordination and subversion" (14). Within the liberal imaginary, this binary model maps onto another, the religious "versus" the secular, which is what makes the religious commitments and practices of Mahmood's subjects so unintelligible to secular scholars and progressives like Mahmood herself. To her credit, she does not exempt herself from critique. In many ways *Politics of Piety* is as much an analysis of forms of women's religious agency as an auto-analysis of what it means to suspend one's own viscerally felt intuitions about the world, risking discomfort so as to encounter others and other lifeworlds on their terms, not "our own."

It is not clear that Mahmood ultimately manages to make this leap of—is it?—faith, but even her failure is brilliantly instructive. With respect to the relationship I am seeking to establish between the rise of affect studies and the rise of a particular kind of religious politics, Mahmood's study is richly suggestive for a number of reasons. For one thing, the historical spark behind *Politics of Piety* coincides with the periodization I am venturing: circa 1979. Although the book is focused on the contemporary Islamist movement in

Egypt, she traces its genesis to a "set of puzzles [she] inherited from [her] involvement in progressive left politics in Pakistan, the land of [her] birth" (ix). She cites two developments as key: crises in Pakistani national identity and political consciousness spiked by the military dictatorship of Zia ul-Haq (1977–1988), who engaged in strategic "Islamicizing" of Pakistan to consolidate his hold on power; and the Iranian revolution, which at once "confounded" Mahmood's and her contemporaries' "expectations of the role Islam could play in a situation of revolutionary change" and "seemed to extinguish the fragile hope that secular leftist politics represented in the region" (x). For another, she is bracingly honest about the affective responses driving and also impeding her analysis of the piety movement and its conservative values: namely, her own dis-ease, fear, repugnance.[7] The book is a kind of working through of unhappy feelings in hopes of arriving somewhere else. Hope is an affective response, too.

This coupling—of hope and fear—is itself part of the deep feeling structure of secular modernity. In a foundational text not just for religious studies, but for the invention of secular modernity "itself," *The Natural History of Religion* (1757), David Hume conceptualizes religion as a "universal" feature of human experience. He wants to set its origins on empirically demonstrable grounds: with an "origin in human nature" not in some divine (and unverifiable) source or sources. Religion, according to Hume, is an attempt to make sense out of the disorganized sensations emanating from the natural world. He conceives religion as a second-order formation arising out of, and responding to, the "ordinary affections of human life," chiefly:

> the anxious concern for happiness, the dread of future misery, the terror of death, the thirst of revenge, the appetite for food and other necessaries. Agitated by hopes and fears of this nature, especially the latter, men scrutinize, with a trembling curiosity, the course of future causes, and examine the various and contrary events of human life. And in this disordered scene, with eyes still more disordered and astonished, they see the first obscure traces of divinity. (28)

Of this list of "ordinary affections," hope, fear, and anxiety are the most crucial to Hume—if sheer repetition of the terms in subsequent passages is measure of their import.

In his own close reading of this text, Robert J. Baird neatly summarizes the *coup de raison* that Hume performs: Hume establishes religion as principally "an emotive (i.e., psychophysical) reality" that generates (false) propositional claims about the natural world (Baird 169–170). Religion is at once a false theory about the world and a way of experiencing it. In Baird's gloss, religion constitutes "an ongoing account, a phenomenology of sorts" of hope, fear, anxiety, and the like (170). For Hume, religion's propositional claims are to be subject to empirical evidence, set upon the foundations, then, of reason alone. Evaluation of the evidence must be done from outside religion, from the standpoint of dispassionate secular reason. In a sense, religion will become the holding place for secular modernity's own disavowed hopes, fears, and anxieties. How so? As Baird also points out, Hume constructs the category of "religion" (i.e., what counts as religion) by analogy to Protestantism. This means that the secular rationality that deduces like from like is, from the start, ensnared in the emotive reality—the feeling structures—of a particular religion.

Arguably, echoes of Hume's stress on hope and fear, and the Protestant genealogy they are imbricated in, can be heard in President George W. Bush's ready conversion of "war on terrorism" into a "war on *terror*."[8] The post-9/11 mobilization of U.S. public feelings toward the project of war wavered between Christian and secular languages of justification—a wavering well captured in President George W. Bush's own early use of the language of "crusade."[9] But even after Bush backed off this particular metaphor, and the history of Christian war against Islam it invoked, resonances of religious war and civilizational clash remained active as states of feeling.[10] What does it mean to declare war on a feeling? How does such a declaration articulate space for some affective formations—and the condensation of subjective experience and, even, subjectivities around them—and exclude some others? What are the stakes of being outside of, in excess to, organized public feelings? And what connection might be drawn to the secularization thesis and the Enlightenment narrative that have long portrayed religion as modernity's excess?

This narrative aligns secular modernity with reason, progress, freedom, universalism over and against religion, which is framed as particularistic, violent, dogmatic, atavistic, and emotionally "off," as my performance studies colleague José Muñoz has importantly argued with respect to "feeling brown."[11] Although narrated as a universal project—as, indeed, the project of universalism—secularism, in its dominant (and dominating) form, remains tied to a particular religion, Christianity, and a particular history of origins in Enlightenment Europe. In our joint work, Jakobsen and I have named this formation "Christian secularism" to mark the particular religious, geographic, and political histories imported into and by the "universal" claims of the secularization thesis (*Secularisms* 9).[12] As Jakobsen and I clarify, we are not proposing that this secularism is really religion in disguise (Christianity). Rather, we are marking the specific context within which dominant secularism—the version of secularism that gets to pass itself off as the unmarked, universal—developed. In a question pertinent to my exploration here, Jakobsen and I ask: "If what gives secularism its moral import is its promise of universality and reasonableness as distinct from the narrowness and fanaticism of religion, what does it mean that this universalism and the rationality that it embodies are actually particular (to European history) and religious (Protestant) in form?" (Jakobsen and Pellegrini, *Secularisms* 3). Does this imply Christian secularism as a structure of feeling?

In *Marxism and Literature*, Raymond Williams proposes "structures of feeling" as a way to describe "pre-emergent" phenomena, that is, experiences that are "active and pressing but not yet fully articulated" (126). He uses the word "feeling" in order to "emphasize a distinction from more formal concepts of 'world-view' or 'ideology'" (132). But he is not abandoning these concepts and concerns so much as pushing us to investigate and take seriously the way "formal or systematic beliefs" are embedded in, and arise out of, concrete relations and experiences:

> We are talking about characteristic elements of impulse, restraint, and tone; specifically affective elements of consciousness and relationships: not feeling against thought, but thought as felt and feeling as thought: practical consciousness of a present kind, in a living and interrelating continuity. We are then defining these elements as a "structure": as a set, with specific internal relations, at once interlocking and in tension. Yet we are also defining a social experience which is still in *process*, often indeed not yet recognized as social but taken to be private, idiosyncratic, and even isolating, but which in analysis (though rarely otherwise) has its emergent, connecting, and dominant characteristics, indeed its hierarchies. (132)

For Williams, "structures of feeling" are what is missed by the habitual turn of thought that reduces culture and society—the "social," as he also names it—to fixed forms and the past tense: the already-known. This reduction or flattening is a dominant mode of historical and political analysis—of "knowledge-power," to use a more Foucauldian terminology. It converts relations, practices, institutions in which we are actively involved and actively constituted as subjects-who-know into, as Williams emphasizes, "formed wholes" with defined elements. In so doing, this form of historical analysis contributes to the petrification—the reification—of daily life. Further, for Williams, this reduction of actively experienced social relations to fixed and fully formed wholes enacts a "separation of the social from the personal" (128). To be more pointed: it separates the personal from the political.

In the face of this sequestration, Williams searches for other ways of naming "the undeniable experience of the present: not only the temporal present, the realization of this and that instant, but the specificity of present being, the inalienably physical, within which we may indeed discern and acknowledge institutions, formations, positions, but not always as fixed products, defining products" (128). Structures of feeling are that conceptual *and* experiential horizon.

There is much to provoke in this analysis. Williams helpfully opens a space between received ideas, categories of experience, and beliefs, on the one side, and the messier, variegated ways people live out social relations, on the other. The habits of thought Williams is describing, which separate the social from the personal, the institutional from the living pulse of unfolding experience, sound an awful lot like the secular fantasy that (1) religion consists in institutional forms and belief structures and (2) social harmony is best achieved through the elevation of secular reason and religion's relegation to the private. If this is a fair extrapolation, then these dominant modes of thought themselves call to be critically re-thought as structures of feeling.

In secular thinking religion is the place where affect is most solicited, most contained (privatization), and most stigmatized. This is why so many committed secularists can value religion as a deeply personal matter even as they think religion should be bracketed or at least minimized from political debates in the public square: religious feelings are held to be impervious to rational persuasion. It is not that religion is "just" a matter of affect (far from it). It is rather that in Christian secular framings, the identification of feelings with religion; or of religion *as* feelings, nothing more than feelings; or—if there is to be something more—of religion as irrational belief blocks us from identifying what feelings the secular mobilizes and draws upon. For starters: hope, fear, anxiety, terror.[13]

Put another way, if we are to offer a history of the present, we need to analyze secularism as a structure of feeling that constructs and privileges particular forms of subjectivity, social belonging, and social knowledge. Let me enlist Foucault on this point: structures of feeling can serve to transmit and codify relations of dominance; they can also serve as spaces—points of "virtual fracture"—in which we might become other than who we thought we were (36). They might even be doing both at the same time. Progressives, whether secular or religious, are mistaken if we think that transformation and transgression are always and only for "the left."

In my own precinct of academe, performance studies, it has become a commonplace to underscore, in nearly reverential terms, the utopian promise of live performance and the role of minoritarian feeling in conjuring new lifeworlds on the margins of the dominant. This hope for performance—this hoped-for performative?—is one I have made claims for in my own writing over the last decade.[14] I thus share this faith in performance's power to transform its audience into something more . . . into a public, perhaps? Or, even, a revolution? However, in my own recent work on Hell Houses, I have come to question some of my own organizing understandings and galvanizing hopes regarding the public work feelings can do ("Signaling").[15] In what follows, I will summarize some of the main points of my arguments about Hell Houses, moving to resituate my earlier analysis of Hell Houses' "structure of feelings" within a larger set of concerns about national affect.

Hell Houses are evangelical riffs on the secular haunted houses staged by communities and schools throughout the U.S. during the Halloween season. Where haunted houses offer fright for entertainment's sake, Hell Houses play for higher stakes: they want to scare you to Jesus. In a typical Hell House, demon tour guides take the audience though a series of bloody staged tableaux depicting sinners whose bad choices (homosexuality, abortion, suicide, and, above all, rejection of Christ's saving grace) lead them straight to hell.

Hell Houses probably date back to the first "Scaremare" mounted by Jerry Falwell's Thomas Road Baptist Church, in Lynchburg, Virginia, in 1972. Today, they are most identified with the Assemblies of God, a Pentecostal denomination. Hell Houses first gained national attention via George Ratliff's 2001 documentary *Hell House*. This documentary focused on the annual Hell House staged by Trinity Church of the Assemblies of God, in Cedar Hill, Texas. Each year, between eleven thousand and fifteen thousand people flock to this Dallas suburb to attend Trinity Church's Hell House.

But it is another Assemblies of God church that has likely done the most to brand Hell Houses around the country—and beyond. The New Destiny Christian Center is located in the Denver suburb of Thornton, Colorado. The senior pastor for that church, Keenan Roberts, has carefully cultivated an online presence for Hell House Outreach. In 1996, Pastor Keenan—as his congregants call him—began selling Hell House Outreach Kits (the 2011 edition costs $299); they have sold approximately eight hundred outreach kits over the past decade.

Hell House Outreach brilliantly joins marketing, missionizing, and media know-how. Starting with the 2006 version of the outreach kit, all the components are on disc, including: a how-to guide to production; a DVD of a *Hell House* performance; and a compact disc soundtrack containing sound effects and music to amp up the fear factor of specific scenes—"from the voice of Suicide to Lucifer's bone-chilling introduction to Hell House to a myriad of others you absolutely cannot find anywhere else," the website promises.

This fear factor is part entertainment, but bigger part spiritual pedagogy. The scenes of a gay man being dragged off to hell after his death bed refusal to accept Christ into his heart or of the teen suicide who has everything going for him (from good grades to popularity) but still feels empty inside are played neither for laughs nor cheap thrills. Hell Houses' use of fear to proselytize to young people has attracted criticism. For example, in the run-up to the 2006 Halloween season, the National Gay and Lesbian Task Force released a report accusing Hell Houses and their purveyors of spreading a message of bigotry and homophobia (Kennedy and Cianciotto 8). Hell Houses have come under criticism from Christian groups as well, such as the Colorado Council of Churches, for engaging in fear-based theology that distorts the Christian message.

But Hell Houses openly court controversy; the media-driven firestorms actually help to get the message out to a broader audience. Moreover, the literally thousands of men, women, and teenagers across the country who take part in Hell House ministries each year do not think of themselves as spreading hate or intolerance; nor do they see themselves as *unreasonably* manipulating people's fears. In any case, asks Pastor Keenan, "Who decided that fear is not an effective teacher?"[16]

He has a point. If we look to public school classrooms around the country—to driver's ed films with their cautionary (and blood-spattered) depictions of traffic accidents caused by immature drivers or to the lessons in "stranger danger" and "good touch, bad touch" routinely taught as part of "age-appropriate" sex education—we can see that fear plays a large role in secular pedagogies of responsible, safe personhood.[17] Although the content of this fear-based education may differ sharply, the anxieties and concerns it seeks to solicit and bind may have more overlap than usually recognized. Such pedagogy does not just teach us *what* to be scared of; it teaches us *how* to be afraid: the phenomenology of fear. This wavering between what and how is also the oscillation between the war on terror and the war *of* terror: orange alerts that do not just tell us the threat level, but teach us to be afraid; the performance of airport security that turns everyday objects, down to the last tube of toothpaste, into potential terrorist weapons.

If Hell Houses traffic in fear, they also offer hope on the other side of the journey. This is salvation as "structure of feeling." Hell Houses' ability to win over converts or spark spiritual rededication depends less on theological pronouncements or pre-existing beliefs, though these may prime someone to receive the message. However, for conviction to seize hold, something more is required. This "something" is affective congruence; the participant is invested (or *re*invested) in feeling structures that can knit together disparate, even contradictory, experiences, bodily sensations, feelings, and thoughts.

For its adherents, a Hell House sutures gaps, soothes contradictions, and produces resonance amid discord.[18] Pastor Keenan himself analogizes the work of his Hell House to the responsibilities of good parenting: "God's word is very explicit about where to play and where not to play. That doesn't make him or us judgmental for communicating, 'Play here or don't play there.' And good parents are the same way." Pastor Keenan here draws what is to him a clear distinction between being hateful and being painfully, even aggressively, honest.

Rather than dismissing Pastor Keenan's proclamation that he doesn't "hate people" and does not believe that Hell Houses' condemnation of homosexuality "is a hateful message" as hypocritical (or as strategically performed for his East Coast interviewers), it is far more useful, analytically and politically, to take him at his word. First, accusations of hypocrisy may make the accuser feel better, but after pronouncing *j'accuse*, there is really nothing else left to say. Hypocrisy is a kind of analytic dead end. Second, taking Pastor Keenan seriously when he distances himself from hate opens up important, if also discomforting, links between Hell Houses' structures of religious feeling and the larger feeling culture not just of evangelicals but of the U.S. public square more broadly. This larger feeling culture is tolerance. Tolerance is a Christian secular structure of feeling; it may even be our national affect. Tolerance is embedded in a long and specifically Protestant history of religious toleration at the same time that it also structures social relations for and in the secular state.

As Jakobsen and I argue elsewhere, tolerance—and "love the sinner, hate the sin" is a neat encapsulation of it—allows people to espouse punitive judgments and promote discriminatory policies against their neighbors and fellow citizens, all the while experiencing themselves as "tolerant" and "open-minded" (*Love the Sin*). This dynamic of tolerance does more to explain the success of Proposition 8 in California than does decrying the slim majority of California voters who passed this anti-gay marriage amendment as "religious zealots" and/or "haters."

The religious communities that stage Hell Houses feel themselves to be under attack and in need of buffering, too. Thus, if we calculate the success of Hell Houses in terms of how many people are saved for the first time, then we are missing out on a much larger story about what performances do for their participants. To be sure, for the makers of Hell Houses, the performances are a form of missionary outreach, an attempt to offer the blessings of salvation to as wide an audience as possible. But they are also performances in the ongoing making and remaking of life-saving communities of belonging—for the here and now of this world and not just the next one. Hell Houses offer a way to reconfirm belief and reconsolidate identity in the face of what many evangelicals experience as secular hegemony.

Nevertheless, it is important to distinguish here between being minoritized, that is ascribed *as* "a minority" by dominant culture, and identifying oneself and one's group as *in* the minority. Different degrees of accuracy obtain.[19] This feeling of marginalization remains active and galvanizing despite the undeniable impact conservative Christianity has had on electoral politics and policy-making in the U.S. over the past two decades. The structure of Christian secularism helps to make sense of this double articulation. Christian conservatives develop their cultural power both by drawing on their connection to the religious aspect of a hegemonic Christian secularism *and* by asserting they are marginalized and even oppressed by this same secularism (Jakobsen with Pellegrini "Introduction" 15).[20]

The "same" feeling structure can work, and be put to work, in different ways. Minoritarian feelings are neither fully determined by dominant structures of feeling (tolerance and fear are two I have specifically addressed in this chapter) nor wholly independent of them, existing in some autonomous realm.[21] Rather, we should think in terms of complex "assemblages," to repurpose a term Jasbir Puar repurposes from Deleuze.

This complexity also helps illuminate some queer convergences between Hell House performances and (other?) forms of queer world-making through performance. In a jointly written essay "'Preaching to the Converted,'" performance studies scholar David Román and performance artist Tim Miller defend the value of performing for one's "own." Drawing on an explicitly religious vocabulary, they argue that "conversion . . . demands a continual testing of identity, if only as a means to affirm it" (Román and Miller 212). This affirmation is made, again and again, not despite but precisely in the face of all that rages against it. That is, conversion is not a defense against vulnerability; it admits it as identity's unstable ground. If queer theatre is "preaching to the converted," as its critics sometimes sneer, this is precisely what Román and Miller want to valorize: the reiteration of community through the binding power of performance. This is what Hell Houses aim at as well.

The value of performing for one's own, the rich worlds that are made and made again, suggests another contributing factor for the affective return post-1979. On the one hand, I have identified an anxiety and, even, a fear about religion. However, we could equally see a turn to affect as a desire for the forms of world-making and plenitude and excess that have otherwise been set down as religion's provenance. We could even speak of a competition for the converted between these sites of affective plenitude. But this rivalry verging on affect envy need not be so bruising. I will at least acknowledge my own envy—not fear, not repugnance—for the affective surplus on display behind the scenes of Hell House performances: the camaraderie and sense of shared purpose and shared pleasure that grace cast and crew. Queer performances and—does this go too far?—some quarters of academic affect studies may actually function as realms of secular enchantment, supplying forms of affective experience resistant to the flattening effects of secular rationality. This resistance does not tell us in advance what kinds of politics or political subjects will be mobilized through affect. Nor does it map out how affective affinities might be mobilized across creedal or ideological differences.[22] But one thing is clear: religion "itself" is not the problem; progressives have nothing to fear but fear itself.

This chapter originally appeared in *Women & Performance: A Journal of Feminist Theory* 19.2 (2009): 205–218.

NOTES

1. For developed arguments on this point, see the essays collected in Jakobsen and Pellegrini, *Secularisms*.
2. In this paragraph, and the three that follow, I am largely paraphrasing our jointly written essay.
3. Qtd. in Stephanson 30. Emphasis in original.
4. I have benefited here from Susan F. Harding's nuanced arguments regarding the impact Jerry Falwell, and what she terms "Falwellianism," made on U.S. academic culture. See Harding.
5. For an extended argument about the conflation of religion with morality, see Jakobsen and Pellegrini, *Love the Sin*.
6. For a fascinating historical account of American feminists' post-1979 preoccupation with the oppression of "Muslim women" and with clitoridectomy, which many American and European feminist activists mistakenly identified

with Islam, see McAlister. This essay importantly traces transcultural feminist circuits of anxiety about and interest in "bad" religion.

7. For "dis-ease" and "fear," see Mahmood xi; for her admission of her repugnance, see 37.
8. From the very first military actions taken under the Obama Presidency (remote-controlled missile strikes into Pakistan), in early 2009, we have seen that "regime change" in the U.S. has not reshaped the war on terror, let alone brought it to an end, in ways that many progressive critics of the Bush administration's policies might have expected or hoped.
9. Bush invoked the language of crusade in a press conference on 16 September 2001: "This is a new kind of—a new kind of evil. And we understand. And the American people are beginning to understand. This crusade, this war on terrorism is going to take a while." See Suskind.
10. These resonances were kept alive by various cultural commentators, such as Andrew Sullivan, and by some Christian religious leaders, such as Franklin Graham, son of evangelical leader Billy Graham. See Jakobsen, "Is Secularism," esp. 60–61.
11. Muñoz's analysis of states and performances of feeling in excess of the national has been formative for my own thought.
12. See also Jakobsen's independent discussion of Christian secularism in "Sex, Secularism," esp. 20–21.
13. I am grateful to Elizabeth Freeman for helping me to un-knot the ideas of this paragraph.
14. See, for example, my discussion of performance artist Holly Hughes's *Preaching to the Perverted* ("(Laughter)").
15. Much of the analysis of Hell Houses that follows is condensed from this essay, though with important new emphases and additions.
16. See Roberts. Unless otherwise indicated, all quotations of Roberts are from this interview.
17. My thanks to Jill Casid for these pointers, and especially for recalling to me the harrowing delights of the splatter film genre so central to high school driver's education courses.
18. I borrow the term "resonance" from Linda Kintz's important discussion of the emotional texture of right-wing Christian politics. See Kintz, esp. 6–7.
19. On this point, see Jakobsen and Pellegrini, *Love the Sin* 118–119.
20. Elizabeth A. Castelli has recently tracked the emergence of a modern Christian persecution complex, which combines a long history of Christian martyrological discourses with the galvanizing rhetorics of contemporary identity politics.
21. My thanks to both Janet Jakobsen and Jasbir Puar for many long conversations on these points.
22. I am grateful to Jane Bennett for shaping conversation about affect-envy and secular realms of enchantment and to William Connolly for underscoring the issue of mobilizing affective affinities across creedal difference.

WORKS CITED

Baird, Robert J. "Late Secularism." *Secularisms*. Ed. Janet R. Jakobsen and Ann Pellegrini. Durham: Duke, 2008. 162–177. Print.

Castelli, Elizabeth A. "Persecution Complexes: Identity Politics and the 'War on Christians.'" *differences* 18.3 (2007): 152–180. Print.

Foucault, Michel. "Critical Theory/Intellectual History." *Politics, Philosophy, Culture: Interviews and Other Writings 1977–1984*. Ed. Lawrence D. Kritzman. New York: Routledge, 1988. 17–46. Print.

Harding, Susan F. "American Protestant Moralism and the Secular Imagination: From Temperance to the Moral Majority." *Social Research* 76.4 (2009): 1277-1306. Print.

Hume, David. *The Natural History of Religion*. Ed. H. E. Root. Stanford: Stanford UP, 1957. Print.

Jakobsen, Janet R. "Can Homosexuals End Western Civilization as We Know It? Family Values in a Global Economy." *Queer Globalizations: Citizenship and the Afterlife of Colonialism*. Ed. Arnaldo Cruz-Malavé and Martin F. Manalansan. New York: New York UP, 2002. 49–70. Print.

———. "Is Secularism Less Violent than Religion?" *Interventions: Activists and Academics Respond to Violence*. Ed. Elizabeth A. Castelli and Jakobsen. New York: Palgrave, 2004. 53–67. Print.

———. "Sex, Secularism, and the 'War on Terrorism': The Role of Sexuality in Multi-Issue Organizing." *A Companion to Lesbian, Gay, Bisexual, Transgender, and Queer Studies*. Ed. George E. Haggerty and Molly McGarry. Oxford: Blackwell, 2007. 17–37. Print.

Jakobsen, Janet R., with Ann Pellegrini. Introduction. *World Secularisms at the Millennium*. Ed. Jakobsen and Pellegrini. Special issue of *Social Text* 64 (2000): 1–27. Print.

Jakobsen, Janet R., and Ann Pellegrini. *Love the Sin: Sexual Regulation and the Limits of Religious Tolerance*. New York: New York UP, 2003. Print.

———, eds. *Secularisms*. Durham: Duke UP, 2008. Print.

Jameson, Fredric. "Postmodernism, or The Cultural Logic of Late Capitalism." *New Left Review* 1.146 (1984): 53–92. Print.

———. "Reification and Utopia in Mass Culture." *Social Text* 1 (1979): 130–148. Print.

Kennedy, Sarah, and Jason Cianciotto. *Homophobia at "Hell House": Literally Demonizing Lesbian, Gay, Bisexual, and Transgender Youth*. Washington, DC: National Gay and Lesbian Task Force Policy Institute, 2006. Web. 13 Dec. 2006.

Kintz, Linda. *Between Jesus and the Market: The Emotions that Matter in Right-Wing America*. Durham: Duke, 1998. Print.

Mahmood, Saba. *Politics of Piety: The Islamic Revival and the Feminist Subject*. Princeton: Princeton UP, 2005. Print.

McAlister, Melani. "Suffering Sisters? American Feminists and the Problem of Female Genital Surgeries." *Americanism: New Perspectives on the History of an Ideal*. Ed. Michael Kazin and Joe McCartin. Chapel Hill: U of North Carolina P, 2006. 242–260. Print.

Muñoz, José Esteban. "Feeling Brown: Ethnicity and Affect in Ricardo Bracho's The Sweetest Hangover (and Other STDs)." *Theatre Journal* 52.1 (2000): 67–79. Print.

Pellegrini, Ann. "(Laughter)." *Psychoanalysis and Performance*. Ed. Adrian Kear and Patrick Campbell. London: Routledge, 2001. 179–193. Print.

———. "'Signaling through the Flames': Hell House Performance and Structures of Religious Feeling." *American Quarterly* 59.3 (2007): 921–945. Print.

Pellegrini, Ann, and Jasbir K. Puar. "Affect." *Social Text* 100 (2009): 35–38. Print.

Puar, Jasbir K. *Terrorist Assemblages: Homonationalism in Queer Times*. Durham: Duke UP, 2007. Print.

Roberts, Keenan. Personal interview by Debra Levine and Ann Pellegrini. 29 Oct. 2006.

Román, David, and Tim Miller. "'Preaching to the Converted.'" *The Queerest Art: Essays on Lesbian and Gay Theater*. Ed. Alisa Solomon and Framji Minwalla. New York: New York UP, 2002. 203–226. Print.

Stephanson, Anders. "Regarding Postmodernism: A Conversation with Fredric Jameson." *Social Text* 17 (1987): 29–54. Print.

Suskind, Ron. "Faith, Certainty and the Presidency of George W. Bush." *The New York Times Magazine* 17 Oct. 2004: n. pag. Web. 17 March 2009.

Williams, Raymond. *Marxism and Literature*. Oxford: Oxford UP, 1977. Print.

14 About[/]Doing

Religion and Theatre in the Academy

Lance Gharavi

"How do you get to Carnegie Hall?" goes the old joke. The punch-line has never been "Go to college." Nevertheless, the institutionalization of "practice" in the field of theatre sits more comfortably, or at least more securely, in North American universities today than it did in the early days of the discipline's academic emergence from the fields of oral interpretation, rhetoric, and literature. The same cannot be said of the status of practice in the field of religious studies. There, the academic discourse around that term has become increasingly fraught in the last two decades, creating sharp divisions that seem, at times, to threaten the very continuation of the discipline itself.

Although it is dangerous to assume too much parallelism in disciplinary discourses that use similar or identical terms—there are crucially different histories of disciplinary formation, different cultural and institutional contexts, different constructions of goals, etc.—both the fields of religious studies and of theatre/performance studies evince an ongoing tension around the concept of practice in the academy. In both cases, these tensions emerged historically as part of a messy process of disciplinary formation involving several intersecting and contesting discourses across multiple cultural and institutional sites. Both processes involved an uneasy coincidence of practice forms—theology for religious studies, various professional and technical knowledges for theatre studies—with the anti-professional, anti-vocational nineteenth-century German model of *Wissenschaft*, a conceit that used the legitimating discourse of science to define and defend the academy as a place for the pursuit of "pure" knowledge.

But a critical distinction between religious studies and theatre/performance studies, as these fields currently exist in North America, is that, in the former, there is a strong and vocal movement—variously successful and embattled—to eschew, critique, and denounce the *practice* within the academy of the subject under concern. The critique constitutes a passionate struggle on the part of an articulate and loose-knit cadre of religious studies scholars over the identity of their field. These scholars seek to draw a "sharp, bright line" that will serve to circumscribe the borders of their discipline; and they draw this line specifically in relation to "practice" or "doing." "First," claims Ivan Strenski, "religious studies is about *studying* religion, not *doing* it" ("Proper Object" 149). Similarly, Russell T. McCutcheon decries many in his field for "confusing [religion's] practice with its study" (*Manufacturing* 200).

Study of/practice of distinctions are, of course, familiar to those in the field of theatre and performance studies. As messy, deceptive, and unproductive as these oppositions are, as much as the perceived gulf between them may be mourned (genuinely or no), and as frequently as hybrid and "bridging" modalities may be sought, such distinctions are used, however tenuously, to demarcate various intra-disciplinary positions and are institutionalized in graduate degrees (e.g., PhD/MFA). But Strenski, McCutcheon, and other scholars[1] on their side of the debate over practice are not simply calling for sharp and absolute intra-disciplinary distinctions, but rather for the banishment of the practice and doing of religion from the field—and from the university—entirely. The stakes involved in the border disputes over practice are, in other words, far higher in religious studies than in departments of theatre and performance.

Those who urge the elimination of practice from the field of religion are frequently referred to (by themselves and their opponents) as "reductionists." In this context, reductionism is a position that holds that references to ahistorical and transcendental terms (e.g., the sacred, myth, religious experience, etc.) have no academically legitimate explanatory power in relation to religion. For the reductionists, the study of religion must be "reduced" to socio-cultural explanations characteristic of the social sciences.[2]

The reductionist critique of the practice of religion in the academy has two principal targets. The first of these is theology. Reductionists argue that theology has no place in the academic study of religion—either in the classroom or as part of the research methodology of faculty—because it is beholden to those institutions or communities that are the objects of study. It therefore cannot retain the objectivity that reductionists cite as the hallmark of academic inquiry. Theology, they argue, is a clear case of "doing" religion. It constitutes religious practice. Some within theological circles have responded by drawing a distinction between confessional theology and "academic theology." Practitioners of the latter argue that their mode of theology is removed from obligation to religious communities and involves the rigorous analysis and critique of religious beliefs in terms that are defensible within the norms of the academy.[3] Such claims by academic theologians, however, rarely hold weight with reductionists.[4] This is, in part, because of the relation between academic theology and the second target of reductionist critique: the discourse on *sui generis* religion.

But this discourse is only a "second target" in a very provisional sense. The discourse on *sui generis* religion is, for the reductionists, a kind of crypto-theology. It holds that religious feeling, faith, or consciousness is interior and unavailable for analysis, that it is primary and irreducible, and that it is the job of the scholar to recover and study this non-empirical content by attending to and interpreting its expressions in interpersonally available forms like rituals, myths, symbols, and institutions. For the reductionists, the discourse on *sui generis* religion *is* religion insofar as it depends on positing as real an ahistorical something that lies behind and is expressed through empirically accessible religious forms and practices. The reductionist critique further conflates this discourse with the universalist and egalitarian aspirations of liberal humanism and with the liberal arts. This critique is not limited to the production of research in the field—where it is subject to peer review—but also applies to the classroom. In the latter, the discourse on *sui generis* religion thrives by situating the religious studies classroom as a site where students explore their culture's "deepest values" and learn to understand and appreciate those of other cultures. But, McCutcheon argues, to "appreciate" the experiences and values of others is, in this context, to reproduce them, and such reproduction cannot be the aim of scholarly inquiry ("Critical Trends" 326). Such exploratory reproduction itself generates a kind of liberal humanistic religion where what is honored is a transcendent mystery that is the ultimate referent of all religions and of religion *as such*. The reductionist critique of the discourse on *sui generis* religion amounts to an accusation that the latter constitutes not the study, but the *practice* of religion—an ecumenical theology of religious pluralism—within the otherwise strictly secular territory of the academy.

I am broadly sympathetic to reductionist perspectives with regard to religious studies. I advocate for the *study* of religion from within a theatre and performance studies context; I do not advocate for religion *per se*. And I do draw a distinction between the two, however provisional, ad hoc, strategic, and contingent such distinctions may be. I have found invoking study of/practice of distinctions vitally important in advocating to my colleagues the need for our discipline to attend to religion. It is useful in allaying a certain anxiety that I often note in my colleagues whenever I raise the issue—an anxiety that my advocacy will inevitably lead to my blurting out, "Say, have you heard the Good News?" or, more likely given my surname, "Deathtotheinfidel!" But although I find these distinctions useful, I am nevertheless wary of the consequences that reductionist arguments may have for the field of theatre and performance studies, and for the academy at large. Narrowly, reductionist arguments have serious implications for research and teaching conducted at the intersections and interstices of religion and theatre/performance. Those who engage in such work should be aware of the tense fractures in the ground on which they tread. There is a good deal of *sui generis* discourse around various religious or quasi-religious studio practices and theoretical concepts (yogic philosophy and practice, myth, ritual exercises, talk of "energy" or "communion," the irreducibility of the artist's or audience's experience, etc.) that might benefit from the insights gleaned by reductionist disputes. More broadly, these arguments are significant insofar as they constitute a polemic against the academic practice of the object of study, against liberal arts/humanities approaches as crypto-theological (and thus inappropriate modes for inquiry within the public university), and finally, against the endorsement of subjectivity and "insider" perspectives in research and pedagogy. While I believe that much that is salutary has come from this debate, I also find much of it problematic. Although the distinctions insisted upon by reductionists have an undeniable strategic value and cachet within the academy, I am skeptical of their plausibility and beneficence as serious analytic categories.[5] Ultimately, I would endorse a more pragmatic and strategic approach to trading in such distinctions.

To amplify the distinctions they draw between themselves and theologians (crypto- or otherwise), reductionists invoke the legitimating authority of science; they call for the *scientific* (or sometimes the *social*-scientific) study of religion. In so doing, the reductionist critique inevitably re-asserts a set of familiar binaries. That is, in staking their identity on an absolute (and mutually constitutive) opposition of science and religion, reductionist arguments release a series of additional binaries that are historically linked to this opposition: logic/emotion, rational/irrational, evidence/faith, objective/subjective, knowledge/belief, freedom/obedience, etc. These binaries are explicitly replicated in the study of/practice of distinctions that vex theatre and performance studies. The scholar is rational, logical, skeptical, disembodied, and objective; the artist is irrational, emotional, gullible, bodied, and subjective.

These binaries are historically and culturally gendered. They are part of a prescriptive and androcentric ideology that produces social reality. As Randi R. Warne has observed, the Western intensification of the science/religion conflict brought about by Darwin in the nineteenth century coincided with a crucial and formative social development. The rise of the industrial state and growth of the middle class produced an ideology of the human community as divided into "spheres" demarcated as "public" and "private" ("Making" 255). These separate spheres were gendered and the science/religion conflict mapped onto them. The public sphere—which encompassed workplace, government, commerce, science, etc.—was the domain of the male, while the private sphere—home, morality, religion, etc.—was the domain of the female.[6] Insofar as reductionists explicitly argue against theology and the discourse of *sui generis* religion in *public* (as opposed to private) colleges and universities, and insofar as they endorse academic inquiry as a necessarily objective and public mode in contrast to the subjective and private character of religion, they thereby participate in (re)producing, naturalizing, and ontologizing the very divisions that generate and sustain the prescriptive ideology of separate spheres. Such a perspective feminizes religion (and, by implication, the academic opponents of the reductionists), interpellating it as the object of the objective and probing masculinized gaze of science. This prescriptive gender ideology has been authorized by the scientific study of religion since its origins in Max Muller's nineteenth-century *Religionswissenschaft* (Warne, "Gender" 150), and continues to distinguish the still-male-dominated field of religious studies in the twenty-first century.

Some feminist scholars of religion have responded to the enduring androcentricism of religious studies by deploying essentialist arguments based on valorizing "women's experience" and subjectivity as a methodological and interpretive tool. But such approaches tend to produce "woman" as a universalized category, and are thus subject to familiar critiques from women of color, as well as from queer, classed, non-Western, and/or historically colonized perspectives. Moreover, such approaches simply invert the terms of androcentric binaries, leaving them intact, reproducing and further ontologizing them. A more constructive approach would be to focus on the historically discursive and performative character of such binaries, to highlight how such distinctions give rise to institutionally enforced social arrangements—like the banishment from the academy of the "practice" of religion endorsed by reductionists—arrangements that are naturalized as they emerge through and as academic discourses and performances—that is to say, through and as material *practice* in the academy.

As Shannon Jackson has observed, in the early days of theatre's emergence as an academic discipline distinct from literary studies, "dramatic literature risked association with the feminine [and] the primitive . . . in a way that threatened the profession of literature's redefined story about itself as a masculine, hard science" (51). Throughout her study, Jackson cites a variety of ways in which theatre has been historically feminized within the academy, assigned gendered associations based on a variety of discursive matrices including professional/amateur, commercial/academic, practical/theoretical, scientific/humanistic, etc. These distinctions are invoked to demarcate both inter- and intra-disciplinary borders. Within the discipline are the already-cited gendered binaries frequently associated with the theory/practice or scholar/artist divide. But in theatre and performance studies, and in the arts more generally, the gendering of these divisions is slippery and contingent on who is making the distinction. Sometimes the theorist-scholar is feminized, sometimes the practitioner-artist. As Jackson describes it, "while there is no question that 'theorists' can be associated with the effetely feminine, it also is the case that theoretical rigor can function to ward off the feminized simplicity of pragmatic embodiment" (139). But from the reductionist perspective—which argues for a disciplinary identity formed from the study/practice fault line—there can be little doubt as to which side is feminized. While it is possible to imagine the theologian or pro-*sui generis* scholar of religion inverting the gendered roles by tagging the reductionists with a characterization of effete femininity similar to that with which the artist may tag the theorist, it is important to note that only the reductionists argue for the *exclusion from the university* of their feminized other. As Donald Wiebe, one of the most outspoken critics of theology and the discourse on *sui generis* religion in the academy, puts it, "if the academic study of religion wishes to be taken seriously as a contributor to knowledge about our world, it will have to concede the boundaries set by the ideal of scientific knowledge that characterizes the university" (xiii). Weibe's use of the possessive pronoun "our" is undoubtedly meant to be all-inclusive, but it functions instead to simultaneously generate and mask a crucial division. It posits a "way-the-world-is," an objective world produced by, owned by, and subject to a gaze that is historically marked as male (and white, straight, etc.) and explicitly characteristic of the university; it interpellates the reader as either a possessor of this gaze, or as an other, a feminized "not-us" who must either relinquish her subjectivity or submit to living outside the boundaries of the academy (where she is produced as the male academician's object of knowledge). The reductionists, in aligning themselves with a masculinized science over and against a feminized practice, and thus endorsing and reproducing the historically gendered binaries in which they are enmeshed, constitute their mission as a contest for the gender identity of the academy itself.

But the binaries that orbit reductionist arguments overlay several oppositional subjectivities. For instance, insofar as the study of theology is linked to vocational (as opposed to "purely" academic) interests, the dispute between reductionists and anti-reductionists takes place across a usually unacknowledged class divide similar to the one that invests any dialogue between scholar and artist with such peculiar tensions. In the former dispute, these class-related anxieties are further amplified by the fact that, at least since Marx's famous "opiate" remark, religion has been widely characterized as appealing most strongly to the lower classes.[7] But, in a way more similar to the gendering of "separate spheres," these binaries characterize the discourses that authorized the projects of Western imperialism. They litter the historical record where they have been, and continue to be, repeatedly and strategically deployed as props for colonialist endeavors. Here, masculinized and objective science is linked to technological mastery, sophistication, and evolutionary adulthood. These valorized (self-) characterizations of European and North American cultures produce as their other the feminized, irrational, and "primitive" cultures that languish in an evolutionary childhood. This other is constructed as definitionally subordinate and thus the appropriate object of knowledge, subject to all the domination and control that such knowing implies.

To be sure, reductionists (appropriately and importantly) accuse the discourse on *sui generis* religion of tripping over its own colonialist embeddedness. McCutcheon cites the way in which the 1963 self-immolation by the Vietnamese Buddhist monk, Thich Quang Duc, was described by the American media and by religious studies scholars in terms that constitute it as a specifically religious (as opposed to political) act, performed in response to specifically religious (again, as opposed to political) motivations. The act was one of "religious sacrifice" or "religious suicide." Such interpretations, claim McCutcheon, are typical of the dominance of the *sui generis* discourse in the West. By focusing only on the religious character of Thich Quang Duc's protest, these interpretations elide an array of complex political, historical, and social factors, de-contextualizing and de-politicizing the event in a way that served the interests of U.S. imperialism. McCutcheon uses this event as an example of the ways in which the discourse on *sui generis* religion is complicit in the exercise of power, privilege, and domination. It is "part of a complex system of power and control, specializing in the deployment of interpretive strategies—the politics of representation" (*Manufacturing* 177).

While the work of McCutcheon and his reductionist colleagues has been valuable in uncovering the heretofore-unexamined politics of religious discourses and practices, including critiques that invoke post-colonialist methodologies, their endorsement of objectivity in its strong form and their resultant elision of their own subjectivity and embeddedness leave them vulnerable to the very same critiques they deploy. In theatre scholarship, modernist accounts of artistic production valorized the individual "genius" of the artist and his (usually his) existential struggles, autonomizing and de-politicizing the creative act in a manner analogous to the "religious suicide" reading critiqued by McCutcheon. In contrast, more recent scholarship often fictionalizes autonomous agency (sometimes under the banner of a misapplied performativity), but only conditionally. Agency is relegated only to the scholar who interprets the performance of the (conscientiously) historically situated actor, who herself is without agency. But in this operation, the scholar's interpretation is given privilege and situated outside the "complex system of power and control." For a Western scholar to interpret an act or practice of a colonized people in terms that reflect and refract the proclivities and hermeneutic obsessions of the scholar (in McCutcheon's case, political and socio-cultural explanations) who is him/herself always already producing such interpretations within an institutional structure that materially rewards such productions—that is, within a "complex system of power and control" that produces the scholar, and that is, in turn, sustained by the scholar's productions—itself performatively reenacts (albeit at a non-negligible remove) the scene of imperial domination. It "restores the behavior" (to bowdlerize and misappropriate Schechner's nomenclature) of the colonialist act and sustains its successful run.

I do not mean to fall into absurd exaggerations by appearing to lay responsibility for the legacies of colonialisms in the laps of McCutcheon and his reductionist colleagues. Their efforts to bring a rigorous political analysis to bear on religious studies constitute a crucial corrective and an updating for the field. But their positional obligations—vis-à-vis their dispute with theology and the discourse on *sui generis* religion—to objectivity in its strong sense result in a strange irony. In trying to avoid accepting the assumptions of one kind of transcendent (the transcendent embraced by those whom they study), they stumble into adopting another: the transcendent subjectivity of the scholar. This is commonly known as the "god's eye view," but this god is a god created by and for a specific set of subject positions: white, male, straight, Western, economically privileged, etc. These positions are normative; they are positioned as the standards against which all are judged and to which all must aspire. Any attempt to assert a position outside of this perspective is marked as "interested," "invested," "embedded," or "advocacy," and thereby definitionally marginal at best (e.g., feminism), or outside the acceptable boundaries of academic inquiry at worst (e.g., theology). This places the reductionists in an odd relationship with certain strains of cultural studies, and with aspects of theatre and performance in the academy. To be marked as "woman," as "Latino," as "artist," as "queer," as "Jew," or as "Muslim" is always to be marked as embedded, invested, and interested, even (or especially) in the academy. But self-consciously embedded "insider perspectives" are widely accepted methodologies in cultural studies areas like Chicana/o studies and women's studies. "Interestedness" and "advocacy" are inalienable aspects of the work of the scholar-artist and the emerging area of performance/practice-as-research. These accepted modes of academic production threaten to destabilize the normative stance taken by the reductionists. They threaten the construction and preservation of a singular operative identity, a perspectival and methodological homogeneity for the academy that produces "outsiders" and "insiders." Perception of such threat attaches itself to, and is expressed as, cultural anxieties that are not necessarily specific to the university milieu. Donald Wiebe, for instance, criticizes the discourse on *sui generis* religion for failing "to live up to the obligations of all '*naturalized citizens*' of [the university], namely, the obligations of neutrality and objectivity" (164, emphasis added).

Wiebe's adoption of nativist rhetoric—of the kind then so prevalent among anti-immigration groups—is frankly telling. That these words were published at a time when North American universities—their faculty and student demographics—were becoming increasingly diverse, increasingly welcoming populations heretofore under-represented in the academy, is suggestive of the nature of, and material source for, reductionist anxieties. The discourse on *sui generis* religion—and any other party marked as "interested"—is a threat to the purity of the naturalized body of the academy. In Wiebe's argument, the reductionist advocacy of strict disinterestedness that has characterized the discourse on the scientific study of religion explicitly takes on the racial connotations that were embedded in it from its origins.

There is thus a kind of refreshing frankness to the argument that D. G. Hart makes in his book *The University Gets Religion*. Hart ties the emergence of religious studies departments to the "therapeutic assumptions and identity politics" that led to the creation of academic departments formed around various social identities: women, African American, Latina/o, Native American, gay/lesbian, etc. (248). Hart frames the introduction of these departments as a capitulation on the part of university administrators to pressure from interested groups who felt their points of view had been unfairly excluded from the academy. In calling for the exclusion of religion (i.e., not just theology, but also the discourse on *sui generis* religion) from the academy, Hart suggests that, in the interest of fairness and consistency, "other special interest-group areas of study" should likewise be excluded (249). As justification for such exclusion, he invokes a particular understanding of the university's identity and mission. He quotes Alan Wolfe: the university "ought not to be in the business of healing the afflicted or comforting the aggrieved" (249). Neither, argues Hart, quoting Louis Menand, is it the university's mission to "discover ways of correcting inequities and attitudes that persist in society as a whole" (249). The university, in other words, is not in the business of nation-building. This is the meaning of "disinterested."

But the argument from disinterestedness masks the manner in which the university—in its research and teaching—is always already enmeshed in normative and socially therapeutic practices. Scholars and artists have historically been expected to subsume their "alterity" into a set of discursively naturalized standards defined by and as white, male, straight, and privileged. This is the normative position constructed as "neutral" or "disinterested." Despite the excellent and important work that has been done in theatre and performance studies, this situation still persists in the discipline, especially in actor-training programs that aim to eliminate aspects of students' voice and movement deemed "culturally specific," (the implication being that "white Mid-Westerner" is culturally neutral). Those who argue against this practice are engaging "therapeutic assumptions" and seeking to correct "inequities and attitudes that persist in society as a whole." Those who defend the practice claim to do so in the name of the professional interests of the student: "That's what the industry expects." Cultural "neutrality," they argue, makes the student more employable. And they are correct. But while I admit that the argument against vocal "neutrality" training constitutes a form of "nation-building," I also submit that the counter-argument is likewise therapeutic insofar as it functions to sustain and maintenance the existing social order, protecting and authorizing those already existing "inequities and attitudes." Similarly, Hart's arguments against social advocacy, interestedness, and therapy at the university elide the existence of an always already (covertly) operative advocacy, interestedness, and therapy. Academic "disinterestedness" is always interested.

In his widely cited and thorough critique of the discourse on *sui generis* religion, *Manufacturing Religion*, McCutcheon adopts the methodology employed by Edward Herman and Noam Chomsky in *Manufacturing Consent* to analyze the way in which this discourse constructs religion as an irreducible category. Such a construction, argues McCutcheon, serves to authorize hegemonic operations, participating in the "coordination, articulation, and experience of dominance" (ix). But McCutcheon's emphasis on the manufacturing operations of the discourse on *sui generis* religion masks the fact that McCutcheon and his reductionist colleagues are doing some manufacturing of their own. By insisting on a "sharp, bright line" between practice and study, reductionists manufacture both religion and the university as mutually constitutive opposites. Religion is the university's other. Religion, the university, and the respective constituents of each emerge as the productive effect of the reductionist's ideology. "Ideology," writes Alan Sinfield, "produces, makes plausible, concepts and systems to explain who we are, who the others are, how the world works" (32). The reductionist ideology serves to produce and make plausible the inviolable homogeneity of the university's identity as subject over religion's object. Further, in proclaiming the reducibility of religion, reductionists insist that, "insider" protests notwithstanding, religion is not a privileged discourse. "Privilege," in this context, is a class-inflected code-word that acts as a political lever, giving egalitarian-empowered carte-blanche to the dominating gaze of the scholar. It is an Enlightenment-inspired ideology—with a grim historical legacy—that leaves no territory outside the domination of the academic's exercise of power-knowledge. From such a position, "insider" resistance or protests have, by definition, no academic or argumentative legitimacy. They are only further data for reductive analysis.

Political arguments aside, perhaps the most serious problem with the reductionist position lies in the circularity of its principal argument. In launching their critique on proponents of *sui generis* religion, reductionists often begin by citing Jonathan Z. Smith's widely accepted observation that religion is "solely the creation of the scholar's study"(xi). Beyond this contingent, disciplinary taxon, there is no religion as such. The discourse on *sui generis* religion is, according to the reductionist critique, a denial of Smith's observation. But in its critique of the discourse on *sui generis* religion, the reductionist argues that this discourse is inappropriate in the academy because it constitutes, in fact, the practice of religion *as such*. Reductionists thus end up endorsing the terms of the very position they are critiquing.[8]

It is, I believe, because of his recognition of the necessity to escape the circularity of reductionism's central objection to the discourse on *sui generis* religion that McCutcheon, in an essay largely dedicated to a rigorous marshalling of the reductionist critique (although, in this instance, McCutcheon cites the object of his critique as the "liberal humanist" approach characteristic of the liberal arts), makes a special plea for a definition of religion ("Critical Trends" 324). And this is crucial, for without a reductionist, *non-essentialist* definition of religion, one that can operate in the "inter-subjectively observable world," one that rejects hermeneutics and the liberal humanist approaches that McCutcheon claims dominate departments of religious studies, reductionism is fighting a phantom. Worse, it is practicing that against which it preaches (i.e., practice).

The reductionist position constitutes an uneasy marriage of empiricist scientism and Foucaultian historicity, a methodology usually employed with a barefaced lack of irony. Yet it is one thing to make a living (much less a good argument) trading in critical analyses based on historicity and discursive formations, but quite another to avoid being tripped up by them. Perhaps the answer to the problematics of the "strong" sense of objectivity, and the associated assertion of "strong" oppositions (e.g., university/religion, study of/practice of, disinterested/interested) that inevitably deconstruct themselves, is to adopt a position of "anti-strength." That is to say, perhaps there is a position that resists both objectivity in its strong sense, and theology and subjectivity in their strong senses: a kind of self-aware embeddedness with "soft" objectivity. But such conceptual "bridges," as Catherine Bell observes, are "readily destabilized by the logical extremes to which they are pegged" (11). A better solution might involve the adoption of a kind of philosophical pragmatism—a perspective of academic realpolitik. For if one wishes to avoid elevating objectivity, science, disinterestedness, and university "norms" (or their opposites) to the kind of thing under reductionist critique (i.e., ahistorical essences that transcend discursive formations and the operations of power and hegemony), then a more honest approach would be to admit the rhetorical character of such critiques, the pragmatic, material, and strategic interests they serve, and their inescapable historicity and discursive constitution.

In the debate over the discipline of religious studies, reductionist critiques constitute both the production of the object of knowledge (in his concern that naming his object "religion" involves hypostasizing religion as such, McCutcheon sometimes prefers calling this object simply an "intriguing aspect of human communities") and of the knower. They demarcate what counts as knowledge and appoint those who can legitimately speak knowledgably. All of these are, of necessity, exclusionary operations ineluctably bound up with the power produced by, and productive of, such knowledge. In the academy, such power has distinctly material consequences—tenure, promotion, grants, publication, fellowships, appointments, research leaves, sabbaticals, awards, etc.—and associated cultural capital. A more pragmatic perspective would constitute an admission that these debates involve a jockeying for position in the contest for the resource slices of the university pie. Such a pragmatic approach—one that avoids either taking sides or searching for some precarious middle ground—may effectively cut the Gordian knot of the reductionist/anti-reductionist dispute. The power-knowledge matrix I have cited, and its associated material and cultural capital, is amoral, irrational, and extra-legal; it can operate only within and behind an epistemological scaffold that masks it, that naturalizes it, and that authorizes its productive functions. Regardless of the position one takes in this study/practice argument, the same purpose is served: the epistemological scaffold is strengthened. "All that capital asks of us," writes Baudrillard, "is to receive it as rational or to combat it in the name of rationality, to receive it as moral or combat it in the name of morality" (15). Insofar as reductionists endorse a thorough and rigorous political analysis in religious studies, they might acknowledge the political enmeshment of their own position, and opt for the end-run around the study/practice dispute offered by pragmatism. This wouldn't necessarily involve giving up or even conceding ground, merely (to extend the territorial metaphor) a recognition of the ground, and the grounds on which, they are contesting. It would involve a kind of recognition that theatre and performance studies understands well: that the dispute is a performative, a *practice* that produces a ground that is subsequently mistaken for foundation.

To their credit, most reductionists readily acknowledge that their efforts constitute a struggle for disciplinary identity and legitimacy within the academy. At times, they even admit to the pragmatic and mundane professional concerns that drive their mission. McCutcheon, citing a 1994 article by Sam Gill, connects the dominance of the discourse on *sui generis* religion to "the budgetary problems experienced by many U.S. departments of religious studies during the 1990s" ("Critical Trends" 318). Not coincidentally, it was during this period of fiscal crisis that the reductionist polemic against *sui generis* religion began to take on an acute urgency. "[T]heories are not lofty, purely intellectual items," states McCutcheon, "[t]hey have practical, institutional, and political implications" ("Critical Trends" 318). Here, McCutcheon tacitly acknowledges that the reductionist's intra-disciplinary polemic is a struggle for material resources and cultural capital, a fight for occupational and economic survival in the academic marketplace. It is a networked series of local struggles for the sustaining of material and personal livelihoods in an acutely competitive arena.

The struggle for cultural capital and for a sustaining share of the limited resources of the university is certainly a struggle that theatre and performance studies—and all the disciplines within "the arts"—can well understand. This struggle has become particularly dire in light of the financial crises currently assailing U.S. universities. It may be fairly observed that theatre and performance studies' efforts at self-justification, their arguments for material resources within the academy, have not occasioned the kind of painfully divisive disciplinary fusillades characteristic of the conflict between reductionists and anti-reductionists in religious studies. But here, my hedge about the dangers of cross-disciplinary comparisons of terms like "practice" becomes critical. The distinctive genealogy of religious studies in the U.S. vexes its struggle for academic legitimacy to a degree that theatre and performance studies cannot apprehend.

The debate over state support of the arts in the U.S. has been broad, but has focused most acutely on so-called "experimental" or "avant-garde" forms, traditions that, although this fact goes (mostly) unspoken, have been historically sustained—some might say "unnaturally" so, for such sustenance functions to resist the avant-garde's self-definition as unsustainable in the presumably "natural" eco-system of the market—through the efforts and practices of faculty at public universities. Controversies over public support of the arts—e.g., the famous "NEA Four"—are familiar battlefields in the U.S. culture wars. But these controversies take place on comparatively weak legal grounds (and invoke comparatively anemic responses) when placed next to the discourse surrounding the supposedly constitutional separation of church and state (a discourse that, ironically, inverts the right/left positions of the state-supported arts dispute). The 1963 Supreme Court decision in *Abington Township School District v. Schempp* became the "*fiat lux*" of religious studies programs in U.S. public universities, endorsing as it did a legal distinction between the study of and practice of religion. The legal and constitutional aspects of this distinction in the U.S. thus constitute the "gun on the table" in the dispute between reductionists and anti-reductionists. This situation raises the stakes to an alarming degree, amplifying the dispute along lines that have culture war anchor-points. However vexed it may become, the study of/practice of distinction in theatre and performance has no analogously strong legal weapon on its table, no similar crowbar that might pry open the distinction to such an extent as to threaten disciplinary integrity. And even if it did, theatre and performance scholars have, by and large, historically endorsed state-supported arts in the U.S. and, occasional grumbling aside, the practice of the arts in the academy.

The reductionists argue that legitimacy within the academy is predicated on an assimilation of the norms of scientific—or, at least, social-scientific—epistemology. In this, they refer back to the founding of the scientific study of religion by Max Muller in Germany under the *Wissenschaft* paradigm, and create polemic bulwarks against what they cite as the theology of the liberal arts and humanities. For reductionists, it is this liberal arts mode—a normative agenda that seeks to produce and educate a "cultivated" and "cultured" citizenry in service of a pluralistic and humanistic vision of liberal democracy—its essentialist and universalist tendencies, its troublesome Enlightenment baggage and crypto-theology that so troubles their field and threatens the identity and integrity of the university itself. It is one of those odd ironies of history that the *Wissenschaft* paradigm on the one hand and the *Bildung* model that contributed to the emergence in the U.S. of the liberal arts ideal on the other were both nineteenth-century imports from German universities.

Insofar as the proponents of reductionism, in adopting the scientific model of research as the *de rigueur* academic paradigm, seek to articulate a division between their efforts and the domains of the liberal arts and humanities, then the current state of their own discipline—and other methodologically heterogeneous disciplines like theatre and performance studies—threatens to undo this tenuous division. In order to legitimate itself within a university that exhibits, in material ways, a distinct preference for the paradigms of scientific inquiry, these scholars have attempted to install their field within the conventions of scientific research, borrowing language, perspectives, methods, and rhetoric as a hedge against fuzzy and transcendentally inflected humanism. This strategy includes a constructed sense of rigor, the adoption of models from the natural and social sciences, a rejection of theology, and a dismissal of hermeneutics and other modes associated with the humanities, particularly literature and the arts. The discomfort expressed by reductionist polemics emerges from their field's location along a discursively constructed fault line between the liberal arts/humanities and scientific/social scientific epistemologies and their attendant values, missions, and ideologies. Those in the field of theatre and performance studies may well identify with—if have little sympathy for—the dilemma faced by the reductionists, for theatre occupies an even more acutely divided position. It straddles a fault line between three epistemological modes and missions: professional/technical, liberal arts/humanities,[9] and scientific/social scientific. Each of these modes have been endorsed as appropriate within the public university, whose identity has been constituted by, and as a site for, the contesting epistemologies, pedagogic goals, cultural values, and socio-economic missions of these three historically and discursively contingent perspectives. While a good deal of advocacy for the legitimacy of theatre and performance studies within the academy cleaves to perspectives gleaned from liberal arts/humanities modes, such arguments downplay the potential strength of an argument from methodological heterogeneity. I would suggest that cross-disciplinary dialogue between theatre and performance studies on the one hand, and religious studies on the other, must include an argument for both disciplines as appropriate sites of productively contesting epistemologies and academic missions reflective of the larger heterogeneous identity of the academy itself.

NOTES

1. Other key players include Donald Wiebe, Timothy Fitzgerald, and Robert A. Segal.
2. For an investigation into reductionism with regard to religion and religious studies, see Jones 224–326.
3. For a defense of academic theology, see Brown, 126–139.
4. For an argument against academic theology, see Strenski (2002).
5. See Chesnek 50.
6. The notion of separate spheres served historically to mask the actual work—and the working conditions—of women both inside and outside the home, and to elide the fact that the leadership of religious institutions was exhaustively male-dominated.
7. Stark 241. As a presidential candidate in 2008, Barack Obama stumbled upon this prejudice, creating a media kerfluffle when he remarked that citizens of small towns hit by sustained economic hardship "get bitter" and "cling to guns or religion."
8. To his credit, McCutcheon acknowledges this circularity in *Manufacturing Religion*. See 16 and 160.
9. The current and severe economic downturn in the U.S. has had a disturbingly deleterious effect on departments within the liberal arts and humanities, revealing, for some, the class-based ideology in which these modes are enmeshed (see Cohen). Not coincidentally, debate over the future of the liberal arts and humanities in the academy has become increasingly urgent. See, for example, recent books by Donoghue and Kronman.

WORKS CITED

Baudrillard, Jean. *Simulacra and Simulation.* Trans. Sheila Faria Glaser. Ann Arbor: U of Michigan P, 1994. Print.

Bell, Catherine. "Pragmatic Theory." *Secular Theories on Religion: Current Perspectives.* Ed. Tim Jensen and Mikael Rothstein. Copenhagen: Museum Tusculanum, 2000. 9–20. Print.

Brown, Delwin. "Academic Theology in the University or Why an Ex-Queen's Heir Should Be Made a Subject." *Religious Studies, Theology, and the University: Conflicting Maps, Changing Terrain.* Ed. Linell E. Cady and Brown. Albany: SUNY P, 2002. 126–139. Print.

Chesnek, Christopher. "Our Subject 'Over There'? Scrutinizing the Distance Between Religion and Its Study." *Religious Studies, Theology, and the University: Conflicting Maps, Changing Terrain.* Ed. Linell E. Cady and Delwin Brown. Albany: SUNY P, 2002. 45–64. Print.

Cohen, Patricia. "In Tough Times, the Humanities Must Justify Their Worth." *New York Times.* 25 Feb. 2009: C1. Web. 9 Jan. 2011.

Donoghue, Frank. *The Last Professors: The Corporate University and the Fate of the Humanities.* New York: Fordham UP, 2008. Print.

Gill, Sam. "The Academic Study of Religion." *Journal of the American Academy of Religion.* 62.4 (1994): 965–975. Print.

Hart, D. G. *The University Gets Religion: Religious Studies in American Higher Education.* Baltimore: Johns Hopkins, 1999. Print.

Jackson, Shannon. *Professing Performance: Theatre in the Academy from Philology to Performativity.* Cambridge: Cambridge UP, 2004. Print.

Jones, Richard H. *Reductionism: Analysis and the Fullness of Reality.* Lewisburg: Bucknell UP, 2000. Print.

Kronman, Anthony T. *Education's End: Why Our Colleges and Universities Have Given Up on the Meaning of Life.* New Haven: Yale UP, 2008. Print.

McCutcheon, Russell T. "Critical Trends in the Study of Religion in the United States." *New Approaches to the Study of Religion.* Vol. 1. Ed. Peter Antes, Armin W. Geertz, and Randi R. Warne. Berlin: de Gruyter, 2004. 317–343. Print.

———. *Manufacturing Religion: The Discourse on Sui Generis Religion and the Politics of Nostalgia.* Oxford: Oxford UP, 1997. Print.

Sinfield, Alan. *Faultlines: Cultural Materialism and the Politics of Dissident Reading.* Berkeley: U of California P, 1992. Print.

Smith, Jonathan Z. *Imagining Religion: From Babylon to Jonestown.* Chicago: U of Chicago P, 1982. Print.

Stark, Rodney. "Rationality." *Guide to the Study of Religions.* Ed. Willi Braun and Russell T. McCutcheon. London: Cassell, 2000. 239–258. Print.

Strenski, Ivan. "The Proper Object of the Study of Religion: Why It Is Better to Know Some of the Questions than All of the Answers." *The Future of the Study of Religion.* Ed. Slavica Jakelic and Lori Pearson. Leiden: Brill, 2004. 145–171. Print.

———. "Why 'Theology' Won't Work." *Religious Studies, Theology, and the University: Conflicting Maps, Changing Terrain.* Ed. Linell E. Cady and Delwin Brown. Albany: SUNY P, 2002. 31–44. Print.

Warne, Randi R. "Gender." *Guide to the Study of Religions.* Ed. Willi Braun and Russell T. McCutcheon. London: Cassell, 2000. 140–154. Print.

———. "Making the Gender-Critical Turn." *Secular Theories on Religion: Current Perspectives.* Ed. Tim Jensen and Mikael Rothstein. Copenhagen: Museum Tusculanum, 2000. 249–260. Print.

Wiebe, Donald. *The Politics of Religious Studies: The Continuing Conflict with Theology in the Academy.* New York: St. Martin's, 1999. Print.

15 Performing Coexistence with Good Faith Intolerance

John Fletcher

In May of 2001, Jerusalem's Museum on the Seam (a "socio-political contemporary art museum") premiered the exhibition "Coexistence," a series of fifty three-by-five-meter displays around the theme of "coexistence" by artists from around the world (*Coexistence*, "About the Exhibition"). Among these was the simple, eye-catching piece, *Coexist*, by Polish graphic designer Piotr Mlodozeniec, consisting of a white three-by-five-meter panel with the word *coexist* in black. In place of the letters *C*, *X*, and *T*, Mlodozeniec substitutes an Islamic crescent, a Jewish Star of David, and a Christian cross. A brief quote from Thomas Jefferson accompanies the sign, serving as a caption:

> On the dogmas of religion as distinguished from moral principles, all mankind, from the beginning of the world to this day, have been quarrelling, fighting, burning and torturing one another, for abstractions unintelligible to themselves and to all others, and absolutely beyond the comprehension of the human mind. (Mlodozeniec)[1]

Mlodozeniec's design quickly became one of the exhibition's signature pieces, spotlighted prominently in the Museum's publicity materials and merchandise (*Coexistence*, "Products"). Particularly with the events of the following September, the work's ecumenical tenor gained it widespread attention. Soon after its premiere in Jerusalem, Mlodozeniec's design went viral, mutating into newer, even more inclusive shapes and cropping up in countless venues and formats. You may have seen a version of the design as a bumper sticker yourself (perhaps with a few more characters than the original).

I take the popularity and mass circulation of the Coexist design as indicative of a present-day yearning for interfaith coexistence, for a respite from the "dogmas of religion" and their "quarrelling." This push and the backlash against it form the context of my ongoing research into intersections of left-progressive activist[2] performance and U.S. evangelicalism.[3] Bringing these fields together produces sparks because the progressive left and conservative evangelicalism are so often imagined as locked in intractable conflict over the issue of coexistence in plural democracy; the left works for a tolerant, multi-faith democracy while religions like evangelicalism remain stubbornly insistent on the exclusivity of their worldviews. As an ex-evangelical Christian with decidedly left-progressive leanings, I might be expected to invest my support in the left's pro-tolerance push against ideological intractability. In this essay, however, I argue that tolerance—particularly the popular hope/demand for interfaith tolerance embodied by the Coexist design—can have corrosive effects on the strength and scope of left-progressive activist initiatives. To pursue this line of argument, I examine how Mlodozeniec's design and its messages have been mobilized in particular performance situations. I then contextualize these acts in terms of both evangelical Christian reactions to popular tolerance discourse and current critiques of liberal-democratic tolerance within political philosophy. I conclude by discussing a different performance practice—public theological debates—that some sectors of Christian evangelicalism use to model a different kind of faith act, a performance of what one might call good faith intolerance.

I begin with one of the most visible stagings of the Coexist design, the Irish band U2's incorporation of the symbol into their live show during their 2005–2006 Vertigo Tour. A one point, during a stretch of politically themed numbers, the music transitions from the song "Love and Peace or Else" into the harsh U2 anthem "Sunday, Bloody Sunday," which expresses horror at political and interreligious violence.[4] Bono, the band's lead singer, dons a white headband emblazoned with the Mlodozeniec Coexist graphic and assumes a position in front of a set of snare drums. Marching militaristically in place, he bangs out the harsh, militaristic beat that begins the song before breaking off to sing. In the middle of the piece, Bono speaks directly to the audience. Blogger Kevin Hutchinson describes the scene:

> Bono kneels down, wrists crossed above his head, conjuring images of a hostage, now blindfolded with the CoeXisT band covering his eyes. In the European shows, the CoeXisT sign dominates the giant screen behind the band. And in the midst of "Sunday Bloody Sunday" (which, according to Bono, doesn't just belong to Ireland anymore) Bono points to each religious icon and declares: *"Jesus, Jew, Muhammad, it's true . . . All sons of Abraham. Father Abraham, speak to your sons. Tell them, No more!"* (Hutchinson)[5]

As the audience takes up the "No more!" chant, Bono returns to the chorus: "The real battle just begun/ To fight the battle Jesus won/ On Sunday, Bloody Sunday . . . " (U2). In their study of U2's Vertigo and Elevation tours, political geographers Victoria Morley and Katrinka Somdahl-Sands note that over 30 percent of spectators they surveyed named the "Coexist spectacle" as one of the most dramatic moments of the concert (66).

Writing about Bono's performance, religion scholar Chad E. Seales cites the spectacle as an example of what he calls Bono's "secular soteriology" in which the star enacts "religious practice as secular activism and secular activism as religious practice" (para. 5). Borrowing from evangelical revivalist dramaturgies (call and response, alternating song-and-sermon passages, direct challenges to congregation/audience) while at the same time distancing himself from alignment with any one denomination, Bono casts himself as an avatar of left-progressive political salvation, a "rock 'n' roll messiah" preaching peace, tolerance, and love—all crowned with the Coexist headband. In the Vertigo tour, Mlodozeniec's design combines with Bono's international activist popularity and U2's anthemic call to spiritual-political transcendence. "Coexist" becomes both an aspirational rallying cry (*We, the Abrahamic faiths, can coexist*) and a command (*Coexist in peace, Abrahamic religions!*). Bono, as postmodern-secular messiah, enacts a quasi-religious call to reform or relinquish the prejudices of religion.

By the time the Vertigo tour wrapped up, the design had already dispersed into popular culture, morphing into a number of variations.[6] Perhaps the most widespread variant Coexist design comes from a company called Peacemonger, which sells the sticker and related merchandise online (at www.Peacemonger.org) and at live events. Peacemonger's design expands the ecumenical umbrella to include other faith-based or ideological groups. It keeps the crescent, star, and cross but adds a peace symbol for the O, a "male/female symbol" for the E, a Wicca/Pagan sign for the I, and a Taoist/Confucian yin-yang for S. Online shoppers at Peacemonger.com can find similarly symbolized stickers (and T-shirts, key fobs, magnets, posters, etc.) declaring such messages as "tolerance," "acceptance," "patience," and "diversity."

While obviously a commercial endeavor, Peacemonger asserts that its activities and designs spring from a particular activist vision that transcends profit-making. The company's founder (and eponymous Peacemonger), Jerry Jaspar, writes that he was initially working as an activist on an anti-war (i.e., anti-Iraq invasion) billboard for a local peace group. Balking at the high cost of billboard rental, he switched to designing bumper stickers. "I figured we could have thousands of very small, more permanent billboards in the world for far less money," he explains. The new format led him to develop the symbols-for-letters tactic, a style he dubs "symbolglyphics" (Jaspar does not mention Mlodozeniec). His particular Coexist design came about, relates Jaspar, after a revelation regarding "the root causes for conflict: Religions. I've found mostly we should focus on similarities between these faiths, rather than fighting over who's 'right.'" By focusing on interfaith unity, Jaspar hopes (in a seeming echo of U2's Coexist spectacle) "to engage the world's religions into messages [of] unity and peace between themselves" (Jaspar). Like Bono's spectacle, then, Jaspar's "small, more permanent billboards" at once indict religions for not coexisting (or tolerating, accepting, diversifying, etc.) and challenge them to coexist as neatly and beautifully as his symbolglyphic design.

Granted, from a performance studies perspective, several orders of magnitude separate the act of slapping a Coexist bumper sticker on a car and Bono's elaborate show. But, as Jaspar's account of his design strategies suggests, bumper stickers can function as miniature activist acts. Within the limited scholarly literature on bumper stickers, most critics affirm that, whatever else they may be (e.g., artifacts of material culture, automotive fashion accessories, advertisements), bumper stickers do performative work.[7] They at once announce and enact one's endorsement of a particular cause or attitude, an expression that implicates the displayer (or anyone taken to be the displayer) into the act of endorsement. Essayist Leslie Haynsworth warns, "Maybe to you it doesn't seem like such a bold personal statement simply to speak your mind about one particular issue via this shiny plastic decal on the back of your car. But chances are good that it will seem bold to others" (27). Those who display bumper stickers, she writes, do not neutrally reproduce a message; they invite others to read them as someone who would display *that* sticker, "so to all the other drivers around you, the sticker signifies who you are, what you're like, and what they should think of you" (23). Stickers mark the displayer as a true believer for a particular cause or attitude, someone sufficiently committed to spread the gospel, so to speak, about a particular issue. In cases where stickers communicate politically or cultural charged stances, such implied commitment can have serious consequences for the displayer. Haynsworth relates several stories of motorists who got ticketed by authorities or even run off the road for displaying partisan bumper stickers (Haynsworth 24–27).

Nor do consequences fall solely on those who display provocative messages. In her survey of queer people growing up in the conservative Christian Bible Belt of the U.S., sociologist Bernadette Barton notes the ubiquitous Christian slogans and symbols that saturate the Belt's cultural landscape. For Barton's subjects, these messages, although rarely anti-gay in and of themselves, nevertheless communicate the suffocating hegemony of a "compulsory Christianity" that is actively hostile to non-heterosexuals. The Jesus fish, cross necklaces, Bible-verse-laden T-shirts, "repent or perish" billboards, and "1CROSS + 3NAILS = 4GVN" bumper stickers, argues Barton, "are not value free; they function as shorthand for beliefs, opinions, and ideology. . . . [R]esidents learn to associate even presumably value-neutral Christian symbols like a T-shirt proclaiming 'SAVED' or a cross over a local grocery store with fundamentalist social attitudes." Eventually, she concludes, queer people in the Bible Belt "may begin to read all Christian symbols as signals of homophobia." Barton, who lives in Kentucky with her partner, admits that after a few encounters with non-gay-friendly locals, even she has begun to associate such Christian paraphernalia and semiotics with "a menacing bigotry" on the part of those who display them (82).

Being a Bible Belt gay myself—growing up in Oklahoma as the son of a (former) Southern Baptist pastor, in fact—I can relate to some of the discomfort Barton's subjects communicate. Although I find the portrayal of the Bible Belt as fundamentalist panopticon overstated, when I visit my parents' rural town, I sometimes catch myself looking at local cars. Almost without thinking, I search out messages, and therefore drivers, that I can interpret as "friendly" (i.e., left-leaning) while at the same time noting the types and numbers of less welcoming (i.e., politically/theologically conservative) symbols. And as I take in others' personal-billboard micro-performatives, Peacemonger's Coexist bumper sticker—rare but hardly nonexistent—qualifies as "friendly" along with the yellow equal signs, rainbow stickers, and "Celebrate Diversity" messages that decorate my parents' car. Such tiny, relatively anonymous expressions may operate on wholly other performative scales than Bono's multi-million-dollar sermon, but in the lived environment of the rural Bible Belt, I welcome any gesture toward left-progressive tolerance. And, really, who wouldn't? Who would make a case in favor of a gay or lesbian person's being made to feel unwelcome in civic or social life? Who could, in other words, criticize the value of tolerance?

Cue the evangelicals.

Rather, cue one strand of current evangelical discourse. A few clarifications are in order. I distinguish present-day U.S. evangelicalism from other labels too often used synonymously or casually to name non-left-progressive Christianities, like *fundamentalism*, *religious right*, and *conservative Christianity*. Present-day evangelicalism in the U.S.—and here I refer to the heirs of a mid-century split with fundamentalism[8]—encompasses a wide range of beliefs, practices, and histories. No official evangelical church exists to organize this multiplicity into an ordered whole. I find it most useful, then, to approach evangelicalism as an essentially contested concept (Gallie 168–172), a zone of theological, historical, and sociological convergence[9] defined in part by persistent internal disagreements regarding its self-definition. That is, part of being evangelical means disagreeing with other evangelicals about the core and boundary features of evangelicalism itself. Currently, one of the main debates among evangelicals concerns how best to navigate a simultaneous dedication to upholding strict doctrines about the Bible, salvation, and Christian behavior on the one hand and engaging in active and meaningful outreach to the culture at large on the other.

Such evangelical orthodoxy-versus-outreach struggles crystallize in discussions of tolerance. For some, evangelicalism's reputation for intolerance signals a Christian failure of witness. David Kinnaman and Gabe Lyons, researchers with the evangelical Barna Group, recently published results of their surveys of popular attitudes toward evangelicalism. To their dismay, they found that young adults, a demographic evangelicalism desperately wants to attract, most strongly associate Christianity with terms like *anti-homosexual*, *judgmental*, and *hypocritical* (27). Worse, the researchers discovered that most non-Christians acquire these perceptions from encounters with Christians themselves. "We have become," the authors lament, "famous for what we oppose, rather than who we are for" (26). Although not willing to compromise on theological truth, Kinnaman and Lyons (along with a range of other evangelical ministers) nevertheless call for re-thinking how Christians communicate orthodox belief in outreach to others.

Other sectors of evangelicalism take a less humble approach, labeling accusations of evangelical intolerance as attacks on Christian orthodoxy. Evangelical apologists Josh McDowell and Bob Hostetler, for example, castigate what they call "the new tolerance," which they define as a postmodern attitude that equates all values and points of view without regard for morality or truth (18–20). Whereas traditional tolerance (which they approve of) makes space for the right to believe or say anything in society, the "new" tolerance imposes a restriction in that it forbids any act or thought that suggests disapproval or objection to another's opinions or actions. The new tolerance requires not just forbearance of prohibition but *approval* of any and all truth positions or attitudes. This new-tolerance regime, McDowell and Hostetler argue, prohibits deep, certain convictions, including Christianity's affirmation of its epistemological and moral superiority to other faiths. Normative assertions of right and wrong become, within this regime, unacceptable varieties of hatred, bigotry, and phobia (72–79). For these authors, tolerance functions as a form of anti-Christian thought control aimed at eradicating normative standards for life. McDowell and Hostetler call on evangelicals to reinforce their commitment to Biblical orthodoxy in the face of a cultural current that would invalidate strong belief.

To be clear, I find McDowell and Hostetler's take on postmodernity tendentious, their tone histrionic, and their recommendations off-putting.[10] Yet their criticisms are representative of a larger evangelical backlash against the ideal/imperative of tolerance circulating in U.S. popular culture. Moreover, some of the contentions they level against "the new tolerance" resonate with current scholarly critiques of tolerance as it operates in liberal-democratic theory.

A short summary is in order as I transition between popular and scholarly registers. As I hope is clear, I have focused on performed mobilizations of the Coexist meme not to set up a shallow, straw-man version of tolerance to demolish but because I take such popular performances as symptomatic of a deeper conceptual tension regarding tolerance in plural culture. I have credited the Coexist design's durability in part to its semantic openness, an openness capitalized on in both U2's concert and Peacemonger's personal-billboard merchandise. Coexist performatives issue two utterances simultaneously: "We *can* get along!" and "You *will* get along!" But these two utterances pull against each other. Is tolerance an aspiration to be freely pursued or an imposition to be assumed?

Oddly enough, many political theorists suggest, liberal-democratic tolerance operates as both at once. Here I must simplify. Basically, liberal democracy confronts a conundrum. It must manage the deep conflict between incompatible religious beliefs yet maintain a commitment both to religious freedom and to the plurality of democratic participants. Predominant models of liberal-democratic theory (such as that of Jürgen Habermas or John Rawls) propose a bifurcated schema of tolerance within democratic society. Alessandro Ferrara neatly summarizes this dual taxonomy:

> As we have seen, Habermas converges with Rawls in distinguishing a broad public sphere, where every contribution even if couched in religious terms is legitimate, and a more restricted institutional realm where binding decisions are made (parliaments, courts, governmental agencies, etc.). Between these two realms a filter must be operative, which lets only secular contents and arguments pass through. The problem is where exactly this filter has to be metaphorically located and what it should block. ("Separation" 86)

Prominent liberal-democratic models of tolerance, in other words, work by designating religious faith as a properly private affair. In its private realm, faith and its constituent values stay insulated from state controls, in theory allowing for an endless, coercion-free plurality of faiths to coexist in peace (thus the aspiration of tolerance). But tolerance schemes also quarantine these beliefs as such from spaces of formal, institutional deliberation lest they gum up the democratic exchange of ideas with faith-based exclusivism (thus the imposition of tolerance). Religiously oriented citizens may participate in formal political deliberations, but to do so they must accept a set of ground rules—the filter Ferrara references—that limits the passions or arguments expressed and exchanged to those accessible by and acceptable to all other participants, regardless of faith. With such a bifurcated tolerance scheme, liberal-democratic theory basically hopes to have its cake and eat it too, ensuring the blessings of religious plurality while staving off the nightmare of interreligious strife.

Yet for many religiously oriented citizens, argues Stanley Fish, this toleration scheme proves unrealistic. In practice, he contends, liberal democracy's bifurcated model "means that some ideas—those urged with an unhappy exclusiveness—must either themselves be excluded or be admitted only on the condition that they blunt the edge of their assertiveness, and present themselves for possible correction." (249) As Fish notes (in concert with many evangelical critiques), religious convictions are not personal accessories to be stored in some political dresser drawer and saved for special (private) occasions. Beliefs are comprehensive world-and-life views that by nature set believers' very standards of assent and dissent. From an evangelical perspective, for example, God (through the Bible) determines the legitimacy of liberal tolerance's expectations of faith, not vice versa. By expecting religious convictions to operate subsequent to liberal protocols—protocols coded not merely *public* but also *secular* and *neutral*—tolerance misconstrues the nature of deep religious conviction.

Of course, for many liberal-democratic theorists, religion's refusal to open its prior convictions to revision or to translate its rationales into neutral (i.e., secular) language demonstrates exactly why religious views must remained locked out of institutional-deliberative processes. From this perspective, religion refuses to be *reasonable*. It insists upon its own conceptions of truth and standards of assent as irreducibly *so*, prior to and regardless of the conventions necessary for plural democratic deliberation. Yet, as Lucas Swaine points out, tolerance's constraints apply not to religion *per se* (Unitarian Universalists, Swaine suggests, might adapt easily) but rather to any set of comprehensive convictions resistant to liberal theory's expectations of revisablity and critical reflection. Swaine deems such committed positions *heteronomous* (184).[11] While many faith-based positions are heteronomous, he notes, so too are many activist positions. A committed pacifist, a vegan, an environmentalist, or a Progressive-era suffragist all operate heteronomously. They hold tightly to contested beliefs that are, for them, resistant to revision (Must vegans open themselves to the possibility of supporting foie gras producers?), compartmentalization (Should environmentalists pretend not to be environmentalists while debating carbon emissions policy?), and translation into "neutral" political language (Could pre-1920 suffragists participate "neutrally" in male-only democratic deliberations?). Each of these stances is potentially unreasonable from within the schema of liberal tolerance. "In this context," summarizes Wendy Brown, "a morally passionate citizen"—and not just a religious extremist—"becomes strangely intolerable" (40).

Ferrara expands on this point, claiming that liberal-democratic tolerance's criterion of reasonability falls into a performative contradiction: it is utterly intolerant toward intolerance. That is, liberal-democratic pluralism demands that participants hold every faith commitment loosely, in a condition of reasonable revisability—every belief, that is, except for faith in liberal-democratic pluralism itself. Other modes of ordered plural coexistence are conceivable, Ferrara notes, but what liberal theory refuses "to become fully aware of is that their case for pluralism is but one among a 'plurality of pluralisms', not the one doctrine of pluralism that the other political cultures of the planet ignore at their peril" ("Reflexive" 363). As a result, toleration at the popular level manifests not as a rationally defensible case but as an incoherent attitude that requires no explanation—a Coexist bumper sticker—consisting of permanently suspended moral judgments and a default disapproval of disapproving.

On a more insidious level, such "liberal monopluralism" (Ferrara, "Reflexive" 353) leads to a constriction of politics' imaginative horizons. Tolerance morphs, argues Brown, from being a necessary-but-insufficient condition for democratic politics to serving as the telos of social activism. The bold "I have a dream" of Martin Luther King, Jr., she observes, becomes the modest "Can't we all just get along?" of Rodney King. While tolerance is certainly necessary as a liberal-democratic precondition, Brown concedes, mere coexistence as end-point offers a "terribly thin vision of membership, participation, and social transformation" (86–88). Worse, in Brown's view, is how tolerance as ultimate political goal tends to bundle material inequalities, structural injustices, and historical traumas into a generic category of "difference," which in turn reifies into a generic subject type: the Other. So long as this Other is tolerated (endured but never welcomed), the democratic state can declare "mission accomplished," excusing itself from doing the long, hard work of addressing the conditions that perpetuate injustices.

The Coexist design beautifully encapsulates this attenuated version of heteronomous commitment within liberal-democratic tolerance. In this scheme, coexistence is possible provided that the constituent faiths/commitments shed or hide away every one of their features except for the surface markers of their existence. Different comprehensive convictions can/must live side-by-side only by being flattened into exchangeable symbols on an evocative bumper sticker or worked into a high-emotion spectacle. Moreover, inclusion in the Coexist sign/system obviates the need to confront material, ideological, historical, and theological complications of plurality. Instead of justice or equality, toleration merely requires that "we all just get along." Just coexist. You can do it. You *have* to do it.

Now, I score no great coup by calling a one-word design overly simplistic. But my point is not that the Coexist meme's pop-culture performances get liberal-democratic tolerance wrong. On the contrary, they get it *right*. Coexist's flattened out (yet oh-so-striking) array of symbols works as a surprisingly accurate précis of the dual aspiration-imposition expectations that liberal-democratic tolerance presents to and imposes upon deep, comprehensive, heteronomous commitments. Such faiths may exist in private, but when it comes to institutional deliberations, the secular-neutral faith in liberal-democratic tolerance is the only religion in town.

To be fair, no liberal-democratic theorist (least of all Habermas or Rawls) sets out to create anti-Christian thought police or bumper sticker cosmopolitanism. Habermas in particular has significantly revised his prior theories of religion's role in politics, calling on democracies to recognize that they live in a "post-secular" culture defined by the persistence and insistence of religious faith in public and political life. And, it must be said, calls for coexistence—be they nuanced or simplistic—carry power because stark, close-minded intolerance remains a real problem. As Kinnaman and Lyons point out, evangelicalism has earned its reputation as judgmental and intolerant through a number of harsh, inflexible stances sometimes founded on factually blinkered perspectives.

A quick Internet search, for example, reveals a number of anti-Muslim responses to the Coexist bumper sticker from groups on the religious right (a demographic with significant overlap with U.S. evangelicalism). One of these features Mlodozeniec's simple Islam-Judaism-Christianity design, but with the Islamic crescent now armed with strap-on explosives, suggesting that the real barrier to coexistence is Islam's commitment to violence ("Coexist?").[12] This is interfaith calumny, intolerance in the worst sense. It reflects no doctrinal point of evangelicalism and represents a willful ignorance about Islam. Assumed as an attitude or, worse, as an essential article of faith, such intolerance can foster mass violence on international as well as intra-cultural scales. Faced with the reality of such toxic hatred cloaked in deep, comprehensive moral conviction, tolerance's coercive compartmentalization of heteronomy becomes all the more appealing.

But here I have to tread carefully. Such ugly and (to my mind) clearly reprehensible examples of intolerance, particularly from evangelicals, can all too easily let me overlook the no-compromise intolerances I myself espouse as necessary and good. For instance, as an actor, I believe I could step into the hypothetical shoes of someone who lives within a worldview radically opposed to my own. I could make the imaginative leap to portray, for example, a character deeply convinced that women should not vote or that certain races ought rightfully to be enslaved. What I cannot do is see myself *qua* myself honestly participating in an exchange where the expectation is that I open my own beliefs about the equality of women or the injustice of slavery to revision or reversal. I am utterly intolerant toward such hypothetical-historical stances. Absent something on the order of traumatic brain injury, I cannot imagine a scenario in which I could be swayed to alter my beliefs on these issues. I possess, in essence, deal-breaker convictions, ethical demands that run so deep and which impose such strong demands upon me that they override the protocols of tolerant democratic deliberation. Were the U.S. to rescind suffrage for women or reinstitute nineteenth-century slavery, I would (I hope) choose to violate protocols of tolerance through acts of civil disobedience or direct action.

Such intolerant violations are the very stuff of many of the most powerful and memorable left-progressive activist performances like suffrage marches, workers' strikes, lunch-counter sit-ins, and anti-war demonstrations. Those who enact such violations hold honored places in the history of social change performance. I do not think it too great a leap to consider such deeds as simultaneously activist performances and acts of faith. Although not necessarily religious in origin, the animating energy behind performance activism flows from convictions about the way the world ought to be, deep and comprehensive beliefs that cannot be expressed solely in terms of cool rationality. They are matters of heart and spirit as well as mind. Such convictions, which others have written about in terms of a demand (Critchley), as fidelity to a world-changing event (Badiou), or as ultimate concern (Tillich) frequently transcend loyalty to a status quo of peaceful coexistence. To transform mere coexistence into an ultimate value is to forget that tolerance undergirds, but is not identical to, the Good that activism and politics in a liberal-democratic tradition are meant to establish.

Still, though, a politics consisting of nothing but an endless stream of sharply transgressive acts does no more to realize equality, justice, and freedom than does surrender at the halfway marker of "just getting along." As artists like Augusto Boal have demonstrated, political activism in performance can be more than the agitprop play that excites thoughtful anger or the direct-action disruption that engages oppressions head-to-head. Performance can also operate as a mode of democratic deliberation, modeling ways of realizing and interacting with the lived realities of our neighbors.

In this spirit, I maintain that evangelicalism's struggles over the idea of tolerance and the stigma of being labeled intolerant have something to offer scholars and practitioners of left-progressive activist performance. Specifically, I think that certain sectors of evangelicalism can offer—if not counter-models of liberal democracy, then at least—alternative modes of performed coexistence. In conclusion, then, I want to turn briefly to the genre of evangelical debate.

Here I mean debates sponsored mainly by religiously affiliated groups (e.g., churches, Christian groups on campuses, faith-based colleges and universities) and held in public venues for the benefit of a lay public. The format for such debates varies, but in general they feature a general topic (usually a question, e.g., "Is Theism Rational?"; "Is God a Moral Monster?"; "Should Women Be Ordained?") with two debaters, one to argue the affirmative and one the negative. After delivering prepared opening statements, each debater engages in a series of timed rebuttal speeches, sometimes interspersed with question-and-answer periods.

Most current research about debates concerns televised political debates, a genre wherein debaters deliver practiced catchphrases and sound bite attacks designed for maximum circulation by the mass media. Relatively little work has been done about the theatrical qualities of live debates. Live debates were a vibrant form of popular entertainment, however, in the nineteenth- and early twentieth-century U.S.[13] Nor were these popular debates solely political. E. Brooks Holifield studied one hundred nineteenth-century public theological debates, noting that records of thousands more exist, extending at least into the mid-twentieth century. Practically every imaginable religious group and sub-group active in the U.S.—Protestant versus Catholic, Universalists versus Presbyterian, Calvinist versus Arminian, Mormon versus Christian—seemed to feel the need to test their faith against others in a public forum (502). Debates could last hours, days, or even weeks. The tone could range from serious and refined to shallow and sarcastic (500). A perceived victory could mean mass migrations from one congregation to another, or it could mean simply a challenge to another debate (515). Holifield even discovered the existence of theological debate superstars, "forensic hired guns who traveled from place to place at the invitation of coreligionists besieged by disrespectful neighbors" (503). Although not as popular as it used to be, Holifield notes, the theological debate tradition persists within some sectors of U.S. Protestantism (499).

Specifically, the debate tradition is thriving in evangelicalism.[14] Indeed, with the advent of the Internet, evangelical debate has found a new life in podcasts, YouTube videos, and blogs. The structure remains fairly consistent with nineteenth-century practices. But in terms of purpose, present-day evangelical debates lose the localism that characterized many earlier debates. Their mass circulation online makes them and their interlocutors material for a larger evangelical culture.

Within this evangelical culture, perhaps the best-known debater today—the forensic hired gun of the twenty-first century—is William Lane Craig, a professor of philosophy at the Talbot School of Theology in California. A specialist in apologetics (reasoned defense of faith), Craig bases much of his scholarly philosophical work on developments of classical cosmological arguments for God. Over the last twenty years or so, he has complemented his academic scholarship with works aimed at lay audiences. His debates with such opponents as Sam Harris, Christopher Hitchens, and Bart Ehrman over topics ranging from the rationality of theism to the evidence for Jesus's bodily resurrection to the standard "Does God Exist?" have won him wide notoriety. As a viewing of any of his debates will attest, Craig is a skilled rhetorician. Disrupting popular stereotypes of evangelicals as anti-intellectual Bible-thumpers, Craig draws on an extensive knowledge of the Western philosophical tradition, classical apologetics, Biblical scholarship, and scientific theory to mount sophisticated arguments in favor of Theism, intelligent design, or Biblical reliability—all delivered with a calm, reasoned tone leavened with a sense of humor. His performance style draws more on the conventions of a confident, scholarly lecture than on those of a fiery sermon. And he is utterly comfortable in the forensic conventions of rebuttal and summary, often outmaneuvering opponents who come expecting amateurish pseudo-intellectualism.

A detailed evaluation of the soundness of Craig's arguments lies beyond the scope of this article. To a certain extent, such an evaluation would be beside the point. Craig's debates often play to evangelical audiences full of fans already familiar with his signature arguments. By and large, they come not to be wooed by Craig's persuasive powers or to be swayed by those of his opponent du jour (although, of course, either can happen). Craig's draw for evangelicals instead stems at least in part from his performance of reasoned apologetic competence. He holds his own—and then some—with many of the major critics of religion and Christianity. He *sounds* convincing. He *looks* convincing. He is the opposite of what popular culture expects from someone holding a committed, exclusivist, essentially intolerant faith position. He exemplifies for evangelicals a mode of gracious heteronomy, what evangelical Richard Mouw calls (drawing on Martin Marty) "convicted civility."

Craig's debates, in other words, stage good faith intolerance. Evangelical debate is not (or at least not primarily) a deliberative dialogue or an exploratory interview in which participants pursue a common goal of discovery or mutual understanding. Debaters do not aim for compromise or for mutually beneficial solutions to a problem. They aim for victory (or, at least, survival with integrity). Debate requires that participants be utterly clear in the exclusivity of their claims, particularly how and why that exclusivity sets them apart from their opponents. But it also requires that they listen and appreciate (which is not the same as agree with) the complexity of their opponents' stances. More than that, debate demands that opponents perform both their argumentations and their refutations with an eye toward persuading their audiences.

This latter element is vital. Although I have suggested that Craig's public debates may not generate converts, the modeling function of his debates—demonstrating what an apologetics of convicted civility looks like—aligns with a renewed emphasis across much of U.S. evangelicalism on the art of persuasion. One of the few unifying features across evangelicalism is the conviction that Christian convictions have to be shared, that Christians are to present a winsome witness to the rationality, attractiveness, and goodness of the world-and-life view that they hold. Evangelicals *evangelize*. The worry that evangelicals like Kinnaman and Lyons have about evangelicalism's reputation lies in their realization that, while *committed* and *principled* are positive attributes of a Christian that assist in advancing a meaningful witness, *judgmental* and *intolerant* are not. Craig's ministry to other evangelicals participates in a growing trend of books, workshops, lectures, classes, videos, and curricula all dedicated to equipping evangelicals with day-to-day versions of the skills that Craig demonstrates in his formal, conventionalized encounters with heterodoxy and unbelief. Evangelicals—those participating in this trend, at least—discipline themselves in communicating their faith calmly, listening to others' faiths, and accepting responsibility for ham-fisted or hurtful encounters with other Christians. But they also respect the notion of faith seriously enough to offer critiques of other's beliefs and defenses of their own. Belief, for evangelicals, is neither so insubstantial as to be donned or discarded at will nor so fragile (or dangerous) as to be quarantined from public debate.[15]

None of this, of course, eliminates the deep disagreements that lie between evangelicals and, say, left-progressive, gay United Methodists like me. The world-and-life view that evangelicals learn to spread diverges in many ways from my own commitments regarding the true, the right, and the beautiful. But I argue that Craig's mode of convicted civility, *mutatis mutandis*, serves as a better, more responsible technique of coexistence in pluralized liberal democracy than mere coexistence. Such an evangelical example reminds me that, as a scholar and sometime practitioner of left-progressive activist performance, I have a responsibility not only to believe but also to persuade, to evangelize for the values and views I see as essential. But to the extent that it means that I do not let other beliefs alone simply because they are beliefs, I am called on to be intolerant in good faith.

NOTES

1. For information about the exhibition, see *Coexistence*. The Jefferson quote comes from an 1816 letter to Matthew Carey (see Jefferson).
2. By *activist*, I name a performance's conscious alignment with a broader endeavor to alter a material and/or ideological conditions of the audience's reality. By *left-progressive*, I mean a commitment to realizing, pluralizing, and expanding the liberal-democratic promise of freedoms and civil protections

for all and equal access to power by all. I prefer the term "progressive left" (or "left-progressive") to the more popular (in the U.S.) "liberal." I reserve the latter term to indicate the basic philosophical tradition of John Locke et al., in which the individual's unalienable liberties take priority in political considerations.

3. I will clarify my use of *evangelicalism* later in this essay. Unless otherwise noted, I use *evangelicalism* to mean present-day evangelicalism in the U.S.
4. "Bloody Sunday" specifically refers to a massacre of twenty-six non-violent Irish protesters by British Armed Forces on Sunday, 30 January 1972.
5. Video of the Coexist spectacle is widely available. See "U2-Bloody Sunday" for the moment I relate here (from the Chicago performance). Note that Bono altered the spectacle slightly at each tour stop.
6. Although, according to Hutchinson, U2 used the design without Mlodozeniec's permission, the artist saw the show and approved of its use. Mlodozeniec was less pleased, however, with the numerous web-based companies who began marketing Coexist-based merchandise. Efforts to secure copyright protections on the sign failed (Butler). Today, a web search for "coexist bumper sticker" will yield any number of variations for sale.
7. Dasenbrock proposes an exploration of the rhetoric of bumper stickers based on J. L. Austin's speech act theory.
8. In the mid-twentieth century, "neo-evangelicals" like Billy Graham and Carl Henry (called simply *evangelicals* afterward) broke from Christian fundamentalists (Protestant anti-modernist conservatives), keeping much of their theology but discarding their separatist and anti-cultural tendencies. Marsden provides the standard history of fundamentalism and of evangelicalism's split. Stone examines evangelicalism's definitional and boundary struggles since that split.
9. Bebbington (writing about British evangelicalism) provides an influential four-fold characterization of distinctly evangelical theological tendencies: 1) *Biblicism*: A view of the protestant Bible as the revealed, complete, and coherent Word of God; 2) *crucicentrism*: a focus on Jesus Christ's death on the cross as the centerpiece of the Christian narrative, in which Jesus substitutes himself for human sinners, saving them from an eternal afterlife in Hell; 3) *conversionism*: an insistence that individuals experience a personal transformation—a re-birth—in which they accept the gift of Christ's substitutionary atonement and live as new creations dedicated to living a Christ-like life; and 4) *activism*: an understanding that such a Christ-like life involves *evangelizing*—spreading the news of Christ to those who have not converted, urging them to experience Christian re-birth (2–17).
10. Although I have chosen McDowell and Hostetler as fit representatives of popular evangelical discourse about tolerance, readers should note that evangelicals have also produced sophisticated scholarly critiques of liberal tolerance theory. See, e.g., Gentry.
11. Swaine contrasts heteronomous individuals with autonomous individuals, by which he means the model participants in liberal deliberations, possessed of self-reflective dispositions along with a willingness to revise their views in the face of compelling arguments or pragmatic compromise (185–188).
12. For more anti-Islam variations, see Conservapedia's "Coexist Exhibition."
13. See Silverman for a theatrical reading of the 1858 Lincoln-Douglas debates.
14. Lists of and links to religious debates can be found widely on the Internet. See, e.g., Thrasher. Donahue, Hendon, and Craig all offer links to sound and video files of various debates.
15. It takes two, of course, to model a civil exchange. Although my work focuses mainly on evangelicals, and although many public debates occur between

evangelicals, my conclusions about convicted civility extend to most of the non-evangelicals (e.g., atheists, agnostics, liberal Protestants, Mormons, Roman Catholics, Muslims) who agree to debate Craig or his peers. Many of these other faith/non-faith positions espouse their own versions of "spreading the gospel" and therefore practice comparable varieties of good-faith intolerance.

WORKS CITED

Badiou, Alain. *Ethics: An Essay on the Understanding of Evil.* Trans. Peter Hallward. New York: Verso, 2001. Print.

Barton, Bernadette. "1CROSS + 3NAILS = 4GVN: Compulsory Christianity and Homosexuality in the Bible Belt Panopticon." *Feminist Formations* 23.1 (2011): 70–93. *Project Muse.* Web. 25 May 2011.

Bebbington, David W. *Evangelicalism in Modern Britain: A History from the 1730s to the 1980s.* New York: Routledge, 1989. Print.

Brown, Wendy. *Regulating Aversion: Tolerance in the Age of Identity and Empire.* Princeton: Princeton UP, 2007. Print.

Butler, Susan. "One Design, Many Claims: Can They Coexist?" *Billboard* 7 Aug. 2005: Upfront sec. *Lexisnexis.* Web. 10 May 2011.

"Coexist Exhibition." *Conservapedia.com.* Conservapedia, 22 Apr. 2011. Web. 5 June 2011.

"Coexist? Sticker (Bumper)." Advertisement. *RightWingStuff.com.* CafePress.com, n.d. Web. 5 June 2011.

Coexistence. Museum on the Seam, n.d. Web. 10 May 2011.

Colavecchio-Van Sickler, Shannon. "Bumper sticker evokes road rage." *St. Petersburg Times* (Florida) 10 Mar. 2005, natl. ed.: 1A. *LexisNexis.* Web. 2 June 2011.

Craig, William Lane. *Reasonable Faith with William Lane Craig.* Reasonable Faith, n.d. Web. 5 June 2011.

Critchley, Simon. *Infinitely Demanding: Ethics of Commitment, Politics of Resistance.* New York: Verso, 2007. Print.

Dasenbrock, Reed Way. "A Rhetoric of Bumper Stickers: What Analytic Philosophy Can Contribute to a New Rhetoric." *Defining the New Rhetorics.* Ed. Theresa Enos and Stuart C. Brown. Newbury Park: Sage, 1993. 191–206. Print.

Donahue, Patrick. *BibleDebates.info.* BibleDebates.info, n.d. Web. 5 June 2011.

Ferrara, Alessandro. "Reflexive Pluralism." *Philosophy & Social Criticism* 36.3–4 (2010): 353–364. *Sage Publications.* Web. 23 May 2011.

———. "The Separation of Politics and Religion in a Post-Secular Society." *Philosophy & Social Criticism* 35. 1–2 (2009): 77–91. *Sage Publications.* Web. 23 May 2011.

Fish, Stanley. *The Trouble With Principle.* Cambridge: Harvard UP, 1999. Print.

Gallie, W. B. "Essentially Contested Concepts." *Proceedings of the Aristotelian Society, New Series* 56 (1955–1956): 167–198. *JSTOR.* Web. 11 Mar. 2009.

Gentry, Glenn. "Rawls and Religious Community: Ethical Decision Making in the Public Square." *Christian Bioethics* 13 (2007): 171–181. *Academic Search Complete.* Web. 26 May 2011.

Habermas, Jürgen, et al. *An Awareness of What Is Missing: Faith and Reason in a Secular Age.* Malden: Polity, 2010. Print.

Haynsworth, Leslie. "My Volvo, My Self: The (Largely Unintended) Existential Implications of Bumper Stickers." *Fourth Genre: Explorations in Nonfiction* 10.1 (2008): 21–34. *Project Muse.* Web. 25 May 2011.

Hendon, Joel, ed. *Public Religious Debates: 126 Interesting Public Debates on Religious Subjects*. Highway 9 Church of Christ, n.d. Web. 5 June 2011.

Holifield, E. Brooks. "Theology as Entertainment: Oral Debate in American Religion." *Church History* 67.3 (1998): 499–520. *JSTOR*. Web. 23 May 2011.

Hutchinson, Kevin. "Can't We All Just Coexist? Lawsuits and Controversy over Who Owns the 'CoeXisT' Sign." *@U2*. @U2, 11 July 2005. Web. 10 May 2011.

Jaspar, Jerry. "Our Vision and Origins." *Peacemonger.com*. Peacemonger, n.d. Web. 10 May 2011.

Jefferson, Thomas. "To Matthew Carey." 11 Nov. 1816. *The Works of Thomas Jefferson*, Federal Edition. Vol. 12. Ed. Paul Leicester Ford. New York: Putnam's Sons, 1904–1905. N. pag. *Online Library of Liberty*. Web. 2 June 2011.

Kinnaman, David, and Gabe Lyons. *UnChristian: What a New Generation Really Thinks About Christianity . . . And Why It Matters*. Grand Rapids: Baker, 2007. Print.

Marsden, George. *Fundamentalism and American Culture: The Shaping of Twentieth-Century Evangelicalism*. Oxford: Oxford UP, 1980. Print.

McDowell, Josh, and Bob Hostetler. *The New Tolerance: How a Cultural Movement Threatens to Destroy You, Your Faith, and Your Children*. Carol Stream: Tyndale, 1998. Print.

Mlodozeniec, Piotr. *Coexist*. 2001. Museum on the Seam, Jerusalem. *Museum on the Seam*. Web. 10 May 2011.

Morley, Veronica, and Katrinka Somdahl-Sands. "Music with a Message: U2's Rock Concerts as Spectacular Spaces of Politics." *Aether: The Journal of Media Geography* 7 (2011): 58–74. Web. 1 June 2011.

Mouw, Richard J. "Convicted Civility & Interfaith Dialogue." *Evangelical Interfaith Dialogue* 1.3 (2010): 3 ff. Web. 26 May 2011.

Seales, Chad E. "Burned over Bono: U2's Rock 'n' Roll Messiah and His Religious Politic." *Journal of Religion and Popular Culture* 14 (2006): n.pag. Web. 1 June 2011.

Silverman, Gillian. "'The Best Circus in Town': Embodied Theatrics in the Lincoln-Douglas Debates." *American Literary History* 21.4 (2009): 757–787. *Project Muse*. Web. 25 May 2011.

Smith, Christian. *Christian America? What Evangelicals Really Want*. Berkeley: U of California P, 2000. Print.

Stone, John R. *On the Boundaries of American Evangelicalism: The Postwar Evangelical Coalition*. New York: St. Martin's, 1997. Print.

Swaine, Lucas. "Deliberate and Free: Heteronomy and the Public Sphere." *Philosophy & Social Criticism* 35.1–2 (2009): 183–213. *Sage Publications*. Web. 31 May 2011.

Thrasher, Thomas N. "The Encyclopedia of Religious Debates." *BibleDebates.info*. Patrick Donahue, n.d. Web. 5 June 2011.

Tillich, Paul. "What Faith Is." *The Essential Tillich: An Anthology of the Writings of Paul Tillich*. Ed. F. Forrester Church. New York: Collier, 1987: 13–31. Print.

"U2-Bloody Sunday (Vertigo Tour, Live in Chicago)." *Online Posting*. YouTube, 25 Dec. 2008. Web. 1 June 2011.

U2. Lyrics. "Sunday, Bloody Sunday." U2.com. U2, n.d. Web. 2 June 2011.

Contributors

Henry Bial is an associate professor of theatre and chair of the Department of American Studies at the University of Kansas, where he has also served as director of the Program in Jewish Studies. He is the author of *Acting Jewish: Negotiating Ethnicity on the American Stage and Screen* (U Michigan P, 2005), the editor of *The Performance Studies Reader* (Routledge, 2003, 2nd ed. 2007), and co-editor of *Theatre Historiography: Critical Interventions* (with Scott Magelssen, U Michigan P, 2010) and *Brecht Sourcebook* (with Carol Martin, Routledge, 2000).

Marvin Carlson is the Sidney E. Cohn Distinguished Professor of Theatre, Comparative Literature and Middle Eastern Studies at the Graduate Center of the City University of New York. His most recent book, co-authored with Khalid Amine, is forthcoming from Palgrave and is a history of theatre in Algeria, Tunisia, and Morocco.

Donnalee Dox is an associate professor in the Department of Performance Studies and director of the interdisciplinary Religious Studies Program at Texas A&M University. In addition to a monograph, *The Idea of the Theatre in Latin Christian Thought: Augustine to the Fourteenth Century* (U Michigan P, 2004), she has published articles on medieval intellectual history, Middle Eastern dance, and contemporary spiritual performance. Her work has appeared in *Theatre Journal*, *The Journal of Dramatic Theory and Criticism*, *The Journal of Religion and Theatre*, *Theatre Research International*, *Viator: Medieval and Renaissance Studies*, and *TDR* as well as collections of essays. From 2004 to 2009 she served as associate director of the Melbern G. Glasscock Center for Humanities Research at Texas A&M University.

John Fletcher is an assistant professor of theatre history and women's and gender studies at Louisiana State University in Baton Rouge. Dr. Fletcher pursues research in social change performance, community-based theatre, cultural and political theory, evangelical and fundamentalist Christianity, queer studies, and Spanish Golden Age performance.

His work appears in *Text and Performance Quarterly*, *Ecumenica*, *Theatre Survey*, *Theatre Topics*, and *Laberinto* as well as in the anthologies *Querying Difference in Theatre History* and *Theatre Historiography: Critical Interventions.* Currently, Dr. Fletcher is completing a monograph, *Preaching to Convert*, in which he frames a number of outreach methods by U.S. evangelicals as specimens of activist performance.

Daniel Gerould is the Lucille Lortel Distinguished Professor of Theatre and Comparative Literature at the Graduate Center, City University of New York, and director of publications and academic affairs at the Martin E. Segal Theatre Center. He is editor of the journal *Slavic and East European Performance: Drama—Theatre—Film* and of the twelve-volume Routledge/Harwood Polish and Eastern European Theatre Archive. He has translated twenty-one plays by Stanisław Ignacy Witkiewicz (Witkacy) and written extensively about twentieth-century avant-garde drama and theatre. His books include *Witkacy*, *The Witkiewicz Reader*, *Quick Change: Theatre Essays and Translations*, and *The Guillotine: Its Legend and Lore.*

Lance Gharavi is an associate professor in the School of Theatre and Film at Arizona State University. He is the author of *Western Esotericism in Russian Silver Age Drama: Aleksandr Blok's The Rose and the Cross.* His work has appeared in journals including *Theatre Topics*, *Modern Drama*, *Text and Performance Quarterly*, *The Journal of Dramatic Theory and Criticism*, *PAJ*, and *Esoterica.*

Ronald L. Grimes, director of Ritual Studies International, is co-editor of the Oxford Ritual Studies Series and author of several books on ritual, including *Ritual, Media, and Conflict*, *Rite Out of Place: Ritual, Media, and the Arts*, and *Deeply into the Bone: Re-Inventing Rites of Passage.* He is professor emeritus of religion and culture at Wilfrid Laurier University in Canada, where he taught courses on religion and the performing arts, field research in the study of religion, ritual studies, and indigenous religions. Grimes held the Chair of Ritual Studies at Radboud University Nijmegen, the Netherlands, from 2005 to 2010. For the academic year 2011–2012, he is a senior research scholar and senior lecturer at Yale University, where he is working on a project called "Ritual and the Improvisational Arts."

Gad Kaynar is the chair of the Theatre Arts Department, Tel Aviv University, and a professor of Israeli, German, and Scandinavian theatre and drama, dramaturgy, and performance analysis. He is the author of numerous articles on topics in these fields. His most recent book is a historiographic study on *The Cameri Theatre of Tel-Aviv* (2008). His books *The Reality Convention in Hebrew Theatre* and *Recent German*

Dramaturgy are due to appear in 2012. He is currently secretary general of the Israeli Center of the I.T.I. For his Ibsen translations and research, he has been appointed "Knight First Class of the Royal Norwegian Order of Merit" by King Harald V of Norway.

Anthony Kubiak is a professor of drama at the University of California, Irvine. He is the author of *Agitated States: Performance in the American Theater of Cruelty*, and *Stages of Terror: Terrorism, Ideology, and Coercion as Theatre History*. His more recent work appears in *MLQ*, *Performance Research*, and *PAJ*.

Isis Costa McElroy is an assistant professor of Afro-Brazilian literatures and culture at Arizona State University. She is an Oshosi priestess and a poet/scholar/teacher whose work focuses, among other things, on the languages and the philosophies of the Diaspora as expressed through literature, popular music, oral history, and sacred and secular manifestations and rituals.

Ann Pellegrini is an associate professor of performance studies and religious studies at New York University, where she also directs the Center for the Study of Gender and Sexuality. She is the author of *Performance Anxieties: Staging Psychoanalysis, Staging Race* (Routledge, 1997); co-author, with Janet R. Jakobsen, of *Love the Sin: Sexual Regulation and the Limits of Religious Tolerance* (NYU P, 2003; Beacon, 2004); co-editor, with Daniel Boyarin and Daniel Itzkovitz, of *Queer Theory and the Jewish Question* (Columbia UP, 2003); and co-editor, with Jakobsen, of *Secularisms* (Duke UP, 2008). With José Esteban Muñoz she co-edits the book series "Sexual Cultures" for New York University Press. She is currently completing a new book on queer structures of religious feelings.

Richard Schechner is a university professor and professor of performance studies at Tisch School of the Arts, NYU. Schechner is the editor of *TDR: The Journal of Performance Studies*. He is the author of many books, including *Between Theater and Anthropology*, *Performance Theory*, and *Performance Studies—An Introduction*. He founded The Performance Group and East Coast Artists. He has directed plays in the U.S., Europe, Asia, and Africa. His most recent work is *Imagining O: A Dispersed Performance-in-Progress* at Kent University, UK.

Tamara Underiner is an associate professor and director of graduate studies for the School of Theatre and Film at Arizona State University, where she also directs the PhD program in Theatre and Performance of the Americas. She is a regular attender of the Phoenix Monthly Meeting of the Religious Society of Friends (Quakers).

R. Andrew White is an associate professor of theatre at Valparaiso University, where he teaches courses in acting, voice and diction, movement, and theatre history. He has published articles in *Theatre Survey*, *New England Theatre Journal*, and *Performance and Spirituality*. His article "La pratique du rayonnement selon Mikhaïl Tchekhov ou comment développer un savoir-faire" appears in the anthology *Mikhail Tchekhov: de Moscou à Hollywood, du théâtre au cinéma*, edited by Marie Christine Autant-Mathieu. In addition, he has performed with numerous theatres in Chicago. He holds an MFA in acting from Carnegie-Mellon University and the Moscow Art Theatre School.

Index

9/11: 1–2, 3, 101–102, 225

A

Activism: 101–102, 11, 128, 150, 160, 180, 206, 208, 225–227, 232, 234–238, 242
Adés: 136
Affect: 45, 56, 60, 85n, 89, 110, 195–206
Afoxés: 127–148, 149–150n
  A Chegada Africana: 129
  Embaixada Africana: 129–131, 141
  Filhos da África: 129
  Filhos de Gandhy: 127–148
    Dress of: 142–143
    Gender roles in 134–137, 139
    History of: 137–142
    Sexuality in: 145
    Visit to Udaipur: 146
  Pândegos da África: 129–132
Ahasver: 70
Al-Hakim (Fatimid ruler): 119–120
Al-Hakim, Tewfik: 117, 120
Animism: 61n, 80, 84
Anthroposophy: 63, 67, 69, 71
Armstrong, Karen: 18
Armstrong, Piers: 133, 146, n152
Artaud, Antonin: 7, 180
Asad, Talal: 12, 28–29, 39n
Auslander, Philip: 84
Austin, J. L.: 112n, 238n

B

Bacon, Margaret Hope: 103–105, 109, 112n
Bahia: 127–148, 149–152n
Bakathir, Ali Ahmed: 117–126
Barclay, Robert: 105
Barna Group: 229
Barnes, Kenneth C.: 106
Bell, Catherine: 42–43, 45–46, 49–50, 60–61n, 220
Besant, Annie: 174
Blavatsky, Helena Petrovna: 69, 174
Blok, Alexander: 175, 180
Bloom, Harold: 7, 21n
Boal, Augusto: 234
Bono: 226–227
Brathwaite, Kamau: 147, 149n
Bread and Puppet: 7
Brook, Peter: 7
Brown, Wendy: 232
Bruce, Lenny: 94–95
Buc, Philippe: 29
Buddhism: 3, 79–86, 125, 188, 215
  Vajrayana (Tibetan): 79–80
Bumper stickers, performativity of: 228–229
Bush, George W.: 2, 200, 207n
Butler, Judith: 18–19

C

Candomblé: 127–148
Carnaval, Brazilian: 127–148, 148–151n
Carslon, Marvin: 7, 21n, 126n
Channeling: 44, 52
Chekhov, Michael: 63–77
Christianity: 3–4, 7, 8–9, 28, 35, 45, 63–70, 71, 100–111, n112, 122, 174–176, 197–198, 202–206, 207n, 225–226, 228–230, 233–237, 238–239n
  Bible Belt: 228–229
  Catholicism: 9, 35, 100, 102, 134, 136, 149n, 235, 239n, 230
  Evangelical apologetics: 230
  Evangelism: 229–230, 202–206, 235–237
  Fundamentalist: 8–9, 197–198, 229

Orthodox: 63–70, 176
Quakerism: 100–111, 111–112n
Symbols and signs of: 228
Ciurlionis, Mikalojus: 176–177
Colonialism: 1, 5, 7, 9, 14, 16, 134, 140, 149, 151, 162, 186–187, 190, 208, 215–216
Consciousness: 3, 12, 15, 42, 43, 45, 51, 55, 56, 57, 61–62, 68, 69, 72, 75, 76, 79, 80, 84, 143, 158, 169, 179, 183, 199, 201, 211
Divided: 75
Coquelin, Constant: 68, 74
Craig, William Lane: 236–237
Crusades: 2, 122, 200
Cultural performances: 29–32

D
D'Aquili, Eugene: 47, 54, 55–56
Deleuze, Gilles: 82, 83–84, 86n, 196, 205
Demastes, William: 42–43, 60–61
Derrida, Jacques: 4
Do Catendê, Moa: 146
Dostoyevsky, Fyodor: 66
Drumming ceremonies: 43, 49–60, 61n, 134, 138
Duc, Thich Quang: 215–216

E
Ego: 54–65, 63, 67–68, 71–72, 75
Cosmic: 70–71, 74
Higher: 63, 67–68, 71–72, 75
Egun: 135–136
Egungun societies: 100, 134–135
Elder Nektary: 66–72
Elegun: 136
Ethnography: 8, 32–33, 60n, 173, 198
Evreinov, Nikolai: 173

F
Falwell, Jerry: 197, 203
Fish, Stanley: 11, 231
Fox, George: 103–105
Fundamentalism: 8–10, 21–22n, 119, 188, 197, 229
Christian: 8, 197–198, 229
Hindu: 188
Jewish: 8
Muslim: 8, 119

G
Gandhi, Mahatma (Mohandas Gandhi): 127–148, 188–190
Garfield, Jules (Jacob Julius Garfinkle): 92–93
Geertz, Clifford: 30, 34–35
Geledé societies: 134
Gil, Gilberto: 127–128, 136, 147
Glossolalia: 44
Gnosticism: 174, 176, 181
Goffman, Erving: 31–35, 189
Gogol, Nikolai: 66
Graves, Michael P.: 101, 105–107, 111
Greece, Ancient: 7, 16, 21n, 63–64, 173–174, 181
Greenwood, Ormerod: 106
Grotowski, Jerzy: 7, 181, 182–183
Guattari, Pierre-Félix: 84, 196
Gunga Din: 138–140, 148

H
Hart, D. G.: 217–218
Hasfari, Shmuel: 155–170
Major works of: 155–157, 159–170
Theatrical techniques of: 157–159
Use of *Kiddush* ceremony: 162–170
Haynsworth, Leslie: 228
Hell Houses: 202–205
Hesychasm: 63–74
Hinduism: 9, 127–148, 173, 185–190
BharatiyaJanata Party: 188
In Brazil: 127–148
Fundamentalist: 188
Hindutva: 188
Hirst, Damien: 2
Hume, David: 199–200
Huntington, Samuel P.: 3, 14

I
India: 16, 29–30, 127, 138, 142, 145, 175, 185–190
Islam: 2–3, 8–9, 14, 21n, 27, 36, 117–126, 128, 140–146, 151n, 186–188, 197–198, 206–207n
Anti-Muslim imagery: 233
In Brazil: 128, 140–146, 151n
Fundamentalist: 8, 119
Muslim Brotherhood: 121
Theatrical traditions within: 117–126, 186
Women's piety in: 198
Ito, Michio: 177
Ivanov, Vyacheslov: 175

J
Jackson, Shannon: 214
Jakobsen, Janet R.: 197, 200, 205, 206

Jameson, Fredric: 196
Jaspar, Jerry: 227
Jennings, Theodore W. Jr.: 46
Judaism: 3, 9, 88–98, 98n, 155–170, 198, 233
  Anti-Semitism: 3, 88–89, 92
  Assimilation: 89–91
  Fundamentalist: 8
  Jewish calendar: 90
  Jewish identity: 88–98

K
Kahane, Rabbi Meir: 156
Kali: 139
Kalumba: 51–60
Kandinsky, Vassily: 173
Kantor, Tadeusz: 181–182
Klabunde, Martin: 51–59
Kubiak, Anthony: 18
Kushner, Tony: 7
Kuzmin, Mikhail: 175

L
Laderman, Gary: 50, 56
Landes, Ruth: 135–136
Laughlin, Charles: 47, 54, 55–56
Lazer, Hank: 97
Leadbeater, Charles: 174
Leaveners, the: 107
Liturgy: 7, 28, 36, 105, 140, 182
Living Theatre, The: 7
Lloyd, Benjamin: 71, 107–108

M
Maeterlinck, Maurice: 174, 176, 179, 180, 181
Mahmood, Saba: 198–199
Marxism: 9–10, 63, 80, 121, 126n, 201
Marx, Karl: 19, 63, 201, 215
McCutcheon, Russell T.: 211–220, 223n
Meditation: 17, 51, 56–57, 59, 60n, 63–76, 80–83, 125
Meyerhold, Vsevolod: 175, 178, 179
Miciński, Tadeusz: 175–175, 178, 179
Miller, Tim: 205–206
Mlodozeniec, Piotr: 225–227
Modernism: 9, 10, 172, 180
Mondrian, Piet: 173
Morales, Anamaria: 137–138, 145
Muñoz, José: 195, 200

N
Narain Singh family: 186
New age: 50
Nietzsche, Friedrich: 175
Nil Sorsky (Saint Nilius of Sora): 64–65

O
Oedipus, adaptations of: 120–124, n126
Ogun: 139, 142, 144
Open Theatre, The: 7
Orishas: 128, 132–148
Oro societies: 134–135
Oshala: 128, 135, 140–141, 145
  Águas de Oxalá: 140
Ouaknin, Marc-Alain: 96–97

P
Parry, Evalyn: 107
Peacemonger: 227
Penn, William: 105, 109
Performance, definitions of: 2, 15, 18, 27, 30, 35–36, 112n
Pharmakos: 82–83
Philokalia: 64–65, 73
Pluralism: 12–13, 36, 92, 212, 222, 225, 230–237
Postcolonialism: 1, 5, 14, 186, 216
Postmodernism: 10–11, 14, 42, 45–46, 60, 89, 168–169, 196
  Critique of spirituality within: 45
  Waning of affect: 196
Postsecularism: 14–15
Poststructuralism: 79, 102, 198
Prayer: 3, 30, 48, 52–54, 57, 59, 63, 64–65, 66, 68–69, 71–76, 77
  Jesus Prayer: 64–65, 71–72
Puar, Jasbir: 195–198, 205
Puritanism: 100, 103–105

Q
Quakerism: 100–111, 111–112n
  Beliefs on speech, language: 107–109
  Dress: 109–110
  Social activism: 109–111
Queer theory: 1, 89, 94, 195–206
Quixote, Don: 70, 73–74
Qur'an: 119–126
  Use of quotations from: 119, 122
Qutb, Sayyid: 121–122

R
Rama: 185–190
Ramayana: 186
Ramila of Ramnagar: 185–190

Religion, definitions of: 12, 15, 17, 27–28, 215–219
Religious debate: 90–96, 106, 220, 235–237, 239
Religious studies: 210–223
  Gender critique within: 213–215
  Practice of religion within: 211–212, 214
  Reductionism: 211–223
Malês, Revolt of the: 140–141
Ritual: 8, 17, 19–20, 27–40, 45–61, 85n, 105, 133, 135, 158, 160, 167–169, 182–183, 187, 212
  Definition of: 27–39, 40n
  Dionysian: 173, 175, 178
  Neurological effects of: 47–49, 55–61
  Rites of passage: 33–36, 160
  Ritual vs. theatre: 33–36
Rodrigues, Nina: 129–130
Román, David: 205–206
Rossi, Vincent: 64, 70, 73
Rozanov, Vasily: 66
Russia/Soviet Union: 63–77, 123, 176, 180
  Communism in: 63, 66, 123, 180

S
Saint Augustine: 67, 70
Saint Maximos: 70, 75
Schechner, Richard: 8, 32–36, 47–48, 55, 148
Schneer, David: 89
Schuré, Edouard: 174
Scriabin, Alexander: 173, 177–178
Secularism: 13–15, 158, 162, 195–206, 231
  Christian: 200
  Israeli: 162
September 11, 2001: *see 9/11*
Severn, Hannah: 109–111
Shamanism: 42–43, 50–57
Shawqi, Ahmad: 117–118
Shukla, Pravina: 127–128, 137, 142, 144, 145, 146
Silva, Agnaldo: 135, 144
Singer, Milton: 29–30
Six-Day War: 156, 160
Smith, Jonathan Z.: 16, 219
Soloviev, Vladimir: 66
Soviet Union: *see Russia/Soviet Union*
Spiritualism: 177, 195
Stanton, Leonard J.: 65–68
Steiner, Rudolph: 63, 67, 69–71
Stewart, Jon: 88, 94–95
Stockhausen, Karlheinz: 1–3
Structuralism: 79, 102, 198, 232
Sunyata: 83
Swaine, Lucas: 232
Symbolism: 7, 28, 102, 123, 128, 172–183
  1970s reemergence of: 180–183
  Decline of: 179–180
  Theoretical underpinnings of: 173–174

T
Ta'ziyeh: 117, 186
Tantra: 79–86
Tataryn, Myroslaw I.: 63, 67
Theosophy: 69, 174, 178
Tolerance: 106, 122–123, 152, 163, 167, 189, 203–205, 225–239
Tolstoy, Lev: 18, 66, 76n
Turner, Victor: 8, 31, 32–36

U
U2: 226–227
Umbanda: 146

V
Villiers de l'Isle-Adam, Auguste: 179

W
War on terror: 3, 14, 198, 200, 204
Wiebe, Donald: 214–215, 217
Williams, Raymond: 19, 196, 201
Winkleman, Michael: 55–56
Wissenschaft: 210, 214, 222
Woolman, John: 110–111
Wyspiański, Stanisław: 176, 181

Y
Yeats, William Butler: 177
Yom Kippur War: 156, 160, 167, 168
Yoruba: 100, 129, 134–136, 142, 145, 146, 151n

Z
Žižek, Slavoj: 18–19, 22n